The World Intellectual Property
Organization (WIPO)

Elgar Practical Guides

Rich in practical advice, *Elgar Practical Guides* are handy, concise guides to a range of legal practice areas.

Combining practical insight and step-by-step guidance with the relevant substantive law and procedural rules, the books in this series focus on understanding and navigating the issues that are likely to be encountered in practice. This is facilitated by a range of structural tools including checklists, glossaries, sample documentation and recommended actions.

Elgar Practical Guides are indispensable resources for the busy practitioner and for the non-specialist who requires a first introduction or a reliable turn-to reference book.

Titles in the series include:

Determann's Field Guide to Data Privacy Law
International Corporate Compliance, Second Edition
Lothar Determann

Proceedings Before the European Patent Office
A Practical Guide to Success in Opposition and Appeal
Marcus O. Müller and Cees A.M. Mulder

The World Intellectual Property Organization (WIPO)
A Reference Guide
Carolyn Deere Birkbeck

The World Intellectual Property Organization (WIPO)

A Reference Guide

CAROLYN DEERE BIRKBECK

Global Economic Governance Programme, University of Oxford, UK

Elgar Practical Guides

Cheltenham, UK • Northampton, MA, USA

Published by
Edward Elgar Publishing Limited
The Lypiatts
15 Lansdown Road
Cheltenham
Glos GL50 2JA
UK

Edward Elgar Publishing, Inc.
William Pratt House
9 Dewey Court
Northampton
Massachusetts 01060
USA

A catalogue record for this book
is available from the British Library

Library of Congress Control Number: 2015952687

This book is available electronically in the **Elgar**online
Law subject collection
DOI 10.4337/9781785364785

ISBN 978 1 78536 477 8 (cased)
ISBN 978 1 78536 478 5 (eBook)

Typeset by Servis Filmsetting Ltd, Stockport, Cheshire
Printed and bound in Great Britain by
TJ International Ltd, Padstow, Cornwall

Content overview

List of figures   xi
List of tables   xii
Preface   xiv
Acknowledgement   xvii
List of abbreviations   xviii

1. Introduction   1

2. What is WIPO and what does it do?   7

3. WIPO's governance system: an analytical framework   47

4. WIPO's legal foundations, mandate and purpose   55

5. WIPO's decision-making structure, processes and practices   67

6. WIPO's financial arrangements and the Program and Budget process   106

7. Mechanisms for control, oversight and accountability of the WIPO Secretariat   157

8. External relations and transparency   177

9. Conclusion   195

Appendix 1: Convention Establishing the World Intellectual Property Organization   198
Appendix 2: Agreement between the United Nations and the World Intellectual Property Organization   210
Appendix 3: WIPO General Rules of Procedure   216
Appendix 4: Special Rules of Procedure of the Governing Bodies   227

Appendix 5: Special Rules of Procedure for WIPO Committees   247
Appendix 6: Example of Rules of Procedure for a Diplomatic
             Conference: Marrakesh Treaty   252
Appendix 7: WIPO Financial Regulations and Rules (selected
             excerpts on oversight and audit)   262
Appendix 8: WIPO Staff Regulations and Rules (selected
             excerpts relevant to governance)   277
Appendix 9: WIPO Investigation Policy   292

Bibliography   297
Index   313

Table of contents

List of figures   xi
List of tables   xii
Preface   xiv
Acknowledgement   xvii
List of abbreviations   xviii

1. Introduction   1

2. What is WIPO and what does it do?   7
    2.1   WIPO's origins   7
    2.2   What is WIPO's purpose?   8
    2.3   What does WIPO do in practice?   9
    2.4   The WIPO Secretariat   31
       2.4.1   Leadership and staffing   32
       2.4.2   Headquarters and external offices   44
       2.4.3   Internal organisation   45

3. WIPO's governance system: an analytical framework   47

4. WIPO's legal foundations, mandate and purpose   55
    4.1   The WIPO Convention   55
    4.2   Agreement between the United Nations and WIPO   58
    4.3   The WIPO Development Agenda: a key decision relevant to debates on WIPO's mandate   60

5. WIPO's decision-making structure, processes and practices   67
    5.1   WIPO's complex decision-making structure   67
    5.2   The main organs   69
       5.2.1   The General Assembly   70
       5.2.2   The WIPO Conference   71
       5.2.3   The WIPO Coordination Committee   72
    5.3   The annual WIPO Assemblies and the Governing Bodies of the Unions   73

5.4   WIPO committees and other subsidiary bodies   76
    5.4.1   Committees   76
    5.4.2   Expert committees established by treaty
         provisions   80
    5.4.3   Working groups   80
    5.4.4   Diplomatic conferences   81
5.5   Decision-making procedures, working methods and
    processes   83
    5.5.1   General Rules of Procedure   84
    5.5.2   Special Rules of Procedure   86
    5.5.3   Voting and consensus   87
5.6   Processes for rule-making: treaties and soft law   90
5.7   Mechanisms for coordination across committees   92
    5.7.1   Development Agenda coordination and
         monitoring mechanism   93
5.8   Regional groups, informal consultations and
    consensus-building at WIPO   95
5.9   Role of the Secretariat in Member State deliberations   98
5.10   Practices for Member State representation   99
    5.10.1   National representation   99
    5.10.2   Interaction among members   103
    5.10.3   Interaction with the Secretariat   104

6.   WIPO's financial arrangements and the Program and
Budget process   106
    6.1   Income   107
        6.1.1   Income sources for the regular budget: fees   107
        6.1.2   Income sources for the regular budget:
             Member State contributions, the Unitary
             Contribution System and arrears   123
        6.1.3   Other income sources for WIPO's regular
             budget   129
        6.1.4   Extra-budgetary income and Funds-in-
             Trust   129
    6.2   WIPO Financial Regulations and Rules   130
        6.2.1   Custody of WIPO funds   133
        6.2.2   The WIPO Controller   134
    6.3   Policies on reserves and investments   135
    6.4   Setting and reviewing WIPO's Program and Budget   137
        6.4.1   Organisational priorities: the Program and
             Budget   137
        6.4.2   The Program and Budget process   139

6.4.3   Program and Budget reporting
         requirements   143
6.4.4   Extra-budgetary contributions, gifts and
         donations in the Program and Budget
         process   143
6.5   The unitary presentation of WIPO's budget   145
6.6   Financial arrangements for the Unions and
      allocation of their income   146
6.6.1   Allocation of income and budgeted
         expenditure by Union   148

7.   Mechanisms for control, oversight and accountability of the
     WIPO Secretariat   157
7.1   Audit and oversight mechanisms   157
7.2   Evaluation   162
7.3   Office of the Legal Counsel   163
7.4   Other internal accountability mechanisms   164
7.4.1   Staff accountability   165

8.   External relations and transparency   177
8.1   Relations with the UN system and other
      international organisations   177
8.2   WIPO's unique relationship with private sector
      stakeholders   184
8.3   Guidelines on observers   186
8.4   Transparency and access to documents   190

9.   Conclusion   195

Appendix 1: Convention Establishing the World Intellectual
             Property Organization   198
Appendix 2: Agreement between the United Nations
             and the World Intellectual Property
             Organization   210
Appendix 3: WIPO General Rules of Procedure   216
Appendix 4: Special Rules of Procedure of the Governing
             Bodies   227
Appendix 5: Special Rules of Procedure for WIPO
             Committees   247
Appendix 6: Example of Rules of Procedure for a Diplomatic
             Conference: Marrakesh Treaty   252

Appendix 7: WIPO Financial Regulations and Rules (selected
             excerpts on oversight and audit)   262
Appendix 8: WIPO Staff Regulations and Rules (selected
             excerpts relevant to governance)   277
Appendix 9: WIPO Investigation Policy   292

Bibliography   297
Index   313

Figures

2.1   Growing demands on WIPO governance from 1970–2015   10
2.2   Organigram of the WIPO Secretariat   41
5.1   A view of WIPO's complex governance structure   68
6.1   Share of WIPO's fee income/total income from
      2004/2005 to 2016/2017   107
6.2   Top ten origins of PCT applications (2014)   110
6.3   Top Hague design applicants in 2014   114
6.4   WIPO Program and Budget Mechanism (in use since
      2008/2009)   141

Tables

2.1 WIPO treaties by category and number of ratifications   12

2.2 Membership of WIPO and selected WIPO treaties, as well as the International Union for the Protection of New Varieties of Plants (UPOV) and the WTO   14

2.3 WIPO budget after transfers (expenditures) and development share (in Swiss Francs as estimated by the WIPO Secretariat) 2010–2017   33

2.4 WIPO Directors General and their period of tenure   39

2.5 Examples of Office Instructions relevant to WIPO governance   43

3.1 Examples of major internal and UN reports on WIPO governance since 1998   48

3.2 Key components of WIPO's governance system   50

4.1 Status of ratification of the 1999 amendment to Article 9(3) of the WIPO Convention   57

4.2 Status of ratification of amendments to WIPO-administered treaties (including the WIPO Convention) adopted by the Assemblies of WIPO Member States on 1 October 2003   59

4.3 WIPO Development Agenda recommendations   61

5.1 Development Agenda: coordination mechanisms and monitoring, assessing and reporting modalities   94

6.1 Evolution of WIPO income from 2002/2003 to 2016/2017 (in millions of Swiss Francs)   108

6.2 Top 50 PCT applicants (1995–2014)   111

6.3 Top 50 PCT applicants: businesses, 2014   115

6.4 Top 50 PCT applicants: universities, 2014   118

6.5 Top 30 PCT applicants: government and research institutions, 2014   121

6.6 Contribution classes of members of WIPO, Paris and/or the Berne Unions   124

6.7 WIPO's Strategic Goals   138

6.8 WIPO's 2016/2017 Budget by Program and Union (in thousands of Swiss Francs)   150

7.1 WIPO Staff Regulations and Rules: selected examples of
     Regulations and Rules relevant to governance   168
7.2 WIPO Code of Ethics   172
8.1 Agreement between the World Intellectual Property
     Organization and the World Trade Organization (1995)
     (selected excerpts)   183
8.2 Criteria for admission as permanent observer in WIPO   188

Preface

My decision to publish this Reference Guide follows over a decade of engagement in policy and scholarly discussions of the World Intellectual Property Organization (WIPO) and its activities. It is the first instalment of ongoing research for a forthcoming book on the power politics, dynamics and evolution of WIPO's governance. In the process of that research, I have regularly lamented the absence of a reference work on WIPO's governance. Meanwhile, amidst protracted debates on all manner of issues at WIPO, concerns about governance regularly arises. It is now commonplace for stakeholders and commentators to describe WIPO's governance system as complex and opaque. Member States too complain of their struggle to navigate and piece together the vast and dispersed web of relevant documents. To help fill the gap, I decided to take on the task of compiling a basic reference guide to WIPO's governance system in practical, readily accessible terms for policymakers, stakeholders and scholars.

My research on WIPO benefited greatly from assistance from a number of WIPO staff. The author thanks Edward Kwakwa, WIPO's Legal Counsel, and Christine Castro Hublin, Head of the Legal and Constitutional Affairs Section within the Office of WIPO's Legal Counsel, for their clarification of several aspects of WIPO's governance system and their feedback on drafts of this book.

Over the past several years, I have benefited from conversations with a broad range of WIPO staff and Member States in the context of my work as co-author of a 2011 *External Review of WIPO's Technical Assistance in the Area of Cooperation for Development* (commissioned by the WIPO Secretariat on behalf of Member States in accordance with Development Agenda Recommendation 31) and author of a 2012 *Independent Strategic Review of the WIPO Academy* (commissioned by the Secretariat on its own behalf). Together, these assignments provided me with a privileged insight into the internal workings and dynamics of the organisation, as well as the relationships between staff and Member States. I extend special thanks also to Lise Macleod at the WIPO Library for swift archival assistance and helping to locate a number of WIPO's historical documents, and to Maya Bachner, who was an invaluable guide to the intricacies of WIPO during the External Review process.

Further, my background research for this book drew regularly on news reports and analysis published by *Intellectual Property Watch*, which I founded in 2004 and continue to serve as the Chair of its Board.

I extend great thanks to Ahmed Abdel-Latif and Pedro Roffe, who have been fantastic companions and sounding boards throughout my work on the international intellectual property system and WIPO. I am grateful to each for enriching my work and for their friendship.

This book also benefited from feedback from an informal dialogue with officials from WIPO, delegates from a number of WIPO Member States, and experts hosted by the International Centre for Trade and Sustainable Development in March 2015, where an early draft of this book was distributed for feedback. In the final stages, I also received valuable input from three of Edward Elgar Publishing's independent reviewers.

The Global Economic Governance Programme, jointly hosted by the University of Oxford's Blavatnik School of Government and University College, has been a wonderful home for my work on this book, and my wider research on the global governance of intellectual property and trade. I am immensely grateful to GEG's Director Ngaire Woods, Dean of the Blavatnik School of Government for her support of my work, and to the Ford Foundation and the Old Members of University College for their financial contributions to GEG. I thank all my colleagues at GEG, and particularly Emily Jones (GEG Deputy Director), Reija Fanous, Taylor St. John, Geoffrey Gertz and Alexa Zeitz for their advice and feedback on various drafts, and for their encouragement.

I am grateful to Catherine Saez, Iveta Cherneva and Emma Burnett for editorial and research assistance at various points along the way, and especially to Alexa Zeitz at GEG for her superb help when preparing the final manuscript.

At Edward Elgar Publishing, I thank Luke Adams and Laura Mann for their swift work in moving the manuscript forward and for sharing my conviction that there was indeed a need for this reference guide on WIPO's governance. I am very grateful to Claire Greenwell for her fine editorial attention to the manuscript.

Finally, my work on this book relied on my Dad's remarkable ability (and willingness) to keep all of my technology up to date and running, and to solve the full array of day-to-day problems – IT and other – that arise! The only explanation for such endurance is love, which I return with armfuls of thanks. For their love and patience, my greatest debt is to my super team – Alec, Emily Skye and George.

Acknowledgement

The material referred to in Tables 2.2, 4.1, 4.2, 4.3, 5.1, 6.1, 6.2, 6.3, 6.4, 6.5, 6.6, 6.7, 6.8, 7.1, 7.2, 8.1 and 8.2; Figures 6.1, 6.2, 6.3 and 6.4; and Appendices 1–9 was originally provided by the World Intellectual Property Organization (WIPO). The Secretariat of WIPO assumes no liability or responsibility with regard to the transformation of this data.

Abbreviations

ABC	Accessible Books Consortium
ACE	Advisory Committee on Enforcement
ADG	Assistant Director General
ADR	Alternative dispute resolution
ARDI	Access to Research for Development and Innovation
ARIPO	African Regional Intellectual Property Organization
ASEAN	Association of South East Asian Nations
ASPI	Access to Specialised Patent Information
BIRPI	United International Bureaux for the Protection of Intellectual Property
CDIP	Committee on Development and Intellectual Property
CEB	United Nations Chief Executives Board
CEBs	Central European and Baltic States Group
CERLALC	Regional Center for Book Development in Latin America and the Caribbean
CGI	Committee on Global IP Infrastructure
CHF	Swiss Franc
CWS	Committee on World Intellectual Property Organization Standards
DAG	Development Agenda Group
DDG	Deputy Director General
DSA	Daily subsistence allowance
DSU	Dispute Settlement Understanding
ECOSOC	United Nations Economic and Social Council
FAO	United Nations Food and Agriculture Organization
FITs	Funds-in-Trust
FRR	Financial Regulations and Rules of the World Intellectual Property Organization
GRULAC	Group of Latin American and Caribbean countries
HLCM	United Nations High-Level Committee on Management
IAC	Industry Advisory Commission
IAOC	Independent Advisory Oversight Committee
ICSC	International Civil Service Commission

ICT	Information and Communication Technologies
IFAC	International Federation of Accountants
IGC	Intergovernmental Committee on Intellectual Property and Genetic Resources, Traditional Knowledge and Folklore
IGO	Intergovernmental organisation
ILO	International Labour Organization
IOD	Internal Oversight Division
IP	Intellectual property
IPAS	Industrial Property Automation System
IPC	International Patent Classification
IPSAS	International Public Sector Accounting Standards
IPSASB	International Public Sector Accounting Standards Board
JIU	United Nations Joint Inspection Unit
LDC	Least Developed Country
MDGs	Millennium Development Goals
MOU	Memorandum of Understanding
MTSP	Medium Term Strategic Plan for WIPO, 2010–2015
NGO	Non-governmental organisation
OECD	Organisation for Economic Co-operation and Development
PAC	Policy Advisory Commission
PBC	Program and Budget Committee
PCDIP	Permanent Committee on Cooperation for Development related to IP
PCT	Patent Cooperation Treaty
PLT	Patent Law Treaty
PMSDS	Performance Management and Staff Development System
PPP	Public–private partnerships
R&D	Research and development
RBM	Results-based management
SCCR	Standing Committee on Copyright and Related Rights
SCP	Standing Committee on the Law of Patents
SCT	Standing Committee on Trademarks, Industrial Designs and Geographical Indications
SME	Small and medium-sized enterprises
SMT	Senior Management Team
TRIPS	Trade-Related Aspects of Intellectual Property Rights
UN	United Nations
UNCTAD	United Nations Conference on Trade and Development
UNEP	United Nations Environment Programme

UNESCO	United Nations Educational, Scientific and Cultural Organization
UNIDO	United Nations Industrial Development Organization
UPOV	International Union for the Protection of New Varieties of Plants
WAEMU	West African Economic and Monetary Union
WCT	WIPO Copyright Treaty
WEOG	Western European and Others Group
WHO	World Health Organization
WIPD	World Intellectual Property Declaration
WIPO	World Intellectual Property Organization
WIPOCOS	World Intellectual Property Organization Copyright Management System
WPPT	WIPO Performances and Phonograms Treaty
WTO	World Trade Organization

1 Introduction

The World Intellectual Property Organization (WIPO) is the multilateral system's key agency charged with intellectual property (IP). Over the past five decades, WIPO has taken a lead role in promoting the strengthening of IP rights, as well as their use and enforcement across the world. A United Nations (UN) Specialized Agency, WIPO is the administrator of 26 international IP treaties and boasts a larger budget for supporting the modernisation of IP systems in developing countries than any other single organisation, national or international. WIPO also serves as a forum for intergovernmental negotiations on new legal instruments and for debate on how IP intersects with a range of public policy goals – from public health to food security.

The World Intellectual Property Organization's work occurs amidst a rapidly changing global economy – as evidenced by the rise of the digital economy – where markets and societies are increasingly connected, and the rising power of emerging economies has changed the dynamics of international diplomacy across global policy issues. WIPO's work also occurs in the context of a growing array of political, economic and social debates on IP treaties, laws, policies and practices around the world. Yet, although IP policy and rules are at the heart of many high-stakes battles across the global knowledge economy, WIPO is largely unknown beyond IP experts and is generally neglected in debates on global economic governance.

In its outreach efforts, the WIPO Secretariat describes the organisation as the global forum for IP policy, services, information and cooperation. Dedicated to making IP 'work for everyone,' the Secretariat characterises WIPO's work as driven by the need for an international IP system that is efficient and easily accessible worldwide, and that provides a set of international rules that 'balance the interests of those who produce and consume the fruits of innovation and creativity.'[1] WIPO's

---

1 WIPO, *WIPO: Making IP Work* (WIPO 2014).

pursuit of this ambitious agenda has spurred an expanding portfolio of activities – from norm-setting and policy dialogue to public-private partnerships and technical assistance.

The starting point for this Reference Guide is that the growing importance and influence of WIPO's expanding work must be accompanied by more active and constructive engagement of governments, stakeholders and scholars with the organisation and more critical oversight of its activities. The prospects for improved oversight and deeper, wider engagement in WIPO's work will depend, however, on greater understanding and transparency of the organisation's governance system and action to address its shortfalls. The need to improve WIPO's governance was underscored in 2014 by the UN Joint Inspection Unit (JIU),[2] and a growing number of Member States and stakeholders acknowledge the array of governance challenges facing the organisation.

The governance matters that provoke debate at WIPO include: the complexity of the organisation's governance structure; the relationship between WIPO and the treaty-based Unions it administers; the appropriate role of the Secretariat and stakeholders; decision-making practices and financial arrangements. In recent years, Member States and stakeholders alike have regularly underscored the importance of bolstering WIPO's Member-driven nature; they have also routinely registered their dissatisfaction with inefficient and opaque decision-making processes. In addition, there are ongoing debates about the scope for plurilateral treaty negotiations at WIPO and their implications for the organisation's multilateral character. Views on which governance challenges demand attention vary. Some stakeholders, for instance, call for attention to WIPO's provisions for public participation and transparency, and for clarity on the private sector's role in WIPO. The Secretariat has emphasised the need for higher-level engagement of Member States. While most Member States are in favour of improved efficiency in WIPO decision-making, they struggle to agree on concrete steps to be taken. Some Member States propose getting started on reform through incremental, practical improvements on specific procedural matters, while others insist on a more comprehensive approach to reform. The core governance priority for many developing country Member States is mainstreaming the Development Agenda

---

2 JIU, *Review of Management and Administration in the World Intellectual Property Organization (WIPO)* JIU/REP/2014/2 (UN Joint Inspection Unit 2014) 7.

throughout the organisation and changing the Secretariat's institutional culture.[3]

Unlike other UN agencies, WIPO does not face one common governance challenge – lack of resources. Rather than relying on Member State contributions, WIPO earns over 95 per cent of its income through fees paid in exchange for IP registration services. As the UN's most successful self-financing organisation, WIPO nonetheless faces a range of governance challenges that arise from these unique financial arrangements.

To date, however, there is no consolidated reference text on WIPO's governance. In 2014, for instance, the UN JIU highlighted the absence of a clear or regularly updated overview of WIPO's governance framework. Member States, staff and stakeholders are instead left to locate, navigate and piece together a multitude of dispersed documents, including the WIPO Convention, procedural rules for WIPO's governing bodies, regulations and rules, working methods, and hundreds of proposals and meetings reports, as well as a suite of internal policies. Although the Secretariat and a number of WIPO committees have produced official WIPO documents that cover some aspects of WIPO's governance structure[4] and the organisation's history,[5] these

---

3 See Carolyn Deere Birkbeck, 'Inside View: Strengthening WIPO's Governance for the Next 50 Years: A Time for Action' *Intellectual Property Watch* (26 September 2014); Nick Ashton-Hart, 'Inside Views: How to Reboot WIPO' *Intellectual Property Watch* (12 September 2014); James Boyle, 'A Manifesto on WIPO and the Future of Intellectual Property' (2004) 9 *Duke Law and Technology Review* 1–12; Nandini Kotthapally, 'From World Intellectual Property Organization (WIPO) to World Innovation Promotion Organization (WIPO): Whither WIPO?' (2011) 3(1) *The WIPO Journal* 56–71; Civil Society Coalition, 'Geneva Declaration on the Future of the World Intellectual Property Organization' (2004) <http://www.futureofwipo.org/future ofwipodeclaration.pdf> accessed 7 July 2015; CIEL, *A Citizens' Guide to WIPO* (CIEL 2007); Robin Gross, 'World Intellectual Property Organisation (WIPO): Institutional Overviews' (2007) *Global Information Society Watch* <http://www.giswatch.org> accessed 30 October 2014.

4 See, for instance, the following WIPO documents: WIPO, *Introduction to WIPO: Objectives, Organization Structure and Activities, Development Cooperation Program* WIPO/ACAD/E/94/2 (WIPO 1994); WIPO, *The Governance Structure of WIPO: Memorandum of the International Bureau* A/32/INF/2 (WIPO 1998); WIPO, *Constitutional Reform: Memorandum of the Secretariat* A/33/3 (WIPO 1998); WIPO, *Report of the WIPO Audit Committee since 2008* WO/GA/38/2 (WIPO 2009); WIPO, *WIPO Governance Structure* WO/PBC/18/20 (WIPO 2011); WIPO, *Governance at WIPO: Report Prepared by the WIPO Independent Advisory Oversight Committee* WO/PBC/19/26 (WIPO 2012). Also see WIPO, *WIPO Intellectual Property Handbook: Policy, Law and Use* (WIPO 2004); WIPO, *A Users' Guide: An Introduction to the Organization for Delegates*, Publication No. 1040 (WIPO 2012).

5 See Jacques Secretan, 'L'évolution de structure des unions internationaux pour la protection de la propriété intellectuelle' in BIRPI, *Les Unions Internationale pour la protection de la propriété industrial, littéraire et artistique, 1883–1963* (BIRPI 1962); Árpád Bogsch, *Brief History of the First*

offer a fragmented, incomplete and sometimes out-dated picture. Moreover, such documents do not capture the many informal dimensions of WIPO's governance system, both those that arise where the formal framework is silent or ambiguous, and those that exist alongside formal processes and impact how governance occurs in practice.

In the academic literature, scholars have offered reflections on WIPO's role in the global governance of IP[6] and in the development of international IP law[7] as well as on its response to initiatives such as the WIPO Development Agenda.[8] Only a handful of studies, however, focus specifically on WIPO as an institution – on its evolution,[9] internal culture

---

25 Years of the World Intellectual Property Organization (WIPO 1992); WIPO, *World Intellectual Property Organization: 1992–2007* (WIPO 2003).

6 Academic publications that reflect on WIPO's role in the governance of IP include: Frederick M. Abbott, 'Distributed Governance at the WTO-WIPO: An Evolving Model for Open-Architecture Integrated Governance' (2000) 3(1) *Journal of International Economic Law* 63–81; Frederick M. Abbott, Francis Gurry and Thomas Cottier *The International Intellectual Property System: Commentary and Materials* (Kluwer Law 1999); Graeme B. Dinwoodie, 'The Architecture of the International Intellectual Property System' (2002) 77(3) *Chicago-Kent Law Review* 993–1014; Paul Salmon, 'Cooperation between the World Intellectual Property Organization and the World Trade Organization' (2003) 17 *St. John's Journal of Legal Commentary* 429–42; Ruth L. Okediji, 'The International Relations of Intellectual Property: Narratives of Developing Country Participation in the Global Intellectual Property System' (2003) 7 *Singapore Journal of International and Comparative Law* 315–85; Ruth L. Okediji, 'WIPO–WTO Relations and the Future of Global Intellectual Property Norms' (2008) 39 *Netherlands Yearbook of International Law* 69–125; Graeme Dinwoodie and Rochelle Dreyfuss, 'Designing a Global Intellectual Property System Responsive to Change: The WTO, WIPO and Beyond' (2009) 46(4) *Houston Law Review* 1187–234.

7 For a concise recent study of the evolution and future of WIPO's role in the development of IP treaties, see Daniel Gervais 'Rethinking the International Intellectual Property System: What Role for WIPO?' in *Rethinking International Intellectual Property Law: What Institutional Environment for the Development and Enforcement of IP Law? Global Perspectives and Challenges for the Intellectual Property System, Issue 1* (Geneva and Strasbourg: ICTSD and CEIPI 2015). Also see various contributions in Daniel Gervais (ed.), *International Intellectual Property: A Handbook of Contemporary Research* (Cheltenham, UK: Edward Elgar Publishing 2015).

8 See Carolyn Deere, 'Reforming Governance to Advance the WIPO Development Agenda,' in Jeremy de Beer (ed.), *Implementing WIPO's Development Agenda* (Wilfrid Laurier University Press 2009); Susan K. Sell, 'Everything Old Is New Again: The Development Agenda Now and Then' (2011) 3(1) *The WIPO Journal* 17–23; Peter K. Yu, 'A Tale of Two Development Agendas' (2008) 35 *Ohio Northern University Law Review* 466–573; Francis Gurry, 'The Dispute Resolution Service of the World Intellectual Property Organization' (1999) 2(2) *Journal of International Economic Law* 385–98, 385.

9 Scholarly works on the history of WIPO include: Ulf Anderfelt, *International Patent Legislation and Developing Countries* (Martinus Nijhoff 1971); F-K Beier, 'One Hundred Years of International Cooperation: The Role of the Paris Convention in the Past, Present and Future' (1984) 15(1) *International Review of Industrial Property and Copyright Law* 1–20; Debora J. Halbert 'The World Intellectual Property Organization: Past, Present and Future' (2005) 54(1) *Journal of the Copyright Society of the USA* 253–84.

and political economy.[10] Although these works address some aspects of WIPO's governance framework, and several papers analyse the process of decision-making at WIPO,[11] the task of systematic analysis of WIPO's governance system has thus far escaped the scholarly attention it deserves. As such, there has not yet been any comprehensive scholarly review of WIPO's governance or governance reform efforts.

This book is intended to serve as a factual reference guide to WIPO's governance system. It does not aim to assess WIPO's governance system, analyse the political dynamics of WIPO's governance, or critique the power politics that shape them, although it does seek to offer a much-needed foundation stone for that important work.[12] The book does, nonetheless, highlight some of the key political and informal dimensions of WIPO's governance system and notes where WIPO diverges significantly from other international organisations in terms of policies or practice, such as its self-financing business model. In describing the components of WIPO's governance system, this book refers to recent debates where they are pertinent to understanding the relevance to governance, but it defers for future scholarship the task of assessing the merits of different views points and reform options.

The book opens in Chapter 2 by introducing the origins of WIPO, its current functions and many activities, as well as the WIPO Secretariat

---

10 See James Boyle, 'A Manifesto on WIPO and the Future of Intellectual Property' (2004) 9 *Duke Law and Technology Review* 1–12; Christopher May, *The World Intellectual Property Organization: Resurgence and the Development Agenda* (Routledge 2006); Alexander Stack, *International Patent Law: Cooperation, Harmonization and an Institutional Analysis of WIPO and the WTO* (Edward Elgar Publishing 2011); Andrea Wechsler, 'WIPO and the Public–Private Web of Global Intellectual Property Governance' in Christoph Hermann, Markus Krajewski and Jörg Philipp Terhechte (eds), *2013 European Yearbook of International Economic Law* (Springer 2013) 413–40. In addition, two notable critical assessments of WIPO's governance have been published by NGOs. See Sisule F Musungu and Graham Dutfield, *Multilateral Agreements and a TRIPS-Plus World: The World Intellectual Property Organisation* TRIPS Issues Paper 3 (Quaker United Nations Office (QUNO) and Quaker International Affairs Program (QIAP) 2003) and CIEL, *A Citizens' Guide to WIPO* (CIEL 2007).

11 Edward Kwakwa, 'Some Comments on Rule Making at the World Intellectual Property Organization' (2002) 12(1) *Duke Journal of Comparative and International Law* 179–95; Geoffrey Yu, 'The Structure and Process of Negotiations at the World Intellectual Property Organization' (2007) 82 *Chicago-Kent Law Review* 1443–53, 1452.

12 For political assessments of the current challenges facing WIPO's governance and the reform process to date, see Carolyn Deere Birkbeck, *Governing the World Intellectual Property Organization: The Power Politics of Institutional Crisis and Reform* (Routledge forthcoming 2016). Also see Carolyn Deere Birkbeck, 'Inside View: Strengthening WIPO's Governance for the Next 50 Years: A Time for Action' *Intellectual Property Watch* (26 September 2014).

and its leadership. Chapter 3 presents a framework for analysing WIPO's governance. The subsequent chapters review the core components of WIPO's governance system in five thematic areas: legal foundations, mandate and purpose; structures and processes for decision-making and practices for Member State representation; financial arrangements (including income and budget process); mechanisms for accountability and control of the Secretariat (that is, for oversight, audit and evaluation); and transparency and external relations. Through this review, the book provides examples of how the WIPO Secretariat is both a subject of WIPO's formal governance structure and an actor in the wider governance system that impacts what the organisation does and how. Chapter 9 concludes the book.

The primary sources for the analysis presented in this book were official WIPO documents (including Secretariat reports and minutes of intergovernmental meetings, WIPO treaties and policies, and the WIPO website), as well as informal interviews of WIPO staff and delegates undertaken by the author, and personal observations of WIPO decision-making processes for over a decade. In addition to academic works and analysis by stakeholder organisations, the research drew extensively on reporting by the independent news service *Intellectual Property Watch*.

2 What is WIPO and what does it do?

2.1 WIPO's origins

The origins of WIPO date back to the 1883 Paris Convention for the Protection of Industrial Property and the 1886 Berne Convention for the Protection of Literary and Artistic Works, which together laid the foundations for contemporary international IP regulation.[1] Both conventions provided for the establishment of an 'International Bureau' to provide administrative support to the Unions formed by their respective States Parties. The two bureaux combined in 1893 to create the United International Bureaux for the Protection of Intellectual Property (usually referred to by its French acronym, BIRPI). With the conclusion of further conventions on specialised aspects of IP (such as on trademarks, industrial designs and appellations of origin), the Unions created by several of these treaties were also integrated into BIRPI (that is, the Madrid, Hague, Nice, and Lisbon Unions).

Following the entry into force of the 1967 Convention Establishing the World Intellectual Property Organization (the WIPO Convention), BIRPI was replaced by WIPO in 1970 (for the text of the Convention, see Appendix 1).[2] As an 'umbrella organisation', WIPO 'federated the Unions dealing with intellectual property issues into an expanded

---

1 See F-K Beier, 'One Hundred Years of International Cooperation: The Role of the Paris Convention in the Past, Present and Future' (1984) 15(1) *International Review of Industrial Property and Copyright Law* 1–20; Geoffrey Gaultier, 'The History of AIPPI' in General Secretariat of AIPPI, *1897–1997 Centennial Edition: AIPPI and the Development of Industrial Property Protection 1897–1997* (AIPPI Foundation 1997); John Braithwaite and Peter Drahos, *Global Business Regulation* (CUP 2000) 60.

2 The Convention was adopted by the Parties of the existing Unions. See Convention Establishing the World Intellectual Property Organization (WIPO Convention) 1967 (amended 1979).

international organization.'[3] In 1974, WIPO became a Specialized Agency of the UN system (see Appendix 2).[4]

By 2015, WIPO had 188 Member States, of which over 120 were developing countries.[5] Together, these Member States are responsible for determining the direction, budget and activities of WIPO.[6]

2.2   What is WIPO's purpose?

The WIPO Convention sets out WIPO's general objectives as: 'to promote the protection of intellectual property throughout the world through cooperation among States' and 'to ensure administrative cooperation among the Unions.'[7] The Preamble to the Convention refers to the States' desire to:

> . . . contribute to better understanding and co-operation among States for their mutual benefit on the basis of respect for their sovereignty and equality; encourage creative activity, to promote the protection of intellectual property throughout the world; and modernize and render more efficient the administration of the Unions established in the fields of the protection of industrial property and the protection of literary and artistic works, while fully respecting the independence of each of the Unions.

In 1974, Article 1 of an agreement between WIPO and the UN established WIPO as a Specialized Agency of the UN 'for promoting creative intellectual activity and for facilitating the transfer of technology related to industrial property to . . . the developing countries in order

---

3 See JIU, *Review of Management and Administration in the World Intellectual Property Organization (WIPO)* JIU/REP/2014/2 (UN Joint Inspection Unit 2014) 2.

4 See WIPO, *Agreement between the United Nations and the World Intellectual Property Organization* WIPO Publication No. 111 (WIPO 1975).

5 For a complete current listing of WIPO Member States, see WIPO, 'Member States' <http://www.wipo.int/members/en/> accessed 26 October 2015.

6 To become a WIPO Member, a state must deposit an instrument of ratification or accession with the Director General. The WIPO Convention provides that membership is open to any state that is: a) a member of the Paris Union or Berne Union; b) a member of the UN, or of any of the UN's Specialized Agencies, or of the International Atomic Energy Agency, or that is a party to the Statute of the International Court of Justice; or c) invited by the WIPO General Assembly to become a Member State of the organisation. States already party to the Berne or Paris Conventions must concurrently ratify or accede to at least the administrative provisions of the Stockholm 1967 Act of the Paris Convention or of the 1971 Act of the Berne Convention.

7 See WIPO Convention, Article 3.

to accelerate economic, social and cultural development.'[8] (For the text of the Agreement, see Appendix 2.)

In 2007, WIPO Member States adopted the WIPO Development Agenda, which included 45 recommendations that together aim to make the organisation as a whole and its various activities more focused on the needs of its developing country Member States.[9] (The text of the WIPO Development Agenda can be found in Table 4.3 in Chapter 4.)

Over the years, the WIPO Secretariat has advanced a number of interpretations of the organisation's mission. In 2010, for instance, WIPO described its mission as: 'the promotion of innovation and creativity for the economic, social and cultural development of all countries through a balanced and effective international IP system.'[10] On the home page of WIPO's website, the Secretariat describes the organisation as the 'global forum for IP services, policy, information and cooperation.'[11] In a 2014 brochure on WIPO, the Secretariat further elaborated, describing the organisation as a 'self-funding, specialized agency of the UN, dedicated to making IP work for innovation and creativity.'[12]

2.3   What does WIPO do in practice?

Whereas WIPO was initially created to serve primarily as the secretariat of intergovernmental treaties and treaty negotiations, its activities have increased enormously over the past four decades. The organisation's growing workload has been due in part to the rising use of its global protection system treaties. It also results from the significant diversification of both WIPO's functions and the scope of its activities. As Member State demands on the organisation have grown, and public expectations have expanded, the WIPO Secretariat has

---

8 See WIPO, *Agreement between the United Nations and the World Intellectual Property Organization* WIPO Publication No. 111 (WIPO 1975).

9 See WIPO, *General Report, WIPO Assemblies of Member States, 43rd Series of Meetings* A/43/16 (WIPO 2007) para. 334. For the text of the agenda, see <http://www.wipo.int/ip-development/en/agenda> accessed 1 October 2014.

10 This mission was advanced in WIPO, *Medium Term Strategic Plan, 2010–15* A/48/3 (WIPO 2010).

11 See WIPO website, <http://www.wipo.int> accessed 29 October 2015.

12 See WIPO, *WIPO: Making IP Work* (WIPO 2014).

Increasing Complexity of Intergovernmental Rule-Making and Decision-Making by Member States

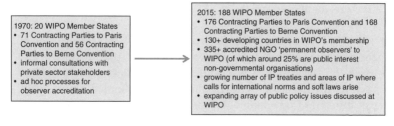

Growing Size of the WIPO Secretariat, Expanding Scope of its Activities and Rising Political Interest in WIPO's Work

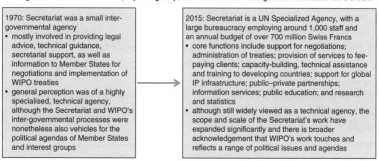

Source: Author's own diagram.

Figure 2.1   Growing demands on WIPO governance from 1970–2015

grown in terms of budget and staff (see Figure 2.1). For the 2016/17 biennium, WIPO Member States approved a budget of over 707 million Swiss Francs.[13]

In practical terms, WIPO's main day-to-day activities can be clustered in two core areas. First, WIPO provides a forum for Member States to pursue legal negotiations and policy discussions that shape international rules and practices on IP, and which occur through its various Committees, supported by the WIPO Secretariat. The agency hosts some 20 intergovernmental committees tasked with different aspects of global IP law and policy. These include committees charged with oversight of existing WIPO treaties and negotiation of new treaties and soft law instruments (such as guidelines), as well as committees focused on issues ranging from IP enforcement to the relationship of IP and development.

---

13 WIPO, *Proposed Program and Budget for the 2016/17 Biennium* A/55/5 Rev. (WIPO 2015).

Second, the WIPO Secretariat is a bureaucracy that provides a range of services to Member States, stakeholders and the public. In this area of WIPO's work, the Secretariat:

1. Administers the 25 intergovernmental IP treaties (plus the WIPO Convention) and their financial arrangements where relevant (see Table 2.1). WIPO's agreements fall into three main categories: 15 IP protection treaties (which define international substantive standards on IP);[14] 4 classification treaties (which aim to organise information concerning inventions, trademarks and industrial designs through an indexed classification system);[15] and 6 global protection system treaties (which establish procedural rules mainly aimed at ensuring that one international registration or filing of an industrial property will have effect in all the countries signatory to the relevant treaties).[16] (See Table 2.2 for the membership of these WIPO treaties.) In addition, WIPO provides administrative and financial services to the International Union for the Protection of New Varieties of Plants (UPOV), an independent intergovernmental organisation established by the International Convention for the

---

14 For each of WIPO's 15 main protection treaties, Member States agree to grant nationals of other countries of the Union the same protection as they grant to their own, and also to follow certain common rules, standards and practices. The 15 protection treaties are the Beijing Treaty on Audiovisual Performances; Berne Convention for the Protection of Literary and Artistic Works; Convention Relating to the Distribution of Programme-Carrying Signals Transmitted by Satellite (Brussels); Madrid Agreement for the Repression of False or Deceptive Indications of Source on Goods; Nairobi Treaty on the Protection of the Olympic Symbol; Paris Convention for the Protection of Industrial Property; Patent Law Treaty; Convention for the Protection of Producers of Phonograms Against Unauthorized Duplication of Their Phonograms; International Convention for the Protection of Performers; Producers of Phonograms and Broadcasting Organizations (Rome); Singapore Treaty on the Law of Trademarks; Trademark Law Treaty; WIPO Copyright Treaty; WIPO Performances and Phonograms Treaty; and the Marrakesh Treaty to Facilitate Access to Published Works for Persons Who Are Blind, Visually Impaired, or Otherwise Print Disabled. The Washington Treaty on Intellectual Property in Respect of Integrated Circuits, which has never entered into force at WIPO, is not included in this list.

15 These are the Locarno Agreement Establishing an International Classification for Industrial Designs; Nice Agreement Concerning the International Classification of Goods and Services for the Purposes of the Registration of Marks; Strasbourg Agreement Concerning the International Patent Classification; and the Vienna Agreement Establishing an International Classification of the Figurative Elements of Marks.

16 These are the Budapest Treaty on the International Recognition of the Deposit of Microorganisms for the Purpose of Patent Procedure; Hague Agreement Concerning the International Deposit of Industrial Designs (including the Geneva Act of 1999); Lisbon Agreement for the Protection of Appellations of Origin and their International Registration; Madrid Agreement Concerning the International Registration of Marks; Protocol Relating to the Madrid Agreement; and the Patent Cooperation Treaty (Washington).

Table 2.1 WIPO treaties by category and number of ratifications

Titles	Purpose	Ratifications
WIPO Convention (1967)	Establishing the World Intellectual Property Organization (WIPO)	188
Protection Treaties	**Purpose**	
Paris Convention (1883)	Concerning protection of industrial property, including patents, marks, industrial designs, utility models, trade names, and the repression of unfair competition	176
Berne Convention (1886)	Concerning the protection of literary and artistic work	168
Madrid Agreement (Source) (1891)	For the repression of false or deceptive indications of the source of goods	36
Rome Convention (1961)	Concerning protection of performances of performers, producers of phonograms and broadcasts of broadcasting organisations	92
Phonograms Convention (1971)	Concerning the protection of phonograms	78
Brussels Convention (1974)	Relating to the distribution of programme-carrying signals transmitted by satellite	37
Nairobi Treaty (1981)	Concerning the protection of the Olympic symbol	52
Washington Treaty (1989)	Concerning intellectual property in respect of integrated circuits	3
Trademark Law Treaty (1994)	Establishing more user-friendly national and regional trademark registration systems	55
WIPO Copyright Treaty (1996)	Introducing new international rules and clarifying the interpretation of certain existing rules in order to respond to the impact of information and communication technologies on the creation and use of literary and artistic works	93
WIPO Performances and Phonograms Treaty (1996)	Introducing new international rules responding to the impacts of information and communication technologies on the production and use of performances and phonograms	94
Patent Law Treaty (2000)	Harmonising and streamlining formal procedures in respect of national and regional patent applications and patents to make such procedures more user-friendly	36
Singapore Treaty (2006)	On the law of trademarks	42
Beijing Audiovisual Treaty (2012)	Protecting the rights of audiovisual performers	10
Marrakesh Treaty (2013)	Facilitating access to published works for persons who are blind, visually impaired or otherwise print disabled	13
Classification Treaties		
Nice Agreement (1957)	Concerning the international classification of goods and services for the purpose of the registration of marks	84

Titles	Purpose	Ratifications
Classification Treaties		
Locarno Agreement (1968)	Establishing a system of classification for industrial designs	54
Strasbourg Agreement (1971)	Establishing the International Patent Classification (IPC) system	62
Vienna Agreement (1973)	Establishing a system of classification for marks	32
Global Protection System Treaties		
Madrid Agreement (Marks) (1891)	Concerning the international registration of marks	55
Hague Agreement (1925) (including the Geneva Act of 1999)	Concerning the international registration of industrial designs	64 (52)
Lisbon Agreement (1958) (including the Geneva Act of 2015)	Concerning the protection of appellations of origin and their international registration	28 (0)
Patent Cooperation Treaty (1970)	Enabling applicants to file an 'international' patent application seeking protection in many countries	148
Budapest Treaty (1977)	Concerning the international recognition of the deposit of microorganisms for the purposes of patent procedure	79
Madrid Protocol (on Registration of Marks) (1989)	Rendering the Madrid system more flexible and more compatible with the domestic legislations of certain countries that had not been able to accede to the Agreement	96

Note: The table does not include the 1989 Film Register Treaty on the international registration of audiovisual works. The operation of the Treaty was discontinued due to lack of demand. The Washington Treaty on the Protection of Integrated Circuits is included in this table given its importance as a treaty substantively incorporated into the TRIPS Agreement, although it is not counted as one of the 15 WIPO protection treaties as it has never entered into force. The Geneva Act of the Lisbon Agreement on Appellations of Origin and Geographical Indication was adopted by a Diplomatic Conference of the Lisbon Union on 20 May 2015. As of December 2015, no country had deposited their instruments of ratification or accession.

Source: WIPO, 'Summary Table of Membership of the World Intellectual Property Organization (WIPO) and the Treaties Administered by WIPO, plus UPOV, WTO and UN' <http://www.wipo.int/treaties/en/summary.jsp> accessed 31 December 2015.

Table 2.2 Membership of WIPO and selected WIPO treaties, as well as the International Union for the Protection of New Varieties of Plants (UPOV) and the WTO

Member State	WIPO Convention	Paris Convention	Berne Convention	Patent Cooperation Treaty	Patent Law Treaty	Rome Convention	Trademark Law Treaty	Hague Agreement (and Geneva Act of Hague)	Madrid Agreement (Marks)	Madrid Protocol	Nice Agreement	Lisbon Agreement	WIPO Copyright Treaty	WIPO Phonograms and Performances Treaty	Beijing Treaty	Locarno Agreement	Marrakesh Treaty	UPOV Convention	World Trade Organization
Afghanistan	X																		
Albania	X	X	X	X	X	X		X (X)	X	X	X	X	X	X				X	X
Algeria	X	X	X	X		X			X		X	X	X	X					
Andorra	X	X	X			X													
Angola	X	X	X	X															
Antigua and Barbuda	X	X	X	X						X									X
Argentina	X	X	X		X	X							X	X				X	X
Armenia	X	X	X	X	X	X		X (X)	X	X	X		X	X		X	X		X
Australia	X	X	X	X		X	X			X	X		X	X		X	X	X	X
Austria	X	X	X	X		X			X	X	X		X	X		X		X	X
Azerbaijan	X	X	X	X		X		X (X)	X	X	X		X	X		X		X	X
Bahamas	X	X	X																
Bahrain	X	X	X	X	X	X	X			X	X		X	X					X

14

Bangladesh	X	X																	X
Barbados	X	X	X				X	X	X	X							X	X	X
Belarus	X	X	X		X		X	X	X	X	X	X					X	X	
Belgium	X	X	X	X	X	X (X)	X	X	X	X	X	X	X	X			X		X
Belize	X	X	X			X													X
Benin	X	X	X			X		X	X	X									X
Bhutan	X	X					X	X											
Bolivia (Plurinational State of)	X	X			X		X			X	X							X	X
Bosnia and Herzegovina	X	X		X	X	X (X)	X	X	X	X	X	X	X	X					
Botswana	X	X	X		X	X (X)	X	X	X						X		X		X
Brazil	X	X	X		X											X		X	X
Brunei Darussalam	X	X	X		X	X (X)													X
Bulgaria	X	X	X			X (X)	X	X	X	X	X	X	X	X			X	X	X
Burkina Faso	X	X	X	X			X	X	X	X	X						X		X
Burundi	X	X			X														X
Cabo Verde	X	X					X												X
Cambodia	X	X						X											X
Cameroon	X		X																X

Member State	WIPO Convention	Paris Convention	Berne Convention	Patent Cooperation Treaty	Patent Law Treaty	Rome Convention	Trademark Law Treaty	Hague Agreement (and Geneva Act of Hague)	Madrid Agreement (Marks)	Madrid Protocol	Nice Agreement	Lisbon Agreement	WIPO Copyright Treaty	WIPO Phonograms and Performances Treaty	Beijing Treaty	Locarno Agreement	Marrakesh Treaty	UPOV Convention	World Trade Organization
Canada	X	X	X	X		X							X	X				X	X
Central African Republic	X	X	X	X															X
Chad	X	X	X	X															X
Chile	X	X	X	X		X	X						X	X				X	X
China	X	X	X	X					X	X	X		X	X	X	X		X	X
Colombia	X	X	X	X		X	X			X			X	X	X			X	X
Comoros	X	X	X	X															
Congo	X	X	X	X		X						X							X
Costa Rica	X	X	X	X		X	X					X	X	X				X	X
Côte d'Ivoire	X	X	X	X			X												X
Croatia	X	X	X	X	X	X		X (X)	X	X	X	X	X	X		X		X	X
Cuba	X	X	X	X					X	X	X		X			X			X
Cyprus	X	X	X	X		X	X		X	X			X	X					X

16

Country																					
Czech Republic	X	X	X		X	X		X		X	X	X	X	X		X	X		X	X		X
Democratic People's Republic of Korea	X	X	X					X		X	X	X	X	X		X		X				
Democratic Republic of the Congo	X	X	X	X																		X
Denmark	X	X	X		X	X	X	X (X)	X	X	X	X	X	X	X		X	X	X	X	X	X
Djibouti	X	X	X		X			X		X										X		X
Dominica	X	X	X		X					X		X										X
Dominican Republic	X	X	X		X	X		X		X			X		X		X	X		X		X
Ecuador	X	X	X		X	X		X		X		X	X	X	X		X		X	X		X
Egypt	X	X	X		X			X (X)	X	X	X	X	X	X			X					X
El Salvador	X	X	X		X	X		X		X			X	X	X	X						X
Equatorial Guinea	X	X	X							X												
Eritrea	X				X																	
Estonia	X	X	X		X	X		X (X)	X	X	X	X	X	X	X		X	X		X	X	X
Ethiopia	X																					
Fiji	X		X	X				X														X

17

Member State	WIPO Convention	Paris Convention	Berne Convention	Patent Cooperation Treaty	Patent Law Treaty	Rome Convention	Trademark Law Treaty	Hague Agreement (and Geneva Act of Hague)	Madrid Agreement (Marks)	Madrid Protocol	Nice Agreement	Lisbon Agreement	WIPO Copyright Treaty	WIPO Phonograms and Performances Treaty	Beijing Treaty	Locarno Agreement	Marrakesh Treaty	UPOV Convention	World Trade Organization
Finland	×	×	×	×	×	×		× (X)		×	×		×	×		×		×	×
former Yugoslav Republic of Macedonia	×	×	×	×	×	×		× (X)	×	×	×	×	×	×		×		×	×
France	×	×	×	×	×	×	×	× (X)	×	×			×	×		×		×	×
Gabon	×	×	×	×				×					×	×					×
Gambia	×	×	×	×															×
Georgia	×	×	×	×		×		× (X)	×	×	×	×	×	×		×		×	×
Germany	×	×	×	×		×	×	× (X)		×	×		×	×				×	×
Ghana	×	×	×	×				× (X)		×			×	×					×
Greece	×	×	×	×		×		×			×		×	×					×
Grenada	×	×	×	×		×										×			×
Guatemala	×	×	×	×									×	×					×
Guinea	×	×	×	×			×				×		×	×		×			×

Country																		
Guinea-Bissau	X	X	X															X
Guyana	X	X	X														X	X
Haiti	X	X	X					X										X
Holy See	X	X	X															
Honduras	X	X	X		X	X			X	X	X		X	X				X
Hungary	X	X	X		X	X	X (X)	X	X	X	X	X	X	X		X	X	X
Iceland	X	X	X			X	X (X)	X	X		X		X			X	X	X
India	X	X	X					X	X	X					X			X
Indonesia	X	X	X		X	X			X		X		X	X				X
Iran (Islamic Republic of)	X	X	X					X	X	X	X		X	X			X	
Iraq	X	X																
Ireland	X	X	X	X	X	X		X	X	X	X		X	X		X	X	X
Israel	X	X	X		X			X	X	X	X					X	X	X
Italy	X	X	X		X	X	X	X	X	X	X		X	X		X	X	X
Jamaica	X	X			X	X			X	X	X		X	X				X
Japan	X	X	X		X	X	X (X)	X	X	X	X		X	X	X	X	X	X
Jordan	X	X	X		X				X	X	X		X	X			X	X
Kazakhstan	X	X	X		X	X			X	X	X		X	X		X		
Kenya	X	X	X					X									X	X
Kiribati	X																	

19

Member State	WIPO Convention	Paris Convention	Berne Convention	Patent Cooperation Treaty	Patent Law Treaty	Rome Convention	Trademark Law Treaty	Hague Agreement (and Geneva Act of Hague)	Madrid Agreement (Marks)	Madrid Protocol	Nice Agreement	Lisbon Agreement	WIPO Copyright Treaty	WIPO Phonograms and Performances Treaty	Beijing Treaty	Locarno Agreement	Marrakesh Treaty	UPOV Convention	World Trade Organization
Kuwait	×	×	×																×
Kyrgyzstan	×	×	×	×	×	×	×	X (X)	×	×	×		×	×		×		×	×
Lao People's Democratic Republic	×	×	×	×															×
Latvia	×	×	×	×	×	×	×	X (X)	×	×	×		×	×		×		×	×
Lebanon	×	×	×			×					×								
Lesotho	×	×	×	×		×			×	×									×
Liberia	×	×	×	×		×			×	×									
Libya	×	×	×	×		×													
Liechtenstein	×	×	×	×	×	×	×	X (X)	×	×	×		×	×					×
Lithuania	×	×	×	×	×	×	×	X (X)		×	×		×	×				×	×
Luxembourg	×	×	×	×		×	×	X (X)	×	×	×		×	×					×
Madagascar	×	×	×	×						×			×	×					×

20

Country	C1	C2	C3	C4	C5	C6	C7	C8	C9	C10	C11	C12	C13	C14	C15	C16	C17	C18	C19	C20
Malawi	X	X	X	X	X							X					X			X
Malaysia	X	X	X	X	X							X								X
Maldives	X		X																	X
Mali	X	X	X	X	X				X					X	X			X		X
Malta	X	X	X	X	X									X	X					X
Marshall Islands																				
Mauritania	X	X	X	X	X															X
Mauritius	X	X	X	X																X
Mexico		X	X	X	X		X					X	X	X	X		X	X	X	X
Micronesia (Federated States of)		X		X																
Monaco	X	X	X	X	X		X	X	X (X)	X	X	X								
Mongolia	X	X	X	X	X				X (X)	X	X	X					X	X		X
Montenegro	X	X	X	X	X	X	X	X	X (X)	X	X	X	X	X	X		X			X
Morocco	X	X	X	X	X			X	X	X	X			X	X				X	X
Mozambique	X	X	X	X	X					X	X	X								X
Myanmar	X																			X
Namibia	X	X	X	X	X				X (X)	X	X									X
Nauru																				

Member State	WIPO Convention	Paris Convention	Berne Convention	Patent Cooperation Treaty	Patent Law Treaty	Rome Convention	Trademark Law Treaty	Hague Agreement (and Geneva Act of Hague)	Madrid Agreement (Marks)	Madrid Protocol	Nice Agreement	Lisbon Agreement	WIPO Copyright Treaty	WIPO Phonograms and Performances Treaty	Beijing Treaty	Locarno Agreement	Marrakesh Treaty	UPOV Convention	World Trade Organization
Nepal	X	X	X																X
Netherlands	X	X	X	X	X	X	X	X	X	X	X		X	X		X		X	X
New Zealand	X	X	X	X						X	X							X	X
Nicaragua	X	X	X	X		X	X					X	X	X					X
Niger	X	X	X	X	X	X		X											X
Nigeria	X	X	X	X		X													X
Niue	X																		
Norway	X	X	X	X	X	X	X	X (X)		X	X		X	X		X		X	X
Oman	X	X	X	X				X (X)		X								X	X
Pakistan	X	X	X	X															X
Palau																			
Panama	X	X	X	X		X	X						X	X				X	X
Papua New Guinea	X	X		X															X

Paraguay	X	X	X			X							X	X			X	X	X
Peru	X	X	X	X		X	X					X	X	X				X	X
Philippines	X	X	X	X		X				X			X	X					X
Poland	X	X	X	X		X		X (X)	X	X	X		X	X		X		X	X
Portugal	X	X	X	X		X			X	X	X	X	X	X				X	X
Qatar	X	X	X	X									X	X	X				X
Republic of Korea	X	X	X	X		X	X	X (X)		X	X		X	X		X	X	X	X
Republic of Moldova	X	X	X	X	X	X	X	X (X)		X	X	X	X	X	X	X		X	X
Romania	X	X	X	X	X	X	X	X (X)		X	X		X	X		X		X	X
Russian Federation	X	X	X	X	X	X	X			X	X		X	X	X	X		X	X
Rwanda	X	X	X	X				X (X)		X									X
Saint Kitts and Nevis	X	X	X	X							X								X
Saint Lucia	X	X	X	X		X					X		X	X					X
Saint Vincent and the Grenadines	X	X	X	X										X					X
Samoa	X	X	X																X
San Marino	X	X		X					X	X									

Member State	WIPO Convention	Paris Convention	Berne Convention	Patent Cooperation Treaty	Patent Law Treaty	Rome Convention	Trademark Law Treaty	Hague Agreement (and Geneva Act of Hague)	Madrid Agreement (Marks)	Madrid Protocol	Nice Agreement	Lisbon Agreement	WIPO Copyright Treaty	WIPO Phonograms and Performances Treaty	Beijing Treaty	Locarno Agreement	Marrakesh Treaty	UPOV Convention	World Trade Organization
Sao Tome and Principe	×	×		×				× (X)		×									
Saudi Arabia	×	×	×	×	×														×
Senegal	×	×	×	×				×											×
Serbia	×	×	×	×	×	×	×	× (X)	×	×	×	×	×	×		×		×	
Seychelles	×	×		×				× (X)											×
Sierra Leone	×	×	×	×					×	×									×
Singapore	×	×	×	×				× (X)		×							×		×
Slovakia	×	×	×	×	×	×	×		×	×	×	×	×	×	×	×		×	×
Slovenia	×	×		×	×	×	×	× (X)	×	×	×		×	×		×		×	×
Solomon Islands																			×
Somalia	×																		
South Africa	×	×	×	×														×	×

24

South Sudan																			
Spain	X	X	X	X	X	X	X	X (X)	X	X	X		X	X		X		X	X
Sri Lanka	X	X	X	X			X												X
Sudan	X	X	X	X					X	X									
Suriname	X	X	X					X			X								X
Swaziland	X	X	X	X					X										X
Sweden	X	X	X	X	X	X			X		X		X	X		X		X	X
Switzerland	X	X	X	X	X	X	X	X (X)	X		X		X	X		X		X	X
Syrian Arab Republic	X	X	X	X		X		X (X)	X		X				X				
Tajikistan	X	X	X	X		X		X (X)	X		X		X	X		X			X
Thailand	X	X	X	X															X
Timor-Leste																			
Togo	X	X	X	X		X							X	X					X
Tonga	X	X	X																X
Trinidad and Tobago	X	X	X	X			X				X		X	X		X		X	X
Tunisia	X	X	X	X				X (X)	X		X	X						X	X
Turkey	X	X	X	X		X	X	X (X)	X		X		X	X		X		X	X
Turkmenistan	X	X		X				(X)	X		X					X			
Tuvalu	X																		

Member State	WIPO Convention	Paris Convention	Berne Convention	Patent Cooperation Treaty	Patent Law Treaty	Rome Convention	Trademark Law Treaty	Hague Agreement (and Geneva Act of Hague)	Madrid Agreement (Marks)	Madrid Protocol	Nice Agreement	Lisbon Agreement	WIPO Copyright Treaty	WIPO Phonograms and Performances Treaty	Beijing Treaty	Locarno Agreement	Marrakesh Treaty	UPOV Convention	World Trade Organization
Uganda	X	X		X															X
Ukraine	X	X	X	X	X	X	X	X (X)			X		X	X	X	X		X	X
United Arab Emirates	X	X	X	X		X			X				X	X			X		X
United Kingdom	X	X	X	X	X	X	X		X		X		X	X		X		X	X
United Republic of Tanzania	X	X	X	X							X								X
United States of America	X	X	X	X	X		X	X (X)	X		X		X	X				X	X
Uruguay	X	X	X	X		X					X		X	X		X	X	X	X
Uzbekistan	X	X	X	X	X		X		X		X					X		X	
Vanuatu	X		X																X

Venezuela (Bolivarian Republic of)	X	X				X													X
Viet Nam	X	X	X	X		X	X											X	X
Yemen	X	X	X																X
Zambia	X	X	X	X			X												X
Zimbabwe	X	X	X	X			X												X
African Intellectual Property Organization (OAPI)							X	X (X)											
European Union (EU)							X	X (X)					X	X				X	X
Hong Kong, China																			X
Macao, China																			X
Taiwan Province of China																			X
Total	188	176	168	148	36	92	55	64 (52)	55	94	84	28	93	94	10	54	13	72	161

Source: WIPO, 'Summary Table of Membership of the World Intellectual Property Organization (WIPO) and the Treaties Administered by WIPO, plus UPOV, WTO and UN' <http://www.wipo.int/treaties/en/summary.jsp> accessed 31 December 2015.

Protection of New Varieties of Plants, and the Director General of WIPO simultaneously serves as UPOV's Secretary-General.[17] The Rome, Phonograms (Geneva) and Satellites (Brussels) Conventions are co-administered by WIPO, UNESCO and the International Labour Organization (ILO).[18]

Notably, all but two of the world's multilateral IP treaties are WIPO agreements. The exceptions are the 1994 World Trade Organization (WTO) Agreement on Trade-Related Aspects of Intellectual Property Rights (TRIPS)[19] and the 1954 United Nations Educational, Scientific and Cultural Organization (UNESCO) Universal Copyright Convention.[20]

Even though TRIPS is now considered the world's most comprehensive and powerful multilateral IP agreement (because it obliges countries to adopt minimum standards of protection across most types of IP and has an effective enforcement mechanism in the form of the WTO's Dispute Settlement Understanding),[21] it did not supersede WIPO agreements. Rather, TRIPS incorporates and builds on the provisions of four WIPO agreements as the source

17 For more information, see UPOV, 'About UPOV' <http://www.upov.int/about/en> accessed 1 September 2015.

18 For the latter two Conventions, this is without much consequence, as they do not provide for any assembly or other body. The Rome Convention provides for a separate Intergovernmental Committee to consider questions concerning the convention. The Rome Convention does not, however, provide for the institution of a Union or a budget. The Intergovernmental Committee, consisting of the representatives of 12 Contracting State, has its own Rules of Procedure. Although the Rules call for a meeting every odd-calendar year, the Committee's practice has varied; it was convened in 1999, 2001, 2005, and 2009 and held successively at the headquarters of the three organisations (Article 32 of the Rome Convention). The sessions of the Intergovernmental Committee have been in suspense since 2009, pending new and substantial developments in relation to ongoing WIPO discussions on the protection of audiovisual performers and broadcasting organisations on the grounds that these could affect the Rome Convention's legal framework.

19 The TRIPS Agreement was adopted as part of the Final Act of the Uruguay Round of GATT Negotiations in 1994. For full text of the Agreement, see WTO, 'TRIPS: Agreement on Trade-Related Aspects of Intellectual Property Rights 1994' <https://www.wto.org/english/docs_e/legal_e/27-trips.pdf> accessed 30 October 2015.

20 UNESCO, 'UNESCO Universal Copyright Convention 1954' <http://portal.unesco.org/en/ev.php-URL_ID=15381&URL_DO=DO_TOPIC&URL_SECTION=201.html> accessed 30 October 2015.

21 The TRIPS Agreement is subject to the WTO's Dispute Settlement Understanding (DSU), which enables a WTO Member to launch dispute settlement proceedings when it believes another member government is violating an agreement or a commitment that it has made in the WTO, such as those included in the TRIPS Agreement. For more information on the DSU, see WTO, 'Dispute Settlement' <www.wto.org/english/tratop_e/dispu_e/dispu_e.htm> accessed 30 October 2015.

of its rules.[22] Further, the global protection system treaties (in other words, the Patent Cooperation Treaty (PCT), the Madrid treaty and its Protocol, and the Hague, Lisbon and Budapest treaties) remain unique to WIPO. Since TRIPS emerged in 1994, WIPO Member States have concluded eight multilateral IP negotiations, resulting in the WIPO Copyright Treaty, the WIPO Performances and Phonograms Treaty, the Geneva Act of the Hague Agreement, the Patent Law Treaty, the Singapore Treaty on the Law of Trademarks, the Beijing Treaty on Audiovisual Performances, the Marrakesh Treaty (for the visually impaired), and the Geneva Act of the Lisbon Agreement (see Table 2.1).

2. Provides a range of services for users of the IP system. The Secretariat offers treaty-related services that help fee-paying applicants and holders of IP rights to protect their IP across borders. WIPO enables applicants to seek patent protection, for instance, and to register trademarks and appellations of origin in multiple countries by filing one international application through the organisation. It also facilitates registration of industrial designs in multiple countries with minimum formalities and expense. In addition, WIPO's Arbitration and Mediation Center offers alternative dispute resolution (ADR) procedures to help businesses, associations and their legal counsels to resolve IP disputes outside courts,[23] most prominently relating to abusive registration and use of Internet domain names (or 'cybersquatting').[24]

---

22 The TRIPS Agreement incorporates the Berne, Paris and Rome Conventions as well as the substantive provisions of WIPO's Washington (Integrated Circuits) Treaty of 1989, which never entered into force at WIPO. See Carlos M Correa (ed), *Research Handbook on the Protection of Intellectual Property under WTO Rules* (Edward Elgar Publishing 2010).

23 The WIPO Center maintains a detailed database of 1,500 independent arbitrators, mediators and experts (neutrals) from more than 70 countries, with further neutrals added to meet the specific needs of each case it administers. Cases submitted include both contractual disputes (for example, patent and software licenses) and non-contractual disputes (for example, patent infringement) under the WIPO Mediation, Arbitration, Expedited Arbitration and Expert Determination Rules, which parties may adopt by including model WIPO clauses in contracts and by concluding WIPO submission agreements. To view examples of such clauses and agreements, see WIPO, 'Recommended WIPO Contract Clauses and Submission Agreements' <http://www.wipo.int/amc/en/clauses/> accessed 30 October 2015.

24 Most prominently, this occurs through the Uniform Domain Name Dispute Resolution Policy (UDRP), see WIPO, 'WIPO Guide to the Uniform Domain Name Dispute Resolution Policy (UDRP)' <http://www.wipo.int/amc/en/domains/guide/> accessed 30 October 2015.

3. Supports global infrastructure for the IP system through services to patent offices and copyright agencies, such as systems that enable patent offices to share documents, including search and examination documentation, to facilitate a more efficient international examination process for patent applications.[25] It also provides systems for the modernisation of offices such as WIPO's Industrial Property Automation System (IPAS) and the WIPO Copyright Management System (WIPOCOS).[26]

4. Provides information services through a series of global databases of patent documents (Patent Scope), brands (Global Brands Database), marks (ROMARIN) and laws and treaties (WIPO Lex), as well as statistics and economic research on IP and innovation.[27]

5. Provides assistance to developing countries, including legal assistance on IP legislation, policy advice, and training and institutional support for national and regional IP offices. In 1995, WIPO and the WTO forged an agreement, wherein WIPO undertook to provide assistance to developing countries for the implementation of the TRIPS Agreement.[28]

6. Hosts a number of multi-stakeholder platforms and public–private partnerships (PPPs), such as WIPO Green (an online marketplace that promotes innovation and diffusion of green technologies by connecting technology and service providers), WIPO Re:Search (a consortium of public and private sector organisations that aims to share IP and expertise with the global health research community to promote the development of new drugs, vaccines and diagnostics) and the Accessible Books Consortium (ABC) (a partnership of WIPO, organisations serving people with print disabilities and

---

25 WIPO tools that facilitate these activities include its Digital Access Service (DAS), the WIPO Centralized Access to Search and Examination (CASE) system, and its classification systems. On the latter, see WIPO, 'WIPO International Classifications' <http://www.wipo.int/classifications/en> accessed 30 October 2015.

26 See: WIPO, 'WIPOCOS: Software for Collective Management of Copyright and Related Rights' <http://www.wipo.int/copyright/en/initiatives/wipocos.html> accessed 21 July 2015; WIPO, 'Technical Assistance: Business Software Solutions for IP Offices' <http://www.wipo.int/global_ip/en/activities/technicalassistance> accessed 21 July 2015.

27 See: WIPO, 'Patentscope' <http://www.wipo.int/patentscope/search/en/search.jsf> accessed 7 July 2015; WIPO, 'About WIPO Lex' <http://www.wipo.int/wipolex/en/about.html> accessed 7 July 2015.

28 See WTO, 'WTO–WIPO Cooperation Agreement 1995' <http://www.wto.org/english/tratop_e/trips_e/wtowip_e.htm> accessed 30 October 2015.

organisations of publishers and authors that aims to increase the number and availability of books in accessible formats for people who are blind or visually impaired), as well as initiatives to improve Access to Research for Development and Innovation (ARDI) and Access to Specialised Patent Information (ASPI) in developing countries.[29]

2.4   The WIPO Secretariat

The Secretariat of WIPO is responsible for the planning and delivery of the work program approved by Member States. Although the term 'Secretariat' has been used increasingly since the year 2000, the WIPO Secretariat has traditionally been referred to as the International Bureau, such as in the WIPO Convention, and is still referred to that way by the governing bodies of the WIPO-administered international IP treaties and in their official documentation.

The WIPO Convention sets out a number of functions for WIPO (see Article 4 and section 4.1) and certain responsibilities of the Director General (see Article 9), but it does not have an Article that explicitly defines particular tasks for the Secretariat. The functions envisaged in the Convention do, however, give implicit guidance on the Secretariat's role.

As outlined above in section 2.3, the Secretariat currently undertakes work to support a broad range of functions – from administering treaties and delivering technical assistance to servicing negotiations among Member States on new international norms – most but not all of which are mentioned in the WIPO Convention. In several of these areas, there has been considerable debate about the over-riding purpose of WIPO's work and the Secretariat's activities, with critics arguing that the WIPO Convention, now almost 40 years old, does not properly capture contemporary priorities and challenges or reflect the 1974 WIPO-UN Agreement and more recent developments such as the WIPO Development Agenda. In practice, Member States have not

---

29 For the WIPO Secretariat's view on the importance of these voluntary initiatives as a comple ment and alternative to traditional treaty-based modes of international cooperation for achieving shared policy objectives, see WIPO, *Address of the Director General: WIPO Assemblies 2014* (WIPO 2014) and WIPO, *Report of the Director General to the WIPO Assemblies: The Year in Review*, WIPO Publication 1040/14 (WIPO 2014). For information on each initiative, see WIPO, 'Multi-Stakeholder Platforms' <http://www.wipo.int/cooperation/en/multi_stakeholder_ platforms/> accessed 25 October 2015.

limited the Secretariat to the functions or purposes envisaged in the Convention. Some ongoing Secretariat activities are not specifically provided for in the Convention (such as the pursuit of PPPs and the provision of dispute settlement services) and several functions have expanded in scope (WIPO's portfolio of development cooperation activities, for instance, goes far beyond the legal assistance envisaged in the Convention).

Details of the Secretariat's strategic goals, work program, expected results and associated budgets are contained in WIPO's biennial Program and Budget documents.[30] (See Table 2.3 for an overview of WIPO's budget by Program. For discussion of the process for elaborating the Program and Budget, see Chapter 6).

2.4.1   Leadership and staffing

The Director General of WIPO is the executive head and representative of the Secretariat. The WIPO Convention makes the Director General responsible for the preparation of draft Program and Budget documents as well as periodical reports on activities, and also calls on him or her to serve as *ex-officio* secretary to the many WIPO bodies and committees (Article 9). Appointed by the WIPO General Assembly upon nomination by the Coordination Committee for a 6-year term, the Director General is eligible for reappointment once for a further 6 years.[31] (For more on the appointment process, see Chapter 5, section 5.2.3).

The Director General reports to the General Assembly and is responsible for carrying out its instructions. The Director General is charged with providing strategic direction for WIPO's programs, ensuring delivery of results in line with the organisation's

---

30 For the most recent Program and Budget, see WIPO, *Proposed Program and Budget for the 2016/17 Biennium* A/55/5 Rev. (WIPO 2015).

31 See WIPO Convention, Articles 8(v) and 6(2)(i). The WIPO Convention establishes that the period and conditions of appointments shall be fixed by the General Assembly, but does not set a limit on the tenure of the Director General (see Article 9). Also see WIPO, *Policies and Practices for the Nomination and Appointment of Directors General* WO/GA/23/6 (WIPO 1998) para. 5; and WIPO, *Report: adopted by Member States, 23rd Session of the WIPO General Assembly* WO/GA/23/7 (WIPO 1998) para. 22. Notably, Member States amended Article 9(3) of the WIPO Convention in 1999, stipulating that the maximum term of appointment of a Director General shall be 12 years. Although the amendment has not yet entered into force, the presumption among Member States and the Secretariat appears to be that the General Assembly's 1999 decision is nonetheless to be followed in practice.

Table 2.3 WIPO budget after transfers (expenditures) and development share (in Swiss Francs as estimated by the WIPO Secretariat) 2010–2017

Programs (Relevant Shares of Program Resources)	New Programs and Program Names	Expenditures 2010/11	Development Share of Expenditures 2010/11	Expenditures 2012/13	Development Share of Expenditures 2012/13	Expenditures 2014/15	Development Share of Expenditures 2014/15	Proposed Budget 2016/17	Development share of Proposed Budget 2016/17
Patents	Patent Law	4751	—	5163	3560	5155	4516	5291	3546
Trademarks, Industrial Designs and Geographical Indications		5729	2136	5654	1979	5539	2909	4854	2319
Copyright and Related Rights		16040	8476	19426	14832	16805	14197	16733	13443
Traditional Knowledge, Traditional Cultural Expressions and Genetic Resources		6621	5959	6630	5603	6372	5088	6115	4891
The PCT System		173824	2768	175893	5026	196964	5978	208209	5845
Madrid, Hague and Lisbon Systems	Madrid and Lisbon Systems (since 2012/13), Madrid System (since 2016/17)	56932	1864	50622	5309	55274	6638	58106	11117

Programs (Relevant Shares of Program Resources)	New Programs and Program Names	Expenditures 2010/11	Development Share of Expenditures 2010/11	Expenditures 2012/13	Development Share of Expenditures 2012/13	Expenditures 2014/15	Development Share of Expenditures 2014/15	Proposed Budget 2016/17	Development share of Proposed Budget 2016/17
	Hague System (from 2012/13)			6 906		7 704		7 572	
	Lisbon System (from 2016/17)							1 335	534
WIPO Arbitration and Mediation Center		9 493		9 975	282	11 221	151	11 358	594
Development Agenda Coordination		5 269	5 269	4 132	4 132	3 677	3 677	3 671	3 671
Africa, Arab, Asia and the Pacific, Latin America and the Caribbean Countries, LDCs		36 584	35 534	33 126	33 126	32 383	32 383	31 907	31 907
Small and Medium-Sized Enterprises (SMEs)	SMEs and Innovation (from 2012/2013); SMEs and	5 195	8 739	9 816	9 816	5 508	5 508	6 083	6 083

Entrepreneurship Support (from 2016/17)								
Cooperation with Certain Countries in Europe and Asia / Transition and Developed Countries (from 2016/17)	6 460	6 460	6 348	6 348	8 349	7 055	13 083	6 368
The WIPO Academy	9 492	9 492	11 856	11 856	11 484	11 484	13 083	13 083
International Classifications and WIPO IP Standards	7 029	197	6 976	1 058	7 197	1 379	7 070	1 078
Global IP Information Services	10 715	–	–	–	–	–	–	–
Global Databases	–	138	4 302	1 075	4 810	1 202	5 758	1 440
Services for Access to Information and Knowledge	–	1 224	7 634	7 634	7 049	6 310	6 990	5 445
IP Office Modernization / Business Solutions for IP Offices	7 212	5 712	8 104	6 501	11 995	9 921	13 806	11 896

Programs (Relevant Shares of Program Resources)	New Programs and Program Names	Expenditures 2010/11	Development Share of Expenditures 2010/11	Expenditures 2012/13	Development Share of Expenditures 2012/13	Expenditures 2014/15	Development Share of Expenditures 2014/15	Proposed Budget 2016/17	Development share of Proposed Budget 2016/17
Economic Studies, Statistics and Analysis	Economics and Statistics	3 935	2 621	5 198	1 611	4 893	807	6 072	1 525
Building Respect for IP		3 017	3 017	2 884	2 384	4 207	3 779	3 752	3 207
IP and Global Challenges		10 087	3 914	7 048	4 497	6 576	4 720	6 323	4 981
Communications		15 836	11 877	16 269	7 648	16 539	5 550	16 483	5 566
External Offices and Relations	External Relations, Partnerships and External Offices	11 350	4 840	10 349	4 055	13 144	5 479	12 395	8 920
Executive Management	Executive Management	18 262	–	18 338	2 082	20 306	2 283	20 675	2 346
Finance, Budget and Program Management	Program and Resource Management	17 687	–	19 074	691	28 181	–	33 276	–

Internal Audit and Oversight	Internal Oversight	3815	–	4837	1753	5062	480	5358	963
Human Resources Management and Development		20443	–	21907	–	24633	–	24617	–
Administrative Support Services	General Support Services	52649	–	40000	–	47436	826	47216	730
Information and Communication Technology		44495	–	47977	–	46345	–	52032	–
Conference and Language Service		37701	–	37691	–	40151	–	38925	–
Security (Safety and)	Information Assurance, Safety and Security (from 2016/17)	10198	–	10814	–	10792	–	17733	–
New Construction	(discontinued in 2016/17)	6326	–	7144	–	823	–		

Programs (Relevant Shares of Program Resources)	New Programs and Program Names	Expenditures 2010/11	Development Share of Expenditures 2010/11	Expenditures 2012/13	Development Share of Expenditures 2012/13	Expenditures 2014/15	Development Share of Expenditures 2014/15	Proposed Budget 2016/17	Development share of Proposed Budget 2016/17
Funds earmarked for Development Agenda		4 540							
Unallocated		1 491		26 319		7 422		6 319	
GRAND TOTAL		**618 637**	**120 236**	**648 411**	**142 859**	**673 993**	**142 321**	**707 036**	**151 500**
Resources devoted to development activities as percentage of total budget			**19.4%**		**20.9%**		**20.9%**		**21.1%**

Note: The grand totals are as provided in the original WIPO documents and reflect rounding of numbers. In 2010/11, 4,540 thousand Swiss Francs were earmarked for the Development Agenda. The 2010/11 total for the development share of expenditure excludes Development Agenda project resources, which for that biennium were accounted for in a separate budget line. From 2012/13, the Program amounts integrated funds earmarked for Development Agenda projects. The expenditures columns reflect WIPO figures on the budget after transfers. The final expenditures for each biennium often differ to those presented in the Program and Budget documents approved by Member States, either due to factors arising in the implementation of a Program that may lead to allocated funds not being spent or to the transfer of resources between Programs by the Director General (a possibility provided for, with certain conditions, in WIPO's Financial Regulations and Rules, as discussed in Chapter 6).

Sources: WIPO Program and Budget for 2010/2011, 2012/2013, 2014/2015, and 2016/17.

Table 2.4 WIPO Directors General and their period of tenure

Director General	Period of Tenure
Georg Bodenhausen (The Netherlands)	1970–73
Árpád Bogsch (United States)	1973–97
Kamil Idris (Sudan)	1997–2008
Francis Gurry (Australia)	2008–term ends in September 2020

nine Strategic Goals, the Program and Budget, and agreed work plans; and managing the budget, activities, and human and financial resources of the organisation. Despite the possibility of long tenure for Directors General at WIPO, there is no provision for annual or mid-term reviews or feedback from Member States on their performance.[32]

Since its creation, WIPO has had four Directors General (see Table 2.4). During Georg Bodenhausen's tenure from 1970 to 1973, Árpád Bogsch served as WIPO's Deputy Director General and was elected to the post of Director General in November 1973.[33] Upon Bogsch's retirement some 24 years later in 1997, Kamil Idris was elected to be WIPO's Director General and was then reappointed for a further 6 years in 2003. In late 2007, however, Idris submitted his early resignation amidst complaints of misconduct.[34] The current Director

---

32 A study on leadership practices in international organisations conducted jointly by the World Economic Forum and Oxford's Blavatnik School of Government proposes that 'best practices' and structures that facilitate good, accountable and effective leadership in international organisations include: clear, transparent performance expectations set by leaders for themselves; a performance management program that includes annual performance appraisals and feedback on performance, as well as the possibility for coaching and development to address weaknesses over time; remuneration or benefits tied to outcomes of the performance management program; consideration of performance management criteria in the re-election process; and incentive structures that encourage leadership to engage with a diverse range of stakeholders. See Global Agenda Council on Institutional Governance Systems, *Effective Leadership in International Organizations* (World Economic Forum and Blavatnik School of Government 2015).

33 Notably, Bogsch was also a Deputy Director of WIPO, and was responsible for overseeing much of the transformation of BIRPI into WIPO. He was also on the US delegation to BIRPI at the time of the first discussions of this transformation; in this capacity, he led a Working Group that prepared the first formal proposals in this respect. See BIRPI, *Report of the Working Group on the Plan of Reorganisation of BIRPI* BPCP/I/2 (BIRPI 1962); BIRPI, *Joint Meeting of the Permanent Bureau of the Paris Union and the Permanent Committee of the Berne Union* (BIRPI 1962).

34 See JIU, *Review of the Management and Administration in WIPO: Budget, Oversight and Related Issues* JIU/REP/2005/1 (UN Joint Inspection Unit 2005).

General, Francis Gurry, was elected to serve for 6 years from the time of Idris' departure in 2008. In 2014, Gurry was re-elected for a second term until 2020.

The Director General is supported by a Senior Management Team (SMT), which consisted in 2015 of four Deputy Directors General (DDGs) and four Assistant Directors General (ADGs) (including the Chief of Staff). (See Figure 2.2 for an organigram of the WIPO Secretariat). Although the Director General appoints the DDGs, this occurs only after the approval of his or her nominations by the WIPO Coordination Committee (as established by Article 9(7) of the WIPO Convention) (for more on the Coordination Committee's role and the process, see section 5.2.3).[35] The Director General appoints the ADGs but is required by the WIPO Staff Regulations and Rules to take into account the advice of the Coordination Committee (in accordance with Regulation 4.8).

The posts of DDG and ADG are generally considered to be political appointments. The first step in the DDG selection process has traditionally been a Secretariat communication inviting Member States wishing to nominate candidates to submit proposals. In 2014, however, the WIPO Director General took the unprecedented step of combining this practice with a 'call for applications' published on WIPO's website inviting interested individuals to submit applications directly (that is, individuals could present their own candidacies). The final set of DDG appointments generally reflects a combination of merit-based considerations (qualifications, experience and skills) and personal political considerations on the part of the Director General, as well as Member State expectations and pressures regarding geographical representation, rotation and representation of one of their

---

35 Regarding the procedure for nomination and selection of DDGs, Article 9(7) of the WIPO Convention states: 'The Director General ... shall appoint the Deputy Directors General after approval by the Coordination Committee. The conditions of employment shall be fixed by the staff regulations to be approved by the Coordination Committee on the proposal of the Director General. The paramount consideration in the employment of the staff and in the determination of the conditions of service shall be the necessity of securing the highest standards of efficiency, competence, and integrity. Due regard shall be paid to the importance of recruiting the staff on as wide a geographical basis as possible.' Regulation 4(8) of the WIPO Staff Regulations and Rules also provides that the Director General shall appoint Assistant Directors General 'taking into account the advice of' the Coordination Committee. Article 9(2) refers to the Director General being assisted by two or more Deputy Directors General. No further clarification is made on the number of Deputy Directors General.

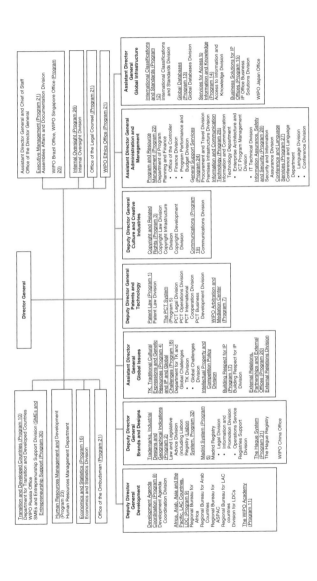

Note: This organigram presents a visual overview of how the core responsibility for WIPO's 32 Programs is allocated across the Secretariat's organisational units, noting the key Sectors, departments and divisions of the organisation, including those that report directly to the Director General. In this diagram, each Program is located within the Sector where the Program Manager is housed, although many Programs rely on collaboration among divisions from several WIPO Sectors.

Source: Author's own diagram based on WIPO, *Proposed Program and Budget 2016/17* A55/5 Rev. (WIPO 2015) 243 and WIPO, 'WIPO Organigram' <http://www.wipo.int/export/sites/www/about-wipo/en/pdf/organigram/_visio-org_en.pdf> accessed 1 December 2015.

Figure 2.2   Organigram of the WIPO Secretariat

national citizens in the organisation's Senior Management Team.[36] In 2014, the WIPO Director General also gave his Chief of Staff a 'personal promotion' to the rank of ADG in recognition of his service (but underlined that this additional ADG post would not constitute a precedent as to the future number of DDGs or ADGs). The practice of personal promotions on the part of the Director General similarly exists in other UN organisations, such as the ILO and WHO, and personal promotions at senior staff levels have long been part of the organisation's culture. However, the extensive use of personal promotions by previous WIPO Directors General raised concerns that the practice was overused and indeed abused as a vehicle for personal and political favours.[37] Member States have subsequently been in favour of a more accountable, merit-based approach to human resource management, although this has not ruled out the Director General's discretionary power to grant personal promotions where warranted, or the potential for politically-motivated appointments.

The terms of office for the current SMT coincide with the mandate of the Director General (or six months after the end of the Director General's appointment should his term of office come to an end more than six months before its stated term on 30 September 2020).[38]

The SMT meets as an executive management committee on a regular but confidential basis. In conducting its work, the SMT requires individual Directors across the organisation to prepare and submit Quarterly Management Reports for its consideration. These reports are not usually accessible to the staff at large, except at the discretion of individual Directors who may choose to draft and share them with their staff.

---

36 Although the Director Generals proposal does not explicitly mention political considerations, Member States frequently refer to them in their discussion of the proposals, as noted in the relevant reports of the Coordination Committee. See for instance WIPO, *Appointment of Deputy Directors General and Assistant Directors General: Document prepared by the Director General* WO/CC/70/2 (WIPO 2014). Also see WIPO, *Appointment of Deputy Directors General and Assistant Directors General: Document prepared by the Secretariat*, WIPO Coordination Committee WO/CC/70 (WIPO: 2014).

37 See JIU, *Review of the Management and Administration in WIPO: Budget, Oversight and Related Issues* JIU/REP/2005/1 (New York: UN Joint Inspection Unit 2005). In 2007, the issue of personal promotions arose in the course of an independent expert assessment conducted by PricewaterhouseCoopers, the final report of which can be found in WIPO, *Final Report of the Desk-to-Desk Assessment of the Human and Financial resources of the World Intellectual Property Organization: prepared by the Secretariat*, WO/GA/34/1 (WIPO 2007).

38 See WIPO, *Appointment of Deputy Directors General and Assistant Directors General: Document prepared by the Director General* WO/CC/70/2 (WIPO 2014).

Table 2.5 Examples of Office Instructions relevant to WIPO governance

Subject	Office Instruction Number
WIPO Ethics Office	Office Instruction 25/2010
WIPO Code of Ethics	Office Instruction 84/2012
The Office of the Ombudsperson	Office Instruction 32/2009
Policy to protect against retaliation for cooperating in an oversight activity or reporting misconduct or other wrongdoing ('Whistleblower Protection Policy')	Office Instruction 58/2012
Personal Accountability and Financial Liability Office	Office Instruction 43/2013
Honors and Gifts	Office Instruction 2/2013
Policy on preventing and deterring corruption, fraud, collusion, money laundering and the financing of terrorism	Office Instruction 13/2013

There is no document setting out the SMT's terms of reference, working methods or decision-making process. There has been no consistent practice over time with regard to the existence and availability of the SMT agenda or minutes or to the circulation of a report or decisions to SMT members. Neither the agenda of SMT meetings nor a summary of decisions is routinely available to Member States or staff. Communication of the results of SMT meetings to WIPO Directors (mid-level management) and staff occurs instead at the discretion of individual SMT Members or through Office Instructions where relevant.[39]

The issuance of an Office Instruction is a key tool used by the Director General to communicate and implement internal management decisions (Table 2.5 offers a sampling of governance-related Office Instructions issued by the incumbent Director General). Such Office Instructions can include announcements of new organisational structures and staff, as well as new policies introduced by management (see, for example, the text of the Office Instruction on the WIPO Code of Ethics in Table 7.2 in Chapter 7). Office instructions are internal Secretariat documents, but the Secretariat can make them available to Member States or even to the public on request.

WIPO recruits staff employed in its higher and professional categories on the basis of the UN system's principle of equitable geographic distribution, and other staff are drawn from a range of countries across

---

39 JIU, *Review of Management and Administration in the World Intellectual Property Organization (WIPO)* JIU/REP/2014/2 (UN Joint Inspection Unit 2014) 14–15.

the world.[40] The number of staff at WIPO has grown from a staff count of 544 in 1992[41] to 1,247 in mid-2015.[42] The geographical diversity of staff has grown from 58 nationalities in 1992 to over 114 nationalities in 2015.[43]

2.4.2   Headquarters and external offices

The World Intellectual Property Organization's headquarters in Geneva has grown in size. WIPO's first headquarters building was completed in 1978. In 1998, construction of an adjacent, supplementary headquarters building in Geneva began. In 2008, space requirements led to the start of work on an additional WIPO administrative building (which was inaugurated in 2011) and a new conference hall (which was inaugurated in 2014), both on the same Geneva campus.[44] The organisation enjoys a number of privileges and immunities as granted under the 1947 Convention on Privileges and Immunities of Specialized Agencies of the United Nations[45] and its 1970 Headquarters Agreement with the Swiss Federal Council, notably being exempt from paying most forms of direct and indirect taxation.

The number and location of WIPO's external offices have evolved over time. As of 2015, WIPO had external offices in Brazil, China, Japan, the Russian Federation and Singapore (established in 2010, 2014, 2006, 2014 and 2005 respectively), as well as a Coordination Office

---

40 See WIPO, *WIPO Intellectual Property Handbook: Policy, Law and Use* (WIPO 2004) 9.

41 See WIPO, *World Intellectual Property Organization: 1992–2007* (WIPO 2003) 15.

42 The latter figure includes staff in regular-funded posts and those financed under reserves and FITs, as well as temporary staff. It also includes interns and fellows, short-term general staff, consultants, individual contractors and short-term translators, who are referred to as 'non-staff'. See WIPO, *Annual Report on Human Resources, Prepared by the Director General* WO/CC/71/2 Rev. (WIPO 2015), Annex 1, 3. By contrast, BIRPI had just 19 officials in 1933 and 51 officials by 1962, of which 31 were permanent staff. See BIRPI, *Observations of BIRPI on their Draft Reorganisation* BPCP/I/2 (BIRPI 1962) 4.

43 See WIPO, *Annual Report on Human Resources, Prepared by the Director General* WO/CC/71/2 Rev. (WIPO 2015) Annex 1, 10, and WIPO, *WIPO Overview* WIPO Publication No. 1007/E/11 (WIPO 2011).

44 WIPO, *Progress Report on the New Construction Project and the New Conference Hall Project: Prepared by the Secretariat* A/54/11 (WIPO 2014). Also see WIPO, *WIPO: Financial Supervision Audit Relating to Construction Projects and New Security Measures, Report of the External Auditor: Swiss Federal Audit Office* WO/PBC/19/18 Appendix (WIPO 2012).

45 Edward Kwakwa and Marie-Lea Rols, 'The Privileges and Immunities of the World Intellectual Property Organization: Practice and Challenges', in Niels Blokker and Nico Schrijver (eds) *Immunity of International Organizations* (Brill Nijhoff 2015).

in New York, charged with liaison between the WIPO headquarters and the UN.[46] Although the external offices (except the New York Coordination Office) are similarly described in Secretariat documents as WIPO Service Centres, the specific priorities and activities of each of the external offices vary, as do their budgets, staffing levels and external partnerships.[47] To address the absence of a policy to guide the establishment and activities of external offices, WIPO Member States adopted 'Guiding Principles Regarding WIPO External Offices' in 2015 and decided that no more than three new external offices would be opened per biennium for the 2016/17 and 2018/19 biennia, with a priority given to Africa.[48] According to the WIPO Financial Regulations and Rules (see Chapter 6, section 6.2), the external offices obtain funds through remittances from headquarters, which are designed to cover cash requirements of the offices for the subsequent two and a half months.[49]

2.4.3 Internal organisation

Within the WIPO Secretariat, the internal organisational structure for managing its activities has changed several times over the past decade. At present, the work of implementing WIPO's 32 Programs is divided among seven organisational Sectors (such as the Development Sector, Brands and Designs Sector, Global Issues Sector, Culture and Creative Industries Sector and the Patents and Technology Sector) and a number of departments and divisions report directly to the Director General (see Figure 2.2 and Table 2.3).[50] Over half of the Programs rely on the engagement and cooperation of divisions in more than one Sector for their implementation.[51] High among the tasks of the Secretariat in many of these Programs is to support and

---

46 Former WIPO offices in Washington and Brussels have been closed for several years.

47 See WIPO, *Proposed Program and Budget for the 2016/17 Biennium* A/55/5 Rev. (WIPO 2015) 137–42.

48 See WIPO, *List of Decisions: Document Prepared by the Secretariat, Assemblies of the Member States of WIPO, Fifty-Fifth Series of Meetings, 5–14 October 2015* A/55/IN/11 (WIPO 2015).

49 WIPO Financial Rule 104.5 states that: 'In the absence of a special authorization from the Controller, those remittances shall not exceed the amount required to bring cash balances up to the levels necessary to meet the recipient liaison office's estimated cash requirements for the next two and a half months.'

50 The number and name of Programs changes according to the priorities set in the biennial Program and Budget process. In the 2016/17 Program and Budget, Member States approved 32 Programs. See WIPO, *Proposed Program and Budget for the 2016/17 Biennium* A/55/5 Rev. (WIPO 2015).

51 The remaining Programs are each implemented by an individual Sector. Some Sectors, such as the Global Challenges Sector, have responsibilities for expected results across many Programs.

serve the various WIPO committees and treaties, particularly in regard to the revision of treaties and development of new ones, for which the Secretariat acts to support cooperation and negotiations among Member States.

3 WIPO's governance system: an analytical framework

The Member States of WIPO have discussed reform of the organisation's governance for over 18 years,[1] provoking debates in a number of WIPO's decision-making and advisory bodies,[2] as well as among stakeholders and within the Secretariat. The discussions have also given rise to a number of reports and reviews of WIPO governance that form part of the organisation's official records (see Table 3.1) and highlight the shifting focus of debate over time.

In this book, the term 'governance system' refers to the web of treaty provisions, rules, regulations, policies and practices that impact how WIPO Member States provide strategic direction and oversight of WIPO's activities; exercise authority and control over the organisation; and with stakeholders, hold the Secretariat to account.[3] Whereas much of the official documentation of WIPO's governance focuses on the structure for decision-making,[4] this book proposes a broader approach to WIPO's governance system. It identifies and examines five thematic

---

1 See, for instance, WIPO, *The Governance Structure of WIPO: Memorandum of the International Bureau* A/32/INF/2 (WIPO 1998).

2 Debate on different aspects of governance reform has taken place in several WIPO bodies, most notably the WIPO General Assembly, the Program and Budget Committee (PBC), the Independent Advisory Oversight Committee (IAOC), the Committee on Development and Intellectual Property (CDIP), and to some extent in the Assemblies and Working Groups of the Unions, such as the PCT Union, as well as informally at side events running parallel to formal discussions. For analysis of the evolution and dynamics of this debate, see Carolyn Deere Birkbeck, *Governing the World Intellectual Property Organization: The Power Politics of Institutional Crisis and Reform* (Routledge forthcoming 2016).

3 For examples of the rich academic literature on the governance of international organisations, and related issues of accountability, see: Thomas G Weiss and Rorden Wilkinson (eds), *International Organisation and Global Governance* (Routledge 2013); Monica Blagescu, Lucy de las Casas, and Robert Lloyd, *Pathways to Accountability: The GAP Framework* (One World Trust 2011); Thomas Hale 'Transparency, Accountability and Global Governance' (2008) 14(1) *Global Governance* 73–94; Ngaire Woods, 'Good Governance in International Organizations' (1999) 5(1) *Global Governance* 39–61.

4 See WIPO, *WIPO Governance Structure: Document Prepared by the Secretariat* WO/PBC/17/2. Rev. (WIPO 2011) 2.

Table 3.1 Examples of major internal and UN reports on WIPO governance since 1998

Year	Name	Document Number	Source
1998	The Governance Structure of WIPO: Memorandum of the International Bureau	A/32/INF/2	WIPO Secretariat
1998	Constitutional Reform: Memorandum of the Secretariat	A/33/3	WIPO Secretariat
2002	Final Recommendations of the WIPO General Assembly Working Group on Constitutional Reform	A/37/5	Working Group on Constitutional Reform
2005	Review of the Management and Administration in WIPO: Budget, Oversight and Related Issues	JIU/REP/2005/1	UN Joint Inspection Unit
2007	Desk-to-Desk Assessment Final Report	WO/GA/34/12	PriceWaterhouse Coopers, commissioned by the WIPO Secretariat
2007	Desk-to-Desk Assessment Final Report: Secretariat's Comments	WO/GA/34/12	WIPO Secretariat
2007	Constitutional Matters: Prepared by the Secretariat	A/42/4	WIPO Secretariat
2009	Report of the WIPO Audit Committee since 2008	WO/GA/38/2	WIPO Audit Committee
2011	WIPO Governance Structure	WO/PBC/17/2	WIPO Secretariat
2011	WIPO Governance Structure	WO/PBC/18/20	WIPO Secretariat
2012	Governance at WIPO: Report Prepared by the WIPO Independent Advisory Oversight Committee (IAOC)	WO/PBC/19/26	WIPO IAOC
2014	JIU Report 'Review of Management and Administration in the World Intellectual Property Organization (WIPO)'	JIU/REP/2014/2	UN Joint Inspection Unit
2014	WIPO Secretariat Comments on JIU Report 'Review of Management and Administration in the World Intellectual Property Organization (WIPO)'	WO/PBC/22/20	WIPO Secretariat

Note: The table does not include the numerous background documents that focus specifically on WIPO's Internal Oversight Division, Independent Advisory Oversight Committee and External Auditor.

Source: Table compiled by author.

areas of WIPO's governance system, exploring the core components of each as follows (also see Table 3.2):

1. Mandate and purpose: The organisation's legal foundations, mandate and purpose as established by the WIPO Convention, described in the WIPO's Agreement with the United Nations, and debated in the context of the WIPO Development Agenda.

2. Decision-making: The organisation's decision-making structures, processes and practices, including the organs and bodies constituted by WIPO-administered treaties, along with the subsidiary committees established by those organs and bodies; rules and processes for decision-making as well as formal and informal mechanisms, practices and customs for consensus-building and consultation among regional groups of Member States; and arrangements for the representation of Member States and composition of their delegations, as well as mechanisms for Member State interaction with each other and the Secretariat.

3. Financing: The organisation's financial arrangements, including its main sources of income (user fees, Member State contributions through the Unitary Contribution System, and extra-budgetary contributions), WIPO's Financial Regulations and Rules, the role of the WPO Controller, policies on investments and reserves, the Program and Budget process and reporting requirements, as well as the financial arrangements for the WIPO-administered Unions.

4. Accountability: The organisation's mechanisms and policies related to oversight, audit, internal control, and evaluation of the Secretariat, including the processes for the development of WIPO's work program and budget (see point 3 above).

5. Transparency and external relations: This includes the organisation's policies on access to documents and meetings, and its relationships with external actors, such as with the wider United Nations system and stakeholders.

For each of the five thematic areas of WIPO's governance system, the primary focus of this book is on the formal conventions, regulations, structures, procedures and policies as formally adopted by WIPO Member States as well as rules and internal policies, decisions and procedures adopted by the WIPO Secretariat. In addition, and as widely

Table 3.2 Key components of WIPO's governance system

Themes	Key Components of WIPO Governance System	Examples of Relevant Rules, Mechanisms, Processes and Practices
Mandate and Purpose	Legal documents establishing the organisation and its mandate, as well as subsequent decisions, statements and agreements adopted by Member States relevant to the interpretation of the organisation's mandate and purpose	The mandate as defined by the 1967 WIPO Convention (see Appendix 1), as well as decisions and statements relevant to mandate and purpose such as the 1974 WIPO–UN Agreement (see Appendix 2) and the 2007 WIPO Development Agenda (see Table 4.3)
Decision-Making Structures, Processes and Practices for Member States	The organs constituted by a WIPO-administered treaty, as well as all the subsidiary bodies established by those organs	Convention-defined organs (such as the General Assembly and the unions established by WIPO treaties) as well as subsidiary WIPO bodies such as Standing Committees, expert committees and working groups (see Figure 5.1)
	Rules, processes and mechanisms for decision-making as well as informal mechanisms, practices and customs for consensus-building and consultation among Member States	WIPO General Rules of Procedure, Special Rules of Procedure for treaty-based bodies and WIPO Committees; Rules of Procedure for Diplomatic Conferences (see Appendices 3–6); coordination mechanisms, such as the Development Agenda Coordination Mechanism (see Table 5.3); working methods adopted by WIPO committees; practices related to voting and consensus-building; financial arrangements for the participation of Member States in WIPO meetings; informal practices related to the composition, consultation and role of regional groups; informal practices related to the selection of chairs; General Assembly decisions and policies related to the admission of observers, documentation and languages; and the Office of the Legal Counsel to the extent that it offers clarifications and interpretations of WIPO's procedural rules

Themes	Key Components of WIPO Governance System	Examples of Relevant Rules, Mechanisms, Processes and Practices
	Representation of Member States	Rules and practices regarding membership of WIPO and its treaties (see Table 2.2), representation at WIPO, composition of delegations, as well as processes and practices for interaction among Member State delegations, and between Member States and the Secretariat
Income and financial arrangements	Arrangements for financing the organisation, including user fees, Member State contributions, and extra-budgetary contributions	Income from Member States and Fees (see Appendix 7, Table 6.1 on income and Table 6.6 on contribution classes); extra-budgetary, voluntary contributions to Funds-in-Trust; Financial Regulations and Rules (see Appendix 7); Rules related to the authority and responsibility of the WIPO Controller, policies on reserves and investments; the Program and Budget process and the unitary presentation of the budget; and financial arrangements for the WIPO-administered Unions
Control and Accountability of the Secretariat	WIPO's work program and budget, including the processes for its development and related accountability mechanisms (such as on reporting and evaluation)	Program and Budget documents (see Table 2.3 for overview of expenditures and budget by Program) and Mechanism (see Figure 6.4); results framework; Program Performance and Validation Reports; Financial Management Reports; management and reporting of Funds-in-Trust (FITs) activities; and WIPO evaluation policies
	Rules, policies and practices related to the accountability of WIPO's chief executive, senior management, and staff for their activities and performance	Rules and practices regarding the selection and role of the Director General and Senior Management; scope for organisational change initiatives (such as the Strategic Realignment Program); staff accountability mechanisms (such as the Staff Regulations and Rules (see Table 7.1 and Appendix 8) and the Code of Ethics (see Table 7.2) including provisions and Office Instructions on issues such as conflict of interest and corruption; policies on procurement and the supplier Code of Conduct; the WIPO

Themes	Key Components of WIPO Governance System	Examples of Relevant Rules, Mechanisms, Processes and Practices
		Staff Association; policies related to staff evaluation, investigation (see Appendix 9) and the WIPO Whistleblower policy
	Accountability mechanisms and policies related to financial oversight, audit, internal financial controls and risk management	WIPO Financial Regulations and Rules including the Internal Oversight Charter (see Table 8.2); the Independent Advisory Oversight Committee (IAOC), the External Auditor, and the Internal Oversight Division (IOD); IOD's evaluation, investigation and audit policies; the Office of the Legal Counsel; and complaint and response mechanisms for users of the WIPO services, procurement activities and WIPO staff
Transparency and External Relations	Relationships with external actors, such as with the wider United Nations system and stakeholders from the private sector, civil society, and scientific and creative communities	The UN-WIPO Agreement, the UN Convention, the WTO–WIPO Cooperation Agreement, Memoranda of Understanding (MOUs) and arrangements for cooperation and joint activities with other UN agencies, international organisations and partners, policies on observers at WIPO meetings (see Table 8.2), and informal practices of consultation and interaction with stakeholders, such as non-governmental organisations (NGOs) representing the private sector, the scientific and creative communities, and civil society
	External and internal transparency, particularly with respect to policies on documents and access to meetings	Policies on access to documents and budget data, translation, access to meetings, the WIPO website and webcasting

Source: Table compiled by the author.

observed in the scholarly literature on international organisations, the analysis in the coming chapters recognises that a number of 'informal' factors also impact how governance occurs in practice, as well as the prospects for organisational change. Examples of such informal factors include consensus-building processes, organisational culture, bureaucratic inertia, the quality of leadership, and the diffusion of ideas within networks of technical experts that include the staff of international organisations and Member State officials.[5] As is the case for most international organisations, each of the five core components of WIPO's governance has both formal and informal dimensions, and has evolved over time.

The analysis in the following chapters underscores the ways in which informal practices and customs are, de facto, part of WIPO's governance system. Chapter 5 of this book, for instance, observes that WIPO Member States and the Secretariat regularly use 'regional groups' of countries as vehicles through which to build consensus and consult on decisions. It notes that the Director General has a number of strategies for informal interaction with Member States, including through breakfasts with groups of ambassadors, meetings with individual heads of IP offices, visits to officials and ministers in national capitals, and the addition of high-level meetings to engage ministers in WIPO's work. Further, although WIPO's General Rules of Procedure provide the framework for formal intergovernmental meetings, Member States routinely derogate from these Rules, such as in the case of summaries by chairs of various WIPO committees. In addition, several of the existing provisions in the General Rules of Procedure have been superseded by new policies (such as on languages) adopted since the last updating of the Rules.

In the following chapters, the WIPO Secretariat is analysed as the subject of WIPO's governance structure (in other words, acknowledging that Member States formally have authority over the Secretariat), and as an actor that can also sometimes form part of the system governing what WIPO does and how. The Secretariat has demonstrated in numerous instances its ability to shape the organisation's priorities and to influence treaty-making processes and Member State decision-making on what the bureaucracy itself should do. While a detailed account of WIPO's internal management and administration is beyond the

---

5 See, for instance, Michael N Barnett and Martha Finnemore, 'The Politics, Power and Pathologies of International Organizations' (1999) 53(4) *International Organization* 699–732; Michael N Barnett and Martha Finnemore, *Rules for the World: International Organizations in Global Politics* (Cornell University Press 2004); Jutta Joachim, Bob Reinalda and Bertjan Verbeek, *International Organizations and Implementation: Enforcers, Managers, Authorities?* (Routledge 2008); and John Mathiason, *Invisible Governance: International Secretariats in Global Politics* (Kumarian Press 2007).

scope of this book, the analysis recognises that internal decisions can impact and alter WIPO's governance system and that the Secretariat has considerable scope for independent action. Actions by the Director General to establish advisory groups, change staff and financial rules, and forge external partnerships, as well as decisions on staff and the process of decision-making by Senior Management all have a governance dimension. They can, for instance, influence the organisation's agenda; the substantive direction of its activities and their implementation; internal transparency and accountability; and the powers of the Director General; and they can serve as tools for managing internal political challenges. Similarly, changes in internal practices with regard to evaluation of the organisation's activities and improved availability of data can each be considered 'governance-related' as they improve the basis for transparency and accountability to Member States.

4 WIPO's legal foundations, mandate and purpose

This chapter sets out WIPO's legal foundations, as established by the WIPO Convention, and its status as a UN Specialized Agency in line with WIPO's agreement with the United Nations. On mandate and purpose, it shows that in addition to the WIPO Convention, the UN-WIPO agreement and the WIPO Development Agenda are also relevant.

4.1 The WIPO Convention

The World Intellectual Property Organization's founding legal instrument is the 1967 WIPO Convention; it defines the roles and functions of WIPO's main or 'principal' organs through which Member States exercise their governance responsibilities (see Appendix 1). The WIPO Convention is 'administrative' in the sense that it does not establish any substantive or procedural standards for various categories of IP (these are taken up by the other 25 treaties administered by WIPO).[1] Further, membership of WIPO does not lead to any obligations concerning other treaties administered by WIPO. The WIPO Convention has been ratified by each of WIPO's 188 Member States (for WIPO's membership, see Table 2.2 in Chapter 2).

To achieve the objectives as set out in Article 1 of the WIPO Convention, Article 4 envisioned seven functions for WIPO: (i) to promote the development of measures designed to facilitate the efficient protection of intellectual property throughout the world and to harmonise national legislation in this field; (ii) to perform the administrative tasks of the Paris Union, the Special Unions established in relation with that Union, and the Berne Union; (iii) to assume, or participate in, the administration of any other international agreement designed to

---

1 Frederick M Abbott, Francis Gurry and Thomas Cottier, *The International Intellectual Property System: Commentary and Materials* (Kluwer Law 1999) 303.

promote the protection of intellectual property; (iv) to encourage the conclusion of international agreements designed to promote the protection of intellectual property; (v) to offer its cooperation to Member States requesting legal-technical assistance in the field of intellectual property; (vi) to assemble and disseminate information concerning the protection of IP, and to carry out, promote and publish studies in this field; and (vii) to maintain services facilitating the international protection of intellectual property and, where appropriate, provide for registration in this field and the publication of the data concerning the registrations.

The Member States of WIPO adopted their first amendment to the WIPO Convention on 28 September 1979 (entering into force on 25 June 1984), with the aim of aligning WIPO's budget process with the practice of biennial budgets prevalent elsewhere in the UN system. WIPO Member States subsequently approved four further amendments to the Convention. In 1998, for instance, Member States approved an amendment to Article 9(3) of the Convention, which they adopted in September 1999, to limit the term of appointment of the Director General to a maximum of 12 years (see section 2.4.1). In September 2003, Member States approved three further amendments, related to: (i) the abolition of the WIPO Conference (see Chapter 5); (ii) a change in the periodicity of the ordinary sessions of the WIPO General Assembly, and the other Assemblies of the Unions, from biannual to annual meetings; and (iii) formal adoption of the unitary contribution system (which Member States had adopted in practice since 1993) and new contribution classes (as adopted in 1989, 1991 and 1993), thereby simplifying the system for Member State contributions (see Chapter 6).[2] The 2003 decisions required not only amendments to the WIPO Convention but also to other WIPO-administered treaties impacted by the decisions, such as the Berne and Paris Conventions. Although the 1999 and 2003 amendments have not yet entered into force (only 52 and 15 notifications of acceptance have been deposited by Member States respectively), the decisions are nonetheless reflected in WIPO's relevant practices (as discussed in Chapter 5). (See Tables 4.1 and 4.2 for the status of ratification of these amendments.)

---

2 See WIPO, *WIPO Intellectual Property Handbook: Policy, Law and Use* (WIPO 2004) 9. Also see WIPO, *Final Recommendations of the WIPO General Assembly Working Group on Constitutional Reform* A/37/5 (WIPO 2002).

Table 4.1 Status of ratification of the 1999 amendment to Article 9(3) of the WIPO Convention*

Member State	Date on which State Deposited its Notification of Acceptance
Andorra	12 January 2001
Argentina	23 August 2004
Australia	16 December 2008
Belarus	7 July 2011
Benin	19 January 2000
Brazil	3 January 2000
Burkina Faso	28 February 2000
Canada	11 August 2000
China	1 May 2000
Cuba	12 July 2002
Democratic People's Republic of Korea	24 March 2000
Denmark	7 January 2000
Dominica	6 April 2000
Ecuador	21 December 1999
El Salvador	10 November 2003
Finland	28 March 2000
Former Yugoslav Republic of Macedonia	26 April 2000
France	21 March 2007
Germany	11 April 2003
Guatemala	14 November 2001
Holy See	16 December 1999
India	22 September 2000
Ireland	16 March 2001
Italy	19 September 2008
Japan	9 July 2002
Jordan	1 February 2000
Kyrgyzstan	26 February 2002
Luxembourg	24 January 2003
Madagascar	24 January 2000
Mauritius	12 January 2000

Member State	Date on which State Deposited its Notification of Acceptance
Netherlands	10 April 2003
Niger	29 January 2001
Nigeria	31 May 2000
Panama	23 February 2000
Poland	13 November 2000
Republic of Korea	20 April 2000
Republic of Moldova	27 September 2001
Saint Lucia	10 January 2000
Saudi Arabia	30 March 2000
Senegal	23 February 2000
Slovenia	21 May 2001
Spain	10 November 2000
Sri Lanka	14 March 2000
Sweden	28 February 2008
Switzerland	28 June 2001
Thailand	21 August 2000
Turkey	19 May 2000
Uganda	1 February 1999
United Kingdom	14 October 2002
United Republic of Tanzania	16 March 2000
United States of America	14 December 2007
Vietnam	20 January 2000
(52)	

Note: * Status as on 15 October 2015. The said amendment shall enter into force 1 month after written notifications of acceptance have been received by the Director General from three-fourths of the Member States of WIPO in accordance with Article 17(3) of the WIPO Convention. The total number of Member States of WIPO when this amendment was adopted stood at 171. The total number of notifications of acceptance required from Member States for its entry into force is 129.

4.2   Agreement between the United Nations and WIPO

In 1974, Article 1 of WIPO's agreement with the UN established the organisation's new status as a UN Specialized Agency 'for promoting

Table 4.2 Status of ratification of amendments to WIPO-administered treaties (including the WIPO Convention) adopted by the Assemblies of WIPO Member States on 1 October 2003*

Member State	Date on which State Deposited its Notification of Acceptance
Australia	16 December 2008
Denmark	13 October 2004
Finland	10 November 2004
Mauritius	3 December 2004
Mexico	3 August 2007
Monaco	8 April 2004
Morocco	31 May 2011
Netherlands	16 October 2008
Republic of Korea	21 April 2004
Saint Lucia	4 June 2004
Saudi Arabia	9 March 2004
Slovenia	1 August 2007
Spain	10 February 2012
Sweden	28 February 2008
Tonga	16 September 2004
(15)	

Note: * Status as on 15 October 2015. The said amendments are: (i) the abolition of the WIPO Conference, (ii) the formalisation of the unitary contribution system and changes in contribution classes, and (iii) a change in the periodicity of the ordinary sessions of the WIPO General Assembly and the other Assemblies of the Unions administered by WIPO. The said amendments shall enter into force one month after written notifications of acceptance have been received by the Director General from three-fourths of the Member States of WIPO in accordance with the relevant provisions of the WIPO-administered treaties.

creative intellectual activity and for facilitating the transfer of technology related to industrial property to . . . the developing countries in order to accelerate economic, social and cultural development.'[3] The UN-WIPO agreement entered into effect on 17 December 1974, upon its approval by the General Assembly of the United Nations and the General Assembly of WIPO (see Appendix 2 for the text of the UN-WIPO agreement). A Protocol incorporating the agreement was

---

3 See WIPO, *Agreement between the United Nations and the World Intellectual Property Organization* WIPO Publication No. 111 (WIPO 1975).

subsequently signed on 21 January 1975 by the two executive heads of the organisations, namely Kurt Waldheim, Secretary-General of the United Nations and Árpád Bogsch, Director General of WIPO. The agreement includes provisions on a range of matters, such as coordination, reporting and sharing of data within the UN system. The agreement formalised WIPO's participation in the UN staff remuneration and pension systems, and gave WIPO's leadership and senior staff clearer professional standing in regard to their interaction and cooperation with other UN organisations. The agreement also provides that relevant WIPO staff can be issued with a UN 'laissez-passer' travel document. (For a more detailed review of the Agreement's key provisions, see Chapter 8, section 8.1.)

4.3   The WIPO Development Agenda: a key decision relevant to debates on WIPO's mandate

The 2007 approval by WIPO Member States of the WIPO Development Agenda had numerous implications for the organisation's governance system. The WIPO Development Agenda included 45 recommendations that aim to mainstream development throughout WIPO's work, divided into six clusters: Cluster A – technical assistance and capacity building; Cluster B – norm-setting flexibilities, public policy and public domain; Cluster C – technology transfer, information and communication technologies (ICT) and access to knowledge; Cluster D – assessment, evaluation and impact studies; Cluster E – institutional matters including mandate and governance; and Cluster F – other issues (see Table 4.3).

The WIPO Development Agenda is regularly invoked by developing countries in a range of deliberations when arguments about WIPO's mandate arise. They argue that the adoption of the Development Agenda affirmed the centrality of development objectives to WIPO's purpose, insisting that the organisation's commitment and responsiveness to the needs of developing countries must be a core benchmark against which WIPO's performance and accountability are assessed.[4] The adoption of the Development Agenda has been described as the first formal acknowledgement by the organisation of the 'importance of moving away from an agenda essentially limited to promotion and

---

4   Susan K Sell, 'Everything Old Is New Again: The Development Agenda Now and Then' (2011) 3(1) *The WIPO Journal* 17–23.

Table 4.3 WIPO Development Agenda recommendations

Cluster A: Technical Assistance and Capacity Building
1. * WIPO technical assistance shall be, inter alia, development-oriented, demand-driven and transparent, taking into account the priorities and the special needs of developing countries, especially LDCs, as well as the different levels of development of Member States and activities should include time frames for completion. In this regard, design, delivery mechanisms and evaluation processes of technical assistance programs should be country specific
2. Provide additional assistance to WIPO through donor funding, and establish Trust-Funds or other voluntary funds within WIPO specifically for LDCs, while continuing to accord high priority to finance activities in Africa through budgetary and extra-budgetary resources, to promote, inter alia, the legal, commercial, cultural, and economic exploitation of intellectual property in these countries
3. * Increase human and financial allocation for technical assistance programs in WIPO for promoting an, inter alia, development-oriented IP culture, with an emphasis on introducing intellectual property at different academic levels and on generating greater public awareness on IP
4. * Place particular emphasis on the needs of SMEs and institutions dealing with scientific research and cultural industries and assist Member States, at their request, in setting up appropriate national strategies in the field of IP
5. WIPO shall display general information on all technical assistance activities on its website, and shall provide, on request from Member States, details of specific activities, with the consent of the Member State(s) and other recipients concerned, for which the activity was implemented
6. * WIPO's technical assistance staff and consultants shall continue to be neutral and accountable, by paying particular attention to the existing Code of Ethics, and by avoiding potential conflicts of interest. WIPO shall draw up and make widely known to the Member States a roster of consultants for technical assistance available with WIPO
7. * Promote measures that will help countries deal with IP-related anti-competitive practices, by providing technical cooperation to developing countries, especially LDCs, at their request, in order to better understand the interface between intellectual property rights and competition policies
8. Request WIPO to develop agreements with research institutions and with private enterprises with a view to facilitating the national offices of developing countries, especially LDCs, as well as their regional and sub-regional IP organisations to access specialised databases for the purposes of patent searches
9. Request WIPO to create, in coordination with Member States, a database to match specific IP-related development needs with available resources, thereby expanding the scope of its technical assistance programs, aimed at bridging the digital divide

Cluster A: Technical Assistance and Capacity Building
10. To assist Member States to develop and improve national IP institutional capacity through further development of infrastructure and other facilities with a view to making national IP institutions more efficient and promote fair balance between IP protection and the public interest. This technical assistance should also be extended to sub-regional and regional organisations dealing with IP
11. * To assist Member States to strengthen national capacity for protection of domestic creations, innovations and inventions and to support development of national scientific and technological infrastructure, where appropriate, in accordance with WIPO's mandate
12. * To further mainstream development considerations into WIPO's substantive and technical assistance activities and debates, in accordance with its mandate
13. * WIPO's legislative assistance shall be, inter alia, development-oriented and demand-driven, taking into account the priorities and the special needs of developing countries, especially LDCs, as well as the different levels of development of Member States and activities should include time frames for completion
14. * Within the framework of the agreement between WIPO and the WTO, WIPO shall make available advice to developing countries and LDCs, on the implementation and operation of the rights and obligations and the understanding and use of flexibilities contained in the TRIPS Agreement
Cluster B: Norm-Setting, Flexibilities, Public Policy and Public Domain
15. * Norm-setting activities shall: be inclusive and member-driven; take into account different levels of development; take into consideration a balance between costs and benefits; be a participatory process, which takes into consideration the interests and priorities of all WIPO Member States and the viewpoints of other stakeholders, including accredited intergovernmental organisations and non-governmental organisations; and be in line with the principle of neutrality of the WIPO Secretariat
16. * Consider the preservation of the public domain within WIPO's normative processes and deepen the analysis of the implications and benefits of a rich and accessible public domain
17. * In its activities, including norm-setting, WIPO should take into account the flexibilities in international IP agreements, especially those which are of interest to developing countries and LDCs
18. * To urge the IGC to accelerate the process on the protection of genetic resources, traditional knowledge and folklore, without prejudice to any outcome, including the possible development of an international instrument or instruments
19. * To initiate discussions on how, within WIPO's mandate, to further facilitate access to knowledge and technology for developing countries and LDCs to foster creativity and innovation and to strengthen such existing activities within WIPO

Cluster B: Norm-Setting, Flexibilities, Public Policy and Public Domain
20. To promote norm-setting activities related to IP that support a robust public domain in WIPO's Member States, including the possibility of preparing guidelines which could assist interested Member States in identifying subject matters that have fallen into the public domain within their respective jurisdictions
21. * WIPO shall conduct informal, open and balanced consultations, as appropriate, prior to any new norm-setting activities, through a member-driven process, promoting the participation of experts from Member States, particularly developing countries and LDCs
22. WIPO's norm-setting activities should be supportive of the development goals agreed within the UN system, including those contained in the Millennium Declaration. The WIPO Secretariat, without prejudice to the outcome of Member States considerations, should address in its working documents for norm-setting activities, as appropriate and as directed by Member States, issues such as: (i) safeguarding national implementation of intellectual property rules; (ii) links between IP and competition; (iii) IP-related transfer of technology; (iv) potential flexibilities, exceptions and limitations for Member States; and (v) the possibility of additional special provisions for developing countries and LDCs
23. To consider how to better promote pro-competitive IP licensing practices, particularly with a view to fostering creativity, innovation and the transfer and dissemination of technology to interested countries, in particular developing countries and LDCs
Cluster C: Technology Transfer, Information and Communication Technologies (ICT) and Access to Knowledge
24. To request WIPO, within its mandate, to expand the scope of its activities aimed at bridging the digital divide, in accordance with the outcomes of the World Summit on the Information Society (WSIS) also taking into account the significance of the Digital Solidarity Fund (DSF)
25. To explore IP-related policies and initiatives necessary to promote the transfer and dissemination of technology, to the benefit of developing countries and to take appropriate measures to enable developing countries to fully understand and benefit from different provisions, pertaining to flexibilities provided for in international agreements, as appropriate
26. To encourage Member States, especially developed countries, to urge their research and scientific institutions to enhance cooperation and exchange with research and development institutions in developing countries, especially LDCs
27. Facilitating IP-related aspects of ICT for growth and development. Provide for, in an appropriate WIPO body, discussions focused on the importance of IP-related aspects of ICT, and its role in economic and cultural development, with specific attention focused on assisting Member States to identify practical IP-related strategies to use ICT for economic, social and cultural development

Cluster C: Technology Transfer, Information and Communication Technologies (ICT) and Access to Knowledge

28. To explore supportive IP-related policies and measures Member States, especially developed countries, could adopt for promoting transfer and dissemination of technology to developing countries

29. To include discussions on IP-related technology transfer issues within the mandate of an appropriate WIPO body

30. WIPO should cooperate with other intergovernmental organisations to provide to developing countries, including LDCs, upon request, advice on how to gain access to and make use of IP-related information on technology, particularly in areas of special interest to the requesting parties

31. To undertake initiatives agreed by Member States, which contribute to transfer of technology to developing countries, such as requesting WIPO to facilitate better access to publicly available patent information

32. To have within WIPO opportunity for exchange of national and regional experiences and information on the links between IP rights and competition policies

Cluster D: Assessment, Evaluation and Impact Studies

33. To request WIPO to develop an effective yearly review and evaluation mechanism for the assessment of all its development-oriented activities, including those related to technical assistance, establishing for that purpose specific indicators and benchmarks, where appropriate

34. With a view to assisting Member States in creating substantial national programs, to request WIPO to conduct a study on constraints to intellectual property protection in the informal economy, including the tangible costs and benefits of IP protection in particular in relation to generation of employment

35. * To request WIPO to undertake, upon request of Member States, new studies to assess the economic, social and cultural impact of the use of intellectual property systems in these states

36. To exchange experiences on open collaborative projects such as the Human Genome Project as well as on IP models

37. * Upon request and as directed by Member States, WIPO may conduct studies on the protection of intellectual property, to identify the possible links and impacts between IP and development

38. To strengthen WIPO's capacity to perform objective assessments of the impact of the organisation's activities on development

Cluster E: Institutional Matters Including Mandate and Governance

39. To request WIPO, within its core competence and mission, to assist developing countries, especially African countries, in cooperation with relevant international organisations, by conducting studies on brain drain and make recommendations accordingly

Cluster E: Institutional Matters Including Mandate and Governance
40. To request WIPO to intensify its cooperation on IP-related issues with UN agencies, according to Member States' orientation, in particular UNCTAD, UNEP, WHO, UNIDO, UNESCO and other relevant international organisations, especially WTO in order to strengthen the coordination for maximum efficiency in undertaking development programs
41. To conduct a review of current WIPO technical assistance activities in the area of cooperation and development
42. * To enhance measures that ensure wide participation of civil society at large in WIPO activities in accordance with its criteria regarding NGO acceptance and accreditation, keeping the issue under review
43. To consider how to improve WIPO's role in finding partners to fund and execute projects for IP-related assistance in a transparent and member-driven process and without prejudice to ongoing WIPO activities
44. * In accordance with WIPO's member-driven nature as a United Nations Specialized Agency, formal and informal meetings or consultations relating to norm-setting activities in WIPO, organised by the International Bureau, upon request of the Member States, should be held primarily in Geneva, in a manner open and transparent to all Member States. Where such meetings are to take place outside of Geneva, Member States shall be informed through official channels, well in advance, and consulted on the draft agenda and program
Cluster F: Other Issues
45. To approach intellectual property enforcement in the context of broader societal interests and especially development-oriented concerns, with a view that 'the protection and enforcement of intellectual property rights should contribute to the promotion of technological innovation and to the transfer and dissemination of technology, to the mutual advantage of producers and users of technological knowledge and in a manner conducive to social and economic welfare, and to a balance of rights and obligations,' in accordance with Article 7 of the TRIPS Agreement

Note: Recommendations with an asterisk were identified by the 2007 General Assembly for immediate implementation.

Source: See WIPO, 'The 45 Adopted Recommendations under the WIPO Development Agenda'' <http://www.wipo.int/ip-development/en/agenda/recommendations.html> accessed 30 October 2015.

protection of intellectual property rights, to embracing the need to assist developing countries in different aspects of this crucial area.'[5]

Also on the governance front, the General Assembly agreed to create a Committee on Development and IP (CDIP) to oversee the implementation of the Development Agenda recommendations and undertake further work.[6] In addition, a number of the Development Agenda recommendations specifically relate to WIPO'S governance and mandate, most notably those in Cluster E on institutional matters. Several recommendations in other Clusters also have governance implications, such as those designed to boost the transparency, development-orientation and accountability of the organisation's activities and norms. Specific examples of components of the WIPO Development Agenda particularly relevant to WIPO's governance include recommendations for implementing a yearly review and evaluation mechanism for all WIPO's development-oriented activities; strengthening capacity to perform objective assessments of the development impact of WIPO's activities; intensifying cooperation with UN agencies; reviewing WIPO technical assistance to developing countries; enhancing participation of civil society in WIPO activities; improving WIPO's role in finding partners for its activities in developing countries; boosting transparency and openness of meetings related to norm-setting; and creating a public, online roster of consultants and database of technical assistance projects. In addition, in 2010, WIPO Member States adopted a Development Agenda Coordination Mechanism to improve monitoring and coordination of the efforts to mainstream development considerations throughout WIPO's work (discussed in Chapter 5).

---

5 See JIU, *Review of Management and Administration in the World Intellectual Property Organization (WIPO)* JIU/REP/2014/2 (UN Joint Inspection Unit 2014).

6 See WIPO, *General Report of the 2007 WIPO Assemblies* A/43/16 (WIPO 2007) para. 334. The existence of a WIPO Member State body focused specifically on development issues was not novel. Although the CDIP had an expanded mandate, its antecedent was the Permanent Committee on Cooperation for Development Related to Intellectual Property (PCIPD), which was an advisory body focused on technical assistance created in 1998 that reported to the WIPO Conference and met in four sessions held between 1998 and 2005. In 2005, Member States agreed to an Intersessional Intergovernmental Meeting on a Development Agenda for WIPO, which met over three sessions. At the 2005 Assemblies, Member States agreed to constitute a Provisional Committee on Proposals Related to a WIPO Development Agenda (PCDA) to take forward discussions on the Development Agenda proposals. Member States also agreed that the PCIPD would cease to exist. The PCDA held four sessions from 2006 to 2007.

5 WIPO's decision-making structure, processes and practices

The World Intellectual Property Organization's decision-making structure is often described as complex. In 2014, for instance, a UN Joint Inspection Unit report observed that WIPO has 'one of the most complex governance structures' in the UN system.[1] This complexity arises in part from WIPO's historical origins and evolution; most notably from the amalgamation of several existing treaty-based structures into WIPO and the progressive adding of new treaties.

5.1 WIPO's complex decision-making structure

The World Intellectual Property Organization's main decision-making organs coexist with the governing bodies of the Unions created by a number of WIPO-administered IP treaties, several of which date back to the late 19th century.[2] Further, the main convention-based organs established by the WIPO Convention are complemented by several layers of subsidiary bodies also involved in decision-making and/or negotiations, including committees, expert committees established by treaty provisions, and working groups. Some of these bodies focus on governance matters (such as the Program and Budget Committee (PBC) and the Independent Advisory Oversight Committee (IAOC)), and others on more substantive and technical matters of IP. (Figure 5.1 presents a visual view of the WIPO's decision-making structure, focusing on the composition and relationships of WIPO's main decision-making organs, subsidiary bodies, and the governing bodies of a number of WIPO treaties.) Diplomatic conferences are further important components of WIPO's governance system. Although Member State views vary on the role and significance of coordination mechanisms such as the Development Agenda Coordination Mechanism, it is discussed in

---

1 JIU, *Review of Management and Administration in the World Intellectual Property Organization (WIPO)* JIU/REP/2014/2 (UN Joint Inspection Unit 2014) 5.

2 See WIPO, *WIPO Governance Structure* WO/PBC/18/20 (WIPO 2011).

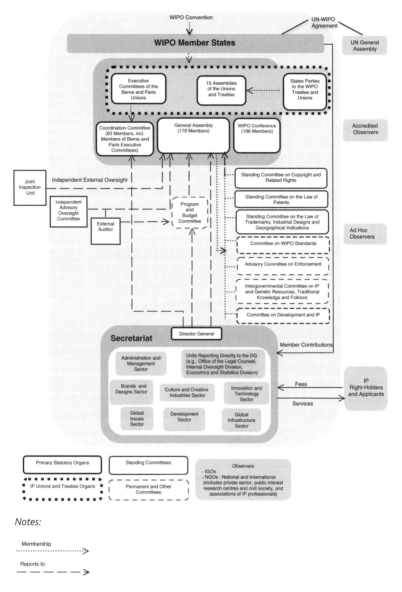

Source: Author's own diagram.

Figure 5.1 A view of WIPO's complex governance structure

this chapter as a component of WIPO's governance system due to its focus on coordination across WIPO's decision-making structure (see section 5.7). Each of these elements is discussed below.

5.2   The main organs

The World Intellectual Property Organization's three main decision-making organs, as defined by the 1967 WIPO Convention, are the WIPO General Assembly (179 Member States), the WIPO Conference (188 members) and the WIPO Coordination Committee (83 members). For each of these core organs, one delegate, who may be assisted by alternate delegates, advisors and experts, can represent each Member State.[3]

Each of the organs established by the WIPO Convention, as well as the governing bodies created by other WIPO treaties (discussed in section 5.3 below), can only be formally modified through amendments to the relevant treaties, which subsequently enter into force after accession/ratification by the required number of members, according to their respective constitutional processes.[4] Although the mandates of WIPO's main organs can not be formally changed through decisions made by the General Assembly, some Member State decisions and practices have nonetheless informally and incrementally altered how decision-making occurs in the main organs, and which of these main organs, or other committees, serves in reality as the venue for discussion of different agenda items.

Notably, whereas many international organisations have an executive committee or board comprised of a sub-group of member states (most of which consist of between 30 and 50 member states representing different geographic or economic groupings of countries) that meet several times a year to guide and oversee the organisation, WIPO does not have such an executive organ among its convention-based or statutory governing bodies.[5] In practice, however, the Program and Budget Committee

---

3   See, for instance, Article 6(1) of the WIPO Convention.
4   See WIPO, *The Governance Structure of WIPO: Memorandum of the International Bureau* A/32/INF/2 (WIPO 1998) 7.
5   For a review of practices related to executive boards and committees, and to subsidiary bodies dealing with administrative and/or budgetary issues, see WIPO, *Report of the WIPO Audit Committee since 2008* WO/GA/38/2 (WIPO 2009) Appendix 1. This information was subsequently updated in WIPO, *WIPO Governance Structure: Document Prepared by the Secretariat* WO/PBC/17/2.Rev. (WIPO 2011) Annex III.

(PBC), one of the General Assembly's subsidiary bodies, performs many of the powerful functions (but not all) that such executive bodies are commonly charged with (the PBC is discussed in detail below).[6]

5.2.1   The General Assembly

The General Assembly is WIPO's highest legislative body. Its 179 members represent all states party to the WIPO Convention that are also members of any of the WIPO-administered Unions (that is, the Assembly thus does not include all WIPO Member States).[7] The main tasks of the General Assembly are to: (i) appoint the Director General upon nomination by the Coordination Committee; (ii) review and approve reports of the Director General and give the incumbent all necessary instructions on strategic matters and policy issues; (iii) review and approve the reports and activities of the Coordination Committee and give instructions to that Committee; (iv) adopt the biennial budget of expenses common to the Unions; (v) approve the measures concerning the administration of the international agreements; (vi) adopt the financial regulations of the organisation; (vii) determine the working languages of the Secretariat; (viii) invite states to become party to the WIPO Convention; and (ix) determine which states that are not members of WIPO and which intergovernmental organisations and international NGOs should be admitted to its meetings as observers.

The General Assembly generally meets as part of the annual Assemblies of the Member States of WIPO, a practice enabled by alternating between biennial 'ordinary' sessions called for by the Convention and 'extraordinary' sessions.[8] Additional 'extraordinary' sessions of the General Assembly are also sometimes held for particular purposes (for example, to conclude unfinished agenda items from earlier sessions, such as the approval of the Program and Budget or the appointment of the Director General). The General Assembly adopts the final decisions on the recommendations of all subsidiary bodies, such as the PBC and the Standing Committee on Copyright and Related Rights

---

6 See JIU, *Review of Management and Administration in the World Intellectual Property Organization (WIPO)* JIU/REP/2014/2 (UN Joint Inspection Unit 2014) 7.

7 The General Assembly does not include the following eight states, which are not members of the Paris and Berne Unions: Afghanistan, Eritrea, Ethiopia, Kiribati, Kuwait, Maldives, Myanmar, Niue and Somalia.

8 Without extraordinary sessions, there would be only a biennial ordinary session.

(SCCR), that report to it. The Chair of the General Assembly is elected for a 2-year term.

5.2.2   The WIPO Conference

On paper, the WIPO Conference is WIPO's second highest decision-making body. It comprises all 188 States party to the WIPO Convention, irrespective of whether they are also members of WIPO-administered Unions (meaning that the Conference has more members than the General Assembly). The tasks originally set out for the Conference included serving as a forum for discussion among members of matters of general interest in the field of IP; in that context the Conference was empowered to adopt recommendations. The Conference was also entrusted with responsibility for amending the WIPO Convention (proposals for such amendments may be initiated by any WIPO Member State, the Coordination Committee or the Director General).[9] In practice, however, the Conference meets at the same time in the same room as the General Assembly, and rarely considers any separate items of business.[10] That is, the functional division of work originally envisaged between the General Assembly and the Conference has rarely occurred. Indeed, WIPO Member States agreed in 2003 to amend the WIPO Convention to abolish the Conference, which will occur when the amendment comes into force (which requires ratification by three-quarters of WIPO's Member States).[11] The last time the Conference met separately on a substantive agenda item was in 2005 on matters concerning the Permanent Committee on Cooperation for Development related to IP (PCDIP). Nonetheless the Conference is still an important and relevant part of WIPO's governance system. At the 2013 Assemblies, debate on the quorum necessary to take a decision on WIPO's Program and Budget led the WIPO Legal Counsel to clarify that as the Program and

---

9 The tasks originally set out for the WIPO Conference in Article 7(2) are to: '(i) discuss matters of general interest in the field of intellectual property and [may] adopt recommendations relating to such matters, having regard for the competence and autonomy of the Unions; (ii) adopt the biennial budget of the Conference; (iii) within the limits of the budget of the Conference, establish the biennial program of legal technical assistance; (iv) adopt amendments to [the WIPO] Convention as provided in Article 17; (v) determine which States not Members of the Organization and which intergovernmental and international non-governmental organisations shall be admitted to its meetings as observers; and (vi) exercise such other functions as are appropriate under [the WIPO] Convention.'

10 Normally, the only ostensible difference in the proceedings is the difference in presiding officer.

11 See WIPO, *Final Texts of Proposed Amendments to the Convention Establishing the World Intellectual Property Organization: Document Prepared by the Secretariat* A/39/2 (WIPO 2003).

Budget requires adoption by the Member States of WIPO and all of the Unions, the plenary session that adopts the Program and Budget has in practice been the WIPO Conference, at which time the General Assembly and other relevant Assemblies simultaneously make their decision (see section 6.4.2).[12]

5.2.3 The WIPO Coordination Committee

The WIPO Coordination Committee has 83 Member States. Its members consist of those states party to the WIPO Convention that are also members of the Executive Committees of the Paris Union, the Berne Union or both.[13] The functions of the Coordination Committee are both advisory and executive. They include: (i) giving advice to the organs of the Unions, the General Assembly, the Conference and the Director General on all administrative, financial and other matters of common interest, and in particular on the budgetary expenses common to the Unions; (ii) preparing the draft agenda of the General Assembly and the Conference; (iii) preparing the draft agenda and draft program and budget of the Conference; and (iv) nominating a candidate for Director General to the General Assembly.[14] Any WIPO Member that is not a member of the Coordination Committee may observe its meetings, 'having the right to take part in the debates but without the right to vote.'[15] The existence of the Coordination Committee highlights that WIPO's founders perceived the organisation's two core treaties, the Paris and Berne Conventions, and its treaty-making functions, as central to the organisation's purpose and activities. As such, the WIPO Convention did not eliminate the Unions of the existing treaties or diminish their autonomy or responsibilities.

On a practical basis, among the Coordination Committee's most important, regular responsibilities are WIPO's human resources, including the nomination of candidates for Director General, the approval of nominations for WIPO's Deputy Directors General, advice on pro-

---

12 WIPO, *General Report: adopted by the Assemblies* A/51/20 (Geneva: WIPO 2013) 108–11.

13 Subject to the rule that only a number equal to one-quarter of the Assembly members that elected the respective Executive Committees of the Unions can be part of the Coordination Committee. The number of members of the Coordination Committee increases when there are new accessions to the Paris and/or Berne Conventions.

14 See Article 8(3) of the WIPO Convention. Other functions include approving the Director General's choice of Deputy Directors General before their appointment.

15 See Article 8(7) of the WIPO Convention.

posed Assistant Directors General, and approval of changes to WIPO Staff Regulations. On the choice of Director General, in some years the Committee has only received one nomination to consider, and in other instances, the nomination has followed a formal election process conducted by the Coordination Committee. In 1998, the Generally Assembly decided in favour of a transparent process where the nomination is made if possible by consensus, while recognising that consultations and voting will likely be a necessary means for building such consensus. The procedures for voting, which occurs by secret ballot in several steps with a view to the gradual reduction of the number of candidates to a short list of three, are clearly set out. However, the informal processes for consensus-building around candidates are not transparent nor are the criteria used by Member States. In practice, a mix of factors is relevant to the emergence of top candidates, including: a candidate's individual campaign strategy; the degree to which candidates receive effective support from their country of origin; power politics and political jockeying among Member States; considerations of regional representation and rotation in WIPO's leadership (and of the regional composition of leadership appointments across international organisations); trade offs by Member States between the choice of Director General and other substantive priorities at WIPO; the degree of support from regional groups; and the merits and experience of the candidates.[16] (see section 2.4.1).

5.3 The annual WIPO Assemblies and the Governing Bodies of the Unions

In total, there are 20 WIPO bodies[17] that meet in ordinary or extraordinary sessions annually or bi-annually. The sessions of these bodies are referred to collectively as the Annual Meeting of the Assemblies

---

16 The WIPO General Assembly adopted procedures in this repsect in 1998, which are reproduced in WIPO, *Information Concerning Procedures, Membership and Voting : Memorandum prepared by the Secretariat* WO/CC/69/INF/1 (WIPO 2014).

17 These bodies are: the WIPO General Assembly, the WIPO Conference, the WIPO Coordination Committee, the Paris Union Assembly, the Paris Union Executive Committee, the Berne Union Assembly, the Berne Union Executive Committee, the Madrid Union Assembly, the Hague Union Assembly, the Nice Union Assembly, the Lisbon Union Assembly, the Locarno Union Assembly, the IPC (International Patent Classification) Union Assembly, the PCT (Patent Cooperation Treaty) Union Assembly, the Budapest Union Assembly, the Vienna Union Assembly, the WCT (WIPO Copyright Treaty) Assembly, the WPPT (WIPO Performances and Phonograms Treaty) Assembly, the Singapore Treaty on the Law of Trademarks Assembly and the PLT (Patent Law Treaty) Assembly.

of Member States,[18] which normally occurs over a ten-day period in September/October.

In addition to the three main organs, some 13 of the treaties administered by WIPO establish a Union of their parties,[19] such as the Paris Union,[20] with a number of responsibilities relevant to the treaty, such as amending the agreement and formulating related rules and regulations.[21] Each Union has an Assembly and in some cases Executive Committees charged with the execution of their respective treaties and related agreements (any Union may also establish Working Groups, Committees and ad hoc groups).[22] (See Table 2.2 for the membership

---

18 The general rule is that the main organs meet in ordinary session once every 2 years, and in extraordinary session once every 2 years. In effect, they meet every year, alternating between ordinary and extraordinary sessions. There are exceptions to the general rule, such as the Coordination Committee and the Paris and Berne Executive Committees, which meet in ordinary session every year.

19 The WIPO Secretariat notes that: 'In 1991, the Assembly of the Union for the International Registration of Marks (the TRT Union) decided to "freeze" the TRT and to suspend future ordinary sessions of the TRT Union Assembly . . . The Assembly of the Union for the International Registration of Audiovisual Works (the FRT Union) similarly suspended, in 1993, ordinary sessions of the FRT Union Assembly . . . For all practical purposes, these Assemblies can no longer be considered to be part of the governance structure of WIPO.' See WIPO, *WIPO Governance Structure: Document Prepared by the Secretariat* WO/PBC/17/2.Rev. (WIPO 2011) 4.

20 The name of the Union is, in most cases, taken from the place where the text of the treaty was first adopted (thus, for instance, the Berne Union).

21 The WIPO Secretariat notes that some of the governing bodies that were envisaged at the time the relevant treaties were adopted 'have not yet been constituted', such as the Executive Committee of the PCT Union. See WIPO, *WIPO Governance Structure: Document Prepared by the Secretariat* WO/PBC/17/2.Rev. (WIPO 2011) 4.

22 In the case of treaties first concluded before the 1967 Stockholm Diplomatic Conference, the earlier Acts created Conferences of Representatives (the predecessor bodies of the Assemblies of those Unions, which were introduced in the 1967 Acts of those treaties that were revised at that Diplomatic Conference). These conferences still exist in cases where there are states party to an Act earlier than the Stockholm Act (but not yet party to the Stockholm Act). The number of states belonging to those bodies is small, and declining as states progressively accede to the Stockholm Acts of the relevant treaties. Examples are the Conference of Representatives of the Paris Union, of which the Dominican Republic and Nigeria are the only members, and the Conference of Representatives of the Berne Union, of which Lebanon, Madagascar and New Zealand are the only members. The Conference of Representatives for the Paris Union, Berne Union, Nice Union and the Hague Union met for the last time in 2000, along with the Lisbon Union Council. The WIPO Secretariat has noted that: 'In practical terms, given the fact that the powers conferred on the Conferences of Representatives by their constituent instruments were extremely limited, that the bodies have never considered any item of substantive business, and that their convening has tended to be a formality only, all these bodies can no longer be considered part of the governance structure of WIPO.' See WIPO, *WIPO Governance Structure: Document Prepared by the Secretariat* WO/PBC/17/2.Rev. (WIPO 2011) 4; WIPO, *WIPO Intellectual Property Handbook: Policy, Law and Use* (WIPO 2004) 11.

of WIPO and the WIPO's treaty-based Unions and Appendix 4 for Special Rules of Procedure for the governing bodies of the various Unions and their Executive Committees).

The practice of the Assemblies has evolved such that in lieu of a series of separate meetings, the Secretariat presents the draft agendas of the 20 Assemblies and other bodies in a consolidated, single agenda. (When a matter concerns more than one Assembly or body, such a matter constitutes a single item).[23] For over 15 years, the Chair of the General Assembly has presided over most of the Assemblies, except for matters that are the responsibility of the Coordination Committee, over which the Chair of that Committee presides, and for matters that concern only a particular Union, where the chair of the relevant governing body presides. In practice, the great majority of the proceedings of the combined Assemblies proceed as though it were a unitary Assembly. Notably, members of WIPO's treaty-specific Unions remain responsible for adopting decisions and reports directly related to their activities through their respective Assemblies; for instance, treaty-related decisions adopted by members of the Paris, Berne or Lisbon Unions do not need subsequent approval by the WIPO General Assembly. However, where such decisions have budgetary or program implications for the WIPO Secretariat, this may require action from other WIPO committees, such as the Program and Budget Committee, which in turn may require approval by the General Assembly.

Drafted by the Secretariat, the General Report of the Assemblies refers to each of the items on the consolidated agenda of the 20 Assemblies and other bodies of Member States. The General Report includes a detailed record of the deliberations and decisions on many agenda items; it also, however, refers in many instances to reports adopted by other bodies (such as the General Assembly, the Coordination Committee and the governing bodies of the WIPO Unions) on agenda items where they have specific responsibility.

The final agenda item before the close of the annual Assemblies deals with the adoption by Member States of the reports of each of the Assemblies and other bodies. The Chair of the General Council presides for the adoption of the General Report of the Assemblies and the

---

23 See for instance, WIPO, *Draft Consolidated and Annotated Agenda*, W/54/1 PROV.4 (WIPO 2014).

Report of the General Assembly, whereas the adoption of the reports by each of the concerned Assemblies or bodies is presided over by their respective Chairs. In 2014 and 2015, however, the Chair of the General Assembly announced that due to the lateness of the meeting and the many statements made by delegations, the Secretariat's draft reports would instead be sent to Member States and posted on WIPO's website. In each of these years, the Chair specified a period within which comments should be submitted to the Secretariat, after which the final reports would be deemed adopted.[24]

5.4   WIPO committees and other subsidiary bodies

A second tier of WIPO's governance is formed by committees and other subsidiary bodies constituted under one or more of the main convention-based organs, such as the General Assembly. These subsidiary bodies include Committees, expert committees established by treaty provisions, and working groups.

5.4.1   Committees

At present, WIPO has eight subsidiary bodies that are formally known as 'Committees'. With the exception of the Program and Budget Committee (PBC), each of these committees is open to all Member States, which normally send relevant national officials and experts, and to accredited intergovernmental organisations (IGOs) and observers. Most, but not all, of the committees introduced below have adopted Special Rules of Procedure (see section 5.5.1 and Appendix 5). The mandate and activities of such Committees can be created, adapted or ended by the WIPO General Assembly.

The list of Committees that comprise WIPO's subsidiary bodies is as follows:

1.   The Program and Budget Committee (PBC), a subsidiary organ created by the General Assembly, is responsible for all budgetary and financial aspects of WIPO.[25] In practice, the PBC is one

---

24 See WIPO, *Draft General Report: Prepared by the Secretariat* A/54/13/PROV (WIPO 2014) 112.

25 The PBC was created in 1998, following a proposal by the Secretariat in its 1998/9 proposed Program and Budget to merge the Budget Committee and Premises Committee. While the

of WIPO's most powerful bodies, dealing with program, budget, finance, premises, and personnel resources, and also increasingly with governance matters. Since 2007, the membership of the PBC has been 53 Member States (up from 35 Member States in 2002). The General Assembly appoints PBC Members for a 2-year term.[26]

Neither the General Assembly nor the PBC has, however, adopted formal Special Rules of Procedure regarding the Committee's membership, the reappointment of countries or term limits. Some countries have served continuously for over 10 years or for numerous terms. There are also no formal criteria to guide the election of PBC members nor is there a formal quota for the number of seats by regional groups. In practice, the PBC submits a proposal on the composition of its membership to the General Assembly on the basis of informal consultations among regional groups, taking into consideration calls by a number of delegations to improve the geographical representation of the PBC. The WIPO General Assembly subsequently elects the members.[27] By tradition, Switzerland is an *ex officio* member of the PBC.

In budget years, the PBC meets twice in formal sessions (and also once in an informal session). In non-budget years, the PBC has one formal session per year.[28] Although non-members of the PBC, WIPO's External Auditor and members of WIPO's Independent

---

General Assembly decision that created the PBC specified the Committee's mandate as one of dealing with program, budget, premises and finance, the WIPO Financial Regulations and Rules define the PBC more broadly as 'the Committee constituted by the General Assembly to deal with program, budget, *personnel resources*, premises and finance' (emphasis added).

26 In October 2015, the WIPO General Assembly unanimously elected the following states as members of the Program and Budget Committee for the period from October 2015 to October 2017: Argentina, Armenia, Azerbaijan, Bangladesh, Belarus, Brazil, Cameroon, Canada, Chile, China, Colombia (2015/16), Congo, Czech Republic, Ecuador, Egypt, El Salvador, Estonia (2016/17), Ethiopia, France, Germany, Greece, Guatemala, Hungary, India, Iran (Islamic Republic of), Italy, Japan, Latvia (2015/16), Malaysia, Mexico, Morocco, Nigeria, Pakistan, Panama, Poland, Republic of Korea, Romania, Russian Federation, Senegal, Singapore, Slovakia, Slovenia, South Africa, Spain, Sri Lanka, Sweden, Switzerland (*ex officio*), Tajikistan, Trinidad and Tobago (2016/17), Turkey, Uganda, United Kingdom, United States of America, Vietnam and Zimbabwe.

27 See, for instance, WIPO, *Composition of the Program and Budget Committee: Document Prepared by the Secretariat* WO/GA/40/1 (WIPO 2014).

28 This practice is in line with the Mechanism for the Preparation of the Program and Budget, approved at the 2006 Assemblies. See WIPO, *Report Adopted by the Assemblies of the 42nd Series of Meetings* A/42/14 (WIPO 2006). Also see WIPO, *Report on, and Recommendations Adopted by, the Ninth and Tenth Sessions of the Program and Budget Committee* A/42/9 (WIPO 2006); WIPO, *Proposals on a New Mechanism to Further Involve Member States in the Preparation and Follow*

Advisory Oversight Committee (IAOC – described below) are able to observe its meetings, they have no decision-making powers. Neither IGO nor NGO observers are admitted to PBC sessions. (Video-on-demand recordings of the formal proceedings of the September 2014 and 2015 sessions can be viewed on WIPO's website, and some earlier sessions were available through webcasting);

2.   Three Standing Committees established by the General Assembly in 1998 with specific mandates on substantive and policy-related issues, which report to the General Assembly and generally meet twice a year. These committees are the Standing Committee on Copyright and Related Rights (SCCR), created to examine matters of substantive law or harmonisation in the field of copyright and related rights;[29] the Standing Committee on the Law of Patents (SCP), established to serve as a forum to discuss issues, facilitate coordination and provide guidance concerning the progressive international development of patent law;[30] and the Standing Committee on Trademarks, Industrial Designs and Geographical Indications (SCT), created to serve as a forum to discuss issues, facilitate coordination and provide guidance on the progressive development of international law on trademarks, industrial designs and geographical indications, including the harmonisation of national laws and procedures.[31] Notably, these standing committees sometimes address topics that are simultaneously the subject of WIPO treaties, which can raise concerns about the relationship between the work of the committees, which are open to all WIPO Members, and the deliberations of WIPO's treaty-based Unions, the membership of which is limited to the parties to the respective treaties. At the SCT, for instance, Member States regularly discuss issues related to appellations of origin that are the subject of the

   Up of the Program and Budget: Document Prepared by the Secretariat, WO/PBC/10/5 (WIPO 2006), Annex IV and V.

29 The SCCR is composed of all Member States of WIPO and/or of the Berne Union. Certain UN member states that are non-members of WIPO and/or the Berne Union, as well as a number of accredited IGOs and NGOs, are admitted as observers.

30 The SCP is composed of all member states of WIPO and/or of the Paris Union. Certain UN member states that are not members of WIPO and/or the Paris Union, as well as a number of accredited IGOs and NGOs, also participate in the SCP as observers.

31 The SCT is open to all members of WIPO or the Paris Union. A special rule of procedure extends membership without the right to vote to the European Union. In addition, certain member states of the UN that are not members of WIPO or the Paris Union, as well as accredited IGOs and NGOs, may participate as observers.

Lisbon Treaty and have recently been the subject of negotiations among members of the Lisbon Union (see section 5.3.4);

3. The Advisory Committee on Enforcement (ACE), tasked in 2002 with 'coordinating with certain organizations and the private sector to combat counterfeiting and piracy activities; public education; assistance; coordination to undertake national and regional training programs for all relevant stakeholders and exchange of information on enforcement issues through the establishment of an Electronic Forum.' Notably, the Committee's mandate excludes norm-setting, and is largely limited to technical assistance and coordination;[32]

4. The Intergovernmental Committee on Intellectual Property and Genetic Resources, Traditional Knowledge and Folklore (IGC), created by the General Assembly in 2000 for the purpose of discussions on genetic resources, traditional knowledge and folklore. The IGC relies on the periodic renewal of its mandate by the General Assembly, meaning that it is not formally classified as a Standing Committee;[33]

5. The Committee on Development and Intellectual Property (CDIP), established by the General Assembly in 2007 to develop a work program for implementation of the adopted Development Agenda recommendations; (b) monitor, assess, discuss and report on the implementation of those recommendations in coordination with relevant WIPO bodies; and (c) discuss IP and development related issues as agreed by the Committee, as well as those decided by the General Assembly;[34] and

6. The Committee on WIPO Standards (CWS), established in 2010 by the General Assembly to 'continue to work on the revision and development of WIPO standards relating to intellectual property information.'[35]

---

32 See WIPO, *Report Adopted by the Assemblies of the 28th Session* WO/GA/28/7 (WIPO 2002) paras 82–120.

33 See WIPO, *Matters Concerning Intellectual Property and Genetic Resources, Traditional Knowledge and Folklore* WO/GA/26/6 (WIPO 2000); and WIPO, *Report Adopted by the Assemblies of the 26th Session* WO/GA/26/10 (WIPO 2000).

34 The CDIP was established in October 2007 to: See WIPO, *General Report of the 2007 WIPO Assemblies* A/43/16 (WIPO 2007) para. 334.

35 The CWS replaced the former Standing Committee on Information Technologies (SCIT), which had agreed earlier that it should be replaced by two bodies: the CWS and the Committee on

5.4.2   Expert committees established by treaty provisions

The four WIPO international classification treaties (see Table 2.1),[36] each establish permanent Committees of Experts that meet to discuss and adopt revisions to the classifications established by each treaty.[37] The committees comprise representatives of each member of the Unions established by these treaties. Representatives of other intergovernmental organisations and international NGOs may also be invited to attend.[38]

5.4.3   Working groups

Each of WIPO's main organs, committees, or committees of experts can establish working groups.[39] In general, working groups are intended to have limited missions and duration, and are created to facilitate the discussion and resolution of particular questions that, because of the technical or confidential nature of the questions, are more appropriately dealt with in a small group.[40] An example of such

---

Global IP Infrastructure (CGI). The 2010 General Assembly decision affirmed that the CWS would continue the work of the SCIT's former Standards and Documentation Working Group (SDWG). It also clarified that '[t]he mandate of the CGI would be to discuss matters concerning global intellectual property infrastructure that do not fall into the mandate of the CWS. Such matters include development of good practices, common tools and coherent approaches to various projects for strengthening international cooperation and interchange of data and information of intellectual property.' See WIPO, *Standing Committee on Information Technology: Document Prepared by the Secretariat* WO/GA/38/10 (WIPO 2009). As of the end of 2015, the CGI has never met.

36   Also see Chapter 2, footnote 15.

37   For instance, Article 3(5) of the Nice Agreement states that: 'Proposals for changes in the Classification may be made by the competent Office of any country of the Special Union, the International Bureau, any intergovernmental organization represented in the Committee of Experts pursuant to paragraph (2)*(b)* and any country or organization specially invited by the Committee of Experts to submit such proposals.'

38   Article 3(2) of the Nice Agreement, for instance, provides that: '*(a)* The Director General may, and, if requested by the Committee of Experts, shall, invite countries outside the Special Union which are members of the Organization or party to the Paris Convention for the Protection of Industrial Property to be represented by observers at meetings of the Committee of Experts. *(b)* The Director General shall invite intergovernmental organizations specialized in the field of marks, of which at least one of the member countries is a country of the Special Union, to be represented by observers at meetings of the Committee of Experts. *(c)* The Director General may, and, if requested by the Committee of Experts, shall, invite representatives of other intergovernmental organizations and international non-governmental organizations to participate in discussions of interest to them.'

39   The WIPO General Rules of Procedure (Rule 12) make provision for the establishment of such working groups for specific purposes.

40   Further examples of working groups established in recent years include: the Working Group

a group was a Working Group on Audit Committee Related Matters, which was established by the PBC and met in 2010. The governing bodies of WIPO's treaties can also create working groups. In 2007, for instance, the PCT Assembly established a PCT Working Group to do preparatory work on matters for submission to the Assembly, such as proposals for amendment of the PCT regulations.[41]

5.4.4 Diplomatic conferences

A diplomatic conference is a high-level meeting of Member States, convened with the sole purpose of finalising negotiations on a new treaty or treaty revisions. For each diplomatic conference, States adopt Rules of Procedure for the Diplomatic Conference.[42] See Appendix 6 for an example of such Rules of Procedure, adopted for the Diplomatic Conference on the Marrakesh Treaty.

If one of WIPO's standing or permanent committees determines that sufficient progress has been made to move towards treaty adoption, the General Assembly can decide to convene a diplomatic conference, which is open to equal participation by all WIPO Member States. The Assemblies of the Unions established by several WIPO-administered treaties may also decide to convene a diplomatic conference, such as for revising a treaty or adopting a new act of a treaty, without the need for approval by the WIPO General Assembly. In 2015, for instance, the 28 members of the Lisbon Union convened a diplomatic conference to adopt a new 'Geneva Act' of the Lisbon Agreement, the text of which had been under development since 2008.[43] The Assembly of the Union in question can in the Rules of Procedure it adopts for the diplomatic conference limit participation to members of that Union; it also has the power decide whether to open the negotiations to non-members

---

on the Review of Rule 3(4) to (6) of the Regulations Under the Singapore Treaty on the Law of Trademarks, the Working Group on the Legal Development of the Madrid System for the International Registration of Marks, the Working Group on the Development of the Lisbon System, and the Working Group on the Reform of the PCT (2001–2007).

41 See PCT Union-Assembly, *Report Adopted by the Assembly of the 36th Session* PCT/A/36/13 (WIPO 2007).

42 See, for instance, WIPO, *Rules of Procedure of the Diplomatic Conference, Prepared for the Diplomatic Conference to Conclude a Treaty to Facilitate Access to Published Works by Visually Impaired Persons and Persons with Print Disabilities* VIP/DC/2 (WIPO 2013).

43 The Diplomatic Conference for the Adoption of a New Act of the Lisbon Agreement for the Protection of Appellations of Origin and their International Registration took place from 11 to 21 May 2015 and adopted the Geneva Act of the Lisbon Agreement on Appellations of Origin and Geographical Indications.

as observers or as equal participants. That said, as the hosting of a diplomatic conference relies on a range of support activities from the WIPO Secretariat, the General Assembly (via the Program and Budget Committee) has the potential to influence whether, when and how negotiations proceed via decisions it makes on the allocation of the organisation's financial resources. The General Assembly's scope for influence could be lower, however, where the resources involved are minimal and/or could be obtained from already allocated budget lines.

Debate among WIPO Member States on the Lisbon Union's decision to convene the 2015 diplomatic conference highlights the complex relationship between WIPO's Unions – which are in effect plurilateral agreements among those Member States interested in joining – and the wider organisation. A number of WIPO Member States that are not members of the Lisbon Union (such as the United States, South Korea and Japan) opposed the convening of the diplomatic conference on several grounds. In so doing, they argued that the draft text did not reflect the diversity of economic interests at stake across WIPO's membership and that the subject of geographical indications was simultaneously under discussion in WIPO's SCT and under negotiation at the World Trade Organization. Further, they argued that the substance of the negotiating text reflected more than merely a revision of the Lisbon agreement (which could be negotiated among Lisbon members) but would in fact create a new WIPO treaty (which they argued would be a matter for the entire WIPO membership). The United States also objected to the allocation of resources from WIPO's general budget to help cover the costs of a diplomatic conference in which the majority of WIPO's membership was not able to have a voting role.[44]

These debates highlight that numerous governance questions exist with regard to diplomatic conferences, such as how the distinction is to be made between a new treaty and treaty revision; whether a diplomatic conference can be convened exclusively for a formal treaty negotiation or for other types of instruments and treaty revisions as well; which Member States should be involved in decisions to convene a diplomatic conference and granted a voting role in negotiations; and on what terms resources from WIPO's general budget

---

44 For an overview of the debate, see William New, 'Special Feature: Differences over GIs Threaten 2016/17 WIPO Budget Approval' *Intellectual Property Watch* (30 July 2015).

should be allocated to administer Unions to which only a minority of WIPO's membership belonged.[45] (For further discussion on these financial arrangements, see Chapter 6, section 6.6). Ultimately, the Lisbon Union refused to revise the rules of procedure for its 2015 diplomatic conference to enable all WIPO Member States to participate in the same capacity, irrespective of whether they were Lisbon members;[46] instead, non-Lisbon WIPO members were classified as 'observer delegations' to the diplomatic conference, giving them the right to contribute to negotiations but not to vote on the final language of the new Geneva Act.[47]

5.5   Decision-making procedures, working methods and processes

The rules governing the procedure of the WIPO Assemblies and other bodies, including the Unions administered by WIPO, are found in three types of documents: (i) the treaties establishing WIPO and the Unions; (ii) the WIPO General Rules of Procedure, which Member States adopted to govern the meetings of all bodies convened under the auspices of WIPO;[48] and (iii) Special Rules of Procedure, which can be adopted by any of WIPO's main organs and subsidiary bodies to supplement or adapt the General Rules of Procedure.[49] As noted above, diplomatic conferences establish their own rules of procedure (see section 5.3.4). In addition, WIPO Committees often establish working methods. Together, the numerous rules of procedure and working methods play a crucial role in the outcomes of WIPO deliberations as Member States sometimes

---

45 WIPO, *Draft Report: Prepared by the Secretariat, WIPO General Assembly, Forty-Seventh Session, 5 to 14 October 2015* WO/GA/47/19 Prov. (WIPO 2015) 19–22 and 63–5.

46 See Catherine Saez, 'United States Hopeful Lisbon Members Will Open Diplomatic Conference to All' *Intellectual Property Watch* (7 May 2015).

47 See WIPO, *Rules of Procedure: As Adopted on 11 May 2015 by the Diplomatic Conference, Diplomatic Conference for the Adoption of a New Act of the Lisbon Agreement for the Protection of Appellations of Origin and their International Registration* LI/DC/2 (WIPO 2015).

48 These rules were adopted in 1970 and amended in 1973, 1976 and 1979. The latest 1979 version of the rules is contained in WIPO, *WIPO General Rules of Procedure* WIPO Publication 339 Rev. 3. (WIPO 1998). The Rules govern the meetings of all bodies convened under the auspices of WIPO to the extent that any such body does not adopt special rules of procedure (see Rule 1(1) of the WIPO General Rules of Procedure). Regrettably, although this document can be found on WIPO's website under publications, it is not available directly from any of the sections of WIPO's website on governance and management.

49 See Rule 1 on the application of the General Rules of Procedure.

seek to advance their interests by make strategic use of the Rules, as well as their ambiguities and silence on a number of procedural matters;[50] in some instance, the Rules themselves can become the central point of contention.

5.5.1 General Rules of Procedure

The WIPO General Rules of Procedure set out meeting procedures related to planning, participation and voting; the roles and responsibilities of chairs and the Secretariat; the conduct of business; languages and interpretation; and the admission of observers (see Appendix 3 for the full text of the General Rules of Procedure).[51] Within the WIPO Secretariat, the Office of the Legal Counsel is the custodian of the General Rules of Procedure and responsible for proposing updated rules to Member States where necessary, or drafting them on the request of Member States. WIPO's Legal Counsel is regularly called upon during intergovernmental meetings at WIPO to respond to questions that arise in regard to the meaning and application of the General Rules of Procedure, and to interpret the Rules, such as where requests for a vote arise.

The General Rules of Procedure Rules were last amended in 1979. Meanwhile, the Rules no longer reflect many of the actual practices followed by Member States and the Secretariat. In some instances, Member States have adopted new policies (such as policies on translation and languages) that supersede provisions in the General

---

50 CIEL, *A Citizens' Guide to WIPO* (CIEL 2007) 31–2.

51 Among others, the rules provide that the Director General shall fix the date, duration and place of each session of WIPO bodies (Rule 3(1)) and prepare the draft agenda for all ordinary sessions (any state member of a body may, at least 1 month before the session, request the inclusion of supplementary items in the draft agenda) (Rule 5). The rules also provide that each Member State can be represented by one or more delegates, who may be assisted by alternates, advisors, and experts (Rule 7). Further, there are provisions regarding the conduct of meetings. The Rules provide, for instance, that the chairman of a session opens and closes meetings, directs the discussions, accords the right to speak, puts questions to the vote and announces decisions (Rule 13). The chairman may also propose limiting the time allowed to speakers and the number of times each delegation may speak on any question, close the list of speakers, and the debate, as well as suspend or adjourn debate or the meeting (see Rule 13). The Director General or a designated staff member of the International Bureau can speak with the approval of the Chairman, at any time during a session and make statements on any subject under discussion (Rule 15). Further, proposals for the adoption of amendments to the drafts submitted to the session and all other proposals may be submitted orally or in writing by any delegation, although the session can only decide to debate and vote on the proposal if it is in writing (Rule 21).

Rules or the Rules have been effectively ignored by Member States, and/or where the Rules have been overtaken by the practices Member States use. Further, there are many matters on which the Rules are silent or ambiguous.

Despite the considerable influence that the chairpersons of inter-governmental meetings at WIPO can have on the direction, dura-tion, format and outcome of meetings, the General Rules are silent on selection criteria or guidelines for the conduct of chairs, for instance. A further matter on which the General Rules are silent is the increasingly common practice in WIPO Committees whereby the Chair produces his or her own summary of the meeting and its outcomes under their own responsibility. While it is normal pro-cedure for committee members to formally adopt a general report of their meeting, and sometimes a summary of key decisions taken, the Rules make no provision for the practice of a chair's summary. Although such reports are often issued with a WIPO document number and become part of the organisation's records, neither the prospect of a chair's summary nor the possibility of its approval by members is mentioned in the General Rules of Procedure, meaning that the official status of such summaries and the views contained therein is unclear. An additional example of the ambiguities that arise in regard to procedural matters at WIPO relates to the practice that has emerged according to which Member States follow a single consolidated agenda for WIPO's annual Assemblies. Although this approach has clear advantages in terms of efficiency, and the General Rules of Procedure provide for joint sessions of WIPO bodies on common agenda items (and include Rules on who should Chair such meetings), the Rules make no provision for the single consolidated agenda for the entire Assemblies, meaning that where questions arise about which bodies should make decisions, what quorum is needed, and where responsibility lies, the result is often confusion and frustration among Member States.

Finally, the provisions of the General Rules of Procedure and those of the Special Rules of Procedure of WIPO's main organs, treaty-based governing bodies, and subsidiary bodies vary widely, as do their prac-tices. For instance, on the election of officers, Chapter 3 of the General Rules states that a chair and vice-chair should be selected at the start of each ordinary session and remain in office until the election of new chairs, and should not be immediately eligible for re-election in the office they have held. In the case of the General Assembly and other governing bodies, such as the Paris and Berne Unions, the relevant treaties provide that chairs are appointed for a 2-year term. The chairs of the Coordination Committee as well as the Paris and Berne Executive Committees are, however, elected for 1 year. In practice, the tenure of chairpersons varies among WIPO's subsidiary committees. In the standing committees, for instance, some chairs are elected for 1 year only, while other chairs are appointed for only one meeting or are re-elected several times over.

5.5.2   Special Rules of Procedure

Most of WIPO's main organs and governing bodies have adopted Special Rules of Procedure that supplement and/or adapt the General Rules (see Appendix 4 for Special Rules of Procedure for WIPO Governing Bodies),[52] as have some subsidiary bodies (see Appendix 5 for examples of Special Rules of Procedure for WIPO Committees adopted by the General Assembly or the Committees, along with references to source documents).[53] Notably, the Special Rules adopted by various WIPO governing and subsidiary bodies are not readily available on the WIPO website. There is no WIPO publication that contains all such Special Rules of Procedure adopted by WIPO's Committees; they can instead only be discerned through a detailed process of comparing the various Secretariat proposals for consideration by relevant committees, reports of Member State discussions in committee meetings and their Annexes, minutes of the Committees, including various Secretariat proposals, and the reports on final decisions.

In general, the Rules for each Committee similarly establish the terms of service for the Chair and Vice-Chairs (1 year) and their immediately

---

52 The special Rules of Procedure of the WIPO Coordination Committee can, for instance, be found in WIPO, *Special Rules of Procedure of the Governing Bodies: Compilation Prepared by the International Bureau, Twenty-Fifth Series of Meetings* AB/XXV/INF/2 (WIPO 1994), and those of the Assembly of the Berne Union, Assembly of the Paris Union and the PCT Union Assembly, among others, are included in WIPO, *Special Rules of Procedure of the Governing Bodies: Compilation Prepared by the International Bureau, Twenty-Fourth Series of Meetings* AB/XXIV/INF/2 (WIPO 1993). Regrettably, although these documents can be consulted in records held by the WIPO library, they are not publicly available on the WIPO website.

53 For instance, for the IGC, members agreed that WIPO's General Rules of Procedure should apply, save as otherwise provided in two Special Rules of Procedure adopted at its first session in April 2001. Further examples of special rules of procedure, not included in Appendix 5, are those adopted by WIPO committees of experts, such as the Committee of Experts of the Nice Union, see Nice Union, *Draft Revised Rules of Procedure of the Committee of Experts of the Nice Union* CLIM/WG/3/2 (WIPO 2009).

eligibility for their re-election (only the CDIP stipulates a maximum term of 3 consecutive years), the membership of the Committee, and observer status for UN Member States that are neither members of WIPO nor a relevant WIPO Union. For several committees, the Rules also extend membership of the committee (without the right to vote) to the European Communities. The CDIP and the IGC include rules on ad hoc observers as part of their Special Rules (whereas other committees make no special mention of ad hoc observers or do so through decisions made in committee meetings on working methods), and the SCP includes in its Special Rules a decision that the Committee's working documents should be produced in all six official UN languages. The committees have in various sessions also adopted working methods on a variety of matters such as: languages, the number of sessions, the creation of electronic forums, financial support for the participation of delegates from developing countries and certain countries in Europe and Asia, and ad hoc observers.[54] Further, the actual practices followed by committees may diverge from their respective Special Rules (such as in regard to the terms of Chairs or languages) and working methods (such as on the number of sessions). And there are several matters, such as the procedure and criteria for the selection of Chairs, for which Committees have not adopted any Special Rules or working methods.

5.5.3   Voting and consensus

Intergovernmental decision-making at WIPO occurs through a combination of consensus and voting.[55] The WIPO Convention sets out that in the General Assembly, the WIPO Conference and the WIPO Coordination Committee, each Member State has one vote. In practice, voting is used relatively rarely or in specific circumstances, and Member States generally favour decision-making by consensus. On

---

54 See, for instance, WIPO, *Matters Concerning Intellectual Property and Genetic Resources, Traditional Knowledge and Folklore* WO/GA/26/6 (WIPO 2000); WIPO, *Rules of Procedure: Memorandum of the Secretariat, First Session of the Intergovernmental Committee on Intellectual Property and Genetic Resources, Traditional Knowledge and Folklore, 30 April to 3 May 2001* WIPO/GRTKF/IC/1/2 (WIPO 2001); and WIPO, *Matters Concerning the Status of the Advisory Committee(s) on Enforcement: Document Prepared by the Secretariat, WIPO General Assembly, Twenty-Eighth (13th Extraordinary) Session* WO/GA/28/4 (WIPO 2002).

55 See Geoffrey Yu, 'The Structure and Process of Negotiations at the World Intellectual Property Organization' (2007) 82 *Chicago-Kent Law Review* 1443–53, 1452; and Coenraad Visser 'The Policy-Making Dynamics in Intergovernmental Organizations: A Comment on the Remarks of Geoffrey Yu' (2007) 82 *Chicago-Kent Law Review* 1457–8.

this note, both the Secretariat and Member States frequently use a variety of informal processes for consultation, information-sharing and consensus-building, including through the use of regional groups (discussed in sections 5.8 to 5.9 below).

During formal proceedings and informal consultations, Member States also sometimes raise the possibility of calling for a vote as a means to force action on an issue. This potential is particularly prized by developing countries, which represent the majority of WIPO's Member States and so collectively have the possibility of trumping developed country opposition to a given proposal through the force of numbers.

Where voting does occur in WIPO bodies, it is generally guided by WIPO's General Rules of Procedure (voting by the governing bodies of treaty-based Unions is governed by their respective Rules of Procedure). The General Rules state that voting shall normally occur by a show of hands (Rule 26), but provisions are also made for voting by roll-call (Rule 27) and secret ballot (Rule 28), if certain conditions are met. The Rules further state that decisions taken by voting shall normally be made by a simple majority (Rule 35). Before issues are put to a vote, formal discussions, informal consultations and consensus-building efforts usually take place. For WIPO's main organs, the WIPO Convention offers further guidance on voting. Where voting occurs in the General Assembly, decisions require a majority of two-thirds of the votes cast, subject to certain conditions,[56] as is also the case for the WIPO Conference.[57] In the Coordination Committee, however, decisions are made by a simple majority of votes cast.[58] For the General Assembly and Coordination Committee, one-half of their

---

56 For instance, the WIPO Convention states that the approval of measures concerning the administration of any international IP agreement (see Article 4(iii)) requires a three-fourths majority of votes cast, and the approval of an agreement with the UN (under Articles 57 and 63 of the Charter of the United Nations) shall require a majority of nine-tenths of the votes cast (Article 6(3)(f)). Further, the appointment of the Director General (Article 6(2)(i)), the approval of measures concerning the administration of international agreements (Article 6(2)(v)) and the transfer of headquarters (Article 10) require a majority not only in the General Assembly but also in the Assemblies of the Paris Union and the Berne Union.

57 Subject to Article 18 of the Convention. See Article 7(3) of the WIPO Convention.

58 See Article 8(5) and (6) of the WIPO Convention. The Convention also provides in Article 8(6)(b) that: 'Even if a simple majority is obtained, any member of the Coordination Committee may, immediately after the vote, request that the votes be the subject of a special recount in the following manner: two separate lists shall be prepared, one containing the names of the States members of the Executive Committee of the Paris Union and the other the names of the States members of the Executive Committee of the Berne Union; the vote of each State shall be inscribed opposite its

respective Member States constitutes a quorum,[59] while for the WIPO Conference only one-third of its Member States is required.

In governing bodies such as the General Assembly, and in subsidiary bodies such as the PBC, only those countries not in arrears are eligible to vote. The potential linkage between the right to vote and Member State contributions is an important matter for Member States to be aware of, particularly where votes on matters related to the governance of the organisation arise. In 1998 and 2008, the Coordination Committee agreed that all Coordination Committee Member States could vote in respect of the selection of the Director General, irrespective of whether their financial contribution to WIPO is in arrears.

The practice among WIPO Member States with regard to voting is varied. Voting by a show of hands is the most commonly used possibility, and is sometimes used in Committees to gauge the degree of consensus among Member States as a way to move deliberations to a close; a show of hands is also sometimes used as the method for suspending meeting sessions, such as where the agenda of the meeting has not been completed. Although Member States vote via secret ballot for specific matters such as the selection of the Director General (see section 5.2.3) and appointment of the External Auditor,[60] formal requests for votes by roll-call or secret ballot in the ongoing work of WIPO's various decision-making bodies have otherwise emerged only a handful of times over the past decade. At the 2007 Assemblies, for instance, the General Assembly voted once in regard to the WIPO Program and Budget for the 2008/09 biennium (the result was that Member States did not approve the draft Program and Budget and an extraordinary session of the General Assembly was later convened to complete deliberations on that agenda item), and the PCT Assembly has voted in regard to a proposed reduction in PCT fees. At the level

---

name in each list in which it appears. Should this special recount indicate that a simple majority has not been obtained in each of those lists, the proposal shall not be considered as carried.'

59 Notwithstanding the provisions of WIPO Convention Article 6(3)(b) if, in any session, less than one-half, but more or equal to one-third of General Assembly members are present, the Assembly may make decisions, but these decisions only take effect pending the following. First, after a 3-month period following receipt of a letter on the matter from the Secretariat, those states that were not represented have not expressed in writing their vote or abstention. Second, at the expiration of this period, the number of responses from states means that the appropriate quorum was attained, as well as the required majority.

60 For instance, the selection panel for the appointment of the WIPO External Auditor uses a secret ballot to make their decision. See WIPO, *Report of the Selection Panel for the Appointment of the WIPO External Auditor* WO/GA/40/3 (WIPO 2011).

of WIPO's subsidiary bodies, Egypt proposed a vote by roll-call in a
2011 CDIP session. Supported by a group of developing countries,
the request related to the adoption of a CDIP project on South-South
cooperation on IP and development, on which despite significant and
lengthy debate, Member States had not been able to reach consensus. A group of developed countries called instead for a secret ballot.
Ultimately no vote occurred and the Members instead suspended the
session by a show of hands.[61] The surrounding discussion within the
Committee, and with the WIPO Legal Counsel, underlined different
interpretations among Member States on the conditions set out in
WIPO's General Rules of Procedure for secret ballots (and also that
a time-dimension can be relevant because preparation of the secret
ballot requires administrative work and thus time on the part the
Secretariat).

5.6   Processes for rule-making: treaties and soft law

The World Intellectual Property Organization is involved in two types
of rule-making: those related to treaty-making or revision, and those
related to the development of new treaties and of 'soft law' norms.[62]

The treaty-making process begins with agreement among the membership on the need to develop a treaty on a particular subject.[63] The
WIPO Secretariat or a committee of experts prepares draft articles as
the basis for negotiations and discussions and, where applicable, draft
rules and/or regulations. Member States also sometimes present draft
articles for discussion. These drafts are then submitted to the relevant
committee or working group where they are discussed in an interactive
process until there is some consensus on most of the articles. When
the Secretariat or the committee discussing the subject perceives
that sufficient consensus exists for agreement on a final treaty text,

---

61 See WIPO, *Draft Report: prepared by the Secretariat, Committee on Development and
    Intellectual Property (CDIP) Seventh Session, 2 to 6 May 2011* CDIP/7/8 PROV. (WIPO 2011).

62 The term soft law is generally used to refer to certain categories of technically non-binding norms,
    but which states nonetheless follow in practice or to which at least they subscribe. See Edward
    Kwakwa, 'Some Comments on Rule Making at the World Intellectual Property Organization'
    (2002) 12(1) *Duke Journal of Comparative and International Law* 179–95, 187.

63 This paragraph summarises Sisule F Musungu and Graham Dutfield, *Multilateral
    Agreements and a TRIPS-Plus World: The World Intellectual Property Organization* TRIPS Issues
    Paper 3 (Quaker United Nations Office (QUNO) and Quaker International Affairs Program
    (QIAP) 2003), 6.

Member States are asked to authorise the preparation of a diplomatic conference to finalise and adopt the treaty. Once adopted, the treaty is opened for signature and ratification and/or accession by Member States according to their own constitutional processes.[64]

Notably, the pursuit of treaty amendments or new treaties may emerge from decisions taken by either the WIPO General Assembly or WIPO's treaty-specific Unions. For instance, a WIPO General Assembly subsidiary committee, such as the SCCR, may recommend that the General Assembly adopt a decision to begin negotiations for a new treaty or treaty amendments or convene a diplomatic conference to conclude and adopt a treaty. Alternatively, Unions such as the Paris, Lisbon or Berne Union may adopt decisions on treaty-related matters (such as the revision or updating of a treaty), without prior or subsequent approval by the WIPO General Assembly. However, where such decisions have budget or program implications for the WIPO Secretariat (such as the need for additional resources for convening negotiations and diplomatic conferences), this may require action from the WIPO Program and Budget Committee, which in turn may require approval by the General Assembly. Where there is overlap in the subject matter, the relationship between negotiations pursued by the Unions and discussions underway in WIPO's subsidiary bodies may require consideration from Member States. As noted above, matters such as patents, copyright, trademark and geographical indications are the focus of several of WIPO's treaty-based Unions, but are simultaneously under discussion by WIPO committees, like the SCP, the SCCR, and the SCT.

Alongside treaty making, WIPO has increasingly used a soft law approach to develop new IP norms since the late 1990s. These soft law norms can take many forms including recommendations, resolutions, declarations and guidelines, and the procedure for their development varies widely.[65] Examples of soft law norms adopted by WIPO Member States include the 1999 Resolution Concerning Provisions on the Protection of Well-Known Marks[66] and the 2001 Recommendation

---

64 Sisule F Musungu and Graham Dutfield, *Multilateral Agreements and a TRIPS-Plus World: The World Intellectual Property Organization* TRIPS Issues Paper 3 (Quaker United Nations Office (QUNO) and Quaker International Affairs Program (QIAP) 2003), 6.

65 Sisule F Musungu and Graham Dutfield, *Multilateral Agreements and a TRIPS-Plus World: The World Intellectual Property Organization* TRIPS Issues Paper 3 (Quaker United Nations Office (QUNO) and Quaker International Affairs Program (QIAP) 2003), 6–7.

66 See WIPO, *Joint Resolution Concerning Provisions of Well-Known Marks* A/34/13 (WIPO 1999).

Concerning the Provisions on the Protection of Marks, and Other Industrial Property Rights in Signs, on the Internet.[67] The impetus for such soft laws has been in large part to overcome the slow and time-consuming process of treaty making, particularly where circumstances change rapidly.[68] Notably, whereas treaty law only binds those states that ratify it, soft law norms can often be made more generally applicable without requiring ratification.[69]

5.7   Mechanisms for coordination across committees

To promote coordination across key WIPO decision-making bodies, the WIPO Convention envisaged an important role for the WIPO Coordination Committee, tasking it with providing advice to the various organs on matters of common interest to the Unions and the organisation. The coordination of WIPO's work also relies on day-to-day efforts by Member States to make coherent decisions across the various WIPO committees. In addition, the WIPO Program and Budget process (described in Chapter 6) is a vehicle that the Secretariat and Member States can harness to promote synergy and coordination between the agendas of the various WIPO committees, and the work plans of the organisation's Sectors and Divisions.

In terms of coordination between the Unions and the organisation, as noted in section 5.4.4, a particular challenge within WIPO concerns the relationship between deliberations underway in WIPO standing committees (which are open to all WIPO Member States) and negotiations pursued by the Unions of WIPO Treaties (in which only those WIPO Member States that have ratified the treaty at hand have decision-making power).

A key example of a mechanism adopted by Member States in recent years to address challenges of coordination is the Development Agenda Coordination and Monitoring Mechanism discussed below.

---

67 See WIPO, *Proposed Joint Recommendation Concerning Provisions on the Protection of Marks, and Other Industrial Property Rights in Signs, on the Internet* A/36/8 (WIPO 2001).

68 Edward Kwakwa, 'Some Comments on Rule Making at the World Intellectual Property Organization' (2002) 12(1) *Duke Journal of Comparative and International Law* 179–95, 181.

69 Edward Kwakwa, 'Some Comments on Rule Making at the World Intellectual Property Organization' (2002) 12(1) *Duke Journal of Comparative and International Law* 179–95, 182.

5.7.1   Development Agenda coordination and monitoring mechanism

At the 2010 WIPO Assemblies, Member States agreed on a Coordination and Monitoring Mechanism for the WIPO Development Agenda, adopting a series of principles on monitoring, assessing and reporting modalities and on coordination among WIPO committees to ensure that development considerations form an integral part of WIPO's work (see Table 5.1).[70] Among other provisions, the decision instructs the relevant WIPO bodies to include a description of their contributions to the implementation of the respective Development Agenda Recommendations in their annual reports to the Assemblies. The Mechanism also calls on the General Assembly to forward the reports to the CDIP for discussion under the first substantive item of its agenda and to request the relevant WIPO bodies to provide it with any information or clarification on the report that may be required. Member States continue to debate which WIPO bodies should be considered 'relevant.'[71] As of the 2015 WIPO Assemblies, the IGC, SCP, SCT, SCCR, and the ACE each include an account of their activities relevant to the implementation of Development Agenda recommendations in their reports to the General Assembly, but not the PBC or CWS.[72] Debate on the relevance of these two committees continues, however, with developing countries insisting that the work of the PBC and the CWS is indeed relevant to the implementation of the WIPO Development Agenda and that their contributions should thus also be reported.[73]

---

70 See WIPO, 'Coordination Mechanisms and Monitoring, Assessing and Reporting Modalities' <http://www.wipo.int/ip-development/en/agenda/coordination_mechanisms.html> accessed 1 September 2014. Also see WIPO, *Coordination Mechanisms and Monitoring, Assessing and Reporting Modalities: Annex II of the Report of the CDIP* WO/GA/39/7 (WIPO 2010).

71 See WIPO, *Decision on the Committee on Development and IP (CDIP) Matters: Document Prepared by the Secretariat* WO/GA/46/10 (WIPO 2014). For discussion on this matter at the Assemblies, see WIPO, *Draft Report: WIPO General Assembly 46th Session* WO/GA/46/12 Prov. (WIPO 2014).

72 See WIPO, *Description of the Contribution of the Relevant WIPO Bodies to the Implementation of the Respective Development Agenda Recommendations: Document by the Secretariat* WO/GA/46/4 (WIPO 2014).

73 WIPO, *Draft General Report: Prepared by the Secretariat, Assemblies of the Member States of WIPO, Fifty-Fifth Series of Meetings*, A/55/13 PROV. (Geneva: WIPO 2015) 26.

Table 5.1 Development Agenda: coordination mechanisms and monitoring, assessing and reporting modalities

The General Assembly decides:

1 To adopt the following CDIP coordination mechanism principles:
  (a) The aim of the Development Agenda is to ensure that development considerations form an integral part of WIPO's work and the coordination mechanism should promote this aim;
  (b) CDIP, in accordance with its mandate, has the responsibility to monitor, assess, discuss and report on the implementation of all recommendations adopted;
  (c) All WIPO Committees stand on an equal footing and report to the Assemblies;
  (d) To avoid duplication of WIPO's governance arrangements the coordination mechanism should be consistent with, and where practical, use existing governance structures and procedures;
  (e) The coordination of the CDIP with other relevant WIPO bodies should be flexible, efficient, effective, transparent and pragmatic. It should facilitate the work of the CDIP and the respective WIPO bodies;
  (f) The coordination should be within existing budgetary resources of WIPO

2 To establish a CDIP standing agenda item dealing with item (b)* of the CDIP mandate. The agenda item:
  (a) should be the first substantive item on its agenda; and
  (b) shall be allocated sufficient time to complete its deliberations within the meeting schedule

3 To extend, on an exceptional basis, if a clear need is identified, the duration of CDIP sessions, subject to the agreement of all Member States. In addition, during discussion of future work the Committee may consider the duration of the next CDIP meeting

4 To instruct the relevant WIPO bodies to include in their annual report to the Assemblies, a description of their contribution to the implementation of the respective Development Agenda Recommendations. The General Assembly shall forward the reports to the CDIP for discussion under the first substantive item of its Agenda. The General Assembly may request the Chairs of the relevant WIPO bodies to provide it with any information or clarification on the report that may be required

5 To instruct the CDIP to include a review of the implementation of the Development Agenda Recommendations in its report to the General Assembly, to be discussed in the General Assembly under the standing item of the Report of the CDIP, as a sub-item entitled Review of the implementation of the Development Agenda Recommendations

6 To instruct the relevant WIPO bodies to identify the ways in which the Development Agenda Recommendations are being mainstreamed in their work, and urge them to implement the Recommendations accordingly

7 To urge the Director General to facilitate the coordination, assessment, and reporting of all the activities and programs undertaken by the Secretariat with respect to the Development Agenda, and to provide regular updates, through written submissions or oral briefings, on the progress of the implementation of the Development Agenda

---

The General Assembly decides:

Recommendations to the CDIP, the General Assembly and relevant WIPO bodies. In particular, updates should focus on the work undertaken by other relevant WIPO bodies concerning implementation of the Development Agenda Recommendations

8   To request the CDIP to undertake an independent review of the implementation of the Development Agenda Recommendations at the end of the 2012/2013 biennium. Upon consideration of that review, the CDIP may decide on a possible further review. The Terms of Reference and the selection of independent IP and development experts will be agreed by the CDIP

9   To strengthen existing mechanisms within WIPO, such as the Internal Oversight Function, modalities for implementation of WIPO's Evaluation Policy and the Program Performance Reports, in order to effectively support the review and evaluation of the implementation of the Development Agenda Recommendations

10   To include in the WIPO Annual Report to the UN, a report on the implementation of the Development Agenda, pursuant to the Agreement between the UN and WIPO

---

* monitor, assess, discuss and report on the implementation of all recommendations adopted, and for that purpose it shall coordinate with relevant WIPO bodies DISCLAIMER: This document was adopted without paragraph numbers. The numbering was added by the Secretariat for ease of reference.

Source: WIPO, 'Coordination Mechanisms and Monitoring, Assessing and Reporting Modalities' <http://www.wipo.int/ip-development/en/agenda/coordination_mechanisms. html> accessed 1 September 2014.

5.8   Regional groups, informal consultations and consensus-building at WIPO

As in the UN system more broadly, WIPO has a well-established custom of using regional groups and their coordinators as the focal point for informal consultations and consensus-building among Member States, as well as between Member States and the Secretariat. At the UN, regional voting blocs were formed in 1961 as an informal means for sharing the distribution of posts for General Assembly committees.[74] Subsequently, the importance of such groups has expanded significantly across the UN system, although

---

74 In the wider UN system, there are now five unofficial regional groups: the African Group, with 54 member states; the Asia-Pacific Group, with 53 member states; the Eastern European Group, with 23 member states; the Latin American and Caribbean Group (GRULAC), with 33 member states; and the Western European and Others Group (WEOG), with 28 member states, plus 1 member state as observer (the United States).

their roles vary across different UN agencies. Regional groups can, for instance, control elections to UN-related positions; coordinate substantive policy; and form common fronts for negotiations and voting.

At present, there are seven informal 'regional' groups active in WIPO: the Asian group, the African group, the Latin American and Caribbean group (GRULAC), Central Europe and Baltic States group (CEBs), Central Asian and East European States group, Group B (comprising developed countries), and China.

Notably, Group B is not a 'geographic' group. Rather, the group's origin was a 1964 UN decision on the creation of the United Nations Conference on Trade and Development (UNCTAD),[75] where Group B represented Western European and other Organisation for Economic Co-operation and Development (OECD) countries. The composition of other groups is also somewhat confusing. For instance, there are members of the European Union that are included in the CEBs group rather than Group B. Further, China has its own 'regional' group. A further complication is that WIPO's regional group structure is not aligned with its own internal organisational structures, where there is one division charged with 'Cooperation with Certain Countries in Europe and Asia' (Program 10), as well as a separate bureau for cooperation with Arab countries.

Despite the strong emphasis given to regional groups throughout WIPO decision-making processes, neither the WIPO Convention nor the WIPO General Rules of Procedure make any reference to them as part of WIPO's governance system. As such, the WIPO Secretariat does not make available the list of countries included in each group, nor are there guidelines on the composition of the groups, on the roles and responsibilities of their coordinators, or on the modalities for the Secretariat's interaction with them. There are no formal rules or working methods to guide the internal functioning of the

---

75 These lists aimed to serve to balance geographical distribution of representation on the Trade Development Board and other UNCTAD structures. At UNCTAD, List A now consists mostly of countries in the African and Asia-Pacific Groups of the UN. List B consists of countries of the Western European and Others Group. List C consists of countries of the Group of Latin American and Caribbean States (GRULAC). List D consists of countries of Eastern Europe. For the original lists, see UNCTAD, *Proceedings of the United Nations Conference on Trade and Development (II)*, Report by the Secretary-General of the Conference, E/CONF.46/141 (UNCTAD 1964).

groups, which is instead the responsibility of the members. Practices thus vary widely among groups in regard to the selection and rotation of leadership, development of policy positions, transparency, and information-sharing (see section 5.9.2).

In practice, regional groups are key vehicles for interaction among delegates of WIPO Member States and also for liaison with the WIPO Secretariat. Regional groups provide the basis, for instance, for Member State representation in selection panels for WIPO's leadership and in WIPO working groups, for the election of committee chairs, and for many decisions related to the provision of WIPO's financial and technical assistance (such as the selection of Member States for attendance at meetings and participation in training activities).[76] Regional groups are also a vehicle used by the Secretariat and Chairs for consultations related to treaty negotiations and the development of the organisation's Program and Budget. In the formal proceedings of WIPO meetings, regional groups are generally given the floor before individual Member States, and individual countries will generally refer back to the group statement in their own statements. Coordinators designated by each group (referred to as 'regional coordinators') serve as a focal point for interaction within the group and also for liaison with other regional groups and the WIPO Secretariat. They generally convene internal meetings of their group members before and during sessions of WIPO bodies, and speak on behalf of the group in different WIPO discussions and negotiations.[77] Coordinators of regional groups also seek to resolve differences within their group and forge common positions. Regional coordinators are often summoned by Chairs of WIPO's inter-governmental meetings or convened by the Secretariat for informal meetings that occur between or alongside formal sessions of WIPO bodies. For further discussion of Member State interactions, see 5.10.2.

Importantly, while accredited non-governmental organisations can observe some of WIPO's formal proceedings (see section 8.4), they cannot participate in the many off-the-record 'informal' closed-door sessions that occur within and among regional groups of countries where much of the real consensus-building and deal-making at WIPO occurs (although non-governmental stakeholders are sometimes included by Member States as part of their government delegations).

---

76 See Permanent Mission of India to the United Nations Geneva, 'World Intellectual Property Organization (WIPO)' <pmindiaun.org/pages.php?id=326> accessed 8 July 2015.

77 CIEL, *A Citizens' Guide to WIPO* (CIEL 2007), 32–3.

5.9 Role of the Secretariat in Member State deliberations

The WIPO Secretariat plays an important role in WIPO's intergovern-mental deliberations. The day-to-day roles of the Secretariat vis-à-vis decision-making and debate among WIPO Member States include:[78]

1. Drafting agendas and reports for meetings of the various Member State bodies. These documents set out what issues Member States will discuss at their meetings and convey information about the status and progress of work, as well as recommendations for con-sideration by Member States.

2. Taking part in discussions (without the right to vote) and serving as the *ex officio* secretary of these bodies. The WIPO Convention establishes that the Director General and any staff member desig-nated by the incumbent may participate, without the right to vote, in all meetings of the governing bodies and any other committee or working group. The elected chairs of WIPO meetings (a Member State delegate) often rely on the Secretariat for guidance on a range of substantive and procedural issues. The Secretariat can also pro-vide opinions and statements on these issues directly to the meet-ings, and is regularly called upon to do so by meeting chairs or the Member States.

3. Submitting its own documents and proposals, either at the request of Member States or at its own initiative.

4. Organising consultative meetings. The Secretariat convenes con-sultations among Member States or other stakeholders at the request of Member States or at its own initiative to, for instance, 'gather comments and recommendations regarding a particular process; ... promote consideration of emerging issues; and ... encourage progress in ongoing discussions and negotiations.'[79] These consultations include convening meetings of regional groups (see section 5.8) and other informal interactions between the Secretariat and Member States (see section 5.10, particularly section 5.10.3).

---

78 The following paragraphs excerpt from and paraphrase analysis provided in CIEL, *A Citizens' Guide to WIPO* (CIEL 2007), 28–30.

79 CIEL, *A Citizens' Guide to WIPO* (CIEL 2007), 28–30.

5. Replying to Member State requests and questions on legal mat-
    ters relevant to their deliberations, including clarification and
    interpretation of the WIPO Convention, WIPO's General Rules of
    Procedure, Special Rules of Procedure, working methods, and the
    mandates of various committees; the compliance of WIPO with its
    internal rules and applicable rules; and an array of constitutional,
    administrative, and contractual matters.

5.10   Practices for Member State representation

As depicted in Figure 5.1, Member States are a central part of WIPO's
governance system. Although financial contributions by WIPO Member
States are low compared to other international organisations, WIPO's
legal foundation – the WIPO Convention – establishes that Member
States are the stewards of the organisation and that the Secretariat is
accountable to them. WIPO Member States have responsibility for
developing and approving any new treaty or amendments as well as
for approving a broad array of policies and proposals on issues ranging
from WIPO's Work Program and Budget to human resources, as well as
for oversight of its activities. As stewards of a 'member-driven' organisation, it is thus vital to have an overview of how Member States arrange
for their own representation in WIPO deliberations and decision-
making, as well as how they interact and organise among themselves,
and their various modes of interaction with the Secretariat.

5.10.1   National representation

Member States are represented at WIPO by a combination of Geneva-
based diplomats and officials from national capitals. The WIPO
Secretariat's policy is to send official communications to Ministries of
Foreign Affairs (usually charged with oversight of international organi-
sations on behalf of national governments) and to the relevant national
IP authorities.

Geneva-based WIPO delegates are usually diplomatic staff from
Ministries of Foreign Affairs, although they sometimes also hail from
Ministries of Trade or Commerce (the latter delegates usually also
follow WTO deliberations on TRIPS). Where delegates travel from
national capitals to Geneva for WIPO meetings, they predominantly
represent national IP offices (such as in countries where governments
have clustered all of their IP-related authorities in one IP agency),

national patent and trademark offices (which are often combined in industrial property offices) or national copyright offices. A handful of countries also post officials employed by their national IP authorities within diplomatic missions in Geneva, who then represent their agency and country directly in WIPO meetings. Depending on the committee and matter under discussion, countries sometimes also include on their delegations representatives from ministries charged with health, agriculture, environment, indigenous affairs, consumer safety, and development. In addition, for some meetings and events, representatives are judges or other officials from national courts that address IP matters or staff of national collective management organisations. In some instances, Member States have included representatives of private sector organisations, academics, public interest NGOs or other non-government experts on their delegations. In the case of the IGC, some governments have also extended participation in their delegations to representatives of indigenous and local communities.

The size and composition of Member State delegations to WIPO, the seniority of delegates and the regularity of their attendance in particular WIPO bodies vary according to the human resources of Geneva-based embassies; budget decisions by national governments regarding travel to WIPO meetings; and the perceived importance of particular deliberations to Member State interests. While many countries send the head of their IP office to attend the WIPO Assemblies, and ambassadors attend the opening sessions of some WIPO Committees, the day-to-day work of the committees is generally conducted by senior or mid-level staff of Geneva-based missions or representatives of national IP offices. Behind the scenes, the degree of engagement by ambassadors and officials in national capitals with WIPO delegates varies widely, with some receiving extensive instruction and others very little.

For a range of WIPO committee meetings and the Assemblies, the organisation finances the participation of delegations from developing countries and of certain countries in Europe and Asia. Further, WIPO covers the travel expenses and daily subsistence allowance (DSA) of one delegate from each member of the PCT Union and/or Madrid Union upon request to attend the WIPO Assemblies. Notably, the financial support for participation is for all members of the PCT and Madrid Unions, not just developing countries (this practice follows a constitutional requirement in the case of the PCT, and a decision taken by the Madrid Union Assembly as well.) In addition, for some diplomatic conferences, the host government contributes financially to the costs of participation by Member States. For instance, in the case of the 2013 Diplomatic Conference for the conclusion of the Marrakesh Treaty, funding was offered to support delegates from 157 WIPO states that are developed or developing countries, 119 of which were financed by the Government of Morocco.[80]

Notably, whereas Ministers of Health, Commerce or Agriculture often attend at least the opening day of the highest governing bodies of other UN organisations such as WHO, UNCTAD and the FAO, the most senior capital-based officials attending the WIPO Assemblies are generally the heads of IP offices (which are very seldom ministerial appointments). The meetings of WIPO's governing bodies are thus not 'ministerial meetings' (such as those that take place, for instance, at WTO Ministerial Conference), nor are there regular, informal 'mini-ministerial' meetings (such as are common at the WTO). However, on an ad hoc basis, some ministers do attend selected WIPO meetings and diplomatic conferences when of particular national interest. Further, in some years, for instance, a high-level segment has been added to the Assemblies to attract ministerial engagement.

At WIPO, limited ministerial involvement means that many governments delegate significant authority to national IP offices for representation and oversight of the organisation. While at the national level, IP offices report to relevant ministries or executive bodies, in a number of countries they are independent and/or largely self-financing regulatory bodies. Such offices are simultaneously responsible for a wide array of activities, from IP administration, promotion and outreach to devising a legislative agenda for compliance with international treaties as well as policy advice, adjudication of disputes, participation in international norm-setting negotiations, and securing external technical assistance and capacity-building. Indeed, national and regional IP authorities are the primary recipients of WIPO's technical assistance and capacity-building.

Across the suite of WIPO's regular calendar of formal and informal committee meetings and consultations throughout each year, Geneva-based delegates are generally more regularly present than staff of national IP offices. Whereas capital-based delegates, such as from IP

---

80 WIPO, *Report on the Outcome of the Marrakesh Diplomatic Conference to Conclude a Treaty to Facilitate Access to Published Works by Visually Impaired Persons and Persons with Print Disabilities* WO/GA/43/9 (WIPO 2013).

offices, commonly attend meetings related to their specific area of expertise (such as committees on copyright, enforcement or patents), Geneva-based delegates attend a wider array of meetings both across IP issues and the substantive areas of WIPO's work as well as those related to the organisation's operations, financing and governance (such as the PBC). Nonetheless, the Secretariat's main interlocutors for the day-to-day implementation of its work programme are staff of national and regional IP offices, such as the European Patent Office (EPO), the Eurasian Patent Organization, and the African Regional Intellectual Property Organization (ARIPO).

With the growing scope of WIPO's work and the growing reach of IP law and policy, interaction between the Secretariat and Member States is becoming increasingly complicated. Within Member States, different government agencies with distinct mandates and roles in policy-making sometimes have divergent views on appropriate responses to global policy issues and positions with respect to international negotiations. This sometimes leads to confusion about where the overarching policy leadership lies, or should lie. Further, many governments struggle to make and implement coherent policies and to coordinate the many parts of government relevant to IP governance – from courts and IP offices to regulatory bodies and expert networks on issues as diverse as health and safety, customs and competition.[81] In some cases, governments have established consultative bodies or processes that draw together the various government stakeholders. Depending on the WIPO activity at hand, the Secretariat may also be in direct communication with a range of different actors at the national level, from national universities and ministries charged with small business development to national research institutes.

With the growing scope and number of WIPO activities in Member States, the challenges of communication by the Secretariat with the appropriate focal point(s) for interaction have grown. Both national IP offices and Ministries of Foreign Affairs have complained to WIPO about inadequate consultation or information on proposed WIPO activities, sometimes each arguing that they should be the priority channels of communication.

---

81 Ahmed Abdel-Latif, 'Developing Country Coordination in International Intellectual Property Standard-Setting', *TRADE Working Paper 24* (Geneva: South Centre 2005).

5.10.2   Interaction among members

As described in section 5.8, regional groups are core vehicles for inter-action among WIPO Member States.

Given that regional groupings do not always properly allow for the expression of the distinct needs and interests of all countries, and given the existence of other political alliances and shared interests, a number of cross-regional and issue-oriented groups have also expressed views at WIPO. A prominent example of an issue-oriented group or 'coali-tion of interest' was the Group of Friends of Development, which called for the WIPO Development Agenda and included countries from Latin America, Africa, Asia and the Group of Least Developed Countries (LDCs). That grouping subsequently evolved into what is now known as the Development Agenda Group (DAG), which continues to attract a cross-regional group of countries, although its composition has evolved with time, and to call for a greater role in WIPO consulta-tion processes. In addition, although not regularly active at WIPO, the Group of 77 and China have at key political moments intervened in WIPO debates, such as during discussions in 2005 on the future of the WIPO Development Agenda.[82]

Examples of other groups that work together in regard to WIPO include the Association of South East Asian Nations (ASEAN) (which has, for instance, been a recipient of WIPO technical assistance) and the European Union. The European Union participates in WIPO meet-ings as a member with no voting rights, and also in the assemblies of certain treaties adopted in 1996 and later with the possibility to take over and exercise the votes of its member states. Further, informal coalitions of interest or caucuses sometimes arise in the context of issue-specific negotiations within particular committees or are active across a range of committees.

In addition to their interaction through regional groups, delega-tions also exchange views and collaborate informally through infor-mal working meetings and lunchtime discussions, or by attending brainstorming meetings convened by NGOs or others. Ambassadors sometimes interact among each other and direct their delegations

---

82   The Group of 77 (G-77) was established on 15 June 1964, by 77 developing countries signatories of the 'Joint Declaration of the Seventy-Seven Countries' issued at the end of the first session of the United Nations Conference on Trade and Development (UNCTAD) in Geneva. In 2015, the G-77 had 134 members.

from behind the scenes through informal deal-making across issues at stake within WIPO (and sometimes on issues under discussion in other international organisations). For instance, some WIPO members work together through the Geneva Group, an informal body of 16 countries (permanently co-chaired by the US and UK) that possess 'like-mindedness' on administrative and financial matters at the UN.[83] At the Ambassadorial and delegate level, the Group regularly meets before governing body meetings of UN agencies to share information and ensure statements at the various meetings assist in generating action and change in the agencies. In some instances, a sub-group of Geneva Group members has undertaken joint lobbying of the WIPO Secretariat and of non-Geneva Group members on particular WIPO governance and management issues.

5.10.3   Interaction with the Secretariat

Interaction between WIPO Member States and the WIPO Secretariat occurs through a number of channels, including: participation in WIPO meetings; Secretariat-convened informal consultations with regional groups; bilateral meetings between senior national officials and WIPO senior management; bilateral meetings between mid-level officials and mid-level WIPO staff; negotiations of bilateral extra-budgetary contributions to WIPO; negotiations for packages of national technical assistance and capacity-building; the implementation of capacity-building programs; participation in WIPO training activities; and interaction in the course of the day-to-day administration of WIPO's global protection system treaties. The Secretariat also interacts directly with the heads of a number of regional IP authorities, as noted above, on matters of training, technical assistance and cooperation under certain WIPO treaties, such as the PCT.

The senior management of WIPO, and particularly the Director General, also meets on a routine basis with senior officials and minis-

---

83 The Geneva Group functions at three levels: (i) UN Directors; (ii) Mission personnel who focus on governance and management issues or otherwise work directly with the UN and its affiliated agencies and funds and programs; and (iii) Ambassadors, who meet periodically to take a strategic overview of the progress being made at expert level. Convened by the Geneva Group, the UN Directors meet twice a year in a Consultative Level Meeting (CLM). The current members are OECD (including Mexico and the Republic of Korea) as well as Russia. The Geneva Group has focal groups on specific thematic issues such as budgets, human resources policy, buildings and oversight (including audit committees, external and internal audit, and evaluation). See Geneva Group, 'About the Geneva Group' <http://www.thegenevagroup.net/cms/home/about-the-geneva-group.html> accessed 15 October 2014.

ters from WIPO Member States, bilaterally or in small groups, either in Geneva or in national capitals. In addition, the Director General hosts breakfast meetings with ambassadors for the purposes of consultation and briefing them on activities.

As noted above, the Director General convenes informal high-level meetings with individual countries or groups of countries from time to time. To attract political engagement in WIPO, the Secretariat has organised 'high level segments' at some WIPO Assemblies and hosted other ministerial-level events. There have also been instances where the Secretariat has convened informal meetings with a sub-set of Member States to help promote consensus on the work program of the organisation. A controversial example occurred in 2005, when the Director General convened an invitation-only consultation in Morocco to break a political deadlock on proposals for substantive patent harmonisation.[84]

The World Intellectual Property Organization's senior management also interacts with the Geneva Group (mentioned above), providing briefings on key WIPO documents and strategies prior to their formal release. Such briefings provide opportunities for members of the Group to provide input to WIPO and to influence its direction and policies.

Formal written communications between WIPO Member States and the Secretariat can take a number of the forms. The Secretariat may write a letter in the name of a specific Secretariat official to a permanent representative or Ambassador. Alternatively, a '*note verbale*' is a diplomatic communication usually written in the third person and unsigned on the part of the Secretariat to a diplomatic mission of a Member State/IP office (or vice versa), and which usually serves a similar purpose as a memorandum. A further option is a 'circular' that may be written in the third or first person, and is generally signed.[85] Issued by relevant staff of the WIPO Secretariat (such as Assistant Directors General charged with the various WIPO sectors), circulars often provide information to national governments on forthcoming WIPO meetings or extend invitations to them.

---

84 William New, 'India Joins Opposition to Casablanca Meeting Outcome' *Intellectual Property Watch* (4 October 2005).

85 Each '*note verbale*' issued by the WIPO Secretariat has the document code NN, whereas circulars have the code CN, each followed by a document number.

6 WIPO's financial arrangements and the Program and Budget process

The World Intellectual Property Organization is unique among UN organisations as it is almost entirely self-financing, rather than relying on assessed contributions from Member States. For the 2016/17 biennium, WIPO Member States approved a regular budget of 707 million Swiss Francs (CHF) for the organisation (up from 470 million CHF in 2002/03).[1] Within the UN system, WIPO is also notable for the fact that its income streams in regularly exceed budgeted amounts; in 2012/13, for instance, the organisation generated a surplus of 34.6 million CHF,[2] thereby starting the 2014/15 biennium with around 200 million CHF in reserves.

This chapter begins in section 6.1 with an overview of WIPO's income, addressing in turn the three income sources for WIPO's regular budget, namely fees, Member State contributions, and 'other'. In so doing, it introduces WIPO's Unitary Contribution System and the organisation's approach to arrears in Member State contributions. It then describes WIPO's sources of extra-budgetary income and its arrangements for Funds-in-Trust. In section 6.2, the chapter reviews WIPO's Financial Regulations and Rules, followed by its arrangements for the custody of funds and the role of the WIPO Controller. Section 6.3 introduces WIPO's policies on reserves and investments. The process for setting and reviewing WIPO's Program and Budget is taken up in section 6.4, as well as related Secretariat reporting requirements and how extra-budgetary contributions are addressed in the Program and Budget process. The chapter continues with a discussion of the unitary presentation of WIPO's Budget in section 6.5 and concludes in section 6.6 with the financial arrangements for the Unions and how

---

1 See WIPO, *Proposed Program and Budget for the 2016/17 Biennium* A/55/5 Rev. (WIPO 2015); WIPO, *Program and Budget 2014/15* WO/PBC/21/8 (WIPO 2013).

2 See WIPO, *Financial Management Report for the 2012/13 Biennium* WO/PBC/22/6 (WIPO 2014) ii.

their income is managed and allocated in the WIPO Program and Budget.

6.1   Income

6.1.1   Income sources for the regular budget: fees

The World Intellectual Property Organization generates the majority of its revenue through fee-paid services that the Secretariat provides to users of its global protection systems, most notably those created by the Patent Cooperation Treaty (PCT) and the Madrid and Hague treaties (see Figure 6.1). In both absolute terms and as a proportion of WIPO's total income, the revenue from such fees has been growing steadily over time – from 81.44 per cent in 1998 to an estimated 93.8 per cent of WIPO's income for the 2014/15 biennium (see Table 6.1).[3] The origins of WIPO's self-financing business model lie in the income streams from the PCT, which began in June 1978 when the filing of PCT applications commenced. In the 2016/17 biennium, just under 75 per cent of WIPO's income is expected to come from PCT revenues

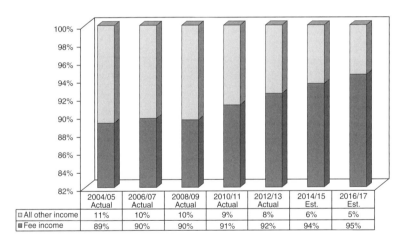

	2004/05 Actual	2006/07 Actual	2008/09 Actual	2010/11 Actual	2012/13 Actual	2014/15 Est.	2016/17 Est.
▫ All other income	11%	10%	10%	9%	8%	6%	5%
■ Fee income	89%	90%	90%	91%	92%	94%	95%

Source: WIPO, *Proposed Program and Budget 2016/17* A55/5 Rev. (WIPO 2015) 19.

Figure 6.1   Share of WIPO's fee income/total income from 2004/2005 to 2016/2017

---

3 See WIPO, *Program and Budget 2014/15* WO/PBC/21/8 (WIPO 2013).

Table 6.1 Evolution of WIPO income from 2002/2003 to 2016/2017 (in millions of Swiss Francs)

Actual Budget	2002/03	2004/05	2006/07	2008/09	2010/11	2012/13	2014/15	2016/17 Estimates
Member State Contributions	34.4	34.4	34.7	34.8	34.8	35.1	35.2	34.7
Fees								
PCT System	348.0	400.6	451.1	443.6	434.8	514.9	570.4	575.9
Madrid System	49.7	60.8	90.3	94.8	99.6	108.0	115.2	128.8
Hague System	8.4	5.0	5.0	5.4	5.9	6.3	7.2	10.3
Lisbon System	0	0	0	0	0	0	0.1	0
Sub-Total Fees	*406.1*	*466.4*	*546.4*	*543.8*	*540.3*	*629.2*	*692.9*	*715.0*
Arbitration	3.2	2.5	3.2	3.3	3.3	3.3	2.7	2.5
Publications	7.1	4.4	2.7	1.1	1.1	1.0	0.7	0.3
Investment revenue	13.1	8.9	15.8	17.8	9.4	3.4	3.0	0
Miscellaneous	6.4	6.0	6.4	6.5	3.9	8.7	6.3	3.8
TOTAL	**470.3**	**522.6**	**609.2**	**607.3**	**592.8**	**680.7**	**740.8**	**756.3**

Sources: WIPO, WIPO Financial Management Report 2012/2013 WO/PBC/22/6 (WIPO 2014), WIPO, Program and Budget 2014/15 WO/PBC/21/8 (WIPO 2013), WIPO, Proposed Program and Budget 2016/17 A55/5 Rev. (WIPO 2015).

alone.[4] The Secretariat estimates that other income will come from the Madrid Union (17.8 per cent), the Hague Union (2 per cent) and the Lisbon Union (0.3 per cent), as well as the Contribution-financed Unions (4.9 per cent), with the remaining 'other' income coming from arbitration fees, publications, interest and miscellaneous income (such as rental income).

The level of the fees payable for services rendered under the PCT, Madrid, Hague and Lisbon systems is determined by the Assembly of the corresponding Union, which updates their respective fee schedules as needed (see Regulation 3.10 of the WIPO Financial Regulations and Rules discussed in section 6.2 below). In some instances, the Unions provide for reductions in certain fees for applicants from eligible countries. For instance, the PCT Schedule of Fees sets out criteria upon which a state is deemed eligible for 90 per cent reductions in certain PCT fees for its applicants.[5]

The income from each Union is allocated to the activities of the respective Union and also to finance a range of the organisation's Programs (see section 6.6 on the financial arrangements for the Unions and their income, as well as the methodology for allocating Union income among WIPO's various Programs). Notably, since 1993, the WIPO Secretariat has produced a single unified presentation of the budget for the organisation as a whole (discussed in section 6.5).

Given the importance of WIPO's global protection systems as the source of most of the organisation's income, it is important from a governance perspective to consider whether and how such users impact decision-making by the Secretariat and/or Member States. As a first step, a profile or breakdown of users underscores a concentration of users from a subset of Member States. Since 1978, the profile of PCT users has changed progressively, featuring applicants from a growing number of the PCT's Contracting States and more intense use by applicants from a core group of emerging economies, such as China

---

4 WIPO, *Proposed Program and Budget for the 2016/17 Biennium* A/55/5 Rev. (WIPO 2015) 188.

5 For the text of the PCT Regulations in force as of 1 July 2015, see PCT, 'PCT Regulations' (WIPO 2015) <http://www.wipo.int/export/sites/www/pct/en/texts/pdf/pct_regs/pdf> accessed 1 November 2015. For the countries eligible for PCT fee reductions, see PCT, 'Schedule of Fees' (WIPO 2015) <http://www.wipo.int/pct/en/texts/rules/rtax.htm> accessed 1 November 2015, and PCT, 'Applicability of 90% Reduction in Certain PCT Fees' (WIPO 2015) <http://www.wipo.int/export/sites/www/pct/en/fees/fee_reduction.pdf> accessed 1 November 2015.

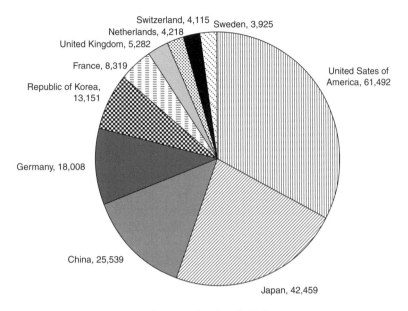

Figure 6.2   Top ten origins of PCT applications (2014)

and the Republic of Korea. Nonetheless, the core users of the PCT system, which represent the source of WIPO's main income stream, hail from a small number of that Union's 148 Member States. Between 1978 and 2011, applicants from the United States and Japan together have accounted for more than half of all PCT applications, and the top eight countries of origin (which include China and the Republic of Korea) combined filed 80 per cent of all PCT applications.[6] In 2014, the United States was by far the top source of PCT applications among WIPO Member States, making it the greatest user of the PCT system (see Figure 6.2).[7]

Further, the top 50 users of the PCT system represent some of the world's largest manufacturing and research and development (R&D) corporations, just as the top ten users of the Hague system are leading corporations in their fields (see Table 6.2 and Figure 6.3). From 1995 to 2014, the 50 applicants listed in Table 6.2 accounted for 18

6 WIPO, *2012 PCT Yearly Review: The International Patent System*, WIPO Publication No. 901E/2012 (WIPO 2012) 18.

7 WIPO, *Patent Cooperation Treaty Yearly Review: The International Patent System 2014*, WIPO Publication No. 901_2014 (WIPO 2015) 36.

Table 6.2 Top 50 PCT applicants (1995–2014)

Rank	Name of Applicant	Main Field of Technology	Origin	Published PCT Applications
1	Koninklijke Philips Electronics N.V.	Audio-visual technology	Netherlands	28 486
2	Panasonic Corporation	Audio-visual technology	Japan	28 224
3	Siemens Aktiengesellschaft	Electrical machinery, apparatus, energy	Germany	21 695
4	Robert Bosch Corporation	Engines, pumps, turbines	Germany	20 577
5	Huawei Technologies Co., Ltd.	Digital communication	China	16 869
6	Telefonaktiebolaget Lm Ericsson (Publ)	Digital communication	Sweden	15 789
7	Qualcomm Incorporated	Digital communication	United States of America	15 326
8	ZTE Corporation	Digital communication	China	14 447
9	Toyota Jidosha Kabushiki Kaisha	Transport	Japan	12 326
10	Sharp Kabushiki Kaisha	Optics	Japan	12 179
11	BASF Se	Organic fine chemistry	Germany	11 853
12	Nokia Corporation	Digital communication	Finland	10 668
13	Procter & Gamble Company	Basic materials chemistry	United States of America	10 563
14	LG Electronics Inc.	Digital communication	Republic of Korea	10 360
15	Mitsubishi Electric Corporation	Electrical machinery, apparatus, energy	Japan	10 167
16	Intel Corporation	Computer technology	United States of America	9 658
17	NEC Corporation	Computer technology	Japan	9 441
18	3M Innovative Properties Company	Optics	United States of America	8 991
19	Samsung Electronics Co., Ltd.	Digital communication	Republic of Korea	8 501
20	Sony Corporation	Audio-visual technology	Japan	8 356
21	Fujitsu Limited	Computer technology	Japan	8 266

Rank	Name of Applicant	Main Field of Technology	Origin	Published PCT Applications
22	Motorola, Inc.	Digital communication	United States of America	8009
23	E.I. Dupont De Nemours and Company	Macromolecular chemistry, polymers	United States of America	7463
24	Microsoft Corporation	Computer technology	United States of America	7191
25	International Business Machines Corporation	Computer technology	United States of America	6821
26	Hewlett-Packard Development Company, L.P.	Computer technology	United States of America	6484
27	University of California	Biotechnology	United States of America	5935
28	Hitachi, Ltd.	Computer technology	Japan	5824
29	General Electric Company	Electrical machinery, apparatus, energy	United States of America	5056
30	Fujifilm Corporation	Optics	Japan	4886
31	Thomson Licensing	Audio-visual technology	France	4696
32	Honeywell International Inc.	Measurement	United States of America	4680
33	Henkel Kommanditgesellschaft Auf Aktien	Basic materials chemistry	Germany	4513
34	Kabushiki Kaisha Toshiba	Electrical machinery, apparatus, energy	Japan	4306
35	Kimberly-Clark Worldwide, Inc.	Medical technology	United States of America	4200
36	Bosch-Siemens Hausgerate Gmbh	Other consumer goods	Germany	4183
37	Daimler AG	Transport	Germany	4122
38	Canon Kabushiki Kaisha	Optics	Japan	4115
39	Commissariat a l'energie atomique et aux energies alternatives	Semiconductors	France	3981
40	Fraunhofer-Gesellschaft zur Forderung der Angewandten Forschung e.V.	Measurement	Germany	3951
41	Applied Materials, Inc.	Semiconductors	United States of America	3745

Rank	Name of Applicant	Main Field of Technology	Origin	Published PCT Applications
42	Novartis AG	Pharmaceuticals	Switzerland	3 712
43	Pioneer Corporation	Audio-visual technology	Japan	3 638
44	Daikin Industries, Ltd.	Thermal processes and apparatus	Japan	3 564
45	Alcatel Lucent	Digital communication	France	3 475
46	Murata Manufacturing Co., Ltd.	Electrical machinery, apparatus, energy	Japan	3 456
47	Corning Incorporated	Optics	United States of America	3 453
48	Dow Global Technologies Inc.	Macromolecular chemistry, polymers	United States of America	3 405
49	Mitsubishi Heavy Industries, Ltd.	Engines, pumps, turbines	Japan	3 390
50	Medtronic, Inc.	Medical technology	United States of America	3 373

Source: WIPO, *Annual Report: Report of the Director General to the WIPO Assemblies* (WIPO 2015) 5.

per cent of total PCT applicants filed over this period.[8] Overall, the medical technology field has had the highest number of PCT applications since 1978, but in 2014 ranked third behind the fields of computer technology, digital communication and electronic machinery.[9] In 2015, WIPO produced breakdowns of the sources of PCT applicants in sub-categories as follows: businesses (85.1 per cent), individuals (7.8 per cent), universities (4.8 per cent) and governments and research institutes (2.3 per cent) (see Tables 6.3, 6.4 and 6.5).[10]

---

8 WIPO, *Patent Cooperation Treaty Yearly Review: The International Patent System 2014*, WIPO Publication No. 901_2014 (WIPO 2015) 16.

9 WIPO, *2012 PCT Yearly Review: The International Patent System*, WIPO Publication No. 901E/2012 (WIPO 2012) 20; and WIPO, *Patent Cooperation Treaty Yearly Review: The International Patent System 2014*, WIPO Publication No. 901_2014 (WIPO 2015) 47.

10 WIPO, *Annual Report: Report of the Director General to the WIPO Assemblies* (WIPO 2015) 4.

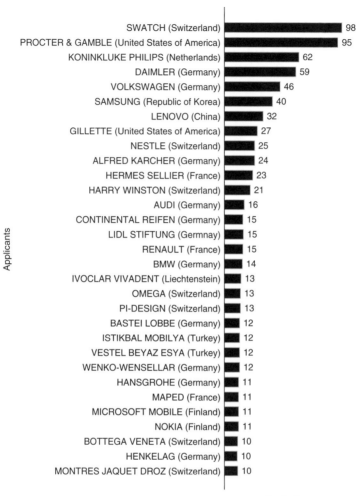

Note: Applicants that filed ten or more international applicants in 2014 are included in the figure.

Source: WIPO, *Hague Yearly Review: International Registration of Industrial Designs* (WIPO 2015) 14.

Figure 6.3   Top Hague design applicants in 2014

Table 6.3 Top 50 PCT applicants: businesses, 2014

Overall Rank	Changed Position from 2013	Applicants	Origin	Applications	Change From 2013
1	2	Huawei Technologies Co., Ltd.	China	3,442	1,332
2	2	Qualcomm Incorporated	United States of America	2,409	351
3	−1	ZTE Corporation	China	2,179	−130
4	−3	Panasonic Corporation	Japan	1,682	−1,157
5	7	Mitsubishi Electric Corporation	Japan	1,593	280
6	−1	Intel Corporation	United States of America	1,539	−332
7	2	Telefonaktiebolaget LM Ericsson (Publ)	Sweden	1,512	44
8	12	Microsoft Corporation	United States of America	1,460	652
9	2	Siemens Aktiengesellschaft	Germany	1,399	51
10	0	Koninklijke Philips Electronics N.V.	Netherlands	1,391	−32
11	2	Samsung Electronics Co., Ltd.	Republic of Korea	1,381	183
12	−4	Toyota Jidosha Kabushiki Kaisha	Japan	1,378	−320
13	−6	Robert Bosch Corporation	Germany	1,371	−438
14	−8	Sharp Kabushiki Kaisha	Japan	1,227	−612
15	−1	NEC Corporation	Japan	1,215	26
16	−1	LG Electronics Inc.	Republic of Korea	1,138	−40
17	36	Tencent Technology (Shenzhen) Company Limited	China	1,086	727
18	−2	Fujifilm Corporation	Japan	1,072	69
19	31	United Technologies Corporation	United States of America	1,013	643
20	−1	Hitachi, Ltd.	Japan	996	141

Overall Rank	Changed Position from 2013	Applicants	Origin	Applications	Change From 2013
21	−4	Sony Corporation	Japan	982	66
22	5	Google Inc.	United States of America	914	284
23	−6	Shenzhen China Star Optoelectronics Technology Co., Ltd	China	904	−12
24	13	Kabushiki Kaisha Toshiba	Japan	856	412
25	−3	Hewlett-Packard Development Company, L.P.	United States of America	826	52
26	9	Halliburton Energy Services, Inc.	United States of America	800	347
27	−4	BASF Se	Germany	780	82
28	0	3M Innovative Properties Company	United States of America	696	91
29	37	Denso Corporation	Japan	665	369
30	−9	Nokia Corporation	Finland	630	−176
31	−6	Nissan Motor Co., Ltd.	Japan	620	−24
32	0	General Electric Company	United States of America	604	86
33	0	Murata Manufacturing Co., Ltd.	Japan	588	75
34	2	LG Chem, Ltd.	Republic of Korea	553	104
35	20	BOE Technology Group Co., Ltd	China	553	200
36	−10	Fujitsu Limited	Japan	552	−85
37	−3	Konica Minolta, Inc.	Japan	519	52
38	−9	Apple Computer, Inc.	United States of America	514	−71
39	−15	International Business Machines Corporation	United States of America	511	−179
40	−2	Mitsubishi Heavy Industries, Ltd.	Japan	487	44

41	7	Procter & Gamble Company	United States of America	474	99
42	–3	Kyocera Corporation	Japan	472	48
43	–1	Dow Global Technologies Inc.	United States of America	470	69
44	11	Yazaki Corporation	Japan	448	103
45	30	Huawei Device Co., Ltd.	China	420	144
46	21	Empire Technology Development LLC	United States of America	411	120
47	19	Terumo Kabushiki Kaisha	Japan	405	113
48	7	Applied Materials, Inc.	United States of America	395	67
49	1	Nitto Denko Corporation	Japan	390	29
50	–22	Alcatel Lucent	France	367	–173

Note: For confidentiality reasons, data are based on publication date.

Source: WIPO, *Patent Cooperation Treaty Yearly Review: The International Patent System 2014* WIPO Publication No. 901_2014 (WIPO 2015) 39.

Table 6.4 Top 50 PCT applicants: universities, 2014

Overall Rank	Changed Position from 2013	Applicants	Origin	Applications	Change from 2013
47	-4	University of California	United States of America	413	15
83	12	Massachusetts Institute of Technology	United States of America	234	15
132	38	University of Texas System	United States of America	154	35
145	19	Harvard University	United States of America	147	26
163	14	Johns Hopkins University	United States of America	135	19
201	11	Leland Stanford Junior University	United States of America	113	12
206	-59	Columbia University	United States of America	112	-21
225	10	California Institute of Technology	United States of America	103	12
249	54	University of Pennsylvania	United States of America	94	22
253	16	Seoul National University	Republic of Korea	92	12
275	-51	Cornell University	United States of America	87	-8
290	-2	Nanyang Technological University	Singapore	82	7
293	-50	University of Florida	United States of America	81	-8
293	69	Kyoto University	Japan	81	23
293	150	Danmarks Tekniske Universitet	Denmark	81	33
304	-18	University of Tokyo	Japan	79	3
305	2	University of Michigan	United States of America	78	7
312	54	Korea University	Republic of Korea	77	20
314	-33	Peking University	China	76	-1
325	77	University of Washington	United States of America	74	21

325	−39	Isis Innovation Limited	United Kingdom	74	−2
332	79	Kyushu University	Japan	72	20
336	17	Tsinghua University	China	70	10
347	−143	Korea Advanced Institute of Science and Technology	Republic of Korea	67	−37
378	33	Osaka University	Japan	62	10
395	143	University of North Carolina	United States of America	59	21
411	−150	Postech Foundation	Republic of Korea	57	−26
411	229	University of Illinois	United States of America	57	25
418	−107	National University of Singapore	Singapore	56	−13
418	−56	Yonsei University	Republic of Korea	56	−2
422	−65	Tohoku University	Japan	55	−4
431	127	Hanyang University	Republic of Korea	54	17
452	121	Duke University	United States of America	51	15
452	−78	New York University	United States of America	51	−5
465	193	Eidgenossische Technische Hochschule Zurich	Switzerland	50	19
488	170	Kyungpook National University	Republic of Korea	48	17
521	162	Ecole Polytechnique Federale De Lausanne	Switzerland	45	15
526	32	Northeastern University	United States of America	44	7
526	1202	China University of Mining and Technolgy	China	44	33
526	114	Emory University	United States of America	44	12

Overall Rank	Changed Position from 2013	Applicants	Origin	Applications	Change from 2013
526	–99	University of Utah	United States of America	44	–6
538	–62	University of Minnesota	United States of America	43	–1
558	–70	University of Southern California	United States of America	41	–2
558	–82	University of Pittsburgh	United States of America	41	–3
558	173	Imperial Innovations Ltd.	United Kingdom	41	13
558	–60	State University of New York	United States of America	41	–1
571	227	University of Rochester	United States of America	40	14
584	–26	Yeda Research and Development Co. Ltd.	Israel	39	2
608	821	University of Houston	United States of America	38	24
608	–70	Northwestern University	United States of America	38	0
624	–126	Vanderbilt University	United States of America	37	–5

Note: The university sector includes all types of educational institutions. For confidentiality reasons, data are based on publication date.

Source: WIPO, *Patent Cooperation Treaty Yearly Review: The International Patent System 2014* WIPO Publication No. 901_2014 (WIPO 2015) 40.

Table 6.5 Top 30 PCT applicants: government and research institutions, 2014

Overall Rank	Changed Position from 2013	Applicants	Origin	Applications	Change from 2013
45	−5	Commissariat a l'energie atomique et aux energies alternatives	France	434	15
63	21	Fraunhofer-Gesellschaft zur Forderung der angewandten Forschung e.V.	Germany	318	70
107	−15	China Academy of Telecommunications Technology	China	196	−31
130	10	Institute of Microelectronics of Chinese Academy of Sciences	China	156	17
136	76	Agency of Science, Technology and Research	Singapore	152	51
139	−21	Centre national de la recherche scientifique (CNRS)	France	150	−15
161	23	Institut national de la sante et de la recherche medicale (INSERM)	France	136	22
191	73	MIMOS Berhad	Malaysia	119	37
192	43	Council of Scientific and Industrial Research	India	117	26
198	45	National Institute of Advanced Industrial Science and Technology	Japan	114	25
262	53	Consejo Superior de Investigaciones Cientificas (CSIC)	Spain	90	22
290	−66	U.S.A., as Represented by the Secretary Dept. of Health and Human Services	United States of America	82	−13
293	69	Korea Institute of Energy Research	Republic of Korea	81	23
352	39	Nederlandse Organisatie voor Toegepast-Natuurwetenschappelijk Onderzoek (TNO)	Netherlands	66	12
374	−41	Korea Institute of Industrial Technology	Republic of Korea	63	−1

Overall Rank	Changed Position from 2013	Applicants	Origin	Applications	Change from 2013
378	13	Korea Electronics Technology Institute	Republic of Korea	62	8
385	17	Battelle Memorial Institute	United States of America	60	7
422	−20	Japan Science and Technology Agency	Japan	55	2
422	−168	Electronics & Telecommunications Research Institute of Korea	Republic of Korea	55	−32
437	73	Cleveland Clinic Foundation	United States of America	53	12
488	195	Sloan-Kettering Institute for Cancer Research	United States of America	48	18
501	139	Korea Research Institute of Chemical Technology	Republic of Korea	47	15
538	−147	Max-Planck-Gesellschaft zur Forderung der Wissenschaften e.V.	Germany	43	−11
550	71	United States of America as Represented by the Secretary of the Navy	United States of America	42	9
608	−197	Commonwealth Scientific and Industrial Research Organisation	Australia	38	−14
608	−98	Mayo Foundation for Medical Education and Research	United States of America	38	−3
645	−115	Korea Institute of Machinery & Materials	Republic of Korea	36	−3
645	−24	Riken (The Institute of Physical and Chemical Research)	Japan	36	3
680	522	Consiglio Nazionale delle Ricerche	Italy	34	17
680	−259	Korea Research Institute of Bioscience and Biotechnology	Republic of Korea	34	−17

Note: Government and research institutions include private non-profit organisations and hospitals. For confidentiality reasons, data are based on publication date.

Source: WIPO, *Patent Cooperation Treaty Yearly Review: The International Patent System 2014* WIPO Publication No. 901_2014 (WIPO 2015) 41.

6.1.2   Income sources for the regular budget: Member State contributions, the Unitary Contribution System and arrears

Membership of WIPO requires both developed and developing country Member States to make contributions, albeit on a modest and sliding scale.[11] See Table 6.6 for the contribution classes of members of WIPO, Paris and/or the Berne Unions. In 2015, the smallest annual assessed Member State contribution to WIPO was around 1,400 CHF while the highest contribution was 1.14 million CHF.[12] Less than 5 per cent of WIPO's regular budget comes from the assessed contributions of Member States. Indeed, the overall proportion of WIPO's income derived from Member State contributions has decreased from 6.6 per cent in 2004/05 to an estimated 4.8 per cent for the 2014/15 biennium (see Table 6.1). Between 2002 and 2015, the total income from Member State contributions increased by less than 1 million CHF (see Table 6.1).[13]

Notably, during his tenure, former Director General Bogsch proposed that in light of WIPO's growing revenue from fees, Member States should consider terminating the system for their contributions. However, at that time and again during discussions of a Working Group on Constitutional Reform (which met from 1999 to 2002), Member States rejected proposals to end their contributions, characterising them as an important affirmation, albeit admittedly somewhat symbolic, of the member-driven character of the organisation, the need for the control and oversight of the Secretariat by Member States, and its accountability to them.[14]

---

11 Most UN organisations similarly determine assessed contributions on a sliding scale based on the country's capacity to pay with a minimum rate for the poorest countries, but all countries formally return one vote. By contrast, for some non-UN international organisations such as the World Bank and IMF voting power is linked to the size of financial contributions: as the majority of member state contributions are made by developed countries and larger developing countries they in turn have more formal voting power and thus influence on decision-making and rules.

12 WIPO, *Financial Management Report for the 2012/13 Biennium* WO/PBC/22/6 (WIPO 2014) 46.

13 See WIPO, *Annual Report 2002* WIPO Publication No. 441 (E) (WIPO 2003) 39; WIPO, *Program and Budget 2014/15* WO/PBC/21/8 (WIPO 2013).

14 The reports of the Working Group include the following: WIPO, *Constitutional Reform, First Session of the Working Group*, 22 to 24 *March* WO/GA/WG-CR/2 (WIPO 2000); WIPO, *Report of the First Session of the Working Group*, 22 to 24 *March* WO/GA/WG-CR/3 (WIPO 2000); WIPO, *Report of the Second Session of the Working Group* WO/GA/WG-CR/2/8 (WIPO 2000); WIPO, *Report of the Third Session of the Working Group*, 3 to 6 *March* 2001 WO/GA/WG-CR/3/6 (WIPO 2001); WIPO, *Report of the Fourth Session of the Working Group*, 11 to 14 *September* WO/GA/WG-CR/4/4 (WIPO 2001); WIPO, *Report of the Fifth Session of the Working Group*, 18 to 22 *February* WO/GA/WG-CR/5/4 (WIPO 2002); and WIPO, *Report of the Sixth*

Table 6.6 Contribution classes of members of WIPO, Paris and/or the Berne Unions

Member	Class	Member	Class
Afghanistan	S*ter*	Colombia	IX
Albania	IX	Comoros	S*ter*
Algeria	IX	Congo	S*bis*
Andorra	IX	Costa Rica	S
Angola	S*ter*	Côte d'Ivoire	S*bis*
Antigua and Barbuda	S*bis*	Croatia	VIII
Argentina	VI*bis*	Cuba	S
Armenia	IX	Cyprus	S
Australia	III	Czech Republic	VI
Austria	IV*bis*	Democratic People's Republic of Korea	S*bis*
Azerbaijan	IX	Democratic Republic of the Congo	S*ter*
Bahamas	S*bis*	Denmark	IV
Bahrain	S	Djibouti	S*ter*
Bangladesh	S*ter*	Dominica	S*bis*
Barbados	S*bis*	Dominican Republic	S
Belarus	IX	Ecuador	S
Belgium	IV	Egypt	IX
Belize	S*bis*	El Salvador	S*bis*
Benin	S*ter*	Equatorial Guinea	S*ter*
Bhutan	S*ter*	Eritrea	S*ter*
Bolivia	S*bis*	Estonia	IX
Bosnia and Herzegovina	S*bis*	Ethiopia	S*ter*
Botswana	S*bis*	Fiji	S*bis*
Brazil	VI*bis*	Finland	IV
Brunei Darussalam	S	former Yugoslav Republic of Macedonia	VIII
Bulgaria	VI*bis*	France	I
Burkina Faso	S*ter*	Gabon	S
Burundi	S*ter*	Gambia	S*ter*
Cabo Verde	S*bis*	Georgia	IX
Cambodia	S*ter*	Germany	I
Cameroon	S*bis*	Ghana	S*bis*
Canada	IV	Greece	VI
Central African Republic	S*ter*	Grenada	S*bis*
Chad	S*ter*	Guatemala	S
Chile	IX	Guinea	S*ter*
China	IV*bis*	Guinea-Bissau	S*ter*

Session of the Working Group, 24 to 28 June WO/GA/WG-GCR/6/3 (WIPO 2002). The Group also made a report to the General Assembly in 2001. The final report of the Group is WIPO, *Final Recommendations of the WIPO General Assembly Working Group on Constitutional Reform* A/37/5 (WIPO 2002).

Member	Class	Member	Class
Guyana	S*bis*	Morocco	S
Haiti	S*ter*	Mozambique	S*ter*
Holy See	IX	Myanmar	S*ter*
Honduras	S*bis*	Namibia	S*bis*
Hungary	VI	Nepal	S*ter*
Iceland	VIII	Netherlands	III
India	VI*bis*	New Zealand	VI
Indonesia	VII	Nicaragua	S*bis*
Iran (Islamic Republic of)	VII	Niger	S*ter*
Iraq	S	Nigeria	S
Ireland	IV	Niue	S*bis*
Israel	VI*bis*	Norway	IV
Italy	III	Oman	IX
Jamaica	S*bis*	Pakistan	S
Japan	I	Panama	S
Jordan	S	Papua New Guinea	S*bis*
Kazakhstan	IX	Paraguay	S*bis*
Kenya	S*bis*	Peru	IX
Kiribati	S*ter*	Philippines	IX
Kuwait	IX	Poland	VI
Kyrgyzstan	IX	Portugal	IV*bis*
Lao People's Democratic Republic	S*ter*	Qatar	IX
Latvia	IX	Republic of Korea	IV*bis*
Lebanon	S	Republic of Moldova	IX
Lesotho	S*ter*	Romania	VI*bis*
Liberia	S*ter*	Russian Federation	IV
Libya	IX	Rwanda	S*ter*
Liechtenstein	VIII	Saint Kitts and Nevis	S*bis*
Lithuania	IX	Saint Lucia	S*bis*
Luxembourg	VII	Saint Vincent and the Grenadines	S*bis*
Madagascar	S*ter*	Samoa	S*bis*
Malawi	S*ter*	San Marino	IX
Malaysia	VIII	Sao Tome and Principe	S*ter*
Maldives	S*bis*	Saudi Arabia	VII
Mali	S*ter*	Senegal	S*ter*
Malta	S*bis*	Serbia	VIII
Mauritania	S*ter*	Seychelles	S*bis*
Mauritius	S*bis*	Sierra Leone	S*ter*
Mexico	IV*bis*	Singapore	IX
Micronesia (Federated States of)	S*bis*	Slovakia	VI
Monaco	VII	Slovenia	VII
Mongolia	S*bis*	Somalia	S*ter*
Montenegro	IX	South Africa	IV*bis*

Member	Class	Member	Class
Spain	IV	Tuvalu	*Ster*
Sri Lanka	S	Uganda	*Ster*
Sudan	*Ster*	Ukraine	IX
Suriname	*Sbis*	United Arab Emirates	IX
Swaziland	*Sbis*	United Kingdom	I
Sweden	III	United Republic of Tanzania	*Ster*
Switzerland	III	United States of America	I
Syrian Arab Republic	S	Uruguay	S
Tajikistan	IX	Uzbekistan	IX
Thailand	IX	Vanuatu	*Ster*
Togo	*Ster*	Venezuela (Bolivarian Republic of)	IX
Tonga	*Sbis*	Viet Nam	S
Trinidad and Tobago	S	Yemen	*Ster*
Tunisia	S	Zambia	*Ster*
Turkey	V*Ibis*	Zimbabwe	*Sbis*
Turkmenistan	IX		

Note: The unitary contribution system, established with effect from 1 January 1994, replaced the separate contribution systems of WIPO and the six Contribution-financed Unions, that is, each state pays one contribution, irrespective of whether it is a member of WIPO or of one or more of the Contribution-financed Unions. Under the unitary contribution system, there are the following classes corresponding to the units of contribution indicated between parentheses: I (25), II (20), III (15), IV (10), IV*bis* (7.5), V (5), VI (3), VI*bis* (2), VII (1), VIII (1/2), IX (1/4), S (1/8), S*bis* (1/16) and S*ter* (1/32). The above table reflects the status on 15 April 2015.

Source: WIPO, 'Contribution Classes of States Members of WIPO and/or the Paris and/or the Berne Unions' <http://www.wipo.int/treaties/en/contribution_classes.html#f2> accessed 8 July 2015.

In 1993, WIPO Member States adopted a Unitary Contribution System[15] to support the general expenses of WIPO and the six Contribution-financed Unions (that is, the Paris, Berne, IPC, Nice, Locarno and Vienna Unions).[16] The Unitary Contribution System was

---

15 This 1993 decision was made by the WIPO Conference and the Assemblies of the Paris and Berne Unions. See WIPO, *WIPO Intellectual Property Handbook: Policy, Law and Use* (WIPO 2004) 9. Also see, for example, WIPO, *Unitary Contribution System for the Six Contribution-Financed Unions and Alignment of the Contributions of Non-Union States* AB/XXIV/5, 31 May 1993 (WIPO 2015), and WIPO, *Constitutional Reform: Memorandum of the Secretariat, Assemblies of the Member States of WIPO, Thirty-Fourth Series of Meetings, 20 to 29 September 1999* A/34/9 (WIPO 1999) para. 19.

16 Each of these six WIPO treaties provide for Member State financing of the operation of the Unions they form and related activities.

intended to encourage wider membership of WIPO and its treaties. Under the system, any country that adheres to the WIPO Convention and any of the Contribution-financed Unions pays a single contribution irrespective of whether it is a member of WIPO, or only of one or more of WIPO's six treaties with Contribution-financed Unions. (That is, Member States replaced the prior system of separate payments for each of the six Contribution-financed Unions and for WIPO for those states that are members of WIPO but not of the Unions). The Hague, Lisbon, Madrid and PCT Unions were not included in the Unitary Contribution System because it was intended that these Unions would be financed through fees from their respective global protection systems (although each treaty also does provide the possibility for Member State contributions). Notably, the 1993 decision did not result in a formal amendment of the WIPO Convention. Rather, a note regarding the adoption of the new contribution was added to the end of the Convention under a sub-heading 'New Contribution System' (see Appendix 1).[17] In 2003, the WIPO Assemblies adopted amendments to various treaties including the WIPO Convention to implement the Unitary Contribution System, but these have not yet entered into force (see sections 6.5 and 6.6 for further discussion relevant to the Unitary Contribution System and the unitary presentation of the budget).

Each WIPO Member State chooses which of 14 contribution classes it will belong to (3 of which are reserved for developing countries only), which in turn determines the amount of its contribution.[18] The amount of the annual contribution payable by each State in each class is calculated by multiplying the number of units of that class by the value, in Swiss Francs, of one contribution unit. That value is fixed by the General Assembly meeting in joint session with the Assemblies of

---

17 The note reads as follows: 'The Governing Bodies of WIPO and the Unions administered by WIPO adopted with effect from January 1, 1994, a new contribution system that replaces the contribution system set forth in Article 11(4)(a), (b) and (c) of the WIPO Convention.' The paragraph continues detailing that it also replaces provisions set forth in 'Article 16(4) (a), (b) and (c) of the Paris Convention, Article 25(4)(a), (b) and (c) of the Berne Convention and the corresponding provisions of the Strasbourg (IPC), Nice, Locarno and Vienna Agreements.'

18 Class I, with the highest contribution, involves the payment of 25 contribution units, whereas Class Ster, with the lowest contribution, involves the payment of 1/32 of one contribution unit. The amount of each state's contribution is the same whether that state is a member only of WIPO, or only of one or more Unions, or of both WIPO and one or more Unions. See WIPO, *Financial Management Report for the 2012/13 Biennium* WO/PBC/22/6 (WIPO 2014) 46–9.

the Contribution-financed Unions (see Regulation 3.3 of the WIPO Financial Regulations and Rules).

The formal rights and obligations of Member States are the same regardless of the contribution class to which they belong.[19] The countries that opt for the highest contribution class are France, Germany, Japan, the United Kingdom and the United States (each of which contribute 25 'units'). Most developing countries have selected classes that require a contribution of between 1 and 1/32 of a unit. The exceptions are countries such as Brazil, India and China, which have opted for higher contribution classes. The contribution amounts designated for each class have been the same for over a decade; that is, there has been no increase or decrease in amounts for each class. Some countries have, however, shifted their contribution class (in 2014, for instance, Belgium shifted class to reduce its annual contribution to WIPO).

Although Member State financial contributions to WIPO are low compared to many other international organisations (and the sums of money at stake are relatively small), if a government is late (in arrears) with their contribution, the political implications can be significant. For instance, WIPO Member States in arrears can be deemed ineligible to vote when key budgetary or governance matters are brought to a vote (see discussion of voting in Chapter 5). At the time of the 2014 WIPO annual Assemblies some 51 Member States (27 per cent of the WIPO membership) were in arrears in the payment of their annual contributions, and 23 Member States, mostly developing countries, had been in arrears for a number of years.[20] In 1991, Member States took a decision to waive a portion of the arrears of least-developed

---

19 WIPO, *WIPO Overview* WIPO Publication No. 1007/E/11 (WIPO 2011).

20 Arrears in contributions are noted in PBC documents each year. See, for instance, WIPO, *Status of the Payment of Contributions as at June 30, 2014: Document Prepared by the Secretariat* WO/ PBC/22/7 (WIPO 2014). Countries in arrears for many years include Bolivia (since 2005), Burundi (since 1994), Central African Republic (since 1994), Chad (since 1994), Comoros (since 2006), Côte d'Ivoire (since 1994), Democratic Republic of Congo (since 1994), the Dominican Republic (since 1994) and (from 1970 to 1993) under the Paris Convention, Guinea (since 1994), Guinea-Bissau (since 1994), Honduras (since 2011), Lebanon (has agreed to an instalment plan for payment of arrears from 1994 to 2006), Mauritania (since 1994), Niger (since 1994), Nigeria (since 1994), Somalia (since 1994), Togo (since 2002). The total amount of arrears in 2014 was 5.6 million CHF (including the unitary contributions and pre-1994 Contribution-financed Unions), representing around 32 per cent of the total amount invoiced for contributions payable for 2014. Some of these amounts, however, relate to 2013/14, and the WIPO Secretariat expects these to be cleared.

countries (that is, for the period prior to 1990).[21] Since 1994, when the unitary contribution system came into effect and more equitable contribution classes for the developing countries were established, arrears in contributions have declined significantly. For instance, the total sum of arrears in regard to the unitary contribution system decreased from 4.37 million CHF in 2003 to 3.3 million CHF in 2015 (and also represents a declining proportion of the organisation's growing overall budget).[22]

6.1.3   Other income sources for WIPO's regular budget

Beyond these two sources of income, WIPO earns a small portion of its regular budget from fees paid for arbitration services, interest and some miscellaneous sources, such as income from WIPO publications and rental income derived from WIPO buildings.

6.1.4   Extra-budgetary income and Funds-in-Trust

As a complement to its regular budget, WIPO also receives some voluntary, extra-budgetary income from Member States and IGOs, usually held as Funds-in-Trust (FITs), most of which is dedicated to development cooperation purposes. Like other international organisations, WIPO is seeking to boost extra-budgetary financial and in-kind contributions from governments as well as philanthropic and other non-governmental sources. The contributions made through FITs have grown from an estimated 14.9 million CHF available for programming in 2010/11 to an estimated 23.3 million CHF available in 2016/17. These estimates represent an increase from 11 per cent to 14 per cent of the total estimated resources available for WIPO's development programming in the respective biennia.[23] The sums noted as

---

21 Notably, according to a 1991 decision taken by the WIPO Conference and the Assemblies of the Paris and Berne Unions, the amount of the arrears in contributions of any least developed country (LDC) relating to years preceding 1990 was placed in a special account, the amount of which was frozen as of 31 December 1989. See WIPO, *Arrears of Contributions of the Least Developed Countries* AB/XXII/20 (WIPO 1991) and WIPO, *General Report: Adopted by the Governing Bodies* AB/XXII/22 (WIPO 1991) para. 127.

22 See, for instance, WIPO, *Status of the Payment of Contributions as at June 30, 2014: Document Prepared by the Secretariat* WO/PBC/22/7 (WIPO 2014) 9 and WIPO, *Status of the Payment of Contributions as at September 1, 2015: Document Prepared by the Secretariat* A/55/8 (WIPO 2015) 8. This reduction is partly explained by the total amount of contributions invoiced, which declined considerably between the years 1997 and 2012.

23 See WIPO, *Program and Budget 2010/11* (WIPO 2009); WIPO, *Program and Budget 2014/15* (WIPO 2013); and WIPO, *Program and Budget 2016/17* A55/5 Rev. (WIPO 2015) 235.

available for each biennium do not necessarily, however, represent new contributions as there is often a balance remaining unspent from prior years and the contributions may provide for activities spanning more than a single biennium. (For the interaction between decision-making on the use and allocation of FITS and WIPO's wider Program and Budget Process, see section 6.4.)

6.2   WIPO Financial Regulations and Rules

The WIPO Financial Regulations and Rules govern the financial activities of the organisation and the Unions administered by it,[24] and are approved by the General Assembly. WIPO's Financial Regulations and its Annexes are regularly amended by Member States (most recently in 2015 in the case of the Annex related to WIPO's Internal Oversight Charter). New draft Regulations are proposed in some instances by the Secretariat to address new challenges or changed circumstances, and also in response to requests from Member States, such as through the PBC or General Assembly. Within the Secretariat, responsibility for working with Member States to draft and propose new Regulations rests with the Controller's Office.

The Financial Rules are established by the Director General in accordance with the provisions of the Financial Regulations and are regularly updated through the Controller's Office. The Director General informs the PBC and General Assembly of any modification in the Rules.[25]

The Financial Regulations and Rules cover a full suite of matters related to purchases and payments for goods and services by the Secretariat. The Regulations and Rules include chapters on matters ranging from the program and budget process, financing (including assessed contributions, fees and voluntary contributions), custody of funds, investments and external borrowing to the use of funds (appropriations,

---

24 See WIPO, *Financial Regulations and Rules (FRR)* (WIPO last amended 30 September 2014) <www.wipo.int/about-wipo/en/pdf/wipo_financial_regulations.pdf> accessed 1 October 2014. These regulations have been applicable since 1 January 2008. Member States amended the Financial Regulations and Rules on 1 October 2009; 1 January 2010; 1 October 2010; 5 October 2011; 9 October 2012; and 30 September 2014. Appendix 7 provides excerpts of those rules and regulations from the FRR selected by the author for being particularly relevant to governance of the organisation.

25 See WIPO, *Draft Report, 46th Session of the WIPO General Assembly* WO/GA/46/12 Prov. (WIPO 2014).

expenditures and procurement), accounting, internal oversight, external audit arrangements, and the role of the Independent Advisory Oversight Committee (IAOC).

All WIPO employees are required to comply with the Financial Regulations and Rules and with Office Instructions issued in connection with them (Rule 101.2). The Rules further specify that any employee who contravenes the Financial Regulations and Rules or corresponding Office Instructions may be held personally accountable and financially liable for his or her actions.

A number of regulations and rules have a clear governance dimension. Chapter 2 of the Financial Regulations and Rules, for instance, addresses the Program and Budget, specifying the authority and responsibility of Member States and the Director General in its preparation, review and approval, as well as its presentation, content and methodology. Chapter 2 also sets out regulations related to supplementary and revised program and budget documents, program and budget performance and evaluation as well as unforeseen and extraordinary expenses. Also relevant from a governance perspective are those regulations and rules related to oversight, external audit and the Independent Advisory Oversight Committee, which are discussed in section 6.4 (also see Appendix 7).

The Financial Regulations and Rules include numerous provisions that clarify the authority, responsibility and role of the Director General. For instance, in Chapter 5 on the utilization of WIPO funds, Regulation 5.5 sets out the scope and limitations on the Director General's ability to transfer funds among WIPO Programs between appropriations. It states that:

> The Director General may make transfers from one program of the program and budget to another for any given financial period, up to the limit of five per cent of the amount corresponding to the biennial appropriation of the receiving program, or to one per cent of the total budget, whichever is higher, when such transfers are necessary to ensure the proper functioning of the services.

In Regulation 5.6, the Director General is given flexibility to make upward or downward adjustments to the resources appropriated for the operations of the PCT, Madrid and Hague systems, and for WIPO programs providing administrative support to these operations, in accordance with the methodology and formula(e) approved by the respective Assemblies of the PCT, Madrid and Hague Unions. Further, in Regulation 5.7, the Director General is given the authority to enter into commitments for future financial periods, provided that such commitments: (i) are for activities which have been approved by the General Assembly and are expected to continue beyond the end of the current financial period; or (ii) are authorised by specific decisions of the General Assembly.

In accordance with these Regulations and Rules, the Director General submits annual financial statements for each calendar year to the External Auditor and the IAOC no later than 31 March (in the year following the end of the year to which they relate) (Regulation 6.5).[26] Rule 106.11 adds that these shall also be transmitted to the PBC. After the annual audit, the Secretariat submits annual financial statements and the report of the External Auditor to the Assemblies of the Member States (Regulation 6.7), prepared in accordance with the International Public Sector Accounting Standards (IPSAS).[27]

Every 2 years, following the end of the biennium, the Director General prepares a Financial Management Report for that financial period (Regulation 6.6).[28] The Secretariat submits the financial

---

26 The financial statements include: (i) a statement of financial position; (ii) a statement of financial performance; (iii) a statement of changes in net assets; (iv) a statement of cash flow; (v) a statement of comparison of budget and actual amounts; and (vi) notes, comprising a summary of significant accounting policies and other explanatory notes.

27 WIPO Member States adopted the IPSAS in 2007, effective 1 January 2010. The IPSAS were developed by the International Public Sector Accounting Standards Board (IPSASB), which is part of the International Federation of Accountants (IFAC). This move was in line with the UN High-Level Committee on Management (HLCM) decision of 30 November 2005. In December 2008, the Member States approved the implementation of a number of further changes to achieve full compliance with the WIPO Financial Regulations and Rules (FRR) and IPSAS, and to achieve a more streamlined, efficient and automated means of requesting, purchasing and paying for goods and services. See WIPO, *Program and Budget 2010/11* (WIPO 2009) Annex VIII; WIPO, *Report by the WIPO Independent Advisory Oversight Committee (IAOC), Prepared by the Secretariat* A/43/5 (WIPO 2013).

28 Regulation 6.6 in the FRR states that the financial management report shall include: (b) A statement of budget and actual income and expenditure for the financial period reported on the same accounting basis as the adopted budget; (c) The income and expenditures of all funds; (d) The status of appropriations, including: (i) the original budget appropriation; (ii) the appropriation as modified by any transfers made by the Director General under Regulation 5.5; (iii) increases or decreases arising from the flexibility adjustments under Regulation 5.6; (iv) credits, if any, other than the appropriations approved by the General Assembly; and (v) the amounts

management reports to the Assemblies for review by all interested states (Regulation 6.7).

6.2.1   Custody of WIPO funds

The World Intellectual Property Organization has four types of internal accounts: (i) a general fund; (ii) working capital funds; (iii) reserve accounts; and (iv) trust funds and special accounts.

The general fund is WIPO's main fund for the purpose of accounting for the organisation's expenditures (Regulation 4.1). It is the repository of all assessed contributions paid by Member States; all fees derived from services provided by the organisation under the PCT, Madrid, Hague and Lisbon systems; and miscellaneous income as well as any advances made from the working capital funds or reserve funds to finance general expenditure.

The WIPO Financial Regulations and Rules provide for the establishment of working capital funds for the organisation as well as for the Paris, Berne, Madrid, Hague, IPC, Nice, PCT, Lisbon, Locarno and Vienna Unions in amounts determined by the Assemblies of the Member States and of the respective Unions (Regulation 4.2). The purpose of such working capital funds is to finance budgetary appropriations that are not yet covered by available liquidity (which was particularly important in the early days of the fee-financed Unions where the future use of their systems was uncertain) and for such other purposes as may be determined by the relevant Assemblies (Regulation 4.3; also see Financial Rule 101.3(q)). In 2015, the Lisbon Union decided to establish a working capital fund as of 1 January 2016, meaning that all of the Unions now have one. The working capital funds for the PCT Union, the Madrid Union and the Hague Union were established in 1983, 1979 and 1978, respectively, and the Contribution-financed Unions have a common working capital fund. In 2015, the PCT Union agreed to return the working capital funds for the PCT Union to the members of the PCT Union through deductions from contribution invoices in 2016/17.

---

charged against those appropriations and/or other credits; (e) Primary financial statements for the financial period prepared on the same accounting basis as the annual financial statements; (f) A report on investments; and (g) A statement on the status of contributions of the Member States. (Note: there was no point numbered (a) in the original Regulation.)

Reserve accounts are used for any surplus of income remaining after the close of a financial period (unless otherwise decided by the General Assembly or the Assembly of the Union concerned) (Regulation 4.7). The General Assembly or the Assembly of the Union concerned decides upon the use of the reserve funds for purposes other than the covering of any deficits (Regulation 4.6).

Finally, the Director General can establish trust funds and special accounts, and also define their purposes and limits. All such funds and accounts must be administered in accordance with the Financial Regulations and Rules (Regulation 4.5). According to Rule 104.1:

> the Controller is authorized to levy a charge on trust funds and special accounts. This charge shall be used to reimburse all, or part of, the indirect costs incurred by the Organization in respect of the generation and administration of trust funds and special accounts. All direct costs of the implementation of programs that are financed by trust funds and special accounts shall be charged against the relevant trust fund and special account.

6.2.2   The WIPO Controller

Across WIPO's Financial Regulations and Rules, there are numerous references to the role and responsibilities of the WIPO Controller, who reports to the WIPO Director General. According to Rule 101.1, the Director General delegates authority and assigns responsibility to the Controller for the implementation of the Financial Regulations and Rules. The Controller may in turn delegate aspects of his/her authority to other officers unless the Director General indicates otherwise. The Controller is also responsible for the organisation and proper working of all WIPO accounting systems, for designating the officers responsible for performing accounting functions (Rule 106.2) and for preparing the Financial Management Report (Rule 106.12). The use of all WIPO funds requires the prior authorization of the Controller, who is also responsible for approving commitments against all future financial periods (Rule 105.1) and all *ex gratia* payments (Rule 105.11). The Controller prepares all proposals for external borrowing (which are then submitted by the Director General, through the Program and Budget Committee, to the General Assembly for approval) (Rule 104.14) and is delegated the authority to make and prudently manage investments in accordance with the investment policy approved by Member States (Rule 104.10). The Controller may determine the maximum amount of the appropriations that it would be prudent to make available for allocation, taking into account the prospects of payment of assessed contributions, the likely level of income from fees, or any other relevant factors (Rule 105.2).[29] Together with the External Auditor, the Controller is also granted important authority with respect to the retention of accounting records. In this respect, Rule 106.13 states that: 'The accounting records shall be supported by financial and property records and other documents which are to be retained in appropriate files and for such periods as may be agreed with the External Auditor, after which, on the authority of the Controller, they may be destroyed.'

6.3   Policies on reserves and investments

The World Intellectual Property Organization is in an extraordinary position compared to other UN organisations in that it has considerable financial reserves. At the end of 2014, WIPO's net assets were over 245.8 million CHF, which exceeded the target level for reserves set by Member States.[30] In 2011, WIPO Member States adopted an investment policy for its budget and reserves.[31] The WIPO Assemblies agreed in 2014 this policy should be reviewed, and a revised policy was adopted in 2015.[32] The WIPO Financial Regulations and Rules are also relevant to the management of WIPO's reserves and investments.

---

29 According to Rule 105.3, authorisations from the Controller may take the form of: (i) an allocation of funds or other authorisation issued to a program manager to plan activities and to initiate action to commit, obligate and expend specified funds for specified purposes during a specified period; and (ii) a staffing table authorisation issued jointly to a program manager and the Director of the Human Resources Management Department (HRMD) to enable the Director of HRMD to fill authorised posts based on requests initiated by the program manager.

30 See WIPO, *Annual Financial Report and Financial Statements 2014: prepared by the Secretariat* A/55/7 (WIPO 2015); WIPO, *Review of WIPO's Financial Situation and its Policies Related to Reserves: Document Prepared by the Secretariat* WO/PBC/22/28 (WIPO 2014) 8.

31 This policy was submitted in accordance with Financial Regulation 4.10, and was approved by the 2011 Assemblies. The 2011 Policy is reproduced in WIPO, *Proposal to Amend the Policy on Investments: Document Prepared by the Secretariat* WO/PBC/22/19 (WIPO 2014) Annex 1.

32 In 2015, the Assemblies of the Member States and of the Union, each as far as it is concerned, approved two investment policies (Operating and Core Cash and Strategic Cash) with two amendments proposed by the PBC. For the PBC decision with two proposed amendments, see WIPO, *List of Decisions: Document Prepared by the Secretariat, Program and Budget Committee, Twenty-Fourth Session, 14 to 18 September 2015* WO/PBC/24/17 (WIPO 2015) 5. For the policies, see WIPO, *Revised Policy on Investments: Prepared by the Secretariat, Program and Budget Committee, Twenty-Fourth Session, 14 to 18 September 2015* WO/PBC/24/10 (WIPO 2015). For the final decisions by the Assemblies, see WIPO, *List of Decisions: Document Prepared by the*

The Director General may make short-term investments of money not needed for immediate requirements in accordance with the organisation's investment policy, as approved by the Member States, and must inform the Program and Budget Committee regularly of any such investments (WIPO Financial Regulation 4.10). The Director General may also make long-term investments of monies standing to the credit of the organisation in accordance with the investment policy and must inform the Program and Budget Committee regularly of any such investments (Regulation 4.11). In this regard, the Regulation states that the Director General may seek the advice of an Advisory Committee on Investments composed of members he or she has appointed, including persons outside the organisation having substantial experience in the financial sector.

The size of WIPO's accumulated surplus/reserves (net assets) has generated ongoing debate among Member States on transparency and clarity regarding the use and amount of these reserves, as well as the conditions under which reserves should be used to finance cash-flow shortages or specific projects, and when this can be done without seeking explicit Member State approval.[33] At present, the planning, utilisation and reporting of WIPO reserves are governed by a combination of the WIPO treaties, WIPO reserves polices (created in 2000, then revised in 2010 and in 2015),[34] and IPSAS accounting standards.

Secretariat, Assemblies of the Member States of WIPO, 55th Series of Meetings of the Member States of WIPO, 5–14 October 2015 A/55/INF/11 (WIPO 2015).

33 In 2014, for instance, WIPO Member States agreed to revisit the target level set by the Member States for the organisation's reserves, as well as the future of WIPO's working capital funds (established with the exception of the Lisbon Union's during the infancies of the various Unions). See WIPO, *Review of WIPO's Financial Situation and its Policies Related to Reserves: Document Prepared by the Secretariat* WO/PBC/22/28 (WIPO 2014) 8; WIPO, *Draft Report, 46th Session of the WIPO General Assembly* WO/GA/46/12 Prov. (WIPO 2014); and WIPO. *General Report: Adopted by the Assemblies, 54th Series of Meetings of the Member States of WIPO, 22 to 30 September 2014* A/54/13 (WIPO 2014) 90–93.

34 The Assemblies and the Unions, each as far as it was concerned, approved the current WIPO Policy Related to Reserves (Net Assets) in 2015. See WIPO, *List of Decisions: Document Prepared by the Secretariat*, Assemblies of the Member States of WIPO, 55th Series of Meetings of the Member States of WIPO, 5 to 14 October 2015, A/55/INF/11 (WIPO 2015). For the text of the policy, see WIPO, *Proposal on a Revised WIPO Policy Related to Reserves: Document Prepared by the Secretariat, Annex 1, 23rd Session of the Program and Budget Committee, 13 to 17 July 2015* WO/PBC/23/8 (WIPO 2015) and the PBC decision, which amended one paragraph, in WIPO, *List of Decisions: Prepared by the Secretariat, 23rd Session of the Program and Budget Committee, 5 to 14 October 2015* WO/PBC/23/9 (WIPO 2015) 6. For earlier versions of the policies, see 'Policy on Reserves and Principles Applied in Respect of the Use of the Reserves' in WIPO, *General Report: WIPO Assemblies of Member States, 48th Series of Meetings* A/48/15 (WIPO 2010) and

6.4   Setting and reviewing WIPO's Program and Budget

The development of WIPO's biennial Program and Budget is the key political and management process that establishes the direction, priorities, and resource allocation framework for all WIPO's Programs and their content. Member State engagement in the Program and Budget process is a key component of their oversight role; it follows then that arrangements for Member State involvement in the process are an important component of WIPO's governance. In addition, decisions on WIPO's Program and Budget can also directly impact the organisation's governance system. In 1998, for instance, the approval of the 1998/99 Program and Budget was the vehicle through which Member States agreed to a number of proposals for the simplification and rationalisation of WIPO's governance structure with regard to the committees constituted by the WIPO Assemblies.[35] Decisions on Program and Budget are also important tools for giving practical effect to the mandates that Member States establish for the WIPO committees because they make resources available for their work.

6.4.1   Organisational priorities: the Program and Budget

As called for in Regulation 2.3 of the WIPO Financial Regulations and Rules, the Secretariat prepares a proposed program and budget document that includes estimates for income and expenditure for the financial period in consolidated form for the organisation as a whole, as well as separately for each Union.

The presentation of WIPO's Program and Budget is organised around the achievement of nine Strategic Goals approved by Member States in December 2009 (see Table 6.7).[36] In keeping with the Secretariat's bolstered commitment to results-based management (RBM) in its

---

in WIPO, *General Report: WIPO Assemblies of Member States, 35th Series of Meetings* A/35/15 (WIPO 2000).

35 WIPO, *Draft Program and Budget 1998/99* A/32/2 (WIPO 1998).

36 The Strategic Goals set the framework for WIPO's Strategic Realignment Program, undertaken by the Secretariat between 2010–12, which aimed to 'make WIPO a responsive, efficient organisation equipped to achieve its Strategic Goals and to provide global leadership on IP issues.' The Strategic Goals are listed in WIPO, *Medium Term Strategic Plan for WIPO, 2010–15* A/48/3 (WIPO 2010), which was developed through interactive consultations between the Secretariat and Member States. Also see WIPO, *WIPO Strategic Realignment Program Roadmap* (WIPO 2011); WIPO, *Taking the Initiative: WIPO Strategic Realignment Program* (WIPO 2012). Both documents are available at: <http://www.wipo.int/about-wipo/en/strategic_realignment/> accessed 1 September 2014.

Table 6.7 WIPO's Strategic Goals

1	Balanced Evolution of the International Normative Framework for IP
2	Provision of Premier Global IP Services
3	Facilitating the Use of IP for Development
4	Coordination and Development of Global IP Infrastructure
5	World Reference Source for IP Information and Analysis
6	International Cooperation on Building Respect for IP
7	Addressing IP in Relation to Global Policy Issues
8	A Responsive Communications Interface between WIPO, its Member States and All Stakeholders
9	An Efficient Administrative and Financial Support Structure to Enable WIPO to Deliver its Programs

Source: WIPO, *Medium Term Strategic Plan for WIPO, 2010–2015* A/48/3 (WIPO 2010).

2009–12 Strategic Realignment Program, the Program and Budget identifies objectives, expected results, and performance measures related to the achievement of these Strategic Goals. The Program and Budget has also been informed by the Secretariat's *Medium Term Strategic Plan for WIPO, 2010–15* (MTSP).[37] The development of the MTSP followed a 2006 Member State decision in favour of a new mechanism to increase the involvement of Member States in the preparation and follow-up of the program and budget; it aimed to provide a high-level strategic framework to guide the preparation of budget documents in 2012/13 and 2014/15. As of the end 2015, the Secretariat had not drafted a follow up MTSP, nor had the prospect been formally discussed with Member States, many of which had contested the earlier process and outcome.

Following a general overview of the organisation's proposed goals, expected results, income and expenditures for the biennium, the core of the program and budget document is divided into separate sections for each WIPO Program. Each of these sections presents a narrative that sets out the content of the Program as well as objectives and expected results during the biennium. They also include tables that summarise the financial and human resources required to achieve the objectives and expected results as well as benchmarks and indicators of achievement, and a table documenting any extra-budgetary resources available to the Program. A number of annexes are included in the

---

37 WIPO, *Medium Term Strategic Plan for WIPO, 2010–15* A/48/3 (WIPO 2010).

Program and Budget document to offer more detailed information, such as on the organisation's finances.[38]

The 2016/17 Program and Budget illustrates how greatly WIPO's workload has grown over the past forty years (such as through the increasing use of its global protection system treaties) as well as the diversification of the organisation's functions and activities in development cooperation, dispute resolution, research and on IP policy issues (as presented in Chapter 2).[39] For an overview of WIPO's Program and Budget from 2010/11 to 2016/17, see Table 2.3 in Chapter 2, which also presents the share of resources by Program that the Secretariat estimates that it devotes to development activities.

From a budgetary standpoint, most of WIPO's activities are part of its regular Budget. The exceptions are activities financed through extra-budgetary sources, such as voluntary contributions to Funds-in-Trust (FITs) for development cooperation for the planning and use of FITs (see section 6.4.4).

6.4.2   The Program and Budget process

The World Intellectual Property Organization's Program and Budget is discussed, revised and approved by the PBC and then the General Assembly on a biennial basis. The preparation of WIPO's Program and Budget is guided by the WIPO Financial Regulations and Rules (see Chapter 2 of the FFR) and by a Program and Budget Mechanism, which Member States approved in 2006. The Mechanism includes several elements, namely that the Director General must submit the draft program and budget to the PBC for discussion, comments, amendment and recommendation by 1 July of the year preceding the financial

---

38 In accordance with Rule 102.2, the proposed program and budget contains: (i) A statement of financial and human resources requirements by proposed program and by nature of expenditure in a consolidated form for the organisation, as well as separately for each Union; for purposes of comparison, the expenditures for the previous financial period, the adopted initial budget and the proposed revised budget for the current financial period indicated alongside the resource requirements estimates for the forthcoming financial period; (ii) A statement of estimated income including income from contributions, fees for services rendered under the PCT, Madrid, Hague and Lisbon systems and income classified as miscellaneous in accordance with Regulation 3.13; (iii) A statement of estimated demand for services under the PCT, Madrid, Hague and Lisbon systems, respectively; and (iv) A detailed organigram of the International Bureau including names of directors and program managers.

39 See WIPO, *WIPO Intellectual Property Handbook: Policy, Law and Use* (WIPO 2004) 5.

period,[40] as well as a process and timeline for the preparation and follow-up of the Program and Budget (Figure 6.4 provides an overview of the process from 2008/09 onward).[41]

In practice, the development of WIPO's Program and Budget occurs through an iterative process – each WIPO Program proposes to the Director General a workplan and corresponding budget based a combination of the following: recommendations of relevant Member State committees; activities and initiatives proposed by Program managers; needs expressed by Member States; and feedback from the Secretariat's senior management. The Secretariat then presents a draft program and budget to the PBC for discussion, comments and recommendations, including possible amendments, which is discussed both informally and formally. After review, the PBC then transmits the proposed program and budget, along with its recommendations, to the Assemblies of the Member States. The document and the PBC recommendations are then forwarded for Member State consideration and adoption at the annual Assemblies of WIPO Member States.

At the Assemblies, the adoption of the Program and Budget requires action from all of the Assemblies of Member States and Unions, and is thus an agenda item for all such bodies. On this point, Regulation 2.8 of the Financial Regulations and Rules specifies that the Assemblies of the Member States and of the Unions as, 'each as far as it is concerned,' adopts the Program and Budget for the following financial period. For such agenda items common to a number of governing bodies, WIPO's General Rules of Procedure call for joint meetings of the relevant bodies, such as routinely occurs in the 'consolidated agenda' for the annual Assemblies (see section 5.3). As such, the General Assembly does indeed make a decision to adopt the Program and Budget, but the other Assemblies also simultaneously adopt it in a joint session, resulting in what is usually reported as a unanimous decision of all of the Assemblies of Member States and of the Unions

---

40 This was achieved through a revision of WIPO's Financial Regulations, which had previously called for the submission of only the budget for observations and possible recommendations. See WIPO, *Report on, and Recommendations Adopted by, the Ninth and Tenth Sessions of the Program and Budget Committee* A/42/9 (WIPO 2006) 3. These two mechanisms were set out in Annex III and Annex IV respectively of WIPO, *Proposals on a New Mechanism to Further Involve Member States in the Preparation and Follow Up of the Program and Budget: Document Prepared by the Secretariat* WO/PBC/10/5 (WIPO 2006).

41 See WIPO, *Report on, and Recommendations Adopted by, the Ninth and Tenth Sessions of the Program and Budget Committee* A/42/9 (WIPO 2006) Annex II, para. 25.

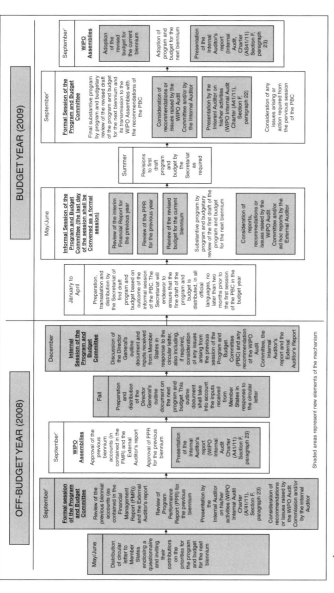

Source: WIPO, *Report on, and Recommendations Adopted by, the Ninth and Tenth Sessions of the Program and Budget Committee* A/42/9 (WIPO 2006) Appendix 4, entitled 'Preparation and Follow Up of Program and Budget – Full Implementation of the New Mechanism From the Next Biennium (2008/09) Onwards.'

Figure 6.4   WIPO Program and Budget Mechanism (in use since 2008/2009)

administered by it.[42] As the Program and Budget requires adoption by the Member States of WIPO and all of the Unions, the plenary session that adopts the Program and Budget has in practice been the Conference not the General Assembly (recalling that the Conference includes all members of WIPO, including those that are not members of Unions, whereas the slightly smaller Assembly includes only those States that are party to both the WIPO Convention and any of the treaties that establish a Union). The quorum for the Conference is one third of the membership, the quorum for the General Assembly is one half (see section 5.5.3). Although the membership is in session as the WIPO Conference, not the General Assembly, the Chair of the General Assembly (not the Chair of the Conference) presides in accordance with the WIPO General Rules of Procedure. Rule 42(2)(i) states that in the case of joint meetings, the presiding Chair will be the Chair of the body that has precedence over the others, with the highest being the General Assembly, followed by the Conference, and then the Coordination Committee.

If the Program and Budget is not adopted before the beginning of the following financial period, Regulation 2.8 further states that: 'the authorization to the Director General to incur obligations and make payments remains at the level of appropriations of the previous financial period.' In several instances, an extraordinary meeting of the relevant Assemblies has been convened to adopt the Program and Budget when consensus was not reached at the annual Assemblies (this occurred most recently in December 2013 with regard to the 2014/15 Program and Budget).

If necessary, the Director General may submit supplementary and revised program and budget proposals. As noted above, the Director General may take some budgetary action without making such proposals, such as transfers among Programs within the limits set in Regulation 5.5 of the Financial Regulations and Rules, as well as flexibility adjustments made in accordance with Regulation 5.6 (see section 6.2). For purposes of disclosure to Member States, however, all such transfers and/or adjustments must be be reflected in supplementary and/or revised program and budget proposals, if and when the Director General submits these proposals (Regulation 2.9). According to Regulation 2.10, supplementary and revised budget proposals are

---

42 WIPO, *General Report: adopted by the Assemblies* A/51/20 (Geneva: WIPO 2013) 108–11.

to reflect changes in the financial and human resources requirements, such as, for example, those associated with activities which the Director General considers to be of the highest urgency and which could not have been foreseen at the time the initial program and budget proposals were prepared. Further, according to Regulation 2.13, the General Assembly and the Assemblies of the Unions, each as far as it is concerned, may 'adopt a decision to authorize the Director General to incur unforeseen and extraordinary expenses which cannot be met from existing appropriations up to such amounts and subject to such limits as included in the authorizing decision.'

6.4.3   Program and Budget reporting requirements

Reporting requirements are an integral part of WIPO's governance system and the Secretariat's management activities. On an annual basis, the Secretariat presents Program Performance Reports to WIPO Member States, which are supplemented by Validation Reports compiled by WIPO's Internal Oversight Division. According to Regulation 2.13 of the FFR, the Program and Performance Report should be based on the program structure, results frameworks, benchmarks and performance indicators contained in the Program and Budget.

As noted above, other reporting activities on the part of the Secretariat include annual financial statements for Member States as well as 2-yearly financial management reports. In addition, WIPO has an online 'Observatory', which is a Member State-only facility that enables governments to review the organisation's financial activities on an ongoing basis.

The WIPO Financial Regulations and Rules call on the Director General to establish a system for planning, conducting and using evaluative information for decision-making (see Regulation 2.15).

6.4.4   Extra-budgetary contributions, gifts and donations in the Program and Budget process

The WIPO Financial Regulations and Rules provide that the Director General may accept voluntary contributions, gifts and donations to the organisation, whether or not in cash, provided that: a) the purposes for which the contributions are made are consistent with the policies, aims and activities of the organisation; and b) the acceptance of contributions that directly or indirectly involve significant additional financial liability for the organisation obtain the consent of the General Assembly (Regulation 3.11). Rule 103.1(b) further specifies that if voluntary contributions, gifts or donations directly or indirectly involve additional financial liability for the organisation, these may be accepted only with the approval of the General Assembly (Rule 103.1(b)).

Voluntary contributions, gifts and donations in cash are accounted for in special accounts, which are commonly referred to as 'Funds-in-Trust' (FITs), for the purposes specified by the donor (see Regulation 3.12). The financial management, accounting and reporting of FITs are subject to WIPO's Financial Regulations and Rules. However, individual donors may also request specific financial accounting and reporting arrangements in the MOU establishing the FIT. The Secretariat and donor bilaterally establish the consultation mechanisms set out in each FIT agreement, and in turn determine arrangements for planning, monitoring, financial reporting and review of FIT activities.

In principle, FIT-financed activities are supposed to be guided by WIPO's Strategic Goals and also by the priorities and results-based management (RBM) framework established in its Program and Budget. Activities financed through Funds-in-Trust are now incorporated into the description of Programs in WIPO's Program and Budget documents, and the extra-budgetary resources available to each Program are provided in a table at the end of each Program description. In addition, a summary table of FITs resources potentially available for programming is presented in an Annex to the Program and Budget document. However, WIPO does not have a specific policy or framework to guide priority setting, allocation and use of FITs and other voluntary contributions, or on matters such as conflicts of interest that may arise in regard to FITs. As noted above, the specific workplans and budget for activities financed by FITs are decided bilaterally between the Secretariat and the donor, and neither reports nor evaluations of these activities are routinely made available to Member States or the public.

To date, WIPO's extra-budgetary donations have largely been from developed country Member States (most prominently Japan followed by France and Italy, as well as Australia, Finland, Portugal and Spain), for the purpose of technical assistance and capacity building activities in third countries. There have also been significant contributions from emerging countries such as Korea, as well as some IGOs and more recently from countries such as Brazil and Mexico, among others. The first Japanese FIT was established in 1987, for instance, and the scale and scope of its activities has expanded since that time, with a total contribution over the period from 1987 to 2015 amounting to over 45 million Swiss Francs.[43] Some countries also maintain national Funds-in-Trust, whereby governments have set aside resources for WIPO activities in their own country, which are noted in an Annex to WIPO's Annual Financial Management Report and Financial Statements.

6.5   The unitary presentation of WIPO's budget

In the WIPO Program and Budget process, the WIPO Secretariat prepares a unitary presentation of the budget of the organisation as a whole, and all of the Unions, both Contribution-financed and fee-financed.[44] The origin of this unitary presentation of the budget was the 1993 General Assembly decision, noted above, in favour of a Unitary Contribution System for the Contribution-financed Unions, which created a unified budget for those Unions.[45] In 2003, WIPO Member States agreed to amend the WIPO Convention and all WIPO treaties to formalise this practice, which had already been in effect since 1994. To aid in the implementation of the Unitary Contribution System, the WIPO Assemblies also agreed as part of their 2003 amendments to delete a provision referring to a 'separate budget' for 'the expenses common to the Unions, and the budget of the Conference,' replacing it with this text: 'the income and expenses of the Union[s]

---

43 Author's calculations based on review of Annexes on FITs in consecutive Program and Budget reports. On Japan's FITs, see WIPO, *The First Twenty Years of the Japan Funds-in-Trust for Industrial Property at WIPO (1987–2007)* (WIPO 2009) 3 (which estimated a contribution of over 25 million Swiss Francs from 1987 to 2007); and WIPO, 'Japan Funds-in-Trust for Industrial Property: Africa & LDCS' <http://www.wipo.int/cooperation/en/funds_in_trust/japan_fitip/> accessed 31 October 2015.

44 This description draws on explanations provided by the Secretariat during the Assembly of the PCT Union on 6 October 2015. See PCT Union, *Draft Report: Prepared by the International Bureau, International Patent Cooperation Union (PCT Union) Assembly, Forty-Seventh Session, 5 to 14 October 2015* WIPO, PCT/A/48/9 Prov. (WIPO 2015) and Catherine Saez, 'At WIPO, A Singular Explanation of a "Non-Unitary" Budget' *Intellectual Property Watch*, 8 October 2015.

45 The Secretariat observes in Note 16.03 on changes to Article 16 of the Paris Convention to implement the 2003 amendments: 'Since the introduction of the unitary contribution system, the budget of the Paris Union is part of the budget of the contribution-financed Unions in the Program and Budget of the organisation and the Unions administered by WIPO.' See WIPO, *Final Texts of Proposed Amendments to the Paris Convention and Other WIPO-Administered Treaties, 39th Assemblies of the Member States of WIPO, 22 September to 1 October 2003* A/39/3 (WIPO 2003) 8.

shall be reflected in the budget of the organisation in a fair and transparent manner.'[46] Although the amendments are not yet in force, in keeping with that decision,[47] the WIPO Secretariat prepares 'a unitary presentation' of the budget of the organisation and all of the Unions administered by WIPO (with both the Contribution-financed and fee-financed Unions' budgets included) within a single document. This 'unitary presentation' is the overarching version of the budget referred to throughout the Program and Budget report: a unitary presentation of the budget is provided both by reference to Program (see Table 2.3) and also by reference to the Strategic Goals and expected results in WIPO's results framework.[48] In addition, the Secretariat provides a separate presentation of the unified budget of the Contribution-financed Unions and of each of the fee-financed Unions, as well as a view of how the Union income is allocated by Program (discussed in section 6.6).

6.6   Financial arrangements for the Unions and allocation of their income

The financial arrangements for WIPO's Contribution-financed Unions and its fee-financed Unions differ. As noted above, following the 1993 decision on the Unitary Contribution System, the Contribution-financed Unions have a unified budget. However, as required by their

---

46 In 2003, the Secretariat explained that: 'Article 11(1) proposes a new enabling provision for the budget consequent upon the adoption of the unitary contribution system. The proposed provision seeks to implement the desire expressed by many delegations in the Working Group on Constitutional Reform that, while the organisation has a unitary contribution system, it should not have a unitary budget in the sense that all income and expenses, regardless of their source or purpose, are mixed without identification. Accordingly, Article 11(1) would require that the budget of the organisation be presented so that the income and expenses of the organisation and of the various Unions be indicated 'in a fair and transparent manner.' See WIPO, *Final Texts of Proposed Amendments to the Convention Establishing the World Intellectual Property Organization: Document Prepared by the Secretariat, 39th Assemblies of the Member States of WIPO, 22 September to 1 October 2003* A/39/2 (WIPO 2003) 24.

47 The practice of the Unitary Contribution System follows a Member State decision, but is not a treaty requirement. Although 15 WIPO Member States had formally accepted the proposed amendments to the WIPO Convention as of October 2015, these amendments will only enter into force 1 month after the Director General has received written notifications of acceptance from three-fourths of the Member States of WIPO. See WIPO, *Options for the Financial Sustainability of the Lisbon Union: Document Prepared by the Secretariat, Program and Budget Committee, Twenty-Fourth Session, Geneva, 14 to 18 September 2015* WO/PBC/24/16 (WIPO 2015), para. 14.

48 See WIPO, *Proposed Program and Budget for the 2016/17 Biennium* A55/5 Rev. (WIPO 2015) 11–12.

respective treaties, each of the fee-financed Unions (Hague, Lisbon, Madrid and PCT) has a separate budget.

The finances of the fee-funded Unions are governed by their respective agreements. Each of these treaties has similar provisions requiring fees and if receipts from other sources (such as fees, publications, gifts, rents and interest) do not suffice to cover the expenses of the Unions, contributions from their respective members. Each treaty also provides for the possibility of a working capital fund for the Unions (see section 6.2 on custody of funds), as well as for advances by the Host State (in other words, the country in which the Union is administered, namely Switzerland) whenever the working capital is insufficient.[49] The growing income of the PCT Union and Madrid Union has enabled each to generate considerable reserves that are kept in separate reserves accounts, as is the case for the Hague Union. In 2015, Member States decided to split the work of the Lisbon and Madrid Unions into two separate Programs meaning that from the 2016/17 biennium onward all of the four fee-financed Unions has separate Programs and associated budgets in the WIPO Program and Budget.[50]

---

49 Prior to the 2016/17 biennium, the Madrid and Lisbon Systems were presented in WIPO's Program and Budget together as Program 6, with a single budget. In the 2016/17 biennium, however, they were split into two separate programs, which are also reflected in relevant budget tables and annexes.

50 In 1993, the WIPO Secretariat stated that: 'while a unitary contribution system, and in consequence, a unitary budget has been introduced in practice for the contribution-financed Unions, separate budgets are still maintained for the PCT Union, the Madrid Union and the Hague Union.' See WIPO, *Constitutional Reform: Memorandum of the Secretariat, Assemblies of the Member States of WIPO, Thirty-Fourth Series of Meetings, 20 to 29 September 1999* A/34/9 (WIPO 1999) para. 58 (iii). For instance, PCT Article 57(1) reads: '(a) The Union shall have a budget; (b) The budget of the Union shall include the income and expenses proper to the Union and its contribution to the budget of expenses common to the Unions administered by the organisation; and (c) Expenses not attributable exclusively to the Union but also to one or more other Unions administered by the organisation shall be considered as expenses common to the Unions. The share of the Union in such common expenses shall be in proportion to the interest the Union has in them.' Similarly, Article 12(1) of the Madrid Agreement (incorporated by reference in Article 12 of the Madrid Protocol) reads: '(a) The Special Union shall have a budget; (b) The budget of the Special Union shall include the income and expenses proper to the Special Union, its contribution to the budget of expenses common to the Unions, and, where applicable, the sum made available to the budget of the Conference of the organisation; and (c) Expenses not attributable exclusively to the Special Union but also to one or more other Unions administered by the organisation shall be considered as expenses common to the Unions. The share of the Special Union in such common expenses shall be in proportion to the interest the Special Union has in them.'

6.6.1 Allocation of income and budgeted expenditure by Union

Any income generated by the Unions (through fees or Member State contributions) flows into custody accounts for that Union (see Regulation 4.1 of the WIPO Financial Regulations and Rules, discussed in section 6.2). Contributions' income is allocated entirely to the Contribution-financed Unions.[51] Fee income from the PCT, Madrid, Hague and Lisbon registration systems is allocated entirely to the respective Unions. Income from publications is allocated to the Contribution-financed, PCT, Madrid, Lisbon and Hague Unions on the basis of the estimated publications revenue for each of the Unions. Income from the Arbitration and Mediation Center is allocated to all Unions based on the assessment of the relative share by Unions. Other income is allocated to all Unions as follows: (i) a share is directly attributable to the Madrid Union on the account of rental income from the Madrid Union building; and (ii) the remaining share is allocated equally across all Unions.

In addition to the unitary presentation of the budget by reference to WIPO Programs (see Table 2.3) and also by reference to expected results, the biennial budget for the organisation is also presented separately for each Union in an Annex to the Program and Budget (in accordance with Rule 102.3 of the WIPO Financial Regulations and Rules). This 'union view' presentation includes an overview of how the Union income is allocated by Program, as well as an overall scenario by Union[52] (see Table 6.8). The authority for allocations of Union income derives from the Member States' approval of the Program and Budget. At present, the methodology for the allocation of the expenditure by Unions among WIPO's various Programs is based on the identification of Union direct and Union indirect expenses.[53] Union direct expenses are the expenses incurred under Union-specific Program activities[54]

---

51 This paragraph draws directly from Annex III of WIPO, *Proposed Program and Budget for the 2016/17 Biennium* A55/5 Rev. (WIPO 2015) 186, para. 5.

52 See, for instance, Table 11 '2016/17 Overall Scenario by Union' in WIPO, *Proposed Program and Budget for the 2016/17 Biennium* A55/5 Rev. (WIPO 2015) 187.

53 For a fuller explanation of 'Union direct' and 'Union indirect' expenses, see WIPO, *Proposed Program and Budget for the 2016/17 Biennium* A55/5 Rev. (WIPO 2015) 185–6, paras 3–4.

54 The Union direct expenses for the Contribution-financed Unions are considered to arise, for instance, in relation to budgeted expenditures for Programs 1 (Patent Law) (partly), 2 (Trademarks, Industrial Designs and Geographical Indications) (partly), 3 (Copyright and Related Rights) (partly), 4 (Traditional Knowledge, Traditional Cultural Expressions and Genetic Resources), 7 (WIPO Arbitration and Mediation Center) (partly), 12 (International Classifications and Standards)

and budgeted expenditures, as well as the attributable share of related administrative and other budgeted expenses.[55] Union indirect expenses are each Union's allocated share of budgeted expenses for Programs not directly related to the activities of the respective Union,[56] together with the share of related administrative and other budgeted expenses.[57]

(partly) and 14 (Services for Access to Information and Knowledge) (partly). The Programs for which the PCT Union is considered to have direct expenses are Programs 1 (Patent Law) (partly), 5 (The PCT System), 7 (WIPO Arbitration and Mediation Center) (partly), 12 (International Classifications and Standards) (partly), 13 (Global Databases) (partly) and 14 (Services for Access to Information and Knowledge) (partly). For the Madrid Union, the Programs are Programs 2 (Trademarks, Industrial Designs and Geographical Indications) (partly), 6 (Madrid System) (partly), 7 (WIPO Arbitration and Mediation Center) (partly), 12 (International Classifications and Standards) (partly), 13 (Global Databases) (partly) and 14 (Services for Access to Information and Knowledge) (partly). For the Hague Union, Union direct expenses relate to Programs 2 (Trademarks, Industrial Designs and Geographical Indications) (partly), 6 (Madrid System) (partly), 7 (WIPO Arbitration and Mediation Center) (partly), 12 (International Classifications and Standards) (partly) and 14 (Services for Access to Information and Knowledge) (partly) and 31 (The Hague System). Finally, the Lisbon Union's direct expenses arise in Programs 6 (Madrid System) (partly), 7 (WIPO Arbitration and Mediation Center) (partly), 14 (Services for Access to Information and Knowledge) (partly) and 32 (Lisbon System). Where expenditures of a Program are only partly allocated to a Union, the basis for allocation is the respective Union's share of this expense as estimated by the program managers of the respective Programs. Where the allocation of a Program is to a single Union, the full cost of that Program is allocated to that Union.

55 The Union direct administrative expenses include a share of all Programs under Strategic Goal IX (Efficient Administrative and Financial Support, which involves Programs 21 to 28) and 'Unallocated.' The Secretariat states that: 'The allocation of budgeted expenditures is determined in a two-step process. In the first step, the total share of direct administrative costs for all Unions is determined on the basis of the total headcount of the direct union-related Programs relative to the total headcount of all Programs other than those under Strategic Goal IX. As a second step, this Union Direct administrative expense is allocated to the respective Unions on the basis of the relative share of each Union's headcount to the total headcount of direct union-related Programs. The two-step process applies to that part of administrative expenditure which is not easily identifiable as linked to a specific union.' See Annex III of WIPO, *Proposed Program and Budget for the 2016/17 Biennium* A55/5 Rev. (WIPO 2015) 186.

56 The following Program activities and budgeted expenditures are considered part of the indirect expenses of the Unions: Programs 1 (Patent Law) (partly), 3 (Copyright and Related Rights) (partly), 8 (Development Agenda Coordination), 9 (Africa, Arab, Asia and the Pacific, Latin America and the Caribbean Countries, Least Developed Countries), 10 (Transition and Developed Countries), 11 (The WIPO Academy), 15 (Business Solutions for IP Offices), 16 (Economics and Statistics), 17 (Building Respect for IP), 18 (IP and Global Challenges), 19 (Communications), 20 (External Relations, Partnerships and External Offices) and 30 (SMEs and Entrepreneurship Support). The share of budgeted expenditures from each of these is allocated to Unions on the basis of their respective biennial capacity to pay.

57 The Union indirect administrative expenses relate to budgeted expenditures under Programs 21 to 28 that have not been allocated to direct Union expenses, as well as the amount budgeted under 'Unallocated' in the proposed budget. The allocation of these budgeted expenditures to the Unions is also done on the basis of their respective capacity to pay (in other words, along the same principles as for indirect Union expenses).

Table 6.8 WIPO's 2016/2017 Budget by Program and Union (in thousands of Swiss Francs)

	Contribution-financed Unions			PCT Union			Madrid Union	
	Amount	% of Prog	% of Union	Amount	% of Prog	% of Union	Amount	% of Prog
1 Patent Law	386	7.3	1.1	4754	89.8	0.9	152	2.9
2 Trademarks, Industrial Designs and Geographical Indications	971	20.0	2.8	–	–	–	3155	65.0
3 Copyright and Related Rights	13299	79.5	38.2	3129	18.7	0.6	305	1.8
4 Traditional knowledge, Traditional Cultural Expressions and Genetic Resources	6115	100.0	17.6	–	–	–	–	–
5 The PCT System	–	–	–	208209	100.0	39.3	–	–
6 Madrid System	–	–	–	–	–	–	57904	99.7
7 WPO Arbitration and Mediation Center	591	5.2	1.7	7201	63.4	1.4	3408	30.0
8 Development Agenda Coordination	65	1.8	0.2	3286	89.5	0.6	321	8.7
9 Africa, Arab, Asia and the pacific Latin America and the Caribbean Countries, Least Developed Countries	564	1.8	1.6	28555	89.5	5.4	2787	8.7
10 Transition and Developed Countries	140	1.8	0.4	7087	89.5	1.3	692	8.7
11 The WIPO Academy	231	1.8	0.7	11708	89.5	2.2	1143	8.7
12 International Classifications and Standards	495	7.0	1.4	6222	88.0	1.2	283	4.0
13 Global Databases	–	–	–	5182	90.0	1.0	576	10.0

	Hague Union			Lisbon Union			Total		
% of Union	Amount	% of Prog	% of Union	Amount	% of Prog	% of Union	Amount	% of Prog	% of Union
0.1	–	–	–	–	–	–	5 291	100.0	0.7
2.5	728	15.0	5.1	–	–	–	4 854	100.0	0.7
0.2	–	–	–	–	–	–	16 733	100.0	2.4
–	–	–	–	–	–	–	6 115	100.0	0.9
–	–	–	–	–	–	–	208 209	100.0	29.4
45.9	190	0.3	1.3	12	0.0	0.6	58 106	100.0	8.2
2.7	136	1.2	0.9	23	0.2	1.0	11 358	100.0	1.6
0.3	–	–	–	–	–	–	3 671	100.0	0.5
2.2	–	–	–	–	–	–	31 907	100.0	4.5
0.5	–	–	–	–	–	–	7 919	100.0	1.1
0.9	–	–	–	–	–	–	13 083	100.0	1.9
0.2	71	1.0	0.5	–	–	–	7 070	100.0	1.0
0.5	–	–	–	–	–	–	5 758	100.0	0.8

	Contribution-financed Unions			PCT Union			Madrid Union	
	Amount	% of Prog	% of Union	Amount	% of Prog	% of Union	Amount	% of Prog
14 Services for Access to Information and Knowledge	94	1.3	0.3	5537	79.2	1.0	1251	17.9
15 Business Solutions for IP Offices	244	1.8	0.7	12356	89.5	2.3	1206	8.7
16 Economics and Statistics	107	1.8	0.3	5434	89.5	1.0	530	8.7
17 Building Respect for IP	66	1.8	0.2	3358	89.5	0.6	328	8.7
18 IP and Global Challenges	112	1.8	0.3	5659	89.5	1.1	552	8.7
19 Communications	292	1.8	0.8	14751	89.5	2.8	1440	8.7
20 External Relations, Partnerships and External Offices	219	1.8	0.6	11093	89.5	2.1	1083	8.7
21 Executive Management	941	4.6	2.7	15327	74.1	2.9	3878	18.8
22 Program and Resource Management	1356	4.1	3.9	22786	68.5	4.3	8025	24.1
23 Human Resources Management and Development	1120	4.6	3.2	18250	74.1	3.4	4617	18.8
24 General Support Services	2149	4.6	6.2	35004	74.1	6.6	8855	18.8
25 Information and Communication Technology	2054	3.9	5.9	38477	73.9	7.3	10346	19.9
26 Internal Oversight	244	4.6	0.7	3972	74.1	0.8	1005	18.8
27 Conference and Language Services	1771	4.6	5.1	28857	74.1	5.5	7300	18.8
28 Information Assurance, Safety and Security	807	4.6	2.3	13146	74.1	2.5	3,326	18.8

% of Union	Hague Union			Lisbon Union			Total		
	Amount	% of Prog	% of Union	Amount	% of Prog	% of Union	Amount	% of Prog	% of Union
1.0	106	1.5	0.7	2	0.0	0.1	6990	100.0	1.0
1.0	–	–	–	–	–	–	13806	100.0	2.0
0.4	–	–	–	–	–	–	6072	100.0	0.9
0.3	–	–	–	–	–	–	3752	100.0	0.5
0.4	–	–	–	–	–	–	6323	100.0	0.9
1.1	–	–	–	–	–	–	16483	100.0	2.3
0.9	–	–	–	–	–	–	12395	100.0	1.8
3.1	458	2.2	3.2	71	0.3	3.3	20675	100.0	2.9
6.4	1006	3.0	7.0	103	0.3	4.7	33276	100.0	4.7
3.7	545	2.2	3.8	85	0.3	3.9	24617	100.0	3.5
7.0	1045	2.2	7.3	163	0.3	7.5	47216	100.0	6.7
8.2	999	1.9	7.0	156	0.3	7.1	52032	100.0	7.4
0.8	119	2.2	0.8	19	0.3	0.8	5358	100.0	0.8
5.8	862	2.2	6.0	135	0.3	6.2	38925	100.0	5.5
2.6	393	2.2	2.7	61	0.3	2.8	17733	100.0	2.5

	Contribution-financed Unions			PCT Union			Madrid Union	
	Amount	% of Prog	% of Union	Amount	% of Prog	% of Union	Amount	% of Prog
30 SMEs and Entrepreneurship Support	108	1.8	0.3	5 444	89.5	1.0	531	8.7
31 The Hague System	–	–	–	–	–	–	–	–
32 Lisbon System	–	–	–	–	–	–	–	–
Unallocated	288	4.6	0.8	4 685	74.1	0.9	1 185	18.8
TOTAL	**34 829**	**4.9**	**100.0**	**529 469**	**74.9**	**100.0**	**126 184**	**17.8**

Note: The totals are provided by WIPO and reflect rounding of numbers.

Source: WIPO, *Proposed Program and Budget for the 2016/17 Biennium* A/55/5 Rev. (WIPO 2015) 188.

For these allocations by Program and Union for the 2016/17 biennium, see Table 6.8.

In 2014 and 2015, questions arose in the Program and Budget Committee and at the Assemblies on the methodology used to allocate income and expenditure by the Unions across WIPO's budget,[58] resulting in a request by the General Assembly for a Secretariat study on potential alternative allocation methodologies for consideration by Member States.[59] The revived interest in the methodology emerged from debates on the financing of the Lisbon Union's operations, which have long been subsidised because the Union has not generated adequate income from fees to cover its expenses.[60] Specifically, some WIPO Member States that are not members of the Lisbon Union opposed the use of WIPO's general resources, and income from the

---

58 WIPO, *List of Decisions: Document Prepared by the Secretariat, Program and Budget Committee, Twenty-Fourth Session, 14 to 18 September 2015* WO/PBC/24/17 (WIPO 2015) 4.

59 WIPO, *List of Decisions: Document Prepared by the Secretariat, Assemblies of the Member States of WIPO, 55th Series of Meetings of the Member States of WIPO, 5 to 14 October 2015* A/55/INF/11 (WIPO 2015) 9.

60 In 2012/13, the Lisbon Union's income was composed of Lisbon fee income, a share of income from the WIPO Arbitration and Mediation Centre and a share of 'other income.' The vast majority of the Lisbon Union's income was from this latter category, and mostly derived from rental income from various WIPO buildings. See WIPO, *Q & A: Proposed Program and Budget 2016/17 (and Other PBC Documents): Document Prepared by the Secretariat, Program and Budget Committee, Twenty-Fourth Session, 14 to 18 September 2015* 9 (WIPO 2015) 39.

	Hague Union			Lisbon Union			Total		
% of Union	Amount	% of Prog	% of Union	Amount	% of Prog	% of Union	Amount	% of Prog	% of Union
0.4	–	–	–	–	–	–	6 083	100.0	0.9
–	7 572	100.0	52.7	–	–	–	7 572	100.0	1.1
–	–	–	–	1 335	100.0	61.0	1 335	100.0	0.2
0.9	140	2.2	1.0	22	0.3	1.0	6 319	100.0	0.9
100.0	14 368	2.0	100.0	2 187	0.3	100.0	707 036	100.0	100.0

PCT in particular, to subsidise the activities of the Lisbon Union.[61] Further, the United States, along with several other WIPO members, specifically objected to the use of such resources to support the hosting of a Diplomatic Conference for the new 'Geneva Act' of the Lisbon Agreement, not only because they opposed the new Act (as discussed in section 5.3.4) but also because the Lisbon Union Assembly would not accommodate their request that Lisbon non-members be given an equal voting role in the Diplomatic Conference, rather than just observer status.[62]

To underscore its point, the United States made a proposal to the 2015 PCT Assembly calling for a decision by the PCT Union Assembly that its fee income and reserves shall not be used to fund the Lisbon Union's direct or indirect expenses, absent specific authorisation from the PCT Union to do so.[63] The United States made a similar proposal

---

61 The US argued, for instance, that the 'WIPO practice of allocating indirect expenses (common expenses) according to a union's "ability to pay" means that underperforming unions are not held responsible for their indirect expenses and the successful unions such as the PCT and Madrid Unions are forced to pay an increased amount of all of the unions' indirect expenses.' See WIPO, *Understanding of the United States on the Unitary Contribution System and the Unitary Budget as they Relate to the Lisbon Agreement: Document Prepared by the Secretariat* A/55/INF/10 (WIPO 2015).

62 WIPO, *Report: 17th Session of the Coordination Committee, 22 to 30 September 2014* WO/CC/70/5 (WIPO 2014) paras 42–65.

63 For the US proposal, see PCT Union, *Matters Concerning the Lisbon Union: Proposal of the United States of America to the Patent Cooperation Treaty Assembly* PCT/A/47/8 (WIPO 2015).

to the Assembly of the Madrid Union in regard to the use of its fee income and reserves.[64] In both instances no consensus was reached on the topic, with many Member States voicing concerns that the US proposals would risk unravelling the unified approach to WIPO's Program and Budget.[65] Ultimately, the Lisbon Union Assembly undertook at the Assemblies to eliminate its projected biennial deficit and to raise fees in an effort to boost its financial sustainability. The General Assembly decided that, if these measures were not sufficient to eliminate its projected budget deficit, a loan would be extended from the reserves of the Contribution-financed Unions (but not the PCT or Madrid Unions).[66]

---

64 For the US proposal, see Madrid Union, *Matters Concerning the Madrid and Lisbon Unions: Proposal of the United States of America to the Madrid Assembly* MM/A/49/4 (WIPO 2015). In its proposal to the Madrid Assembly, the United States also proposed that any excess revenue from the Madrid Union be returned to the contracting parties of the applicable agreement.

65 For a summary of the discussion in each Assembly, see PCT Union, *Draft Report: Prepared by the International Bureau, International Patent Cooperation Union (PCT Union) Assembly, 47th Session, 5 to 14 October 2015* WIPO, PCT/A/48/9 Prov. (WIPO 2015), and Madrid Union, *Draft Report: Prepared by the International Bureau, 49th Session of the Assembly of the Special Union for the International Registration of Marks (Madrid Union), 5 to 14 October 2015* MM/A/49/5 Prov. (WIPO 2015).

66 WIPO, *List of Decisions: Document Prepared by the Secretariat, Assemblies of the Member States of WIPO, 55th Series of Meetings, 5 to 14 October 2015* A/55/INF/11 (WIPO 2015) 9.

7 Mechanisms for control, oversight and accountability of the WIPO Secretariat

The World Intellectual Property Organization is the subject of several internal, external and independent oversight mechanisms. This chapter reviews WIPO's audit and oversight mechanisms, its regulations and policies with regard to evaluation, the role and activities of the organisation's Legal Counsel, and other accountability mechanisms, such as those that address the roles, responsibilities and conduct of WIPO staff.

7.1 Audit and oversight mechanisms

The WIPO Independent Advisory Oversight Committee (IAOC) (formerly known as the Audit Committee) is an independent, expert advisory and external oversight body charged with providing 'assurance to Member States on the adequate and effectiveness of internal controls and of internal and external oversight at WIPO.'[1] It also aims to 'assist Member States in their role of oversight and in exercising their governance responsibilities' with respect to WIPO's various operations. Its mandate includes promoting internal controls (including review of the organisation's Financial Regulations, arrangements for

---

1 In September 2005, the WIPO General Assembly approved the proposal of the Working Group of the Program and Budget Committee on the establishment of a WIPO Audit Committee. The WIPO Audit Committee was formed in 2007. In September 2010, the WIPO General Assembly approved proposals to change the title of the Committee into the Independent Advisory Oversight Committee and amend its composition and rotation procedures. The latest revision was approved by the WIPO General Assembly in October 2015, the text of which is contained in WIPO, *Proposed Revision of the Terms of Reference of the WIPO Independent Advisory Oversight Committee (IAOC): Document Prepared by the Secretariat, Program and Budget Committee Twenty-Fourth Session, 14–18 September 2015* WO/PBC/24/4 Annex 1 (WIPO 2015). For earlier revisions, see, for instance, WIPO, *Revised Terms of Reference of the WIPO Audit Committee: Revised WIPO Internal Audit Charter* WO/GA/34/15 (WIPO 2007); WIPO, *Report Adopted by the WIPO General Assembly, 34th Session* WO/GA/34/16 (WIPO 2007); WIPO, *Proposed Revisions to the WIPO Internal Oversight Charter: The Terms of Reference Governing External Audit and the Terms of Reference of the WIPO IAOC* WO/GA/41/10 Rev. Annex II (WIPO 2012).

risk management, ethics and misconduct); providing assurance to the General Assembly (such as by reviewing the internal audit function, promoting effective coordination between the internal and audit function, and the collective coverage of WIPO's various internal oversight functions); overseeing compliance with internal and external oversight recommendations; monitoring the delivery and content of financial statements; and overseeing and supporting investigations. The IAOC makes recommendations to the PBC, as it considers appropriate. The Committee members serve in their personal capacity, without remuneration and independent of the Member States that appoint them.[2]

An External Auditor, appointed by the General Assembly, is responsible for auditing WIPO's accounts and 'may make observations with respect to the efficiency of the financial procedures, the accounting system, the internal financial controls and, in general, the administration and management of the organisation.'[3] The Financial Regulations and Rules state that the External Auditor shall be the Auditor General (or officer holding the equivalent title) of a Member State, and shall be appointed for a term of office of 6 years non-renewable consecutively. Appointed in 2012 for a six-year period, WIPO's External Auditor at the time of publication was the Comptroller and Auditor General of India. The terms of reference governing external audit are contained in Chapter 8 of WIPO's Financial Regulations and Rules (see Appendix 7 for the text of that chapter).

The WIPO Internal Oversight Charter, which is contained in Annex I of WIPO's Financial Regulations and Rules, provides the framework for the internal oversight function at WIPO, which comprises internal audit, evaluation and investigation (see Appendix 7 for a copy of the latest 2014

---

2 IAOC members are, however, reimbursed for any travel and subsistence expenses that are necessarily incurred in relation to participation in quarterly meetings in Geneva, which generally last 4 days, and other official meetings. Also see 2013 WIPO vacancy notice for IAOC members, WIPO, 'Member, WIPO Independent Advisory Oversight Committee (IAOC)' <https://erecruit.wipo.int/public/hrd-cl-vac-view.asp?jobinfo_uid_c=27167&vaclng=en> accessed 8 August 2014. In 2015, the IAOC members were from Zambia (Chair); Hungary (Vice-Chair); India; Germany; the Russian Federation; Uruguay and China. See WIPO, 'WIPO Independent Advisory Oversight Committee' <http://www.wipo.int/about-wipo/en/oversight/iaoc/> accessed 31 October 2015.

3 See Article 11(10) of the WIPO Convention (Appendix 1) and Regulation 8.5 of the WIPO Financial Regulations and Rules (Appendix 7).

version of the Charter).[4] The Charter establishes the mission for WIPO's Internal Oversight Division (IOD), namely: 'to examine and evaluate, in an independent manner, WIPO's control and business systems and processes in order to identify good practices and to provide recommendations for improvement.'[5] The Division reports directly to the Director General. The Charter further states that IOD's purpose is to 'help strengthen accountability, value for money, stewardship, internal control and corporate governance in WIPO.' To this end, the IOD conducts internal audits that assess management controls to ensure cost-efficient and accountable operations (guided by an Internal Audit Strategy, the latest of which covers the period 2015–17);[6] investigations that examining possible wrong-doing and identifying areas where fraudulent activity might occur (see Appendix 9 for WIPO's Investigation Policy); and evaluations of WIPO's activities and programs to improve implementation, performance and planning (see section 7.2). The IOD's annual reports to the WIPO Assemblies summarise its activities and include general information on its audit, investigation and evaluation activities.

The Internal Oversight Charter requires that final internal audit and evaluation reports be submitted to the Director General, with a copy to the IAOC and the External Auditor (paragraph 30). Further, it requires that these reports, as well as reports on management implications resulting from investigations, be published on the WIPO website within 30 days of their issuances (paragraph 31). The Charter further provides that the IOD Director may at his/her discretion withhold a report in its entirety or redact parts of it, if required to protect security, safety or privacy (paragraph 31). Preliminary evaluation reports and final investigation reports are fully confidential. To give these Charter clauses effect, the IOD adopted a Report Publication Policy in 2015.[7]

---

4 See WIPO, *Financial Regulations and Rules* (1 November 2014 edition) <www.wipo.int/about-wipo/en/pdf/wipo_financial_regulations.pdf> accessed 1 October 2015. In October 2015, a revised Annex III of the Financial Regulations and Rules, which covered the terms of reference of the Independent Advisory Oversight Committee (IAOC), was approved by the WIPO General Assembly. For the approved revised text, see WIPO, *Proposed Revision of the Terms of Reference of the WIPO Independent Advisory Oversight Committee (IAOC): Document Prepared by the Secretariat, Program and Budget Committee Twenty-Fourth Session, 14–18 September 2015* WO/PBC/24/4 Annex 1 (WIPO 2015).

5 In 2014, WIPO Member States changed the division's name from the Internal Audit and Oversight Division to the Internal Oversight Division (IOD).

6 This was preceded by a 2012-15 Internal Audit Strategy, which similarly established priorities for internal audit.

7 WIPO, *Internal Oversight Division: Report Publication Policy, First Edition* IOD/PP/2015 (WIPO: 2015).

The 2014 revision to WIPO's Internal Oversight Charter incorporated a significant shift in terms of transparency and accountability because it revised and clarified requirements in respect of the public availability of IOD reports. Internal audit reports were previously neither publicly available nor distributed to Member States, although Member States could consult these on request at the WIPO Headquarters. Only a list of the titles of the latest internal audit reports was publicly available on the WIPO website. Although some IOD evaluation reports since 2010 were already available through IOD's webpage, the revised Internal Oversight Charter and Publication Policy provide a clear framework requiring the routine and timely availability of such reports on WIPO's public website.

The UN's Joint Inspection Unit (JIU) provides independent oversight of agencies in the UN system, such as WIPO, which have accepted the JIU statute. The JIU is mandated to conduct evaluations, inspections and investigations system-wide to:

(a) assist the legislative organs of the participating organisations in meeting their governance responsibilities in respect of their oversight function concerning management of human, financial and other resources by the Secretariats; (b) help improve the efficiency and effectiveness of the respective Secretariats in achieving the legislative mandates and the mission objectives established for the organisations; (c) promote greater coordination between the organisations of the United Nations system; and (d) identify best practices, propose benchmarks and facilitate information-sharing throughout the system.[8]

During the JIU evaluation process, participating UN organisations have opportunities to provide input on JIU reports, review draft reports and recommendations, provide feedback and input to these as appropriate, correct factual errors and provide substantive comments. They may also give overall comments, including on recommendations, once a report has been finalised. Some JIU reports can be specific to a particular UN agency, such as a 2014 JIU report on the management and administration of WIPO, which was preceded by a report on the same topic in 2005.[9] JIU reports may also address the UN system more

---

8 See JIU, 'About Us' <https://www.unjiu.org/en/about-us/Pages/default.aspx> accessed 1 October 2014.

9 JIU, *Review of Management and Administration in the World Intellectual Property Organization*, JIU/REP/2014/2 (UN Joint Inspection Unit 2014) and JIU, *Review of Management and Administration in the World Intellectual Property Organization (WIPO): budget, oversight and related issues*, JIU/REP/2005/1 (UN Joint Inspection Unit 2005).

widely, and are applicable to the suite of UN agencies such as WIPO that comprise that system. JIU reports may include recommendations for the attention of the executive head of a UN agency (such as the Director General of the WIPO Secretariat) and/or recommendations for the attention of legislative bodies (that is, Member State bodies) of UN system organisations (such as WIPO's General Assembly).

The organisation then implements JIU recommendations as appropriate. The JIU has no formal mechanism to require action on the part of the UN agency or its Member States to implement a given recommendation. Staff of the JIU may discuss their findings and recommendations with the agency and its membership, but the JIU relies on Member States to monitor and assess how effectively its recommendations have been implemented. In some instances, the UN agency or Member States may disagree with some JIU findings and their related recommendations. Implementation of recommendations addressed to the Executive Head rely on action taken by the Secretariat, and also sometimes interest and pressure from Member States to spur such action. In the case of recommendations to legislative bodies, the Secretariat is responsible for drawing the attention of Member States to the recommendation, but implementation relies on guidance and/ or decisions by Member States through the relevant legislative body. When the relevant legislative body accepts a particular recommendation addressed to it by the JIU, it may also call for specific action to implement the recommendation by the WIPO Secretariat.

Between 2010 and 2015, the JIU issued 30 reports that were applicable to WIPO.[10] Whereas the 2015 JIU review of WIPO's management and administration addressed a broad range of management, governance and administrative matters, the other 29 reports over this period addressed a wider range of matters relevant to the UN system as a whole – from contract management and resource mobilisation to strategic planning and refurbishment/construction projects.[11] WIPO reports to Member States on its implementation of JIU

---

10 See, for instance, WIPO, *Joint Inspection Unit Report 'Review of Management and Administration in the World Intellectual Property Organization' (JIU/REP/2014/2) Progress Report on the Implementation of Recommendations: Document Prepared by the Secretariat* WO/ PBC/23/4 (WIPO 2015).

11 See, for instance, JIU, *Analysis of the Evaluation Function in the United Nations System* JIU/ REP/2014/6 (UN Joint Inspection Unit 2014); JIU, *Strategic Planning in the United Nations System* JIU/REP/2012/12 (UN Joint Inspection Unit 2012); and JIU, *South-South and Triangular Cooperation in the United Nations System* JIU/REP/2011/3 (UN Joint Inspection Unit 2011).

recommendations addressed both to WIPO specifically[12] and to the UN system and its various agencies in general.[13]

7.2   Evaluation

According to the WIPO Financial Rules and Regulations, the Director General is responsible for establishing a system for planning, conducting and using evaluative information for decision-making (see Regulation 2.15). In practice, however, the evaluation culture at WIPO is nascent, particularly in regard to WIPO's development cooperation activities. This shortcoming has in turn constrained the capacity for Member States to closely monitor, assess and guide WIPO's activities.[14]

Only in the past five years, for instance, has WIPO's IOD begun to conduct evaluations of a number of WIPO's programs and activities, such as through publication of its first ever country portfolio evaluations (which covered Kenya in 2012, Thailand in 2014, and Chile in 2015) as well as its first evaluation of WIPO's work related to achieving one of WIPO's strategic goals (that is, an evaluation related to Strategic Goal VI – International Cooperation on Building Respect for intellectual Property).[15] In September 2015, the Secretariat published a new draft IOD Evaluation Policy for the period 2016–20 for review and eventual approval by the Director General (to replace an earlier evaluation policy that was established in 2007 and revised in 2010). The draft evaluation policy proposed a number of types of evaluations, namely: program evaluations, strategic evaluations from the perspective of each of WIPOs strategic goals; thematic evaluations, and geographical (country or regional) evaluations, as well as project-level and process evaluations.[16]

---

12 See, for instance, WIPO, *Joint Inspection Unit Report 'Review of Management and Administration in the World Intellectual Property Organization' (JIU/REP/2014/2) Progress Report on the Implementation of Recommendations: Document Prepared by the Secretariat* WO/PBC/23/4 (WIPO 2015).

13 WIPO, *Progress Report on the Implementation of the Joint Inspection Unit (JIU) Recommendations for the Review of WIPO Legislative Bodies: Prepared by the Secretariat, Twenty-Fourth Session of the Program and Budget Committee, 14 to 18 September 2015* WO/PBC/24/7 (WIPO 2015).

14 Carolyn Deere Birkbeck and Santiago Roca, *Independent External Review of WIPO Technical Assistance in the Area of Cooperation for Development* CDIP/8/INF/1 (WIPO 2011).

15 WIPO, *Annual Report by the Director of the Internal Oversight Division: Prepared by the Secretariat* WO/GA/47/4 (WIPO 2015).

16 See WIPO, 'Evaluations' <http://www.wipo.int/about-wipo/en/oversight/iaod/evaluation> accessed 1 October 2015, and WIPO, *Internal Oversight Division: Evaluation Policy (Draft) Second Edition* IOD/EP/2015 (WIPO 2015).

For information on the performance of particular WIPO programs, WIPO Member States and stakeholders can also refer to annual Program and Performance Reports prepared by the Secretariat (as well as the validation reports produced by the IOD), which incorporate reports on WIPO's progress on a range of expected results and indicators established by WIPO's results-based management (RBM) framework (see section 6.4.1). In addition, some individual WIPO units and divisions conduct more specific, activity-related evaluations (such as satisfaction surveys of training participants and project evaluations of WIPO Development Agenda projects). However, there is to date no organisation-wide system for collecting data and analysis so generated by Program staff. There is also no system for *ex ante* or *ex post* evaluations of impacts of the various WIPO treaties and proposed treaties, although some WIPO Committees have requested ad hoc evaluations of the outcomes of certain treaty provisions.

Finally, the Office of the WIPO Chief Economist produces and analyses statistics on a number of aspects of the IP system (such as in its biannual World Intellectual Property Report and the Global Innovation Index, published with INSEAD), which may assist Member States in some of their evaluation tasks. In addition, WIPO produces annual reports that provide data on trends, such as the annual report on the international patent system, entitled the *PCT Yearly Review*, which includes a review of the profile of the users of the PCT system.

7.3   Office of the Legal Counsel

The Office of WIPO's Legal Counsel performs a range of functions relevant to the governance and management of WIPO, as well as to the Secretariat's interaction with Member States. The Office is responsible for:

> providing legal advice and assistance to the Director General, to the bodies of the WIPO Member States and to the Secretariat on constitutional, administrative, contractual and general legal matters and in respect of the depositary functions of the WIPO-administered treaties. It is also responsible for ensuring that WIPO fully complies with its internal rules and applicable laws.[17]

---

17 This description draws directly from WIPO's website, see <http://www.wipo.int/about-wipo/en/activities_by_unit/units/olc.html> accessed 15 March 2015.

Examples of activities undertaken by the Office of the Legal Counsel include advising and defending WIPO in judicial proceedings, such as on complaints lodged by WIPO staff with the ILO Administrative Tribunal;[18] drafting and review of contracts entered into by WIPO; and preparation of treaty action notifications, such as notifications addressed to Member States of adherence to or denunciations of treaties.

The Legal Counsel is available to Member States in their inter-governmental meetings to clarify legal matters that arise and to reply to questions that emerge on the decision-making process and structure, such as in regard to the meaning and interpretation of WIPO's General Rules of Procedure and the Special Rules of Procedure for various Governing Bodies and Committees (see Appendices 3, 4 and 5).

7.4   Other internal accountability mechanisms

In 2014, WIPO Member States approved a WIPO 'accountability framework' proposed by the Secretariat to align WIPO with the three-pillar framework developed in a 2005 JIU report aimed at improving accountability frameworks in the UN system.[19] WIPO's framework provides an overview of each of the three pillars, describing their specific elements, systems and mechanisms as listed in brackets as follows:

---

18 The ILO Administrative Tribunal can consider complaints alleging non-observance, in substance or in form, of the terms of appointment of officials and of the provision of staff regulations of international organisations that fall within its jurisdiction. See ILO, 'Administrative Tribunal', <http://www.ilo.org/public/english/tribunal/about/index.htm> accessed 15 September 2015.

19 See WIPO, *Accountability Framework* WO/PBC/22/12 (WIPO 2014) 1. The Joint Inspection Unit's report JIU, *Accountability Frameworks in the United Nations System* JIU/REP/2011/5 (UN Joint Inspection Unit 2011) provided 'a comparative analysis report on various accountability frameworks in the United Nations system' in response to the United Nations General Assembly resolution *Towards an Accountability System in the United Nations* A/RES/64/259 (UN 2010), para. 4. In its report, the JIU recommended that UN organisations without accountability frameworks should develop them as a 'priority inspired by the benchmarks contained in this report' and 'to evaluate their implementation for consideration in 2015.' In 2013, WIPO's then Internal Audit and Oversight Division (IAOD) recommended in its audit on results-based management that the 'WIPO Secretariat should engage with the General Assembly to define and get approval for an accountability framework in line with key components as defined and recommended in the report by the Joint Inspection Unit (JIU/REP/2011/5).'

- Pillar 1: Covenant with Member States, Stakeholders and Users of WIPO's Services (WIPO Agreements and Treaties, WIPO Results Framework);

- Pillar 2: Risk Management and Internal Controls (WIPO's Control Environment, Risk Assessment Policies, Control Activities, Information and Communication, and Monitoring); and

- Pillar 3: Complaints and Response Mechanisms (channels for complaints and response available to users of WIPO Services, Procurement Activities and WIPO Staff).[20]

This book has already reviewed most of the tools available to Member States (and sometimes stakeholders) for promoting accountability of the Secretariat to Member States, including: the Program and Budget process (see Chapter 6); financial reporting processes and requirements (see Chapter 6); and audit and oversight mechanisms (comprised of the Independent Advisory Oversight Committee (IAOC), the External Auditor and the Internal Oversight Division (IOD), which include evaluation and investigation) (as described in sections 7.1 and 7.2).

7.4.1   Staff accountability

A final set of accountability measures relate to regulations, rules, policies and standards applicable to WIPO staff. Such measures have an array of governance implications. Staff practices, the scope for staff action, and procedures for addressing staff complaints may, for instance, impact the specific activities undertaken by the organisation and the accountability of the organisation's senior management as well as the prospects for internal reform and changes to the organisation's internal culture.

As UN employees, WIPO staff are subject to the Standards of Conduct of the International Civil Service, promulgated by the International Civil Service Commission (ICSC).[21] (WIPO staff belong to the UN

---

20 The WIPO website refers to these three components as its 'Accountability System' on its website, see WIPO, 'Oversight' <http://www.wipo.int/about-wipo/en/oversight> accessed 4 October 2014.

21 The latest version of these Standards was adopted in 2013 by the ICSC, updating the version prepared in 1954 and revised in 2001. See ICSC, *Standards of Conduct in the International Civil Service* (International Civil Service Commission 2013). The Standards were approved by

salary system and can participate in the UN pension system (that is, the UN Joint Staff Pension Fund), provided that their participation is not excluded by their letter of appointment. WIPO participates in the UN Safety and Security System and follows UN policy on occupational health.)

The World Intellectual Property Organization's legal framework for human resources consists of: the WIPO Convention (which designates the Coordination Committee as responsible for decisions on human resources matters); the WIPO Staff Regulations and Rules (which set out the conditions of employment for WIPO staff); WIPO Office Instructions on Human Resources policies and practices; the WIPO Financial Regulations and Rules; and Headquarters Agreements with Host States (which can impact issues such as the diplomatic privileges and immunity of WIPO staff, and procedures for waiving these).[22] Since 2010, the performance of staff is managed through WIPO's Performance Management and Staff Development System (PMSDS).[23] WIPO staff are also bound by WIPO's internal Code of Ethics, which was issued by the Secretariat in an Office Instruction in 2012 (see Table 7.2 for the WIPO Code of Ethics).

A number of WIPO's Staff Regulations and Rules, which set out the conditions of employment for WIPO staff, are relevant to WIPO's governance, most notably those relevant to the duties, obligations and privileges of staff; the immunity of staff; principles governing the recruitment, appointment and promotion of staff; and provi-

---

the United Nations General Assembly, see UN, *United Nations Common System: Report of the International Civil Service Commission, Resolution Adopted by the General Assembly on 12 April 2013* A/RES/67/257 (UN 2013), <http://icsc.un.org/resources/pdfs/general/standardsE.pdf> accessed 26 October 2015. The intention of the Standards, as stated in the foreword, is to serve as a behavioural and ethical guide: to inform, to inspire and, when needed, to provide explanations. They reflect the philosophical underpinnings of the international civil service and inform its conscience. They trust that like the previous version, the present Standards become an indispensable part of the culture and heritage of the organisations and are of similarly enduring quality. The Standards include guiding principles (on integrity, tolerance, impartiality, incorruptibility, loyalty to the UN system, and accountability) as well as provisions on issues ranging from post-employment restrictions and conflicts of interest to the role of the Secretariats.

22 On the privileges and immunities of WIPO, see Edward Kwakwa and Marie-Lea Rols, 'The Privileges and Immunities of the World Intellectual Property Organization: Practice and Challenges', in Niels Blokker and Nico Schrijver (eds), *Immunity of International Organizations* (Brill Nijhoff 2015) 115–36.

23 For the PMSDS guidelines, see WIPO, 'Performance Management and Staff Development System Guidelines' <www.wipo.int/export/sites/www/about-wipo/en/strategic_realignment/pdf/pmsds_guidelines.pdf> accessed 1 September 2014.

sions related to termination of employment, disciplinary measures, conflict resolution, and appeals as well as the rules of procedure of appointment boards.[24] Table 7.1 provides an illustrative list of the titles of regulations and rules on such topics, drawn from the Table of Contents of the Staff Regulations and Rules (excerpts of selected regulations and rules listed in Table 7.1 are provided in Appendix 8).

Regulations and rules on such staff matters – and their interpretation – have the potential to empower, or circumscribe the power, of WIPO's senior management and its ability to steward organisational changes approved by Member States. They can also influence management – staff relations, staff morale and staff performance, and thus the internal culture and effectiveness of the organisation. In addition, there are clear links between the provisions of the Staff Regulations and Rules and the wider governance of the organisation where charges of corruption, financial mismanagement and misconduct of either senior management or other staff arise. Further, provisions regarding staff performance, promotion and remuneration may be relevant where there is dissent among staff about the content of work they are expected to perform or where there are different visions – practical or political – between some staff and senior management on how WIPO's mandate and work program should be advanced. The Staff Regulations and Rules can be vehicles that dissenting staff may use to assert their rights, and alternatively may be used by the Secretariat's senior management to reinforce its decisions by underscoring the responsibilities and obligations of staff.

In recent years, WIPO's Staff Regulations and Rules have been the focal point of highly politicised debates on whether senior management and staff have acted appropriately in respect of disputes on promotion, dismissal, status or remuneration. These in turn have sometimes been linked to wider political debates about the management and direction of the organisation; the ability of senior management to pursue mandated organisational changes; the appropriate oversight by Member States of senior management; and controls over

---

24 See WIPO, *Staff Regulations and Rules* (WIPO 2014) as amended by the WIPO Coordination Committee at the 2015 Annual Assemblies, see WIPO, *Amendments to Staff Regulations and Rules: Document Prepared by the Director General* WO/CC/71/4 Rev. (WIPO 2015) and subject to two exceptions noted in WIPO, *List of Decisions: Documents Prepared by the WIPO Secretariat* A/55/INF/11 (WIPO 2015) 19.

Table 7.1 WIPO Staff Regulations and Rules: selected examples of Regulations and Rules relevant to governance

Chapter	Titles of Selected Regulations Relevant to Governance	Titles of Selected Rules Relevant to Governance
Chapter I	**Duties, Obligations and Privileges**	
	Regulation 1.1 Status of Staff Members*	
	Regulation 1.4 Instructions from External Sources*	
	Regulation 1.5 Conduct*	Rule 1.5.1 – Discrimination or Harassment*
		Rule 1.5.2 – Use of Property and Assets*
	Regulation 1.6 Activities and Interests outside the International Bureau*	
	Regulation 1.7 Communication of Information*	Rule 1.7.1 – Confidential Documents, Information or Material*
	Regulation 1.8 Honors and Gifts*	
	Regulation 1.9 Political Activities*	Rule 1.9.1 – Membership of a Political Party
	Regulation 1.10 Privileges and Immunities*	
	Regulation 1.11 Oath or Declaration*	
	Regulation 1.12 Compliance with Local Laws and Private Legal Obligations*	
	Regulation 1.13 Information Requested of Staff Members and Obligation to Supply Such Information*	Rule 1.13.1 – Information to be Supplied by Staff Members*
Chapter II	**Classification**	
	Regulation 2.1 Classification of Posts	
	Regulation 2.2 Reclassification of Posts	
Chapter III	**Salaries and Allowances**	
Chapter IV	**Principles Governing Recruitment, Appointment and Promotion**	
	Regulation 4.1 General Principles*	
	Regulation 4.2 Geographical Distribution and Gender Balance*	
	Regulation 4.3 Transfers	
	Regulation 4.4 Promotion	

Chapter	Titles of Selected Regulations Relevant to Governance	Titles of Selected Rules Relevant to Governance
Chapter IV	**Principles Governing Recruitment, Appointment and Promotion**	
	Regulation 4.7 Nationality*	
	Regulation 4.8 Authority for Appointment*	
	Regulation 4.9 Recruitment*	Rule 4.9.1 – Employment of Members of the Same Family
		Rule 4.9.2 – Appointments under Funds-in-Trust and other Special Agreements*
	Regulation 4.10 Appointment Boards	Rule 4.10.1 – Composition and Rules of Procedure of Appointment Boards
	Regulation 4.15 Types of Appointment*	
	Regulation 4.20 Accountability and Performance Management*	Rule 4.20.1 – Performance Appraisal of Staff Members on Fixed-term, Continuing and Permanent Appointments
Chapter V	**Annual, Special and Home Leave**	
Chapter VI	**Social Security** Regulation 6.1 Pension Fund Regulation 6.2 Health Protection and Insurance	
Chapter VII	**Travel and Removal Expenses**	
Chapter VIII	**Staff Relations**	
	Regulation 8.1 Staff Council*	Rule 8.1.1 – Staff Council*
	Regulation 8.2 Advisory Body*	Rule 8.2.1 – Joint Advisory Group*
		Rule 8.2.2 – Petition by Staff Members*
Chapter IX	**Separation from Service**	
	Regulation 9.1 Separation from Service	
	Regulation 9.2 Termination*	Rule 9.2.2 – Termination of Appointments of Temporary Staff Members*

Chapter	Titles of Selected Regulations Relevant to Governance	Titles of Selected Rules Relevant to Governance
Chapter IX	**Separation from Service**	
	Regulation 9.7 Notice of Termination*	Rule 9.7.1 – Notice of Termination for Temporary Staff Members*
Chapter X	**Disciplinary Measures**	
	Regulation 10.1 Disciplinary Measures*	Rule 10.1.1 – Disciplinary Measures*
		Rule 10.1.2 – Procedure
		Rule 10.1.3 – Temporary Suspension from Duty
		Rule 10.1.4 – Serious Misconduct
		Rule 10.1.5 – Appeal
Chapter XI	**Conflict Resolution**	
	Regulation 11.1 Respectful Workplace*	
	Regulation 11.2 Independence, Impartiality, Conflict of Interest and Confidentiality*	
	Regulation 11.3 Informal Conflict Resolution*	Rule 11.3.1 – Means of Informal Conflict Resolution*
		Rule 11.3.2 – Office of the Ombudsperson*
	Regulation 11.4 Formal Conflict Resolution*	Rule 11.4.1 – Administrative Resolution of Workplace-Related Conflicts and Grievances
		Rule 11.4.2 – Administrative Resolution of Rebuttal of Performance Appraisals
		Rule 11.4.3 – Administrative Resolution of Requests for Review of Other Administrative Decisions
	Appeals	
	Regulation 11.5 Internal Appeal*	Rule 11.5.1 – Appeal Board*
		Rule 11.5.2 – Filing of an Appeal

Chapter	Titles of Selected Regulations Relevant to Governance	Titles of Selected Rules Relevant to Governance
Chapter XI	**Conflict Resolution**	
	Regulation 11.6 Litigious Appeal*	Rule 11.5.3 – Procedure before the Appeal Board Rule 11.6.1 – Administrative Tribunal*
Chapter XII	**General Provisions**	
	Regulation 12.1 Amendments to the Regulations Regulation 12.2 Staff Rules	Rule 12.2.1 – Amendments and Derogations to Staff Rules
	Regulation 12.3 Interpretation of the Staff Rules Regulation 12.6 Delegation of Authority*	
Annex I	**Glossary**	
Annex II	**Salaries and Allowances**	
Annex III	**Selection Procedures for Temporary Appointments**	
Annex IV	**Rules of Procedure of Appointment Boards**	
Annex V	**Specific Rules Applicable to Staff Members in Part-time Employment**	
Annex VI	**Calculation of Time Limits for the Purposes of Chapter X and Chapter XI**	

Notes: * The text of Regulations and Rules marked with an * is provided in Appendix 8. The table presents the titles of all chapters in the Staff Regulations and Rules and annexes, but includes only a sample of Regulations and Rules in various chapters deemed by the author to be particularly relevant to WIPO's governance. The table does not include the titles of all Regulations nor all Rules under each Regulation.

Source: WIPO, *Staff Regulations and Rules* (WIPO 2014) as amended by the WIPO Coordination Committee at the 2015 Annual Assemblies, see WIPO, *Amendments to Staff Regulations and Rules: Document Prepared by the Director General* WO/CC/71/4 Rev. (WIPO 2015) and subject to two exceptions noted in WIPO, *List of Decisions: Documents Prepared by the WIPO Secretariat* A/55/INF/11 (WIPO 2015) 19.

Table 7.2 WIPO Code of Ethics

Preamble	Reaffirming the purposes, values and principles of the World Intellectual Property Organization, as enshrined in the Convention Establishing the World Intellectual Property Organization, and the importance for the Organization of securing the highest standards of efficiency, competence and integrity;
	Taking account of the Organization's core value of environmental, social and governance responsibility established under the Strategic Realignment Program, particularly with respect to acting and performing in an ethical manner;
	Recognizing that it is imperative for the Organization to establish, cultivate, nurture and promote a culture of ethics, which enhances integrity and accountability and thereby strengthens its credibility and that of the personnel working in the Organization;
	Reaffirming the Standards of Conduct for the International Civil Service 2001, as it may be amended from time to time, as well as standards of conduct provided for in the relevant Staff Regulations and Rules;
	The present Code of Ethics sets out the values and principles to guide conduct of personnel of the Organization.
Values	*Independence* – Personnel of the Organization shall maintain their independence and shall not seek or accept instructions, explicit or implicit, from any Government or from any other person or entity external to the Organization, or work to promote the interest of Government or external entity, and shall refrain from any action which might be reasonably considered to reflect negatively on their position as personnel of the Organization responsible only to the Organization.
	Loyalty – Loyalty to the principles of the Organization as stated in the Convention Establishing the World Intellectual Property Organization (WIPO) is of fundamental importance to the discharge of their duties by all personnel. Personnel shall be loyal to the Organization and shall, at all times, undertake and perform their functions and regulate their conduct with the best interests of the Organization only in view.
	Impartiality – Personnel of the Organization, in the performance of their official duties, shall always act with impartiality, objectivity and professionalism. They shall ensure that the expression of their personal views and convictions, including on the policies of particular Governments or external entities, does not compromise or appear to compromise in any manner the performance of their official duties or the interests of the Organization. They shall not act in a way that could lead to biased, or actual or perceived preferential treatment, for or against particular individuals, groups or interests.
	Integrity – Personnel of the Organization shall maintain the highest standards of integrity, including honesty, fairness and incorruptibility, in all matters affecting their official duties and the interests of the Organization. They shall conduct themselves in a manner befitting their status as international civil servants.

Values	*Accountability* – Personnel of the Organization shall be accountable for the proper discharge of their functions and for their decisions and actions. In fulfilling their official duties and responsibilities, personnel of the Organization shall make decisions only in the interests of the Organization. They shall submit themselves to scrutiny as required by their position.
	Respect for human rights – Personnel of the Organization shall fully respect the human rights, dignity and worth of all persons and shall act with respect for gender equality and for diversity, and without regard to ethnic origin, race, religion, political persuasion, sexual orientation and with understanding, tolerance, sensitivity and without any form of discrimination whatsoever.
Principles	*Conflicts of interest* – Personnel of the Organization shall arrange their private interests in a manner that will prevent actual, potential or apparent conflicts of interest from arising, but if such a conflict does arise between their private interests and their official duties and responsibilities, the conflict shall be disclosed immediately and resolved promptly in preserving the best interests of the Organization. Personnel shall also ensure that in all matters internal to the Organization that they undertake and perform their functions and regulate their conduct so as to prevent actual, potential or apparent conflicts of interest between their private interests and their official duties and responsibilities. If such a conflict shall arise, they shall disclose it immediately and resolve it promptly in the best interests of the Organization.
	Abuse of authority – Personnel of the Organization shall not use the authority entrusted to them, in particular by taking advantage of colleagues, beneficiaries, or other individuals or groups, for financial, political, administrative, professional, sexual or other gain. Personnel shall in no case exercise any form of retaliation against colleagues, and in particular managers shall in no case exercise any form of retaliation against their subordinates.
	Commitment to a respectful working environment – Personnel of the Organization shall conduct themselves in such a way as to ensure a safe working environment free of harassment, including from allegations that are made maliciously or with reckless disregard as to their accuracy.
	Gifts, honors, favors or other benefits – Personnel of the Organization shall not solicit or accept gifts, honors, favors and/or other benefits from sources external to the Organization that may bring into question their independence, impartiality, integrity, loyalty and objectivity, unless the acceptance of such gifts, honors, favors and/or other benefits is pursuant to applicable policies and regulations. Personnel of the within the Organization that may bring into question their independence, impartiality, loyalty and integrity in the performance of their functions, except in accordance with applicable policies and regulations.

Principles	*Resources of the Organization* – Personnel of the Organization shall only use or allow the use of the tangible and intangible resources of the Organization, directly or indirectly, including its property, for authorized purposes.
	Confidentiality of Information – Personnel of the Organization shall not use information that is not available to the public for private gain, financial or otherwise, to benefit themselves or others nor shall they disclose such information to the public without authorization. That duty continues to apply after separate from the Organization.
	Post-employment – Personnel of the Organization shall not act in such a manner as to take improper advantage of their official functions and positions, including privileged information obtained from such functions and positions, when seeking employment or appointment after leaving their service with the Organization.
Administration of the Code	The provisions of this Code of Ethics shall extend to all personnel of the Organization. For the purposes of this Code, personnel of the Organization includes staff members of the Organization and related personnel, such as individuals who have entered into agreements with the Organization as holders of Special Services Agreements (SSAs), or as interpreters, translators or revisers, as well as individual contractors or experts on mission.
	The values and principles contained in the present Code of Ethics shall be reflected in the applicable standards of conduct provided for in the relevant Staff Regulations and Rules and other relevant issuances of the Organization.

Source: WIPO, *WIPO Code of Ethics* Office Instruction 84/2012 (WIPO 2012).

the conduct of WIPO's Directors General, as well as the extent of their powers and discretion.

The Staff Regulations and Rules are reviewed on an ongoing basis in light of evolving organisational and staff needs, and amended by Member States through the WIPO Coordination Committee (in the case of Regulations) and by the Director General (in the case of Rules). Before decisions by the WIPO Coordination Committee, the Program and Budget Committee reviews and debates proposed amendments to Regulations in response to proposals from Member States and/or the Secretariat, and makes recommendations to the WIPO Coordination Committee in favour of proposed amendments. The Coordination Committee amended the Staff Regulations in 2012, 2013, 2014 and 2015, for instance. The Staff Rules have been updated under the authority of the Director General on an ongoing basis in response to changing management needs and new policies. Staff are notified of such changes to Rules through Office Instructions. The WIPO Coordination Committee is also notified of such changes in a document prepared by the Director General in advance of the Committee's annual meeting.

As noted above, WIPO staff members are international civil servants. The WIPO Staff Regulations and Rules emphasise that staff obligations 'are not national but exclusively international', and that by 'accepting appointment they pledge themselves to discharge their functions and regulate their conduct only with the interests of the International Bureau in view' (Regulation 1.1). They further require that: 'In the performance of their duties with the International Bureau, staff members shall neither seek nor accept instructions or assistance from any government or from any other authority outside the International Bureau' (Regulation 1.4).

As illustrated in Table 7.1, the WIPO Staff Regulations and Rules contain provisions relevant to the internal justice system, including on disciplinary procedures, terms of dismissal, temporary suspension, serious misconduct, the Ombudsperson's Office and the WIPO Appeal Board (see Appendix 8). WIPO staff have the possibility to express views on management decisions through the WIPO Staff Association. In the case where complainants have exhausted all internal procedures open to them to settle disputes related to the terms of their appointment (such as on complaints of unfair promotion decisions and harassment), WIPO staff have ultimate recourse to the International Labour Organization (ILO) Administrative Tribunal.[25]

Further, in accordance with the WIPO Internal Oversight Charter (see Appendix 7), the IOD may receive complaints or information concerning the possible existence of alleged misconduct, wrongdoing or irregularities, including fraud, waste, abuse of authority, and violation of WIPO regulations and rules. Once an allegation is received, it is registered and evaluated to determine whether an investigation is warranted. If an investigation is needed, it is to be conducted in compliance with the WIPO Internal Oversight Charter and the WIPO Investigation Policy (see Appendix 9).

WIPO also has an Ethics Office, located within the Director General's Office, charged with providing advice and guidance on ethical issues. The Ethics Office is also responsible for WIPO's Whistleblower

---

25 See footnote 18.

Protection Policy, issued by the Secretariat in the form of an Office Instruction in 2012,[26] which aims to provide protection against retaliation for reporting wrong-doing and sets out the organisation's policy on preventing and deterring corruption, fraud, collusion, coercion, money laundering and the financing of terrorism. The Ethics Office publishes an Annual Report (contained in an Annex to the Secretariat's Annual Report on Human Resources). In 2015, some discussion arose on how best to safeguard the independence in the substance of the Ethics Office's work while providing adequately for administrative reporting and formalities: this prompted questions on the structure of the Ethics Office, where within (or outside) the Director General's Executive Office it should be located, and the appropriate reporting lines for the Chief Ethics Officer.[27]

Finally, the WIPO Secretariat has also formulated a Code of Conduct for WIPO Suppliers as a reference for WIPO staff. Based on the UN Suppliers Code of Conduct, it provides guidelines for those WIPO staff involved in procurement activities, as well as for all commercial entities/vendors that wish to do business with WIPO.[28] The Code includes provisions, for instance, on bribery and corruption, conflict of interest, gifts and hospitality, and post-employment restrictions.

---

26 See WIPO, *Office Instruction on the 'Policy to Protect against Retaliation for Cooperating in an Oversight Activity or Reporting Misconduct or Other Wrongdoing ("Whistleblower Protection Policy")' (As May Be Amended from Time to Time)* Office Instruction 58/2012 (WIPO 2012). Also see WIPO, *Accountability Framework* WO/PBC/22/12 (WIPO 2014) 4.

27 Practices in this respect vary among UN agencies. The United Nations Ethics Office is located outside the Executive Office of the Secretary-General to ensure operational independence and to ensure staff are hired through clearly established recruitment procedures (in accordance with UN General Assembly Resolution A/60/568). For an example of Member State discussion of the Ethics Office, see WIPO, *Report: adopted by the Committee, Coordination Committee, Seventieth Session* WO/CC/70/5 (WIPO 2015) 4.

28 For the Code of Conduct for WIPO Suppliers, see <http://www.wipo.int/export/sites/www/procurement/en/docs/code_of_conduct_for_wipo_suppliers.pdf> accessed 15 July 2015.

8 External relations and transparency

Several components of WIPO's governance system have a bearing on the organisation's external relations and transparency. This chapter reviews agreements and practices relevant to WIPO's relations with the UN system and other international organisations; WIPO's unique relationship with private sector stakeholders; its guidelines on observers; and policies and practices with regard to transparency and access to documents.

8.1 Relations with the UN system and other international organisations

The World Intellectual Property Organization's 1974 Agreement with the UN includes a number of concrete provisions regarding the coordination of WIPO's policies and activities with the wider UN system, which are implemented to varying degrees by WIPO's Secretariat and Member States in their respective areas of responsibility (see Appendix 2 for the text of the UN-WIPO Agreement).

In formally establishing WIPO's status as a UN Specialized Agency, Article 1 of the UN-WIPO agreement described the organisation's purpose as 'promoting creative intellectual activity and . . . facilitating the transfer of technology related to industrial property to . . . the developing countries in order to accelerate economic, social and cultural development.'[1] The purpose of cooperation provided for in the Agreement is 'to make fully effective the envisaged coordination of the policies and activities of the UN system, and to participate in UN bodies established for that purpose.' In this spirit, the WIPO Director General participates in the UN Chief Executives Board (CEB) (which meets bi-annually and brings together all executive heads of the UN system) and the UN High-Level Committee on Management (HLCM)

---

1 See WIPO, *Agreement between the United Nations and the World Intellectual Property Organization* WIPO Publication No. 111 (WIPO 1975).

(which is charged with addressing administrative and management issues of common concern to the UN system, and meets twice a year).[2] As noted in the Introduction to this book and Chapter 2, there are diverse views among WIPO Member States and stakeholders, as well as within the Secretariat, on what is and should be the legal and political significance of the UN-WIPO Agreement in relation to WIPO's purpose, mandate and ongoing activities.

The UN-WIPO Agreement also provides for reciprocal representation of UN representatives in all WIPO bodies, and for WIPO to be invited to participate, without the right to vote, in the main committees and organs of the UN General Assembly and the Economic and Social Council, among other UN conferences and meetings (Article 3). At present, 17 UN agencies are accredited as WIPO observers. Further, WIPO and the UN each agree to include items proposed by the other in the provisional agendas of the appropriate bodies items (Article 4).

The Agreement calls on WIPO to submit to the appropriate organ of the organisation all formal recommendations that the United Nations may make to it (Article 5(a)). For several years, a document summarising UN decisions and resolutions relevant to WIPO was included in the documentation for the WIPO Assemblies, but this practice appeared to have stopped in 1999.[3] Since then, WIPO has reported on a more ad hoc basis to Member States on its relationship to the UN system, usually on particular issues. In 2013, for instance, the WIPO Secretariat produced a document on WIPO's contribution to the Millennium Development Goals (MDGs), which includes references to its activities with other UN agencies.[4]

---

2 See WIPO, 'WIPO Director General Francis Gurry to Chair the UN High-Level Committee on Management' *WIPO News Archive* (19 April 2012) <http://www.wipo.int/portal/en/news/2012/ article_0021.html> accessed 15 September 2014. The CEB is the successor of the Administrative Committee on Coordination referred to in Article 2 of the UN-WIPO Agreement.

3 See WIPO, *Resolutions and Decisions of the United Nations, the Administrative Committee on Coordination and the Joint Inspection Unit: Report by the Director General WIPO General Assembly 24th Session* WO/GA/24/3 (WIPO 1999). The report covered the period from July 1997 to July 1999. This report was preceded by several prior biennial reports, including, for instance, WIPO, *Resolutions and Decisions of the United Nations: Report by the Director General WIPO General Assembly 21st Session* WO/GA/XXI/6 (WIPO 1997), which covered the period 31 July 1995 to 1 July 1997, and WIPO, *Resolutions and Decisions of the United Nations: Report by the Director General WIPO General Assembly 16th Session* WO/GA/XVI/3 (WIPO 1995), which covered the period from 16 July 1993 to 31 July 1995.

4 WIPO, *The Measurement of the Millennium Development Goals (MDGs) in Other United Nations Agencies and the Contribution of WIPO to the MDGs: Prepared by the Secretariat* CDIP/12/8 (WIPO 2013).

In Article 6, the Agreement calls on WIPO to submit an annual report to the United Nations on its activities, but this appears not to occur on a regular basis.[5] However, in response to requests from the UN Secretariat or other UN agencies, the WIPO Secretariat provides information on WIPO activities for inclusion in UN reports on various matters and also on WIPO's implementation of the recommendations and resolutions of the UN General Assembly and of other organs of the United Nations.[6]

The UN-WIPO Agreement also includes provisions regarding exchange of information and documents; cooperation in the area of statistical services; assistance to the UN, cooperation in the provision of technical assistance and in promoting and facilitating technology transfer; assistance to the International Court of Justice; relations with other international organisations; administrative cooperation; common personnel arrangements; conformity with UN standards, practices and presentation of budgets; and UN laissez-passer travel documents.

The World Intellectual Property Organization is also part of the UN staff pension system,[7] has accepted the jurisdiction of the ILO Administrative Tribunal (see section 7.4.1), and is a participating organisation in the UN Joint Inspection Unit (JIU). The WIPO Secretariat designates a focal point for interaction with the JIU, such as for the provision of input and feedback on its reports on the UN system. It also reports to Member States on its implementation of UN JIU recommendations addressed to the WIPO Secretariat and/or WIPO Member States specifically as well as those to UN agencies in general.[8]

---

5 For instance, no such reports are available through WIPO's website nor do they feature on the lists of documents presented to the UN General Assembly.

6 Examples include the submission by WIPO of information on its activities to the UN Permanent Forum on Indigenous Issues. See, for instance, UN ECOSOC, *Information Received from the United Nations System and Other Intergovernmental Organizations: Secretariat on the Convention on Biological Diversity and WIPO* E/C.19/2008/4.Add.13 (UN 2008). In 2012, the Permanent Forum held an in-depth dialogue with WIPO, concluding with a number of recommendations to improve indigenous peoples' representation and engagement in WIPO's work. See UN ECOSOC, *Recommendations of the Permanent Forum: Comprehensive Dialogue with the World Intellectual Property Organization* E/C.19/2012/L.4 (UN 2012).

7 The UN Joint Staff Pension Board presents a report to the UN General Assembly and to member organisations at least once every 2 years (which is made available in the UN General Assembly documentation, but not reproduced by the Secretariat).

8 See, for instance, WIPO, *Joint Inspection Unit Report 'Review of Management and Administration in the World Intellectual Property Organization' (JIU/REP/2014/2) Progress Report on the*

Beyond its Agreement with the UN, WIPO does not have a policy or set of guidelines on its partnerships with other agencies in the UN system or other international organisations. The WIPO Convention, however, requires that the WIPO Coordination Committee approve any agreement entered into by WIPO with a view to establishing working relations and cooperation with other intergovernmental organisations (Article 13(1)). Memoranda of Understanding (MOUs) are thus prepared by the WIPO Director General with the relevant head of the organisation, and then presented to the Coordination Committee for approval. The Secretariat has not made a running list of all of its MOUs and the status of their implementation available to Member States or the public.[9]

WIPO has forged, for instance, MOUs with several UN agencies, such as the UN Food and Agriculture Organization (FAO) and the UN Industrial Development Organization (UNIDO), both approved by WIPO Member States in 2010, and the UN Economic and Social Commission for Asia and the Pacific (ESCAP) (approved in 2015) as well as with other international organisations such as the African Regional Intellectual Property Organization (ARIPO) (approved by Member States in 2008), the Regional Center for Book Development in Latin America and the Caribbean (CERLALC (approved in 2015)), and the American Intellectual Property Law Association (AIPLA) (signed in 2002).[10] Where such MOUs exist, they are generally written in very broad terms, and are supplemented by workplans for specific joint activities or collaborations when they arise.[11] WIPO DDGs or other senior WIPO staff also sometimes sign MOUs to advance specific Program activities. The Director of the WIPO Academy has, for

---

Implementation of Recommendations: Document prepared by the Secretariat WO/PBC/23/4 (WIPO 2015).

9 At the 2010 meeting of the WIPO Coordination Committee, Egypt proposed that the Secretariat should prepare for Member States a list of all WIPO MOUs and other such instruments with other organisations. Egypt argued that such a list would help Member States to enhance WIPO's 'cooperation and collaboration with other UN agencies and international organisation, in keeping with the spirit of the Development Agenda Recommendation 40', but no decision to this effect was taken on the production of such a list, and the Secretariat has not otherwise made one publicly available. See WIPO, Report: Adopted by the Coordination Committee WO/CC/63/8/ (WIPO 2010) 2.

10 See, for instance, WIPO, Report: Adopted by the Coordination Committee WO/CC/63/8/ (WIPO 2010) 2.

11 The Secretariat also submits for the approval of the WIPO Coordination Committee all proposed agreements with foreign governments determining the legal status of the WIPO external office in the country concerned.

instance, signed MOUs with universities and other partners for its training activities, the Director of WIPO's Mediation and Arbitration Centre signed an agreement with the Internet Corporation for Assigned Names and Numbers (ICANN) in 2013, and a WIPO DDG signed an agreement with the Hong Kong Trade and Development Council in 2014 to jointly promote the trading of IP through their respective online IP market places.

The Secretariat has also forged cooperation agreements with regional IP organisations such as the European Patent Organisation, signed in 2012,[12] the African Intellectual Property Organization (OAPI) and ARIPO. Although such agreements are usually of a general nature, like MOUs, they provide the framework for specific joint activities and cooperation. Examples of international organisations with which the WIPO Secretariat has forged formal cooperation agreements include the International Criminal Police Organization – Interpol. Noting the 'desirability of cooperation in combatting wilful infringement of IP rights', the 2004 WIPO-Interpol agreement was signed by the two agency heads and includes commitments to sharing expertise in regard to technical assistance, mutual consultation and information exchange on policy issues and matters of common interest, and reciprocal representation at meetings in which the other party has an interest or technical competence.[13] The WIPO-administered Unions may also approve external partnerships. The PCT Assembly has approved a series of partnerships with national and regional IP offices regarding the administration of the PCT, resulting in a number of MOUs between the Secretariat and International Searching and International Preliminary Examining Authorities.[14]

WIPO also makes contributions to the work of other international organisations on an ad hoc basis and participates in a number of cooperative activities, partnerships and projects with UN and international

---

12 WIPO/EPO, 'EPO and WIPO Sign Agreement to Enhance Co-operation' WIPO/EPO Press Release, 3 May 2012 <http://www.wipo.int/pressroom/en/articles/2012/article_0008.html> accessed 26 October 2015.

13 Interpol–WIPO, 'Co-operation Agreement between the International Criminal Police Organization and the World Intellectual Property Organization' <http://www.interpol.int/content/download/9466/69442/version/6/file/WorldIntellectualPropertyOrganization(WIPO).pdf> accessed 26 October 2015.

14 For the text of these agreements, see WIPO, 'ISA and IPEA Agreements' http://www.wipo.int/pct/en/access/isa_ipea_agreements.html> accessed 31 October 2015.

organisations with which it does not have a broader MOU.[15] The WIPO Secretariat has, for instance, conducted a number of joint projects with the WHO and UNITAID, and its activities sometimes involve collaboration among several inter-governmental organisations simultaneously. In 2011, for instance, the WHO, WTO, Interpol and the World Customs Organization participated in a Multi-stakeholder Roundtable on the Technical Assistance against Counterfeit Medicines held at WIPO,[16] and WIPO works with WHO and the WTO on a shared initiative to advance Trilateral Cooperation on Public Health, IP and Trade.[17]

In 1995, WIPO forged an agreement with the WTO that aims to establish a 'mutually supportive relationship' and 'appropriate arrangements for cooperation', including in regard to notification of, access to and translation of national IP laws; implementation of procedures for the protection of national emblems; and technical cooperation (see Table 8.1 for excerpts from the WTO–WIPO Cooperation Agreement).[18] The two organisations subsequently forged several initiatives on technical cooperation, including a 1998 effort to help developing countries meet their 1 January 2000 deadline for implementing the WTO's TRIPS Agreement, a 2001 programme to assist least-developed countries to implement TRIPS, and a 2005 agreement to intensify cooperation for least-developed countries upon the extension of their transition period for TRIPS implementation until 1 July 2013.[19] (WTO Member States subsequently extended the transition period until 2021, and in the case of patents for pharmaceutical products until 2033). The WIPO Secretariat reports annually to the WTO on its activities related to TRIPS implementation,[20] and the two organisations

---

15 The WIPO Secretariat lists a number of recent examples of WIPO's cooperation with various UN agencies in WIPO, *The Measurement of the Millennium Development Goals (MDGs) in Other United Nations Agencies and the Contributions of WIPO to the MDGs* CDIP/12/8 (WIPO 2013).

16 World Customs Organization, 'Capacity Building Cooperation with WTO and WIPO' <http://www.wcoomd.org/en/media/newsroom/2011/january/capacity-building-cooperation-with-wto-and-wipo.aspx> accessed 26 October 2015.

17 Also see WIPO, 'WHO, WIPO, WTO Trilateral Cooperation on Public Health, IP and Trade' <http://www.wipo.int/globalchallenges/en/health/trilateral_cooperation.html> accessed 15 October 2015.

18 See WTO–WIPO Cooperation Agreement 1995 <http://www.wto.org/english/tratop_e/trips_e/wtowip_e.htm> accessed 30 October 2015.

19 See WTO, 'The WTO and World Intellectual Property Organization' <https://www.wto.org/english/thewto_e/coher_e/wto_wipo_e.htm> accessed 15 October 2015.

20 See, for instance, WIPO, *Note on Technical and Legal Assistance of WIPO Relevant to the Implementation of the Agreement on TRIPs* (WIPO 2010).

undertake a number of joint technical cooperation activities. Beyond individual staff efforts, however, no routine procedures or mechanisms exist for coordination among international donors on priorities, needs assessments or plans for assistance by country.

Table 8.1   Agreement between the World Intellectual Property Organization and the World Trade Organization (1995) (selected excerpts)

Article 2. Laws and Regulations	(1) [*Accessibility of Laws and Regulations in the WIPO Collection by WTO Members and Their Nationals*] The International Bureau shall, on request, furnish to WTO Members and to nationals of WTO Members copies of laws and regulations, and copies of translations thereof, that exist in its collection, on the same terms as apply to the Member States of WIPO and to nationals of the Member States of WIPO, respectively
Article 4. Legal-Technical Assistance and Technical Cooperation	(1) [*Availability of Legal-Technical Assistance and Technical Cooperation*] The International Bureau shall make available to developing country WTO Members which are not Member States of WIPO the same legal-technical assistance relating to the TRIPS Agreement as it makes available to Member States of WIPO which are developing countries. The WTO Secretariat shall make available to Member States of WIPO which are developing countries and are not WTO Members the same technical cooperation relating to the TRIPS Agreement as it makes available to developing country WTO Members (2) [*Cooperation between the International Bureau and the WTO Secretariat*] The International Bureau and the WTO Secretariat shall enhance cooperation in their legal-technical assistance and technical cooperation activities relating to the TRIPS Agreement for developing countries, so as to maximize the usefulness of those activities and ensure their mutually supportive nature (3) [*Exchange of Information*] For the purposes of paragraphs (1) and (2), the International Bureau and the WTO Secretariat shall keep in regular contact and exchange non-confidential information

Source: WTO–WIPO Cooperation Agreement 1995 <http://www.wto.org/english/tratop_e/trips_e/wtowip_e.htm> accessed 30 October 2015.

8.2   WIPO's unique relationship with private sector stakeholders

Among UN agencies, WIPO has a unique relationship with the private sector, and in particular with IP right-holders and applicants that pay fees in exchange for treaty-related services provided by the Secretariat (such as registration of IP rights). The fact that user-fees represent the majority of WIPO's income, and that most such users hail from a small sub-set of WIPO's total membership (as discussed in section 6.1), has unsurprisingly generated a view among such users, the sub-set of Member States that account for the greatest proportion of the users and within many of the Secretariat's leadership and staff, that fee-paying users of WIPO's services should be viewed as the organisation's key clients. It is hard to dispute that users of WIPO's services have direct interests in regard to the usefulness, cost, and efficiency of the fee-paying services the Secretariat provides and in regard to the substance of WIPO's normative activities. Strictly speaking, however, the fees that IP right-holders and applicants pay to WIPO are payments in exchange for specific services that the Secretariat provides them. WIPO's governance system does not formally accord such stakeholders any special status, privileges, rights or obligations in respect of decision-making at WIPO, such as on the allocation of resources in the organisation's Program and Budget. Like other WIPO stakeholders, however, organisations that represent fee-paying users of WIPO's services are able to seek accreditation as observers to WIPO meetings.

Although the fact of WIPO's special relationship with the private sector is undisputed, the extent of the private sector's influence and its desirability are hotly debated among Member States and stakeholders. In addition to observer status at WIPO meetings, private sector users of WIPO's services interact with and lobby the Secretariat and Member States through informal, private meetings, participation in WIPO technical assistance activities, and through WIPO events, which they sometimes speak at or co-host. Further, associations of IP-right holders and the companies they represent often have long-standing relationships with national IP offices; they can shape decision-making outcomes at WIPO through their influence on the positions their governments take in WIPO deliberations. A review of WIPO meeting reports confirms that those Member States that are home to the majority of WIPO's fee-paying clients, such as Japan and the United States, regularly promote the interests of particular groups of IP right-holders and professionals, although they face mounting pressures to better serve a broader range of private and public-interest constituents at WIPO. Here, it is important to underscore that a range of private sector actors have interests at WIPO, including large multinational R&D companies; manufacturing, entertainment and software industries; private collective management societies; SMEs; and associations of artists, creators, scientists and inventors, as well as generic producers. Among these, the larger international corporations and industry associations with long-standing relationships with WIPO, have greater resources for engaging with the organisation and lobbying Member States than smaller private sector stakeholders or those more recently engaged in the international IP system and related policy debates.

From 1998 to 2003, WIPO Member States approved the operation of two bodies aimed at giving a direct voice to the private sector and non-state actors, namely a Policy Advisory Commission (PAC) and an Industry Advisory Commission (IAC).[21] The PAC was comprised of 25 eminent people drawn from a range of fields, including politics, diplomacy and administration, which have bearing on IP.[22] The IAC was comprised of 20 top-level representatives from the private sector.[23] Although each of these Commissions ceased to exist after 2003, they are worth noting here because they have had an important and enduring influence on perceptions and expectations among Member States and stakeholders on what the role of the private sector should or should not be at WIPO.

---

21 For a report of their first meetings, see WIPO, *Policy Advisory Commission and Industry Advisory Commission* WO/GA/24/6 (WIPO 1999) Annex 1.

22 Its mandate was to 'enhance the Secretariat's capacity to monitor and respond in a timely, informed and effective manner to international and regional developments in intellectual property, in information technology, and in other fields bearing on WIPO's operations and its policy environment.' Members of the Commission included three former presidents (of Malta, Romania and Portugal), and its chair was HRH Prince El-Hassan of Jordan. The PAC created a taskforce (which met in July 1999 and March 2000) to develop a workplan, which included the review of several studies and presentations, as well as the formulation of a World Intellectual Property Declaration (WIPD). For the declaration, see WIPO, 'Policy Advisory Commission: World Intellectual Property Declaration' <http://www.wipo.int/about-wipo/en/pac/ip_declaration.htm> accessed 26 October 2015.

23 In opening the first IAC meeting, former Director General Kamal Idris stated that he considered it essential that the 'voice of the market sector is heard in order for the organisation is responsive to its [market sector] needs.' Although the role of the IAC was intended as purely advisory, the Director General stated that it was designed to ensure that there is 'a direct input of industry into the policy-making process in WIPO.' See WIPO, *Policy Advisory Commission and Industry Advisory Commission* WO/GA/24/6 Annex 1 (WIPO 1999) 1.

8.3   Guidelines on observers

The WIPO General Rules of Procedure state that the Director General shall invite as observers to the various sessions such states and inter-governmental organisations as are entitled to observer status under a treaty or agreement (Rule 8). The Rules state that such observers may take part in debates at the invitation of the chair, but may not submit proposals, amendments or motions (Rule 24), may not have a vote (Rule 39) and that their expenses shall be borne by the States or organisations that have sent them (Rule 49(2)). In addition, the WIPO Director General may at any time invite States or organisations to send observers to follow the work of an Ad Hoc Committee of Experts (Rule 38(4)).

The World Intellectual Property Organization also has general guide-lines for the admission of three categories of observers to WIPO meetings: intergovernmental organisations, international NGOs and national NGOs (see Table 8.2 for the criteria for admission as perma-nent observer to WIPO).[24] Requests by IGOs and NGOs for observer status are considered on an annual basis at the WIPO Assemblies; they are submitted to the Secretariat, which then presents the request to the General Assembly for approval. Once an intergovernmental organisation is admitted to attend the Assemblies as an observer, it is a WIPO practice that it is also invited to attend as an observer to other meetings of committees, working groups or bodies subsidiary to the Assemblies, if their subject matter seems to be of direct interest to that IGO.[25]

For national and international NGOs, WIPO requires basic informa-tion about the organisation, including its articles of incorporation, list of officers (and their nationality in the case of an international NGO), a complete list of national groups or members, a description of the composition of its members or its governing body or bodies (including geographical distribution in the case of an international

---

24 These guidelines are available on the WIPO website at WIPO, 'Observers' <http://www.wipo.int/members/en/admission/observers.html> accessed 1 August 2014. The granting of observer status to national NGOs was considered and approved at the 2002 WIPO Assemblies. See WIPO, *Admission of Observers: Assemblies of the Member States of WIPO, 37thSeries of Meetings* A/37/8 (WIPO 2002).

25 Catherine Monagle, *Observer Status and Access to Documents: Comparative Analysis across Selected International Organizations* (Berne: Berne Declaration and Development Fund 2011) 7.

NGO), a statement of its objectives and an indication of the field(s) of IP of interest to it. A number of additional principles are observed in extending invitations to national NGOs as observers (see Table 8.2).

As of October 2015, some 72 intergovernmental organisations were accredited with permanent observer status at WIPO (these included 17 UN system organisations, 8 intergovernmental IP organisations, 34 regional intergovernmental organisations, and 12 other intergovernmental organisations) and 330 NGOs (over 250 of which were international NGOs).[26]

Broadly speaking, there are five types of NGOs accredited at WIPO, namely those representing: (i) companies or groups of companies in a particular industry, such as publishers or pharmaceutical companies; (ii) professionals active in the realm of IP, such as patent and copyright lawyers; (iii) collecting societies in the area of copyright; (iv) individual creators, artists, musicians or authors; and (v) public interests, such as organisations concerned with public health, libraries and access to knowledge.

Within the UN system of organisations, WIPO attracts one of the highest rates of private sector interest and participation in its work. Of the 335+ NGOs with status as permanent accredited observers to WIPO, the majority represent private interests, while an estimated 20–25 per cent have a public interest purpose.[27] The attendance and degree of participation by accredited organisations in meetings varies widely; some appear for only very targeted meetings. However, a small number of accredited NGOs regularly attend and engage in a range of different WIPO bodies.

Non-governmental organisations can also request ad hoc observer status with specific WIPO committees (giving those organisations that

---

26 A full list of the 258 international and 79 national NGOs 'accredited observers' at WIPO is available at: WIPO, 'Observers' <http://www.wipo.int/members/en/admission/observers.html> accessed 25 October 2015.

27 Author's calculations based on names and mission statements of organisations. NGOs were classified as either private interest (representing primarily the commercial interests of industry, SMEs, lawyers or individual creators and artists) or public interest where their purpose is primarily to advance public policy or broad social goals.

Table 8.2   Criteria for admission as permanent observer in WIPO

Requests for admission as permanent observers in WIPO must be presented to the International Bureau, addressed to the WIPO Director General or to the WIPO Legal Counsel. The admission of NGOs to observer status lies within the competence of the WIPO General Assembly, which takes decisions on that matter at its sessions held every year. Requests must include the following information:

International Non-Governmental Organisation (NGO)	National Non-Governmental Organisation (NGO)
• Text of its constituent instrument (articles of incorporation, bylaws, and so on);	• Text of its constituent instrument (articles of incorporation, bylaws, and so on);
• Indication of the date and place where it was established;	• Indication of the date and place where it was established;
• List of its officers (showing their nationality);	• List of its officers;
• Complete list of its national groups or members (showing their country of origin);	• Complete list of its national groups or members;
• Description of the composition of the members of its governing body or bodies (including their geographical distribution);	• Description of the composition of the members of its governing body or bodies;
• Statement of its objectives; and	• Statement of its objectives; and
• Indication of the field or fields of intellectual property (for example, copyright and related rights) of interest to it	• Indication of the field or fields of intellectual property (for example, copyright and related rights) of interest to it

In addition, the following principles are observed in extending invitations to national NGOs, as observers:

(i)   The organisation shall be essentially concerned with intellectual property matters falling within the competence of WIPO and shall, in the view of the Director General, be able to offer constructive, substantive contributions to the deliberations of the Assemblies of WIPO;

(ii) The aims and purposes of the organisation shall be in conformity with the spirit, purposes and principles of WIPO and the United Nations;

(iii) The organisation shall have an established headquarters. It shall have democratically adopted statutes, adopted in conformity with the legislation of the Member State from which the NGO originates. One copy of the statutes shall be submitted to WIPO;

(iv) The organisation shall have authority to speak for its members through its authorised representatives and in accordance with the rules governing observer status; and

(v)   The admission of national NGOs to observer status shall be the subject of prior consultations between Member States and the Secretariat.

Source: WIPO, 'Observers' <http://www.wipo.int/members/en/admission/observers.html> accessed 25 October 2015.

do not have permanent observer status the possibility to participate).[28] Two WIPO Committees that are particularly notable for the ad hoc accreditation of NGO observers (in addition to the 335+ permanent NGO observers that are entitled to attend) are the IGC (which has approved over 300 organisations as ad hoc observers) and the CDIP (which has admitted over the course of its sessions several dozen ad hoc observers for a period of one year without implications as to their status for future CDIP meetings). Rules for ad hoc observers vary by committee; whereas ad hoc observer status for the IGC applies to attendance at all subsequent IGC meetings, ad hoc observer status for the CDIP provides access for a period of 1 year only. The IGC, which is WIPO's most participatory body in terms of civil society engagement, has the broadest criteria for ad hoc observers, which can include not only NGOs but also representatives of indigenous and local communities and undertakes more activities than any other WIPO committee to engage NGOs in its work.[29] The WIPO General Assembly has also encouraged Member States 'to include representatives of indigenous and local communities on their delegations' to the IGC.[30] In addition, a Voluntary Fund,[31] designed to facilitate the participation of representatives of local and indigenous communities in the IGC's work, has sponsored more than 80 groups, but now suffers a shortage of funds.[32]

Although the accreditation of NGOs is comparatively swift at WIPO[33] and observers have the right to speak at meetings, address negotiators, and submit documents, they cannot participate in the many

---

28 The requests are submitted each year in a Memorandum of the Director General to the Assemblies on Admission of Observers. See, for instance, WIPO, *Admission of Observers: Document Prepared by the Secretariat, Assemblies of the Member States of WIPO, 55th Series of Meetings, 5 to 14 October 2015* A/55/2 (WIPO 2015).

29 For instance, the IGC has a distinct webpage devoted to proposals, submissions and papers of observers, and the Secretariat offers briefings on the IGC's work to NGOs and civil society.

30 See WIPO, *General Report: WIPO Assemblies of Member States, 37th Series of Meetings* A/37/14 (WIPO 2002) sub para. 290(ii). This call was reiterated in 2003, see WIPO, *Intergovernmental Committee on Intellectual Property and Genetic Resources, Traditional Knowledge and Folklore: Report Prepared by the Secretariat* WIPO/GRTKF/IC/5/15 (WIPO 2003) para. 206.

31 WIPO, *The WIPO Voluntary Fund: A Stronger Voice for Indigenous and Local Communities in WIPO's Work on Traditional Knowledge, Traditional Cultural Expressions and Genetic Resources* WIPO Publication No. 936(E) (WIPO 2007).

32 Catherine Saez, 'New Proposal to Keep Indigenous Peoples on WIPO Traditional Knowledge Committee', *Intellectual Property Watch*, 26 August 2014.

33 UN ECOSOC, by contrast, has a long process for accreditation of observers. With the exception of its ministerial meetings and certain meetings of its dispute settlement bodies, the WTO has

off-the-record 'informal' closed door sessions that occur within and among regional groups of countries, which is where much of the real consensus-building and deal-making occurs at WIPO (see discussion in section 5.5). Observers are generally invited to speak only after Members wishing to speak have done so and if time permits.[34] NGOs can, however, interact with delegates and distribute documents in rooms and halls outside the conference proceedings, and side events can be hosted by accredited NGOs on site, space permitting.

Beyond its guidelines on observers at meetings, WIPO does not have any further guidelines or policy framework for its engagement with stakeholders in other aspects of the organisation's work, such as its multi-stakeholder platforms, technical assistance, training, and events, or for their financial or in-kind support of WIPO's activities.

8.4   Transparency and access to documents

There are several WIPO policies relevant to transparency, most notably in respect of access to WIPO meetings, documents and negotiating texts; the content on the WIPO website; and the public availability of data on the organisation's activities.

In terms of access to meetings, WIPO's Rules of Procedure and guidelines on observers define the terms on which NGOs and intergovernmental organisations actors can participate in WIPO proceedings (as discussed in section 8.3). Other Secretariat practices relevant to stakeholder participation and the transparency of WIPO meetings and activities are 'Information Meetings' hosted on an informal basis on selected activities and issues that are open to Member States and the wider public (including those individuals and organisations not otherwise accredited to attend WIPO meetings), as well as press briefings for accredited journalists. In addition, WIPO's policy on webcasting makes it possible for those stakeholders without observer status or without adequate resources to attend meetings in Geneva to view some formal sessions of

---

no general policy to enable the participation of NGOs and other stakeholders as observers at its regular meetings.

34 Also see Jeremy Malcolm, 'Public Interest Representation in Global IP Policy Institutions' *Program on Information Justice and Intellectual Property (PIJIP) Research Paper No. 6* (American University Washington College of Law 2010). Malcolm observes that in formal meetings, 'civil society interventions are left until last and the time given for them is strictly limited' (and also must be shared with time allotted for the various business NGOs), 16.

WIPO meetings.[35] WIPO provides electronic recording of many conference proceedings as well as live webcasting and recorded meeting content, through video-on-demand, of a growing number of official WIPO
meetings, such as the formal proceedings of the annual Assemblies, the
PBC and Standing Committees.[36] In recent years, the Secretariat made
free public Wi-Fi available in its buildings, which improved the ability of
stakeholders participating in meetings to coordinate among themselves
and to share information in real-time with those not present.

The WIPO Secretariat makes most official documents for intergovernmental sessions available on its website and in hard copies during meetings, as well as draft negotiating texts, although not always proactively.[37]
The WIPO Secretariat generally publishes a summary of gavelled decisions and recommendations swiftly at the end of each meeting, as well as
a detailed meeting report for adoption by Member States. As observed
in Chapter 5, however, on occasions where Member State debate has
resulted in lengthy discussions and extended sessions, the Secretariat
has sometimes not been able to produce the draft report in time for distribution and adoption at the meeting. In 2014 and 2015, for instance,
Member States agreed that the draft reports of the WIPO Assemblies
would be published on WIPO's website and communicated to Member
States in the following month, for comments within two months, and
that the final reports would be deemed adopted one month later.

In the case of treaty negotiations, WIPO provides access to draft negotiating documents before and after each round of negotiation. At the
most recent Marrakesh Diplomatic Conference for a treaty to facilitate access to published works for persons who are visually impaired,
the WIPO Secretariat webcast the negotiations and established lis-
tening rooms where stakeholders could hear discussions underway in
break-out rooms where negotiators were working on specific issues.
When consensus on new language was forged, the new draft text of
the agreement was released to the public.[38] In addition, a system for

---

35 Webcasting was introduced for the first time at the 2010 WIPO Assemblies. See WIPO,
    Webcasting at WIPO: Document Prepared by the Secretariat WO/PBC/18/19 (WIPO 2011).
36 See WIPO, 'Webcasting' <www.wipo.int/webcasting/en> accessed 28 October 2014.
37 Knowledge Ecology International, *Transparency of Negotiating Documents in Selected
    Fora* (KEI 2009) <http://www.keionline.org/misc-docs/4/attachment2_transparency_ustr.pdf>
    accessed 15 August 2014. Also see Jeremy Malcolm, 'Public Interest Representation in Global IP
    Policy Institutions' (2010) *PIJIP Research Paper No. 6.*
38 Sean Flynn, 'Inside Views: WIPO Treaty for the Blind Shows that Transparency Can
    Work (and Is Necessary)' *Intellectual Property Watch* (26 June 2013).

stakeholder consultations and input was established, including stakeholder working groups composed of commercial and non-commercial interests alike, along with published reports and summaries of their deliberations.[39]

A further aspect of transparency relates to the accessibility and manageability of WIPO documents. Here, key issues are the languages in which documents are available to Member States and the public; the overall volume in terms of numbers and length of documents; and ease with which Member States and the public can locate, review and analyse the documentation. Together, these elements can impact the ability of Member States to fulfil their oversight role and the quality of their engagement in WIPO deliberations.

In 2010, WIPO Member States adopted a Policy on Languages, according to which documentation is to be provided in the six official languages of the United Nations (Arabic, Chinese, English, French, Russian and Spanish), for meetings of the WIPO main bodies, committees and working groups, as well as for core and new publications.[40] This policy has been introduced in a phased manner since 2011 and subject to approval of the resource requirements. Notably, the language policy decision noted that the extension of language coverage in the WIPO Committees would be reflected in the language section of the Special Rules of Procedure of the respective WIPO Committees (see paragraph (x) of the decision), which has not occurred to date. In respect of exceptionally voluminous documents and support papers (studies, surveys) commissioned by certain committees, Member States have stated that these should be made available only in the original languages with a summary to be prepared by the Secretariat in all six languages, with the proviso that if a Member State or group of Member States were to express specific interest in one of such documents, the Secretariat would translate its full text in the required language.

As observed above, the WIPO Secretariat produces a large volume of documents for the consideration of Member States. Some documents are produced to meet the requirements of various WIPO

---

39 Ibid.

40 See WIPO, *Policy on Languages at WIPO* WO/PBC/18/15 (Geneva: WIPO 2011); WIPO, *Progress Report on the Implementation of WIPO Language Policy: Prepared by the Secretariat* WO/PBC/21/15 (WIPO 2013) 1–2. For the text of the language policy decision, see WIPO, *Summary of Recommendations Made by the Program and Budget Committee* A/48/24 (2010 WIPO) Annex II.

treaties, regulations and policies adopted by Member States, others respond to specific Member State decisions or requests, and others are produced by the Secretariat on it own initiative. Documents may include background information, proposals or recommendations, as well as meeting reports that detail the full proceedings and summaries of key decisions. The Secretariat also commissions and publishes many surveys and studies at the request of Member States. In 2011, as part of their decision to adopt the WIPO language policy, Member States called for better control and rationalisation of the total volume of WIPO documentation, including through more concise, reduced-length documents. The focus on the volume of documents was partly financially motivated – to reduce the costs of translation – but was also prompted by the recognition that few Member States had the capacity to critically review and respond to the range of documents in a timely manner.[41] As of 2014, the JIU estimated that the average combined length of documents submitted by the Secretariat to Member States each year was over 8,000 pages per year.[42]

A further documentation-related challenge to transparency and oversight at WIPO relates to the practice of extensive cross-referencing among WIPO documents. As noted in a 2014 JIU report, many documents that report on Member State meetings and decisions need to be read in 'conjunction with the (often divergent) comments made orally during the debates and cross-referenced with other background documentation.'[43] Although a common practice in UN documentation systems, this process is onerous and time-consuming, particularly for those not already well-versed in the intricacies of WIPO's decision-making practices. Moreover, this complexity constrains the capacity of many Member States to provide effective oversight and of stakeholders to monitor the organisation's work.

The WIPO website provides a further vehicle for transparency of the organisation's activities: it provides information on official meetings, events, and statistics, as well as access to studies commissioned by the Secretariat and official documents produced by the Secretariat. At present, there is no centralised online database of all such WIPO

---

41 Ibid.

42 JIU, *Review of Management and Administration in the World Intellectual Property Organization (WIPO)* JIU/REP/2014/2 (UN Joint Inspection Unit 2014) 8.

43 JIU, *Review of Management and Administration in the World Intellectual Property Organization (WIPO)* JIU/REP/2014/2 (UN Joint Inspection Unit 2014) 6.

documents that enables effective and efficient text searching, such as of studies undertaken under the auspices of particular WIPO committees. Instead, Member States and the public need to be able to identify the particular WIPO meeting where an issue or study may have been discussed, and then to consult the list of documents for that specific meeting. As of end 2015, the documentation on WIPO meetings available on WIPO's website went back only to the mid-1990s in most instances (for documentation prior to that date, it is possible to consult the WIPO library for archival assistance), and the website remained under revision, such as in regard to translation.

A final aspect of transparency relates to the access of Member States and stakeholders to data about WIPO's activities – their cost, content, expected results and impact. WIPO has three channels for the provision of such data: its periodic financial and program performance reports; internal evaluation, investigation and audit reports; and online information published on the WIPO website. In some areas, WIPO provides access to extensive online databases, such as on national IP laws as well as patent and trademark applications. On the other hand, electronic databases designed to provide information on WIPO's capacity-building activities and consultants lack key substantive information needed to enable Member States and external stakeholders to monitor and make independent assessments of effectiveness (such as on budget, content of activities and evaluation).[44]

---

44 Carolyn Deere Birkbeck and Santiago Roca, *Independent External Review of WIPO Technical Assistance in the Area of Cooperation for Development* CDIP/8/INF/1 (WIPO 2011).

9   Conclusion

This Reference Guide has presented a factual overview of WIPO's complex governance system. The core focus has been on its formal components, such as those found in the WIPO Convention, the organisation's agreement with the UN and in the various rules, regulations and policies adopted by Member States or the Secretariat. The book has also, however, documented areas where governance practices at WIPO diverge from the formal components of its governance framework or where relevant regulations, rules, policies, guidelines or reports are ambiguous, inconsistent or absent. It has provided numerous examples of where and how informal dimensions of WIPO's governance system impact how governance of the organisation and its activities actually occur. The book has underscored, for instance, the prominent role of regional groups of Member States as vehicles for consensus-building and consultation.

Beyond the more common focus on WIPO's decision-making structures and procedures, this Reference guide has taken a wider view of WIPO's governance system, arguing that it also comprises the organisation's formal rules, regulations, policies and informal practices in respect of Member State representation and interaction with the Secretariat; financial arrangements and the Program and Budget process; audit, evaluation and oversight of the Secretariat, its leadership and staff; and external relations, stakeholder participation and transparency.

This Reference Guide has also drawn attention to the potential for WIPO's formal governance structure to shape the informal dimensions of the organisation's governance system, such as the political dynamics of decision-making by Member States and the Secretariat. A clear example relates to WIPO's unique financial arrangements – whereby the core of the organisation's income derives from fees paid by users of its treaty-based services, which although financially attractive for the Secretariat and Member States, gives rise to a special relationship between the WIPO Secretariat and its fee-paying clients. The result is a widely acknowledged tension between the quest to preserve the member-driven character of the organisation, where Member States are the core constituency and focus of accountability, and the pressure to better serve WIPO's core private sector clients (IP applicants and right-holders) and by extension the sub-set of Member States that are the countries of origin for the majority of WIPO's fee-based income.

The WIPO Secretariat is more than a subject of WIPO's governance system; it is also an actor within it. This book has illustrated how the Secretariat can play a role within WIPO's governance system, noting a diversity of ways that it can influence the agenda and decisions of Member States and outcomes of the organisation's work. In addition, the analysis in this book has presented a clear view of WIPO's notoriously complex decision-making structure, setting out the organisation's governing bodies and committees, and describing their relationship to the many WIPO-administered IP treaties and Unions, as well as their respective governance bodies, financial arrangements and memberships.

Although beyond the scope of this Reference Guide, future efforts to understand (and improve) WIPO's governance will require deeper attention to the political, economic and cultural factors at play. Already, debates on the implementation of WIPO's Development Agenda have underscored that institutional culture and leadership; power politics among Member States; pressures from private sector and public interest stakeholder groups; and shifting economic, scientific, technological and cultural trends, as well as new models for innovation and creativity, shape the context for decision-making at WIPO. Together, they impact how WIPO's governance system works in practice and the prospects for organisational change. Similarly, changes in the composition, origins and priorities of the core users of the IP system and the growing array of private and public interest stakeholders interested in WIPO's work have the potential to alter the organisation's governance dynamics.

How does WIPO's governance system impact the potential for Member States to fulfil their oversight functions, provide strategic direction and reach decisions? How does it constrain or enable different kinds of stakeholders in their efforts to hold both Member States and the Secretariat to account? Looking ahead, my hope is that this Reference

Guide will serve as a foundation stone, and as a call to scholars, policymakers and stakeholders alike, for greater attention to WIPO's governance system and political dynamics, and their impact on the organisation's outcomes.

Appendix 1: Convention Establishing the World Intellectual Property Organization

Signed at Stockholm on July 14, 1967 and as amended on September 28, 1979

The Contracting Parties,

Desiring to contribute to better understanding and cooperation among States for their mutual benefit on the basis of respect for their sovereignty and equality, Desiring, in order to encourage creative activity, to promote the protection of intellectual property throughout the world, Desiring to modernize and render more efficient the administration of the Unions established in the fields of the protection of industrial property and the protection of literary and artistic works, while fully respecting the independence of each of the Unions, Agree as follows:

Article 1 Establishment of the Organization

The World Intellectual Property Organization is hereby established.

Article 2 Definitions

For the purposes of this Convention:

(i) "Organization" shall mean the World Intellectual Property Organization (WIPO);

(ii) "International Bureau" shall mean the International Bureau of Intellectual Property;

(iii) "Paris Convention" shall mean the Convention for the Protection of Industrial Property signed on March 20, 1883, including any of its revisions;

(iv) "Berne Convention" shall mean the Convention for the Protection of Literary and Artistic Works signed on September 9, 1886, including any of its revisions;

(v) "Paris Union" shall mean the International Union established by the Paris Convention;

(vi) "Berne Union" shall mean the International Union established by the Berne Convention;

(vii) "Unions" shall mean the Paris Union, the Special Unions and Agreements established in relation with that Union, the Berne Union, and any other international agreement designed to promote the protection of intellectual property whose administration is assumed by the Organization according to Article 4(iii);

(viii) "intellectual property" shall include the rights relating to:

- literary, artistic and scientific works,
- performances of performing artists, phonograms, and broadcasts,
- inventions in all fields of human endeavor,
- scientific discoveries,
- industrial designs,
- trademarks, service marks, and commercial names and designations,

– protection against unfair competition,

and all other rights resulting from intellectual activity in the industrial, scientific, literary or artistic fields.

Article 3 Objectives of the Organization

The objectives of the Organization are:

(i) to promote the protection of intellectual property throughout the world through cooperation among States and, where appropriate, in collaboration with any other international organization,

(ii) to ensure administrative cooperation among the Unions.

Article 4 Functions

In order to attain the objectives described in Article 3, the Organization, through its appropriate organs, and subject to the competence of each of the Unions:

(i) shall promote the development of measures designed to facilitate the efficient protection of intellectual property throughout the world and to harmonize national legislation in this field;

(ii) shall perform the administrative tasks of the Paris Union, the Special Unions established in relation with that Union, and the Berne Union;

(iii) may agree to assume, or participate in, the administration of any other international agreement designed to promote the protection of intellectual property;

(iv) shall encourage the conclusion of international agreements designed to promote the protection of intellectual property;

(v) shall offer its cooperation to States requesting legal-technical assistance in the field of intellectual property;

(vi) shall assemble and disseminate information concerning the protection of intellectual property, carry out and promote studies in this field, and publish the results of such studies;

(vii) shall maintain services facilitating the international protection of intellectual property and, where appropriate, provide for registration in this field and the publication of the data concerning the registrations;

(viii) shall take all other appropriate action.

Article 5 Membership

(1) Membership in the Organization shall be open to any State which is a member of any of the Unions as defined in Article 2(vii).

(2) Membership in the Organization shall be equally open to any State not a member of any of the Unions, provided that:

(i) it is a member of the United Nations, any of the Specialized Agencies brought into relationship with the United Nations, or the International Atomic Energy Agency, or is a party to the Statute of the International Court of Justice, or

(ii) it is invited by the General Assembly to become a party to this Convention.

Article 6 General Assembly

(1)

(a) There shall be a General Assembly consisting of the States party to this Convention which are members of any of the Unions.

(b) The Government of each State shall be represented by one delegate, who may be assisted by alternate delegates, advisors, and experts.

(c) The expenses of each delegation shall be borne by the Government which has appointed it.

(2) The General Assembly shall:

    (i) appoint the Director General upon nomination by the Coordination Committee;

    (ii) review and approve reports of the Director General concerning the Organization and give him all necessary instructions;

    (iii) review and approve the reports and activities of the Coordination Committee and give instructions to such Committee;

    (iv) adopt the biennial budget of expenses common to the Unions;

    (v) approve the measures proposed by the Director General concerning the administration of the international agreements referred to in Article 4(iii);

    (vi) adopt the financial regulations of the Organization;

    (vii) determine the working languages of the Secretariat, taking into consideration the practice of the United Nations;

    (viii) invite States referred to under Article 5(2)(ii) to become party to this Convention;

    (ix) determine which States not Members of the Organization and which inter-governmental and international non-governmental organizations shall be admitted to its meetings as observers;

    (x) exercise such other functions as are appropriate under this Convention.

(3)

(a) Each State, whether member of one or more Unions, shall have one vote in the General Assembly.

(b) One-half of the States members of the General Assembly shall constitute a quorum.

(c) Notwithstanding the provisions of subparagraph (b), if, in any session, the number of States represented is less than one-half but equal to or more than one-third of the States members of the General Assembly, the General Assembly may make decisions but, with the exception of decisions concerning its own procedure, all such decisions shall take effect only if the following conditions are fulfilled. The International Bureau shall communicate the said decisions to the States members of the General Assembly which were not represented and shall invite them to express in writing their vote or abstention within a period of three months from the date of the communication. If, at the expiration of this period, the number of States having thus expressed their vote or abstention attains the number of States which was lacking for attaining the quorum in the session itself, such decisions shall take effect provided that at the same time the required majority still obtains.

(d) Subject to the provisions of subparagraphs (e) and (f), the General Assembly shall make its decisions by a majority of two-thirds of the votes cast.

(e) The approval of measures concerning the administration of international agree-ments referred to in Article 4(iii) shall require a majority of three-fourths of the votes cast.

(f) The approval of an agreement with the United Nations under Articles 57 and 63 of the Charter of the United Nations shall require a majority of nine-tenths of the votes cast.

(g) For the appointment of the Director General (paragraph (2)(i)), the approval of measures proposed by the Director General concerning the administration of international agreements (paragraph (2)(v)), and the transfer of headquarters

(Article 10), the required majority must be attained not only in the General Assembly but also in the Assembly of the Paris Union and the Assembly of the Berne Union.

(h) Abstentions shall not be considered as votes.

 (i) A delegate may represent, and vote in the name of, one State only.

(4)

(a) The General Assembly shall meet once in every second calendar year in ordinary session, upon convocation by the Director General.

(b) The General Assembly shall meet in extraordinary session upon convocation by the Director General either at the request of the Coordination Committee or at the request of one-fourth of the States members of the General Assembly.

(c) Meetings shall be held at the headquarters of the Organization.

(5) States party to this Convention which are not members of any of the Unions shall be admitted to the meetings of the General Assembly as observers.

(6) The General Assembly shall adopt its own rules of procedure.

Article 7 Conference

(1)

(a) There shall be a Conference consisting of the States party to this Convention whether or not they are members of any of the Unions.

(b) The Government of each State shall be represented by one delegate, who may be assisted by alternate delegates, advisors, and experts.

(c) The expenses of each delegation shall be borne by the Government which has appointed it.

(2) The Conference shall:

(i) discuss matters of general interest in the field of intellectual property and may adopt recommendations relating to such matters, having regard for the competence and autonomy of the Unions;

(ii) adopt the biennial budget of the Conference;

(iii) within the limits of the budget of the Conference, establish the biennial program of legal-technical assistance;

(iv) adopt amendments to this Convention as provided in Article 17;

(v) determine which States not Members of the Organization and which inter-governmental and international non-governmental organizations shall be admitted to its meetings as observers;

(vi) exercise such other functions as are appropriate under this Convention.

(3)

(a) Each Member State shall have one vote in the Conference.

(b) One-third of the Member States shall constitute a quorum.

(c) Subject to the provisions of Article 17, the Conference shall make its decisions by a majority of two-thirds of the votes cast.

(d) The amounts of the contributions of States party to this Convention not members of any of the Unions shall be fixed by a vote in which only the delegates of such States shall have the right to vote.

(e) Abstentions shall not be considered as votes.

 (f) A delegate may represent, and vote in the name of, one State only.

(4)

(a) The Conference shall meet in ordinary session, upon convocation by the Director General, during the same period and at the same place as the General Assembly.

(b) The Conference shall meet in extraordinary session, upon convocation by the Director General, at the request of the majority of the Member States.

(5) The Conference shall adopt its own rules of procedure.

Article 8 Coordination Committee

(1)

(a) There shall be a Coordination Committee consisting of the States party to this Convention which are members of the Executive Committee of the Paris Union, or the Executive Committee of the Berne Union, or both. However, if either of these Executive Committees is composed of more than one-fourth of the number of the countries members of the Assembly which elected it, then such Executive Committee shall designate from among its members the States which will be members of the Coordination Committee, in such a way that their number shall not exceed the one-fourth referred to above, it being understood that the country on the territory of which the Organization has its headquarters shall not be included in the computation of the said one-fourth.

(b) The Government of each State member of the Coordination Committee shall be represented by one delegate, who may be assisted by alternate delegates, advisors, and experts.

(c) Whenever the Coordination Committee considers either matters of direct interest to the program or budget of the Conference and its agenda, or proposals for the amendment of this Convention which would affect the rights or obligations of States party to this Convention not members of any of the Unions, one-fourth of such States shall participate in the meetings of the Coordination Committee with the same rights as members of that Committee. The Conference shall, at each of its ordinary sessions, designate these States.

(d) The expenses of each delegation shall be borne by the Government which has appointed it.

(2) If the other Unions administered by the Organization wish to be represented as such in the Coordination Committee, their representatives must be appointed from among the States members of the Coordination Committee.

(3) The Coordination Committee shall:

(i) give advice to the organs of the Unions, the General Assembly, the Conference, and the Director General, on all administrative, financial and other matters of common interest either to two or more of the Unions, or to one or more of the Unions and the Organization, and in particular on the budget of expenses common to the Unions;

(ii) prepare the draft agenda of the General Assembly;

(iii) prepare the draft agenda and the draft program and budget of the Conference;

(iv) [deleted]

(v) when the term of office of the Director General is about to expire, or when there is a vacancy in the post of the Director General, nominate a candidate for appointment to such position by the General Assembly; if the General Assembly does not appoint its nominee, the Coordination Committee shall nominate another candidate; this procedure shall be repeated until the latest nominee is appointed by the General Assembly;

(vi) if the post of the Director General becomes vacant between two sessions of the General Assembly, appoint an Acting Director General for the term preceding the assuming of office by the new Director General;

(vii) perform such other functions as are allocated to it under this Convention.

(4)

    (*a*) The Coordination Committee shall meet once every year in ordinary session, upon convocation by the Director General. It shall normally meet at the headquarters of the Organization.

    (*b*) The Coordination Committee shall meet in extraordinary session, upon convocation by the Director General, either on his own initiative, or at the request of its Chairman or one-fourth of its members.

(5)

    (*a*) Each State, whether a member of one or both of the Executive Committees referred to in paragraph (1)(*a*), shall have one vote in the Coordination Committee.

    (*b*) One-half of the members of the Coordination Committee shall constitute a quorum.

    (*c*) A delegate may represent, and vote in the name of, one State only.

(6)

    (*a*) The Coordination Committee shall express its opinions and make its decisions by a simple majority of the votes cast. Abstentions shall not be considered as votes.

    (*b*) Even if a simple majority is obtained, any member of the Coordination Committee may, immediately after the vote, request that the votes be the subject of a special recount in the following manner: two separate lists shall be prepared, one containing the names of the States members of the Executive Committee of the Paris Union and the other the names of the States members of the Executive Committee of the Berne Union; the vote of each State shall be inscribed opposite its name in each list in which it appears. Should this special recount indicate that a simple majority has not been obtained in each of those lists, the proposal shall not be considered as carried.

(7) Any State Member of the Organization which is not a member of the Coordination Committee may be represented at the meetings of the Committee by observers having the right to take part in the debates but without the right to vote.

(8) The Coordination Committee shall establish its own rules of procedure.

Article 9 International Bureau

(1) The International Bureau shall be the Secretariat of the Organization.

(2) The International Bureau shall be directed by the Director General, assisted by two or more Deputy Directors General.

(3) The Director General shall be appointed for a fixed term, which shall be not less than six years. He shall be eligible for reappointment for fixed terms. The periods of the initial appointment and possible subsequent appointments, as well as all other conditions of the appointment, shall be fixed by the General Assembly.

(4)

    (*a*) The Director General shall be the chief executive of the Organization.

    (*b*) He shall represent the Organization.

    (*c*) He shall report to, and conform to the instructions of, the General Assembly as to the internal and external affairs of the Organization.

(5) The Director General shall prepare the draft programs and budgets and periodical reports on activities. He shall transmit them to the Governments of the interested States and to the competent organs of the Unions and the Organization.

(6) The Director General and any staff member designated by him shall participate, without the right to vote, in all meetings of the General Assembly, the Conference, the Coordination Committee, and any other committee or working group. The Director General or a staff member designated by him shall be ex officio secretary of these bodies.

(7) The Director General shall appoint the staff necessary for the efficient performance of the tasks of the International Bureau. He shall appoint the Deputy Directors General after approval by the Coordination Committee. The conditions of employment shall be fixed by the staff regulations to be approved by the Coordination Committee on the proposal of the Director General. The paramount consideration in the employment of the staff and in the determination of the conditions of service shall be the necessity of securing the highest standards of efficiency, competence, and integrity. Due regard shall be paid to the importance of recruiting the staff on as wide a geographical basis as possible.

(8) The nature of the responsibilities of the Director General and of the staff shall be exclusively international. In the discharge of their duties they shall not seek or receive instructions from any Government or from any authority external to the Organization. They shall refrain from any action which might prejudice their position as international officials. Each Member State undertakes to respect the exclusively international character of the responsibilities of the Director General and the staff, and not to seek to influence them in the discharge of their duties.

Article 10 Headquarters

(1) The headquarters of the Organization shall be at Geneva.

(2) Its transfer may be decided as provided for in Article 6(3)*(d)* and *(g)*.

Article 11 Finances

(1) The Organization shall have two separate budgets: the budget of expenses common to the Unions, and the budget of the Conference.

(2)

    (a) The budget of expenses common to the Unions shall include provision for expenses of interest to several Unions.

    (b) This budget shall be financed from the following sources:

        (i) contributions of the Unions, provided that the amount of the contribution of each Union shall be fixed by the Assembly of that Union, having regard to the interest the Union has in the common expenses;

        (ii) charges due for services performed by the International Bureau not in direct relation with any of the Unions or not received for services rendered by the International Bureau in the field of legal-technical assistance;

        (iii) sale of, or royalties on, the publications of the International Bureau not directly concerning any of the Unions;

        (iv) gifts, bequests, and subventions, given to the Organization, except those referred to in paragraph (3)*(b)*(iv);

        (v) rents, interests, and other miscellaneous income, of the Organization.

(3)

    (a) The budget of the Conference shall include provision for the expenses of holding sessions of the Conference and for the cost of the legal-technical assistance program.

    (b) This budget shall be financed from the following sources:

        (i) contributions of States party to this Convention not members of any of the Unions;

        (ii) any sums made available to this budget by the Unions, provided that the amount of the sum made available by each Union shall be fixed by the Assembly of that Union and that each Union shall be free to abstain from contributing to the said budget;

      (iii) sums received for services rendered by the International Bureau in the field of legal-technical assistance;

      (iv) gifts, bequests, and subventions, given to the Organization for the purposes referred to in subparagraph *(a)*.

(4)

    (a) For the purpose of establishing its contribution towards the budget of the Conference, each State party to this Convention not member of any of the Unions shall belong to a class, and shall pay its annual contributions on the basis of a number of units fixed as follows:

        Class A 10

        Class B 3

        Class C 1

    (b) Each such State shall, concurrently with taking action as provided in Article 14(1), indicate the class to which it wishes to belong. Any such State may change class. If it chooses a lower class, the State must announce it to the Conference at one of its ordinary sessions. Any such change shall take effect at the beginning of the calendar year following the session.

    (c) The annual contribution of each such State shall be an amount in the same proportion to the total sum to be contributed to the budget of the Conference by all such States as the number of its units is to the total of the units of all the said States.

    (d) Contributions shall become due on the first of January of each year.

    (e) If the budget is not adopted before the beginning of a new financial period, the budget shall be at the same level as the budget of the previous year, in accordance with the financial regulations.

(5) Any State party to this Convention not member of any of the Unions which is in arrears in the payment of its financial contributions under the present Article, and any State party to this Convention member of any of the Unions which is in arrears in the payment of its contributions to any of the Unions, shall have no vote in any of the bodies of the Organization of which it is a member, if the amount of its arrears equals or exceeds the amount of the contributions due from it for the preceding two full years. However, any of these bodies may allow such a State to continue to exercise its vote in that body if, and as long as, it is satisfied that the delay in payment arises from exceptional and unavoidable circumstances.

(6) The amount of the fees and charges due for services rendered by the International Bureau in the field of legal-technical assistance shall be established, and shall be reported to the Coordination Committee, by the Director General.

(7) The Organization, with the approval of the Coordination Committee, may receive gifts, bequests, and subventions, directly from Governments, public or private institutions, associations or private persons.

(8)

    (a) The Organization shall have a working capital fund which shall be constituted by a single payment made by the Unions and by each State party to this Convention not member of any Union. If the fund becomes insufficient, it shall be increased.

    (b) The amount of the single payment of each Union and its possible participation in any increase shall be decided by its Assembly.

    (c) The amount of the single payment of each State party to this Convention not member of any Union and its part in any increase shall be a proportion of the contribution of that State for the year in which the fund is established or the increase decided. The proportion and the terms of payment shall be fixed by the Conference on the proposal of the Director General and after it has heard the advice of the Coordination Committee.

(9)

   (a) In the headquarters agreement concluded with the State on the territory of which the Organization has its headquarters, it shall be provided that, whenever the working capital fund is insufficient, such State shall grant advances. The amount of these advances and the conditions on which they are granted shall be the subject of separate agreements, in each case, between such State and the Organization. As long as it remains under the obligation to grant advances, such State shall have an ex officio seat on the Coordination Committee.

   (b) The State referred to in subparagraph (a) and the Organization shall each have the right to denounce the obligation to grant advances, by written notification. Denunciation shall take effect three years after the end of the year in which it has been notified.

(10) The auditing of the accounts shall be effected by one or more Member States, or by external auditors, as provided in the financial regulations. They shall be designated, with their agreement, by the General Assembly.

Article 12 Legal Capacity; Privileges and Immunities

(1) The Organization shall enjoy on the territory of each Member State, in conformity with the laws of that State, such legal capacity as may be necessary for the fulfilment of the Organization's objectives and for the exercise of its functions.

(2) The Organization shall conclude a headquarters agreement with the Swiss Confederation and with any other State in which the headquarters may subsequently be located.

(3) The Organization may conclude bilateral or multilateral agreements with the other Member States with a view to the enjoyment by the Organization, its officials, and representatives of all Member States, of such privileges and immunities as may be necessary for the fulfilment of its objectives and for the exercise of its functions.

(4) The Director General may negotiate and, after approval by the Coordination Committee, shall conclude and sign on behalf of the Organization the agreements referred to in paragraphs (2) and (3).

Article 13 Relations with Other Organizations

(1) The Organization shall, where appropriate, establish working relations and cooperate with other intergovernmental organizations. Any general agreement to such effect entered into with such organizations shall be concluded by the Director General after approval by the Coordination Committee.

(2) The Organization may, on matters within its competence, make suitable arrangements for consultation and cooperation with international non-governmental organizations and, with the consent of the Governments concerned, with national organizations, governmental or non-governmental. Such arrangements shall be made by the Director General after approval by the Coordination Committee.

Article 14 Becoming Party to the Convention

(1) States referred to in Article 5 may become party to this Convention and Member of the Organization by:

   (i) signature without reservation as to ratification, or
   (ii) signature subject to ratification followed by the deposit of an instrument of ratification, or
   (iii) deposit of an instrument of accession.

(2) Notwithstanding any other provision of this Convention, a State party to the Paris Convention, the Berne Convention, or both Conventions, may become party to this

Convention only if it concurrently ratifies or accedes to, or only after it has ratified or acceded to:

either the Stockholm Act of the Paris Convention in its entirety or with only the limitation set forth in Article 20(1)(b)(i) thereof,

or the Stockholm Act of the Berne Convention in its entirety or with only the limitation set forth in Article 28(1)(b)(i) thereof.

(3) Instruments of ratification or accession shall be deposited with the Director General.

Article 15 Entry into Force of the Convention

(1) This Convention shall enter into force three months after ten States members of the Paris Union and seven States members of the Berne Union have taken action as provided in Article 14(1), it being understood that, if a State is a member of both Unions, it will be counted in both groups. On that date, this Convention shall enter into force also in respect of States which, not being members of either of the two Unions, have taken action as provided in Article 14(1) three months or more prior to that date.

(2) In respect to any other State, this Convention shall enter into force three months after the date on which such State takes action as provided in Article 14(1).

Article 16 Reservations

No reservations to this Convention are permitted.

Article 17 Amendments

(1) Proposals for the amendment of this Convention may be initiated by any Member State, by the Coordination Committee, or by the Director General. Such proposals shall be communicated by the Director General to the Member States at least six months in advance of their consideration by the Conference.

(2) Amendments shall be adopted by the Conference. Whenever amendments would affect the rights and obligations of States party to this Convention not members of any of the Unions, such States shall also vote. On all other amendments proposed, only States party to this Convention members of any Union shall vote. Amendments shall be adopted by a simple majority of the votes cast, provided that the Conference shall vote only on such proposals for amendments as have previously been adopted by the Assembly of the Paris Union and the Assembly of the Berne Union according to the rules applicable in each of them regarding the adoption of amendments to the administrative provisions of their respective Conventions.

(3) Any amendment shall enter into force one month after written notifications of acceptance, effected in accordance with their respective constitutional processes, have been received by the Director General from three-fourths of the States Members of the Organization, entitled to vote on the proposal for amendment pursuant to paragraph (2), at the time the Conference adopted the amendment. Any amendment thus accepted shall bind all the States which are Members of the Organization at the time the amendment enters into force or which become Members at a subsequent date, provided that any amendment increasing the financial obligations of Member States shall bind only those States which have notified their acceptance of such amendment.

Article 18 Denunciation

(1) Any Member State may denounce this Convention by notification addressed to the Director General.

(2) Denunciation shall take effect six months after the day on which the Director General has received the notification.

Article 19 Notifications

The Director General shall notify the Governments of all Member States of:

    (i) the date of entry into force of the Convention,

    (ii) signatures and deposits of instruments of ratification or accession,

    (iii) acceptances of an amendment to this Convention, and the date upon which the amendment enters into force,

    (iv) denunciations of this Convention.

Article 20 Final Provisions

(1)

    (a) This Convention shall be signed in a single copy in English, French, Russian and Spanish, all texts being equally authentic, and shall be deposited with the Government of Sweden.

    (b) This Convention shall remain open for signature at Stockholm until January 13, 1968.

(2) Official texts shall be established by the Director General, after consultation with the interested Governments, in German, Italian and Portuguese, and such other languages as the Conference may designate.

(3) The Director General shall transmit two duly certified copies of this Convention and of each amendment adopted by the Conference to the Governments of the States members of the Paris or Berne Unions, to the Government of any other State when it accedes to this Convention, and, on request, to the Government of any other State. The copies of the signed text of the Convention transmitted to the Governments shall be certified by the Government of Sweden.

(4) The Director General shall register this Convention with the Secretariat of the United Nations.

Article 21 Transitional Provisions

(1) Until the first Director General assumes office, references in this Convention to the International Bureau or to the Director General shall be deemed to be references to the United International Bureau for the Protection of Industrial, Literary and Artistic Property (also called the United International Bureau for the Protection of Intellectual Property (BIRPI)), or its Director, respectively.

(2)

    (a) States which are members of any of the Unions but which have not become party to this Convention may, for five years from the date of entry into force of this Convention, exercise, if they so desire, the same rights as if they had become party to this Convention. Any State desiring to exercise such rights shall give written notification to this effect to the Director General; this notification shall be effective on the date of its receipt. Such States shall be deemed to be members of the General Assembly and the Conference until the expiration of the said period.

    (b) Upon expiration of this five-year period, such States shall have no right to vote in the General Assembly, the Conference, and the Coordination Committee.

    (c) Upon becoming party to this Convention, such States shall regain such right to vote.

(3)

    (a) As long as there are States members of the Paris or Berne Unions which have not become party to this Convention, the International Bureau and the Director General shall also function as the United International Bureau for the Protection of Industrial, Literary and Artistic Property, and its Director, respectively.

(b) The staff in the employment of the said Bureaux on the date of entry into force of this Convention shall, during the transitional period referred to in subparagraph (a), be considered as also employed by the International Bureau.

(4)

(a) Once all the States members of the Paris Union have become Members of the Organization, the rights, obligations, and property, of the Bureau of that Union shall devolve on the International Bureau of the Organization.

(b) Once all the States members of the Berne Union have become Members of the Organization, the rights, obligations, and property, of the Bureau of that Union shall devolve on the International Bureau of the Organization.

NEW CONTRIBUTION SYSTEM

The Governing Bodies of WIPO and the Unions administered by WIPO adopted with effect from January 1, 1994, a new contribution system that replaces the contribution system set forth in Article 11(4)(a), (b) and (c) of the WIPO Convention, Article 16(4)(a), (b) and (c) of the Paris Convention, Article 25(4)(a), (b) and (c) of the Berne Convention and the corresponding provisions of the Strasbourg (IPC), Nice, Locarno and Vienna Agreements. Details concerning that system may be obtained from the International Bureau of WIPO.

Appendix 2: Agreement between the United Nations and the World Intellectual Property Organization

This Agreement entered into effect on December 17, 1974. A Protocol incorporating the Agreement was signed by Kurt Waldheim, Secretary-General of the United Nations, and Árpád Bogsch, Director General of the World Intellectual Property Organization, on January 21, 1975.

Preamble
In consideration of the provisions of Article 57 of the Charter of the United Nations and of Article 13, paragraph (1), of the Convention Establishing the World Intellectual Property Organization, the United Nations and the World Intellectual Property Organization agree as follows:

Article 1 Recognition
The United Nations recognizes the World Intellectual Property Organization (hereinafter called the "Organization") as a specialized agency and as being responsible for taking appropriate action in accordance with its basic instrument, treaties and agreements administered by it, *inter alia*, for promoting creative intellectual activity and for facilitating the transfer of technology related to industrial property to the developing countries in order to accelerate economic, social and cultural development, subject to the competence and responsibilities of the United Nations and its organs, particularly the United Nations Conference on Trade and Development, the United Nations Development Programme and the United Nations Industrial Development Organization, as well as of the United Nations Educational, Scientific and Cultural Organization and of other agencies within the United Nations system.

Article 2 Co-ordination and Co-operation
In its relations with the United Nations, its organs and the agencies within the United Nations system, the Organization recognizes the responsibilities for co-ordination of the General Assembly and of the Economic and Social Council under the Charter of the United Nations. Accordingly, the Organization agrees to co-operate in whatever measures may be necessary to make co-ordination of the policies and activities of the United Nations and those of the organs and agencies within the United Nations system fully effective. The Organization agrees further to participate in the work of any United Nations bodies which have been established or may be established for the purpose of facilitating such co-operation and co-ordination, in particular through membership in the Administrative Committee on Co-ordination.

Article 3 Reciprocal Representation
    (a) Representatives of the United Nations shall be invited to attend the sessions of all the bodies of the Organization and all such other meetings convened by the

Organization, and to participate, without the right to vote, in the deliberations of such bodies and at such meetings. Written statements presented by the United Nations shall be distributed by the Organization to its members.

(b) Representatives of the Organization shall be invited to attend meetings and to participate, without the right to vote, in the deliberations of the Economic and Social Council, its commissions and committees, of the main committees and the organs of the General Assembly, and of other conferences and meetings of the United Nations, with respect to items on the agenda relating to intellectual property matters within the scope of the activities of the Organization and other matters of mutual interest. Written statements presented by the Organization shall be distributed by the Secretariat of the United Nations to the members of the above-mentioned bodies, in accordance with the rules of procedure.

(c) Representatives of the Organization shall be invited, for purposes of consultation, to attend meetings of the General Assembly of the United Nations when questions as defined in paragraph (b) above are under discussion.

Article 4 Proposal of Agenda Items

Subject to such preliminary consultation as may be necessary, the Organization shall arrange for the inclusion in the provisional agenda of its appropriate bodies of items proposed by the United Nations, and the Economic and Social Council, its commissions and committees shall arrange for the inclusion in their provisional agenda of items proposed by the Organization.

Article 5 Recommendations of the United Nations

(a) The Organization, having regard to the obligation of the United Nations to promote the objectives set forth in Article 55 of the Charter of the United Nations and the function and power of the Economic and Social Council, under Article 62 of the Charter, to make or initiate studies and reports with respect to international economic, social, cultural, educational, health and related matters and to make recommendations concerning these matters to the specialized agencies concerned, and having regard also to the responsibility of the United Nations, under Articles 58 and 63 of the Charter, to make recommendations for the co-ordination of the policies and activities of such specialized agencies, agrees to arrange for the submission, as soon as possible, to the appropriate organ of the Organization, of all formal recommendations which the United Nations may make to it.

(b) The Organization agrees to enter into consultation with the United Nations upon request with respect to such recommendations, and in due course to report to the United Nations on the action taken by the Organization or by its members to give effect to such recommendations, or on the other results of their consideration.

Article 6 Information and Documents

(a) Subject to such arrangements as may be necessary for the safeguarding of confidential material, full and prompt exchange of appropriate information and documents shall be made between the United Nations and the Organization.

(b) The Organization shall submit to the United Nations an annual report on its activities.

Article 7 Statistical Services

(a) The United Nations and the Organization agree to strive for the maximum co-operation, the elimination of all undesirable duplication between them and the most efficient use of their technical personnel in their respective collection, analysis, publication and dissemination of statistical information. They agree to combine their efforts to secure the greatest possible usefulness and utilization of statistical information and to minimize the burden placed upon Governments and other organizations from which such information may be collected.

(b) The Organization recognizes the United Nations as the central agency for the collection, analysis, publication, standardization and improvement of statistics serving the general purposes of international organizations.

(c) The United Nations recognizes the Organization as an appropriate agency for the collection, analysis, publication, standardization and improvement of statistics within its special sphere, without prejudice to the right of the United Nations, its organs and other agencies within the United Nations system to concern themselves with such statistics in so far as they may be essential for their own purposes or for the improvement of statistics throughout the world.

(d) The United Nations shall, in consultation with the Organization and other agencies within the United Nations system, develop administrative instruments and procedures through which effective statistical co-operation may be secured between the United Nations, the Organization and other agencies within the United Nations system brought into relationship with it.

(e) It is recognized as desirable that the collection of statistical information should not be duplicated by the United Nations or any of the agencies within the United Nations system whenever it is practicable for any of them to utilize information or materials which another may have available.

(f) In order to collect statistical information for general use, it is agreed that data supplied to the Organization for incorporation in its basic statistical series or special reports should, so far as practicable, be made available to the United Nations on request.

(g) It is agreed that data supplied to the United Nations for incorporation in its basic statistical series or special reports should, so far as is practicable and appropriate, be made available to the Organization upon request.

Article 8 Assistance to the United Nations

The Organization shall, in accordance with the Charter of the United Nations and the basic instrument of the Organization, treaties and agreements administered by the Organization, co-operate with the United Nations by furnishing to it such information, special reports and studies, and by rendering such assistance to it, as the United Nations may request.

Article 9 Technical Assistance

The United Nations and the Organization undertake to co-operate in the provision of technical assistance for development in the field of intellectual creation. They also undertake to avoid undesirable duplication of activities and services relating to such technical assistance and agree to take such action as may be necessary to achieve effective co-ordination of their technical assistance activities within the framework of existing co-ordination machinery in the field of technical assistance. To this end, the Organization agrees to give consideration to the common use of available services as far as practicable. The United Nations will make available to the Organization its administrative services in this field for use as requested.

Article 10 Transfer of Technology
The Organization agrees to co-operate within the field of its competence with the United Nations and its organs, particularly the United Nations Conference on Trade and Development, the United Nations Development Programme and the United Nations Industrial Development Organization, as well as the agencies within the United Nations system, in promoting and facilitating the transfer of technology to developing countries in such a manner as to assist these countries in attaining their objectives in the fields of science and technology and trade and development.

Article 11 Trust, Non-Self-Governing and Other Territories
The Organization agrees to co-operate within the field of its competence with the United Nations in giving effect to the principles and obligations set forth in Chapters XI, XII and XIII of the Charter of the United Nations and in the Declaration on the Granting of Independence to Colonial Countries and Peoples, with regard to matters affecting the well-being and development of the peoples of the Trust, Non-Self-Governing and other Territories.

Article 12 International Court of Justice
(a) The Organization agrees to furnish any information which may be requested by the International Court of Justice in pursuance of Article 34 of the Statute of the Court.
(b) The General Assembly of the United Nations authorizes the Organization to request advisory opinions of the International Court of Justice on legal questions arising within the scope of its competence other than questions concerning the mutual relationships of the Organization and the United Nations or other specialized agencies.
(c) Such requests may be addressed to the International Court of Justice by the General Assembly of the Organization, or by the Co-ordination Committee of the Organization acting in pursuance of an authorization by the General Assembly of the Organization.
(d) When requesting the International Court of Justice to give an advisory opinion, the Organization shall inform the Economic and Social Council of the request.

Article 13 Relations with Other International Organizations
Before the conclusion of any formal agreement between the Organization and any other specialized agency, any intergovernmental organization other than a specialized agency or any non-governmental organization, the Organization shall inform the Economic and Social Council of the nature and scope of the proposed agreement; furthermore, the Organization shall inform the Economic and Social Council of any matter of interagency concern within its competence.

Article 14 Administrative Co-operation
(a) The United Nations and the Organization recognize the desirability of co-operation in administrative matters of mutual interest.
(b) Accordingly, the United Nations and the Organization undertake to consult together from time to time concerning these matters, particularly the most efficient use of facilities, staff and services and the appropriate methods of avoiding the establishment and operation of competitive or overlapping facilities and services among the United Nations and the agencies within the United Nations system and the Organization and with a view to securing, within the limits of the Charter of the United Nations and the Convention establishing the Organization, as much uniformity in these matters as shall be found practicable.

(c) The consultations referred to in this article shall be utilized to establish the most equitable manner in which any special services or assistance furnished, on request, by the Organization to the United Nations or by the United Nations to the Organization shall be financed.

Article 15 Personnel Arrangements

(a) The United Nations and the Organization agree to develop, in the interests of uniform standards of international employment and to the extent feasible, common personnel standards, methods and arrangements designed to avoid unjustified differences in terms and conditions of employment, to avoid competition in recruitment of personnel, and to facilitate any mutually desirable and beneficial interchange of personnel.

(b) The United Nations and the Organization agree:

(i) to consult together from time to time concerning matters of mutual interest relating to the terms and conditions of employment of the officers and staff, with a view to securing as much uniformity in these matters as may be feasible;

(ii) to co-operate in the interchange of personnel when desirable, on a temporary or a permanent basis, making due provision for the retention of seniority and pension rights;

(iii) to co-operate, on such terms and conditions as may be agreed, in the operation of a common pension fund;

(iv) to co-operate in the establishment and operation of suitable machinery for the settlement of disputes arising in connexion with the employment of personnel and related matters.

(c) The terms and conditions on which any facilities or services of the Organization or the United Nations in connexion with the matters referred to in this article are to be extended to the other shall, where necessary, be the subject of subsidiary agreements concluded for this purpose after the entry into force of this Agreement.

Article 16 Budgetary and Financial Matters

(a) The Organization recognizes the desirability of establishing close budgetary and financial relationships with the United Nations in order that the administrative operations of the United Nations and the agencies within the United Nations system shall be carried out in the most efficient and economical manner possible, and that the maximum measure of co-ordination and uniformity with respect to these operations shall be secured.

(b) The Organization agrees to conform, as far as may be practicable and appropriate, to standard practices and forms recommended by the United Nations.

(c) In the preparation of the budget of the Organization, the Director General of the Organization shall consult with the Secretary-General of the United Nations with a view to achieving, in so far as is practicable, uniformity in presentation of the budgets of the United Nations and of the agencies within the United Nations system for the purposes of providing a basis for comparison of the several budgets.

(d) The Organization agrees to transmit to the United Nations its draft triennial and annual budgets not later than when the said draft budgets are transmitted to its members so as to give the General Assembly sufficient time to examine the said draft budgets, or budgets, and make such recommendations as it deems desirable.

(e) The United Nations may arrange for studies to be undertaken concerning financial and fiscal questions of interest both to the Organization and to the other agencies

within the United Nations system, with a view to the provision of common services and the securing of uniformity in such matters.

Article 17 United Nations Laissez-Passer
Officials of the Organization shall be entitled, in accordance with such special arrangements as may be concluded between the Secretary-General of the United Nations and the Director General of the Organization, to use the laissez-passer of the United Nations.

Article 18 Implementation of the Agreement
The Secretary-General of the United Nations and the Director General of the Organization may enter into such supplementary arrangements for the implementation of this Agreement as may be found desirable.

Article 19 Amendment and Revision
This Agreement may be amended or revised by agreement between the United Nations and the Organization and any such amendment or revision shall come into force on approval by the General Assembly of the United Nations and the General Assembly of the Organization.

Article 20 Entry into Force
This Agreement shall enter into force on its approval by the General Assembly of the United Nations and the General Assembly of the Organization.

Appendix 3: WIPO General Rules of Procedure

As adopted on September 28, 1970, and amended on November 27, 1973, October 5, 1976, and October 2, 1979

PART I: GENERAL

Rule 1: *Application*
(1) These General Rules of Procedure shall apply to the bodies of the World Intellectual Property Organization (WIPO), to the bodies of the various international Unions whose administrative tasks it performs, to the bodies established under international agreements whose administration it assumes, to the subsidiary bodies of any of the said bodies, and to the ad hoc committees of experts convened by the Director General of WIPO, to the extent that the said General Rules of Procedure are not in conflict with the international treaties having created such bodies or the special rules of procedure of such bodies, subsidiary bodies or committees.
(2) These General Rules of Procedure shall not apply to diplomatic conferences.

Rule 2: *Definitions*
For the purposes of these General Rules of Procedure and the rules of procedure of the bodies and committees referred to in Rule 1(1):
"assembly" shall mean the participants having the right to vote in any meeting of a body, subsidiary body and ad hoc committee of experts to which the General Rules of Procedure apply;
"body" shall mean the General Assembly, the Conference and the Coordination Committee of WIPO, as well as the Assemblies, the Conferences of Representatives and the Executive Committees of the Unions, the Council of the Lisbon Union for the Protection of Appellations of Origin and their International Registration, the Committee of Directors of National Industrial Property Offices of the Madrid Union for the International Registration of Marks, the Committee of Experts of the Locarno Union for the International Classification of Industrial Designs, the Committee of Experts of the Nice Union for the International Classification of Goods and Services for the Purposes of the Registration of Marks, the Committee of Experts of the Special Union for the International Patent Classification, the WIPO Permanent Committee for Development Cooperation Related to Industrial Property, the WIPO Permanent Committee for Development Cooperation Related to Copyright and Neighboring Rights and the WIPO Permanent Committee on Patent Information;
"Director General" shall mean the Director General of WIPO; in all cases where Acts earlier than the Stockholm Acts are still applicable, "Director General" shall mean the Director of BIRPI;
"International Bureau" shall mean the International Bureau of Intellectual Property established by Article 9(1) of the WIPO Convention; in all cases where Acts earlier than the

216

Stockholm Acts are still applicable, "International Bureau" shall also mean the United International Bureaux for the Protection of Intellectual Property (BIRPI);

"Organization" shall mean the World Intellectual Property Organization;

"Union" shall mean any international agreement designed to promote the protection of intellectual property whose administrative tasks are performed or whose administration is assumed by the Organization;

"WIPO" shall mean the World Intellectual Property Organization.

PART II: BODIES OF WIPO AND OF THE UNIONS

Chapter I: Preparation of Sessions. Agenda

Rule 3: *Dates and Place of Sessions*

(1) The opening date of each session, its duration and place shall be fixed by the Director General.

(2) The opening date fixed for an extraordinary session must not be more than four months after the day on which the Director General has received the request to convene that session, except where the author or authors of the said request express their willingness to accept a later date.

Rule 4: *Convocations*

The Director General shall send out letters of convocation not less than two months prior to the opening of the session.

Rule 5: *Agenda*

(1) The Director General shall prepare the draft agenda for ordinary sessions.

(2) The draft agenda for extraordinary sessions shall be established by the person or persons requesting convocation of such sessions.

(3) The Director General shall send out the draft agenda at the same time as the letter of convocation.

(4) Any State member of a body may request the inclusion of supplementary items on the draft agenda. Such requests shall reach the Director General not later than one month before the date fixed for the opening of the session. The Director General shall immediately notify the other States members of that body accordingly.

(5) The assembly shall adopt its agenda at the first meeting of the session.

(6) During the session, the assembly may change the order of the items on its agenda, amend some of those items, or delete them from the agenda.

(7) During the session, the assembly may, by a majority of two-thirds of the votes cast, decide to add new items to the agenda, provided they are of an urgent character. The discussion of any such items shall be deferred for forty-eight hours if any delegation so requests.

Rule 6: *Working Documents*

(1) Each item on the agenda of an ordinary session shall, as a rule, be the subject of a report by the Director General.

(2) Reports and other working documents must be sent out at the same time as the letter of convocation, or as soon thereafter as possible.

Chapter II: Participation in Sessions

Rule 7: *Delegations*

(1) Each State member of a body shall be represented by one or more delegates, who may be assisted by alternates, advisors, and experts.

(2) Each delegation shall have a head of delegation.

(3) Any alternate, advisor or expert may act as delegate by order of the head of his delegation.

(4) Each delegate or alternate shall be accredited by the competent authority of the State which he represents. The Director General shall be notified of the appointment of delegates and alternates in a letter, note or telegram, issuing preferably from the Ministry of Foreign Affairs.

Rule 8: *Observers*

(1) The Director General shall invite such States and intergovernmental organizations to be represented by observers as are entitled to observer status under a treaty or agreement.

(2) In addition, each body shall decide, in a general way or for any particular session or meeting, which other States and organizations shall be invited to be represented by observers.

(3) Observers shall be accredited by the competent authority of their State or the competent representative of their organization, in a letter, note or telegram addressed to the Director General; if they represent a State, such communication shall preferably be effected by the Ministry of Foreign Affairs.

Chapter III: Officers and Secretariat

Rule 9: *Officers*

(1) In the first meeting of each ordinary session, each body shall elect a Chairman and two Vice-Chairmen.

(2) Officers shall remain in office until the election of new officers.

(3) The outgoing Chairman and Vice-Chairmen shall not be immediately eligible for re-election to the office which they have held.

Rule 10: *Acting Chairmen*

(1) If the Chairman dies, if he finds it necessary to be absent, or if the State he represents ceases to be a member of the body concerned, the older of the two Vice-Chairmen shall act in his place.

(2) If, for any of the reasons mentioned in the preceding paragraph, none of the Vice-Chairmen is able to act as Chairman, the body concerned shall elect an Acting Chairman.

Rule 11: *Secretariat*

(1) The Director General, or a staff member of the International Bureau designated by him, shall act as Secretary for all meetings, including those of subsidiary bodies.

(2) The International Bureau shall receive, translate and distribute documents, provide for the interpretation of oral interventions, prepare the draft reports of the sessions, be responsible for the safekeeping of documents in its archives, and, generally, perform all the tasks which the meetings of the body concerned may require and for which it has the necessary means at its disposal.

Chapter IV: Subsidiary Bodies

Rule 12: *Subsidiary Bodies*

(1) Any body may establish committees, working groups or other subsidiary bodies.

(2) Each subsidiary body shall report to the body which established it.

(3) The provisions of these General Rules of Procedure shall, as far as possible, apply also to subsidiary bodies.

Chapter V: Conduct of Business

Rule 13: *General Powers of the Chairman*

(1) The Chairman shall declare the opening and closing of the meetings, direct the discussions, accord the right to speak, put questions to the vote, and announce decisions.

(2) He shall rule on points of order and shall have complete control of the proceedings and over the maintenance of order thereat.

(3) He may propose limiting the time to be allowed to each speaker, limiting the number of times each delegation may speak on any question, closing the list of speakers, and closing the debate.

(4) He may propose the suspension or adjournment of the debate on the question under discussion, or the suspension or adjournment of the meeting.

Rule 14: *Points of Order*

(1) In the course of a debate, any delegation may raise a point of order. It may not speak at the same time on the substance of the matter under discussion.

(2) Such points of order shall be immediately decided by the Chairman.

(3) Any delegation may appeal against the ruling of the Chairman. The appeal shall be immediately put to the vote and the Chairman's ruling shall stand unless overruled by a majority of the delegations.

Rule 15: *Right to Speak*

(1) No person may speak without having previously obtained the permission of the Chairman.

(2) The Chairman shall call upon speakers in the order in which they signify their desire to speak. The Secretariat shall be responsible for drawing up a list of such speakers.

(3) The Chairman of a subsidiary body may be accorded precedence for the purpose of explaining the conclusions arrived at by that subsidiary body.

(4) The Director General, or a staff member of the International Bureau designated by him, may at any time, with the approval of the Chairman, make statements on any subject under discussion.

(5) The Chairman may call a speaker to order if his remarks are not relevant to the subject under discussion.

Rule 16: *Limitation of the Number and Length of Speeches*

(1) Any assembly may limit the number of times each delegation may speak on any question and the time to be allowed to each delegation.

(2) The Chairman may limit the time to be allowed to any person speaking on the adjournment or closure of a debate, proposing the suspension or adjournment of the meeting, speaking on the reconsideration of proposals already adopted or rejected, or explaining the vote of his delegation.

(3) When a speaker exceeds the time allotted to him, the Chairman shall call him to order without delay.

Rule 17: *Closing of List of Speakers*

(1) During the discussion of any matter, the Chairman may announce the list of speakers and, with the consent of the meeting, declare the list closed.

(2) He may, however, accord the right of reply if a speech delivered after he has declared the list closed makes it desirable.

Rule 18: *Adjournment or Closure of Debate*
(1) During the course of a meeting, any delegation may move the adjournment or closure of the debate on the question under discussion whether or not any other participant has signified his wish to speak.
(2) Such motion shall be immediately debated. In addition to the delegation proposing the motion, one other delegation may speak in favor of the motion, and two against it, after which the motion shall immediately be put to the vote.
(3) If the assembly is in favor of the adjournment or closure, the Chairman shall immediately declare the debate adjourned or closed.

Rule 19: *Suspension or Adjournment of the Meeting*
(1) During the course of a meeting, any delegation may move its suspension or adjournment.
(2) Such motions shall not be debated, but shall immediately be put to the vote.

Rule 20: *Order of Procedural Motions*
Subject to the provisions on points of order, the following motions shall have precedence, in the order indicated below, over all other proposals or motions before the meeting:
  (a) to suspend the meeting,
  (b) to adjourn the meeting,
  (c) to adjourn the debate on the question under discussion,
  (d) to close the debate on the question under discussion.

Rule 21: *Proposals by Delegations*
(1) Proposals for the adoption of amendments to the drafts submitted to the assembly, and all other proposals, may be submitted orally or in writing by any delegation.
(2) The assembly may decide to debate and vote on a proposal only if it is submitted in writing.
(3) Unless it decides otherwise, the assembly shall discuss or vote on a written proposal only if it has been translated and distributed in the languages in which the documents of the body concerned must be submitted.

Rule 22: *Withdrawal of Proposals*
(1) A proposal may be withdrawn by the delegation which has made it at any time before voting on it has commenced, provided that it has not been amended.
(2) A proposal thus withdrawn may be immediately reintroduced by any other delegation.

Rule 23: *Reconsideration of Proposals Adopted or Rejected*
(1) When a proposal has been adopted or rejected, it may not be reconsidered unless the assembly so decides by a two-thirds majority.
(2) In addition to the delegation proposing the motion to reconsider, one other delegation may speak in favor of the motion, and two against it, after which the motion shall immediately be put to the vote.

Rule 24: *Observers*
(1) Observers may take part in debates at the invitation of the Chairman.
(2) They may not submit proposals, amendments or motions.

Chapter VI: Voting

Rule 25: *Voting*
Proposals and amendments submitted by a delegation shall be put to the vote only if they are supported by at least one other delegation.

Rule 26: *Method of Voting in General*
Voting shall normally be by a show of hands.

Rule 27: *Voting by Roll-Call*
(1) Voting shall be by roll-call:
- (a) if, when the result of a vote by show of hands is in doubt, the Chairman so decides;
- (b) if at least two delegations so request, either before voting takes place or immediately after a vote by show of hands.

(2) The roll shall be called in the alphabetical order of the names in French of the States represented, beginning with the delegation whose name is drawn by lot by the Chairman.
(3) When voting is by roll-call, the vote of each delegation shall be recorded in the report on the session.

Rule 28: *Voting by Secret Ballot*
(1) All elections and decisions concerning States or individuals shall be voted on by secret ballot if at least two delegations so request.
(2) Voting by secret ballot is governed by special regulations, which form the annex to the present General Rules of Procedure and are an integral part thereof.

Rule 29: *Conduct During Voting*
After the Chairman has announced the beginning of voting, no one shall interrupt the voting except on a point of order in connection with the actual conduct of such voting.

Rule 30: *Division of Proposals and Amendments*
(1) Any delegation may move that parts of a proposal or of an amendment be voted upon separately.
(2) If a delegation opposes such motion, permission to speak on the subject shall be given only to one delegation in favor and two delegations against, after which the motion shall be put to the vote.
(3) If the motion for division is carried, all parts of the proposal or of the amendment, separately approved, shall again be put to the vote together as a whole.
(4) If all the operative parts of the proposal or of the amendment have been rejected, the proposal or the amendment shall be considered to have been rejected as a whole.

Rule 31: *Voting on Proposals*
If two or more proposals relate to the same question, the assembly shall, unless it decides otherwise, vote on the proposals in the order in which they have been submitted.

Rule 32: *Voting on Amendments*
(1) When an amendment to a proposal is moved, the amendment shall be voted on first. A motion is considered an amendment to a proposal if it adds to, deletes from, or revises part of, that proposal.
(2) When two or more amendments to a proposal are moved, they shall be put to the vote in the order in which their substance is more removed from the proposal. If, however, the

adoption of any amendment necessarily implies the rejection of any other amendment or of the original proposal, such amendment or proposal shall not be put to the vote.

(3) If one or more amendments are adopted, the proposal as amended shall be put to the vote.

Rule 33: *Election for a Single Post*
When a single elective place is to be filled and none of the candidates obtains the required majority in the first ballot, additional ballots shall be taken which shall be restricted to the two candidates having obtained the greatest number of votes.

Rule 34: *Election for Several Posts*
(1) When several elective places are to be filled at one time and in the same conditions, the officers or a nominations committee set up for the purpose may submit to the competent assembly a list containing a number of candidates equal to that of the places to be filled. The procedure provided for in paragraph (2) shall be applied if the assembly does not unanimously accept the list thus proposed.

(2) When several elective places are to be filled at one time and in the same conditions, those candidates obtaining the required majority in the first ballot shall be elected. If the number of candidates obtaining such majority is less than the number of places to be filled, there shall be additional ballots to fill the remaining places. The voting shall then be restricted to the candidates obtaining the greatest number of votes in the previous ballot, up to a number which shall not, however, be more than twice the number of places remaining to be filled.

Rule 35: *Required Majority*
Unless expressly provided otherwise in the applicable treaties or in the present General Rules of Procedure, all decisions shall be made by a simple majority.

Rule 36: *Majority and Unanimity. Equally Divided Votes*
(1) In determining whether the required majority or unanimity is attained, only votes actually cast shall be taken into consideration. Abstentions shall not be considered votes.

(2) When, on matters other than elections which require a simple majority, a vote is equally divided, the proposal or amendment shall be considered rejected.

Rule 37: *Explanations of Votes Cast*
(1) The Chairman may allow delegations to explain their votes, either before or after the voting takes place, unless the vote is taken by secret ballot.

(2) Explanations of votes cast shall be recorded in the report on the session.

Rule 38: *Chairmen Not Entitled to Vote*
(1) No Chairman or Acting Chairman shall vote.

(2) Another member of his delegation may vote for the State he represents.

Rule 39: *Observers*
Observers shall not have the right to vote.

Chapter VII: Miscellaneous Provisions
Rule 40: *Languages of Documents*
(1) Documents intended for the various bodies shall be drawn up in English and French. The Director General may, in so far as he considers it advisable and practicable, decide that certain documents shall be drawn up also in Spanish or Russian, or in both of those languages.

(2) The Director General shall decide on the language or languages in which documents intended for subsidiary bodies shall be drawn up.

Rule 41: *Languages of Oral Interventions. Interpretation*
(1) Oral interventions during meetings of the various bodies shall be in English or French, and interpretation shall be provided for in the other language. The Director General may, however, decide that oral interventions may also be made in Spanish or Russian, or in both of those languages; in such cases, interpretation shall be provided for in all the accepted languages.
(2) With regard to the subsidiary bodies, the Director General shall decide on the language or languages in which oral interventions shall be made and for which interpretation shall be provided.
(3) In any meeting in which simultaneous interpretation is provided by the Secretariat in at least two languages, any participant may make oral interventions in another language in so far as he provides for simultaneous interpretation in one of the languages for which interpretation is provided by the Secretariat.

Rule 42: *Joint Meetings*
(1) When two or more bodies of the Organization or of the Unions must examine questions of common interest to them, they shall hold joint meetings.
(2) Every joint meeting shall be presided over by the Chairman of the body which has precedence over the others, such precedence being determined as follows:
> (i) among bodies of WIPO: 1. General Assembly, 2. Conference, 3. Coordination Committee;
> (ii) among bodies of the same Union: 1. Assembly, 2. Conference of Representatives, 3. Executive Committee;
> (iii) among bodies of WIPO and one or more Unions: the WIPO body;
> (iv) among bodies of several Unions: the body of the oldest Union.

Rule 43: *Publicity of Meetings*
(1) Meetings of the WIPO Conference and the WIPO General Assembly and those of the Assemblies of the Unions shall be open, whereas those of the other bodies and of the subsidiary bodies shall be closed.
(2) Any body and any subsidiary body may, for its own purposes, waive the provision of the preceding paragraph in special cases and to the extent desired.

Rule 44: *Report*
(1) At the end of every session the Secretariat shall submit to the assembly a draft report on the work accomplished.
(2) After the session, the report adopted by the assembly shall be transmitted by the Director General to the States and organizations invited to the session.

Rule 45: *Entry into Force and Amendment of Special Rules of Procedure*
(1) The special rules of procedure of each body shall enter into force on being adopted by that body.
(2) Each body may amend its own rules of procedure.

PART III: AD HOC COMMITTEES OF EXPERTS

Rule 46: *Functions*
(1) The Director General shall, in implementation of the program of the Organization or of any Union, convene ad hoc committees of experts (committees, working groups) whose task shall be to make suggestions or give advice on any subject within the competence of the Organization or of such Union.
(2) The terms of reference of ad hoc committees of experts shall be defined in the program of the Organization or of the Union concerned, or, failing this, by the Director General.

Rule 47: *Dates and Place of Meetings*
The Director General shall fix the place and dates of meetings of ad hoc committees of experts.

Rule 48: *Participants*
(1) Experts shall serve in a personal capacity.
(2) They shall be designated individually, either by the Director General or by Governments or international organizations on the invitation of the Director General.
(3) Unless decided otherwise by the Director General, experts may be accompanied by advisors, who may participate in the debates.
(4) The Director General may at any time invite States or organizations to send observers to follow the work of an ad hoc committee of experts.

Rule 49: *Expenses of Participants*
(1) At the time of the convocation, the Director General shall indicate whether and to what extent the travel and subsistence expenses of participants shall be borne by the Organization.
(2) The expenses of observers shall be borne by the States or organizations which have sent them.

Rule 50: *Agenda and Rules of Procedure*
(1) The Director General shall draw up the agenda of each ad hoc committee of experts. He may modify it on his own initiative or at the request of the ad hoc committee of experts.
(2) The provisions of Part II of the General Rules of Procedure shall, as far as possible, serve as rules of procedure for ad hoc committees of experts. To the extent that they apply to such committees, the Director General may modify them in each individual case, either on his own initiative or at the request of the ad hoc committee of experts concerned.

Rule 51: *Languages*
(1) The Director General shall decide on the language or languages in which documents intended for ad hoc committees of experts are drawn up.
(2) The Director General shall decide on the language or languages in which oral interventions must be made and for which interpretation will be provided, in an ad hoc committee of experts.

Rule 52: *Officers of ad hoc Committees of Experts*
(1) During its first meeting, the ad hoc committee of experts shall elect from among its members a Chairman and two Vice-Chairmen.
(2) With the consent of the Director General, the ad hoc committee of experts may elect the Director General himself or another official of the International Bureau as Chairman.

Rule 53: *Voting*
Each member of the ad hoc committee of experts shall have one vote.

Rule 54: *Publicity of Meetings*
(1) Meetings of ad hoc committees of experts shall be closed.
(2) The Director General may waive this rule on his own initiative or at the request of the ad hoc committee of experts.

Rule 55: *Report*
Ad hoc committees of experts shall submit their reports to the Director General, who shall distribute and publicize these documents as he sees fit.

PART IV: FINAL PROVISIONS

Rule 56: *Amendment of General Rules of Procedure*
(1) These General Rules of Procedure may be amended, as far as each body which has adopted them is concerned, by a decision of that body, provided that the said decision is taken as far as possible in joint meeting and that the said body accepts the amendment according to the procedure laid down for amendment of its own rules of procedure.
(2) Any amendment to these General Rules of Procedure shall enter into force for each body which has adopted these General Rules of Procedure when that body has accepted the amendment.

Rule 57: *Entry into Force*
These General Rules of Procedure shall enter into force for each body at the time when it adopts its own rules of procedure referring thereto.

ANNEX

to the General Rules of Procedure of WIPO

Rules for Voting by Secret Ballot

Rule 1. – In order to vote, delegations must be properly accredited.
Rule 2. – Before the ballot begins, the Chairman shall appoint two tellers from among the delegates present. He shall hand them the list of delegations entitled to vote and, where applicable, the list of candidates.
Rule 3. – The Secretariat shall distribute ballot papers and envelopes to the delegations. Ballot papers and envelopes shall be of white paper without distinguishing marks.
Rule 4. – The tellers shall satisfy themselves that the ballot box is empty, and, having locked it, shall hand the key to the Chairman.
Rule 5. – Delegations shall be called in turn by the Secretary of the meeting, in the alphabetical order of the names of the member States in French, beginning with the member State whose name shall have been drawn by lot.
Rule 6. – When their names are called, delegations shall hand their ballot papers, in the envelopes, to a teller, who shall place them in the ballot box.
Rule 7. – To indicate the recording of each member State's vote, the Secretary of the meeting and one of the tellers shall sign or initial the list in the margin opposite the name of the member State in question.
Rule 8. – At the conclusion of the calling, the Chairman shall declare the ballot closed and announce that the votes are to be counted.

Rule 9. – When the Chairman has opened the ballot box, the tellers shall check the number of envelopes. If the number is greater or less than that of the voters, the Chairman shall be informed, and shall then declare the vote invalid and announce that it is necessary to re-open the ballot.

Rule 10. – One of the tellers shall open the envelopes, one by one, read aloud what is written on the ballot paper, and pass it to the other teller. The votes inscribed on the ballot papers shall be entered on lists prepared for that purpose.

Rule 11. – Blank ballot papers shall be considered to be abstentions.

Rule 12. – The following shall be considered invalid:

(a) ballot papers on which there are more names than there are States or persons to be elected;

(b) ballot papers in which the voters have revealed their identity, in particular, by apposing their signature or mentioning the name of the member State they represent;

(c) ballot papers which do not give a clear reply to the question asked.

Rule 13. – A candidate is entitled to only one vote per ballot paper, even if his name appears more than once thereon.

Rule 14. – When the counting of the votes is completed, the Chairman shall announce the results of the ballot in the following order:

number of member States entitled to vote at the session;

number absent;

number of abstentions;

number of invalid ballot papers;

number of votes recorded;

number of votes constituting the required majority;

number of votes for or against the proposal or names of the candidates and number of votes secured by each of them, in descending order of the number of votes.

Rule 15. – The Chairman shall announce the decision resulting from the vote. In particular, he shall declare elected those candidates who have obtained the required majority.

Rule 16. – Immediately after the announcement of the results of the ballot, the ballot papers shall be burnt in the presence of the tellers.

Rule 17. – The lists on which the tellers have recorded the results of the vote shall, after signature by the Chairman and by the tellers, constitute the official record of the ballot, and shall be deposited in the archives of the Organization.

Rule 18. – The Chairman of the meeting shall draw the attention of delegations to these Rules whenever a vote is taken by secret ballot.

Rule 19. – (1) These Rules shall in no way affect the provisions according to which a quorum may, in certain conditions, be attained after the session.

(2) Votes expressed by correspondence shall not be secret.

Appendix 4: Special Rules of Procedure of the Governing Bodies

Source: WIPO, *Special Rules of Procedure of the Governing Bodies: Compilation Prepared by the International Bureau, Governing Bodies of WIPO and the Unions Administered by WIPO, Twenty-Fourth Series of Meetings, Geneva, 20 to 29 September 1993* AB/XXIV/INF/2 (WIPO 1993).

The rules governing the procedure of the Governing Bodies of WIPO and the Unions administered by WIPO consist of provisions in the treaties establishing WIPO and the Unions, the WIPO General Rules of Procedure, and, for each Governing Body, a distinct set of rules, called "Special Rules of Procedure."

This Appendix provides the most recent compilation of the Special Rules of Procedure of the 21 Governing Bodies as prepared by the WIPO Secretariat for the 24th WIPO Assemblies in 1993 in the document cited above. It also contains, as far as the Conferences of Representatives of the Paris, Berne, Hague, Nice Unions and the Council of the Lisbon Union are concerned, the provisions of the treaties or the resolutions which established those Governing Bodies.

1. WIPO GENERAL ASSEMBLY
RULES OF PROCEDURE, adopted on September 28, 1970

Rule 1: Application of the General Rules of Procedure
The Rules of Procedure of the General Assembly shall consist of the General Rules of Procedure of WIPO, supplemented and amended by the provisions set forth hereinafter.

Rule 2: Draft Agenda
For the ordinary sessions of the General Assembly, the Director General shall prepare the draft agenda according to the instructions of the Coordination Committee.

Rule 3: Decisions when a Quorum is not Reached
(1) In the case referred to in Article 6(3)(c) of the WIPO Convention, the Director General shall immediately communicate those decisions which have not yet taken effect to the States members of the General Assembly which were not represented at the session, together with the report of the session and whatever additional explanations may be necessary.

(2) The period of three months allowed to them to express their vote or abstention shall run from the date on which the communication was sent. Replies shall be taken into consideration only if they reach the Director General within the period allowed.

(3) Replies must come either from the Ministry of Foreign Affairs or from a competent authority of the State in question.

Rule 4: Languages
Oral interventions in meetings of the General Assembly may be made in English, French, Spanish or Russian, and interpretation shall be provided in the other three languages.

Rule 5: Publication of the Report
The report on the work of each session, or a summary drawn up by the International Bureau, shall be published in the reviews **La Propriété industrielle**, **Industrial Property**, **Le Droit d'Auteur**, and **Copyright**.

2. WIPO CONFERENCE
RULES OF PROCEDURE, adopted on September 28, 1970

Rule 1: Application of the General Rules of Procedure
The Rules of Procedure of the Conference shall consist of the General Rules of Procedure of WIPO, supplemented and amended by the provisions set forth hereinafter.

Rule 2: Draft Agenda
For the ordinary sessions of the Conference, the Director General shall prepare the draft agenda according to the instructions of the Coordination Committee.

Rule 3: Languages
Oral interventions in meetings of the Conference may be made in English, French, Spanish or Russian, and interpretation shall be provided in the other three languages.

Rule 4: Publication of the Report
The report on the work of each session, or a summary drawn up by the International Bureau, shall be published in the reviews **La Propriété industrielle**, **Industrial Property**, **Le Droit d'Auteur**, and **Copyright**.

3. WIPO COORDINATION COMMITTEE
RULES OF PROCEDURE adopted on September 28, 1970

Rule 1: Application of the General Rules of Procedure
The Rules of Procedure of the Coordination Committee shall consist of the General Rules of Procedure of WIPO, supplemented and amended by the provisions set forth hereinafter.

Rule 2: Composition
(1) The Coordination Committee shall be composed of ordinary members, associate members, and ad hoc members.
(2) Ordinary members shall be States which are ordinary members of the Executive Committee of the Paris Union, or of the Executive Committee of the Berne Union, or of both of the said Committees.
(3) Associate members shall be States which are associate members of the Executive Committee of the Paris Union, or of the Executive Committee of the Berne Union, or of both of the said Committees.
(4) Ad hoc members shall be States elected by the Conference in accordance with Article 8(1)(c) of the WIPO Convention.

Rule 3: Officers
(1) At the first meeting of each ordinary session, the Coordination Committee shall elect a Chairman and two Vice-Chairmen.
(2)

(a) At each ordinary session of odd number [1st, 3rd, 5th, etc.], the Chairman and the second Vice-Chairman shall be elected from among the delegates of the ordinary members of the Executive Committee of the Paris Union and the first Vice-Chairman shall be elected from among the delegates of the ordinary members of the Executive Committee of the Berne Union, provided that as long as the number of associate members of the Executive Committee of the Paris Union is four or more, the second Vice-Chairman shall be elected from among the delegates of the said associate members.

(b) At each ordinary session of even number [2nd, 4th, 6th, etc.], the Chairman and the second Vice-Chairman shall be elected from among the delegates of the ordinary members of the Executive Committee of the Berne Union and the first Vice-Chairman shall be elected from among the delegates of the ordinary members of the Executive Committee of the Paris Union, provided that as long as the number of associate members of the Executive Committee of the Berne Union is four or more, the second Vice-Chairman shall be elected from among the delegates of the said associate members.

Rule 4: Separate Voting
(1) When a vote is not unanimous and it is necessary to know the respective decisions or opinions of ordinary members, associate members, and ad hoc members, the vote shall be taken again separately within each of the groups.
(2) When any question is clearly not within the competence of all the groups of members, the vote shall be taken only within the competent group or groups.

Rule 5: Publication of the Report
The report on the work of each session, or a summary drawn up by the International Bureau, shall be published in the reviews **La Propriété industrielle**, **Industrial Property**, **Le Droit d'Auteur**, and **Copyright.**

4.   PARIS UNION ASSEMBLY
RULES OF PROCEDURE adopted on September 28, 1970

Rule 1: Application of the General Rules of Procedure
The Rules of Procedure of the Assembly of the Paris Union shall consist of the General Rules of Procedure of WIPO, supplemented and amended by the provisions set forth hereinafter.

Rule 2: Draft Agenda
For the ordinary sessions of the Assembly of the Paris Union, the Director General shall prepare the draft agenda according to the instructions of the Executive Committee of the Paris Union.

Rule 3: Election of Ordinary Members of the Executive Committee of the Paris Union
(1) The members of the Executive Committee elected by the Assembly of the Paris Union shall be called ordinary members of that Committee.
(2) Ordinary members of the Executive Committee may be re-elected, but only up to a maximum of two-thirds of such members.

(3) Except where the procedure provided for in Article 34(1) of the General Rules of Procedure is observed, election shall take place in the following manner: the member States shall be called in the alphabetical order of their names in French, after the letter of the alphabet at which the roll-call is to start shall have been drawn by lot; on the calling of the name of each State, the Assembly shall decide whether or not it is re-elected; if necessary, the States last called shall be excluded from re-election if such exclusion is required to ensure that the proportion of two-thirds shall not be exceeded; the Assembly shall then elect the number of new members required to attain the total number to be elected.

Rule 4: Decisions when a Quorum is not Reached

(1) In the case referred to in Article 13(4)(c) of the Paris Convention, the Director General shall immediately communicate those decisions which have not yet taken effect to the States members of the Assembly of the Paris Union which were not represented at the session, together with the report of the session and whatever additional explanations may be necessary.

(2) The period of three months allowed to them to express their vote or abstention shall run from the date on which the communication was sent. Replies shall be taken into consideration only if they reach the Director General within the period allowed.

(3) Replies must come either from the Ministry of Foreign Affairs or from the competent authority of the State in question.

Rule 5: Publication of the Report

The report on the work of each session, or a summary drawn up by the International Bureau, shall be published in the reviews **La Propriété industrielle** and **Industrial Property**.

5.   PARIS UNION CONFERENCE OF REPRESENTATIVES

I.

EXCERPT FROM THE LISBON ACT (1958) OF THE PARIS CONVENTION

"ARTICLE 14

"(5)(a) During the interval between the Diplomatic Conferences of revision, Conferences of representatives of all the countries of the Union shall meet every three years* in order to draw up a report on the foreseeable expenditure of the International Bureau for each three-year period* to come and to consider questions relating to the protection and development of the Union.

"(b) Furthermore, they may modify, by unanimous decision, the maximum annual amount of the expenditure of the International Bureau, provided they meet as Conferences of Plenipotentiaries of all the countries of the Union, convened by the Government of the Swiss Confederation.

"(c) Moreover, the Conferences provided for in paragraph (a) above may be convened between their triennial meetings by either the Director of the International Bureau or the Government of the Swiss Confederation."

*The Conference of Representatives of the Paris Union decided, on September 28, 1979, that, pending the ratification of or accession to Acts of the Paris Convention subsequent to the Lisbon Act by the members of the said Conference of Representatives, the said Conference of Representatives shall meet every two years rather than every three years and that the report on the foreseeable expenditure of the International Bureau shall be drawn up by it for each two-year period rather than each three-year period.

RULES OF PROCEDURE adopted on September 28, 1970

Rule 1: Application of the General Rules of Procedure
The Rules of Procedure of the Conference of Representatives of the Paris Union shall consist of the General Rules of Procedure of WIPO, supplemented and amended by the provisions set forth hereinafter.

Rule 2: Representatives of Member States
(1) Each delegate may represent one State only.
(2) The expenses of each delegation shall be borne by the Government which has appointed it.

Rule 3: Sessions
(1) The Conference of Representatives of the Paris Union shall meet during the same period and at the same place as the Assembly of the Paris Union.
(2) It shall meet in extraordinary session at the request of one-fourth of its members, the associate members of the Executive Committee of the Paris Union, or the Government of the Swiss Confederation, or on the initiative of the Director General.

Rule 4: Matters of General Interest
With respect to matters which are of interest also to other Unions, the Conference of Representatives of the Paris Union shall make its decisions after having heard the advice of the Coordination Committee.

Rule 5: Election of Associate Members of the Executive Committee of the Paris Union
(1)(a) At each ordinary session, the Conference of Representatives of the Paris Union shall elect, from among its members, to the Executive Committee of the Paris Union in the capacity of associate members the number of States equal to one-fourth of the number of its members represented at the session.
(b) However, if the number of States represented at the session is less than twenty, the Conference of Representatives of the Paris Union shall elect, from among its members, to the Executive Committee of the Paris Union in the capacity of associate members the number of States equal to one-fourth of all its members, whether represented at the session or not, provided that the number of States so elected shall not exceed five.
(c) In establishing the number of seats to be filled, remainders after division by four shall be disregarded.
(2) In electing associate members of the Executive Committee of the Paris Union, the Conference of Representatives of the Paris Union shall seek to achieve an equitable geographical distribution, and shall have due regard to the need for all States party to the Special Agreements established in relation with the Paris Union to be among the States constituting the Executive Committee of that Union.
(3) Associate members of the Executive Committee of the Paris Union shall serve from the close of the session of the Conference of Representatives which elected them until the close of the next ordinary session of the Conference of Representatives. Any associate member of the Executive Committee subsequently becoming a member of the Assembly of the Paris Union shall automatically become an ordinary member of the Executive Committee.
(4) Associate members of the Executive Committee of the Paris Union may be re-elected, but only up to a maximum of two-thirds of such members.

(5) Except where the procedure provided for in Article 34(1) of the General Rules of Procedure is observed, election shall take place in the following manner: the member States shall be called in the alphabetical order of their names in French, after the letter of the alphabet at which the roll-call is to start shall have been drawn by lot; on the calling of the name of each State, the Conference of Representatives of the Paris Union shall decide whether or not it is re-elected; if necessary, the States last called shall be excluded from re-election if such exclusion is required to ensure that the proportion of two-thirds shall not be exceeded; the Conference of Representatives of the Paris Union shall then elect the number of new members required to attain the total number to be elected.

Rule 6: Executive Committee of the Paris Union and Coordination Committee of WIPO

(1) Associate members of the Executive Committee of the Paris Union shall take part in the debates of that body in an advisory capacity, and shall express opinions on matters within its competence.

(2) Associate members of the Executive Committee of the Paris Union shall be members of the Coordination C ommittee in the same capacity. They shall take part in the debates of that body in an advisory capacity, and shall express opinions on matters within its competence. In particular, they shall advise the Swiss Government, acting as supervisory authority, on administrative and financial questions and other matters of common interest, particularly in the cases provided for in the Staff Regulations and Financial Regulations.

Rule 7: Majority

Subject to the provisions of Article 14(5)(b) of the Lisbon Act of the Paris Convention, the Conference of Representatives of the Paris Union shall make its decisions by a majority of two-thirds of the votes cast. This rule shall not apply to decisions on procedure.

Rule 8: Publication of the Report

The report on the work of each session, or a summary drawn up by the International Bureau, shall be published in the reviews **La Propriété industrielle** and **Industrial Property**.

6.   PARIS UNION EXECUTIVE COMMITTEE

RULES OF PROCEDURE adopted on September 28, 1970

Rule 1: Application of the General Rules of Procedure

The Rules of Procedure of the Executive Committee of the Paris Union shall consist of the General Rules of Procedure of WIPO, supplemented and amended by the provisions set forth hereinafter.

Rule 2: Composition

(1) The Executive Committee of the Paris Union shall be composed of ordinary members, associate members, and Switzerland in the capacity of ex officio ordinary members.

(2) Ordinary members shall be the States elected by the Assembly of the Paris Union.

(3) Associate members shall be the States elected by the Conference of Representatives of the Paris Union.

Rule 3: Officers

The Chairman and the two Vice-Chairmen of the Executive Committee of the Paris Union shall be elected from among the delegates of the ordinary members. However, as long as the number of associate members is four or more, the second Vice-Chairman shall be elected from among the delegates of associate members.

Rule 4: Associate Members
(1) Associate members of the Executive Committee of the Paris Union shall take part in the debates of that body in an advisory capacity, and shall express opinions on matters within its competence.
(2) Associate members of the Executive Committee of the Paris Union shall be members of the Coordination Committee in the same capacity. They shall take part in the debates of that body in an advisory capacity, and shall express opinions on matters within its competence. In particular, they shall advise the Swiss Government, acting as supervisory authority, on administrative and financial questions and other matters of common interest, particularly in the cases provided for in the Staff Regulations and Financial Regulations.

Rule 5: Separate Voting
(1) When the vote is not unanimous and it is necessary to know the respective decisions or opinions of the ordinary members and the associate members of the Executive Committee of the Paris Union, the vote shall be taken again separately within these two groups of members.
(2) When any question is clearly not within the competence of both groups of members, the vote shall be taken only within the competent group.

Rule 6: Publication of the Report
The report on the work of each session, or a summary drawn up by the International Bureau, shall be published in the reviews **La Propriété industrielle** and **Industrial Property**.

7.   BERNE UNION ASSEMBLY
RULES OF PROCEDURE adopted on September 28, 1970

Rule 1: Application of the General Rules of Procedure
The Rules of Procedure of the Assembly of the Berne Union shall consist of the General Rules of Procedure of WIPO, supplemented and amended by the provisions set forth hereinafter.

Rule 2: Draft Agenda
For the ordinary sessions of the Assembly of the Berne Union, the Director General shall prepare the draft agenda according to the instructions of the Executive Committee of the Berne Union.

Rule 3: Election of Ordinary Members of the Executive Committee of the Berne Union
(1) Members of the Executive Committee elected by the Assembly of the Berne Union shall be called ordinary members of that Committee.
(2) Ordinary members of the Executive Committee thus elected may be re-elected, but only up to a maximum of two-thirds of such members.
(3) Except where the procedure provided for in Article 34(1) of the General Rules of Procedure is observed, election shall take place in the following manner: the member States shall be called in the alphabetical order of their names in French, after the letter of the alphabet at which the roll-call is to start shall have been drawn by lot; on the calling of the name of each State, the Assembly shall decide whether or not it is re-elected; if necessary,

the States last called shall be excluded from re-election if such exclusion is required to ensure that the proportion of two-thirds shall not be exceeded; the Assembly shall then elect the number of new members required to attain the total number to be elected.

Rule 4: Decisions when a Quorum is not Reached
(1) In the case referred to in Article 22(3)(c) of the Berne Convention, the Director General shall immediately communicate those decisions which have not yet taken effect to the States members of the Assembly of the Berne Union which were not represented at the session, together with the report of the session and whatever additional explanations may be necessary.

(2) The period of three months allowed to them to express their vote or abstention shall run from the date on which the communication was sent. Replies shall be taken into consideration only if they reach the Director General within the period allowed.

(3) Replies shall come either from the Ministry of Foreign Affairs or from the competent authority of the State in question.

Rule 5: Publication of the Report
The report on the work of each session, or a summary drawn up by the International Bureau, shall be published in the reviews Le Droit d'Auteur and Copyright.

8.   BERNE UNION CONFERENCE OF REPRESENTATIVES
I.
RESOLUTION ESTABLISHING THE CONFERENCE OF REPRESENTATIVES
adopted on September 28, 1970,
and amended on September 28, 1979

The countries members of the International Union for the Protection of Literary and Artistic Works (Berne Union) which are not members of the Assembly of the said Union,

Meeting in Geneva from September 21 to 28, 1970,

1. Resolve to establish a Conference of Representatives of the Berne Union;

2. Decide that the members of this Conference shall be those member countries of the Berne Union which are not members of the Assembly of the Berne Union, and that any member country of the Berne Union which, in the future, shall become a member of the Assembly of the Berne Union shall automatically cease to be a member of the Conference of Representatives;

3. Decide that the Conference of Representatives shall meet every two years in ordinary session in order to draw up, for each two-year period to come, a report on the foreseeable expenditure of the International Bureau as far as the Berne Union is concerned, and to consider questions relating to the protection and the development of the said Union;

4. Resolve that the Conference of Representatives may modify, by unanimous decision, the maximum annual amount of the expenditure of the International Bureau as far as the countries members of the Conference of Representatives are concerned, provided that it meets as a Conference of Plenipotentiaries upon convocation by the Government of the Swiss Confederation;

5. Resolve that the Conference of Representatives shall establish its own rules of procedure.

RULES OF PROCEDURE adopted on September 28, 1970

Rule 1: Application of the General Rules of Procedure
The Rules of Procedure of the Conference of Representatives of the Berne Union shall consist of the General Rules of Procedure of WIPO, supplemented and amended by the provisions set forth hereinafter.

Rule 2: Representatives of Member States
(1) Each delegate may represent one State only.
(2) The expenses of each delegation shall be borne by the Government which has appointed it.

Rule 3: Sessions
(1) The Conference of Representatives of the Berne Union shall meet during the same period and at the same place as the Assembly of the Berne Union.
(2) It shall meet in extraordinary session at the request of one-fourth of its members, the associate members of the Executive Committee of the Berne Union, or the Government of the Swiss Confederation, or on the initiative of the Director General.

Rule 4: Matters of General Interest
With respect to matters which are of interest also to other Unions, the Conference of Representatives of the Berne Union shall make its decisions only after having heard the advice of the Coordination Committee.

Rule 5: Election of Associate Members of the Executive Committee of the Berne Union
(1)(a) At each ordinary session, the Conference of Representatives of the Berne Union shall elect, from among its members, to the Executive Committee of the Berne Union in the capacity of associate members the number of States equal to one-fourth of the number of its members represented at the session.
   (b) However, if the number of States represented at the session is less than twenty, the Conference of Representatives of the Berne Union shall elect, from among its members, to the Executive Committee of the Berne Union in the capacity of associate members the number of States equal to one-fourth of all its members, whether represented at the session or not, provided that the number of States so elected shall not exceed five.
   (c) In establishing the number of seats to be filled, remainders after division by four shall be disregarded.
(2) In electing associate members of the Executive Committee of the Berne Union, the Conference of Representatives of the Berne Union shall seek to achieve an equitable geographical distribution.
(3) Associate members of the Executive Committee of the Berne Union shall serve from the close of the session of the Conference of Representatives which elected them until the close of the next ordinary session of the Conference of Representatives. Any associate member of the Executive Committee subsequently becoming a member of the Assembly of the Berne Union shall automatically become an ordinary member of the Executive Committee.
(4) Associate members of the Executive Committee of the Berne Union may be re-elected, but only up to a maximum of two-thirds of such members.
(5) Except where the procedure provided for in Article 34(1) of the General Rules of Procedure is observed, election shall take place in the following manner: the member States

shall be called in the alphabetical order of their names in French, after the letter of the alphabet at which the roll-call is to start shall have been drawn by lot; on the calling of the name of each State, the Conference of Representatives of the Berne Union shall decide whether or not it is re-elected; if necessary, the States last called shall be excluded from re-election if such exclusion is required to ensure that the proportion of two-thirds shall not be exceeded; the Conference of Representatives of the Berne Union shall then elect the number of new members required to attain the total number to be elected.

Rule 6: Executive Committee of the Berne Union and Coordination Committee of WIPO

(1) Associate members of the Executive Committee of the Berne Union shall take part in the debates of that body in an advisory capacity, and shall express opinions on matters within its competence.

(2) Associate members of the Executive Committee of the Berne Union shall be members of the Coordination Committee in the same capacity. They shall take part in the debates of that body in an advisory capacity, and shall express opinions on matters within its competence. In particular, they shall advise the Swiss Government, acting as supervisory authority, on administrative and financial questions and other matters of common interest, particularly in the cases provided for in the Staff Regulations and Financial Regulations.

Rule 7: Majority

Subject to the provisions of paragraph 4 of the Resolution of September 28, 1970, the Conference of Representatives of the Berne Union shall make its decisions by a majority of two-thirds of the votes cast. This rule shall not apply to decisions on procedure.

Rule 8: Publication of the Report

The report on the work of each session, or a summary drawn up by the International Bureau, shall be published in the reviews **Le Droit d'Auteur** and **Copyright**.

9.   BERNE UNION EXECUTIVE COMMITTEE
RULES OF PROCEDURE
adopted on September 28, 1970,
and amended on October 24, 1979

Rule 1: Application of the General Rules of Procedure

The Rules of Procedure of the Executive Committee of the Berne Union shall consist of the General Rules of Procedure of WIPO, supplemented and amended by the provisions set forth hereinafter.

Rule 2: Composition

(1) The Executive Committee of the Berne Union shall be composed of ordinary members, associate members, and Switzerland in the capacity of ex officio ordinary member.

(2) Ordinary members shall be the States elected by the Assembly of the Berne Union.

(3) Associate members shall be the States elected by the Conference of Representatives of the Berne Union.

Rule 3: Officers

(1) At the first meeting of each session, the Executive Committee of the Berne Union shall elect a Chairman and two Vice-Chairmen.

(2) The officers thus elected shall remain in office until the election of new officers.

(3) The outgoing Chairman and Vice-Chairmen shall not be immediately eligible for re-election to the office that they have held, except where the election takes place at an extraordinary session.

(4) The Chairman and the two Vice-Chairmen of the Executive Committee of the Berne Union shall be elected from among the delegates of the ordinary members. However, as long as the number of associate members is four or more, the second Vice-Chairman shall be elected from among the delegates of associate members.

Rule 4: Associate Members

(1) Associate members of the Executive Committee of the Berne Union shall take part in the debates of that body in an advisory capacity, and shall express opinions on matters within its competence.

(2) Associate members of the Executive Committee of the Berne Union shall be members of the Coordination Committee in the same capacity. They shall take part in the debates of that body in an advisory capacity, and shall express opinions on matters within its competence. In particular, they shall advise the Swiss Government, acting as supervisory authority, on administrative and financial questions and other matters of common interest, particularly in the cases provided for in the Staff Regulations and Financial Regulations.

Rule 5: Separate Voting

(1) When the vote is not unanimous and it is necessary to know the respective decisions or opinions of the ordinary members and the associate members of the Executive Committee of the Berne Union, the vote shall be taken again separately within these two groups of members.

(2) When any question is clearly not within the competence of both groups of members, the vote shall be taken only within the competent group.

Rule 6: Publication of the Report

The report on the work of each session, or a summary drawn up by the International Bureau, shall be published in the reviews **Le Droit d'Auteur** and **Copyright**.

10. MADRID UNION ASSEMBLY

RULES OF PROCEDURE
adopted on October 2, 1971,
and amended on November 27, 1973,
and on December 15, 1983

Rule 1: Application of the General Rules of Procedure

The Rules of Procedure of the Assembly of the Madrid Union shall consist of the General Rules of Procedure of WIPO, supplemented and amended by the provisions set forth hereinafter.

Rule 2: Decisions When a Quorum is Not Reached

(1) In the case referred to in Article 10(3)(c) of the Stockholm Act of the Madrid Agreement (Marks), the Director General shall immediately communicate those decisions which have not yet taken effect to the States members of the Assembly of the Madrid Union which were not represented at the session, together with the report of the session and whatever additional explanations may be necessary.

(2) The period of three months allowed to them to express their vote or abstention shall run from the date on which the communication was sent. Replies shall be taken into consideration only if they reach the Director General within the period allowed.

(3) Replies must come either from the Ministry of Foreign Affairs or from the competent authority of the State in question.

Rule 3: Expenses
(1) The travel and subsistence expenses of one delegate of each member State shall be borne by the Madrid Union under the following conditions:
- (a) on presentation of the used ticket, the net cost of the rail or air fare (first class) shall be refunded;
- (b) daily subsistence allowances shall be those specified in the United Nations schedule; the number of daily subsistence allowances paid shall correspond to the number of days required for the session, plus one day;
- (c) the fixed sum paid for terminal expenses shall be that specified by the WIPO Staff Regulations and Staff Rules.

(2) Delegates receiving such allowances must state in writing that their travel or subsistence expenses are not refunded from other sources.

Rule 4: Publication of the Report
The report on the work of each session, or a summary drawn up by the International Bureau, shall be published in the reviews **La Propriété industrielle** and **Industrial Property**, and, where appropriate, in the review **Les Marques internationales.**

11.   HAGUE UNION ASSEMBLY
RULES OF PROCEDURE
adopted on September 27, 1976,
and amended on May 28, 1979,
and on October 1, 1985

Rule 1: Application of the General Rules of Procedure
The Rules of Procedure of the Assembly of the Hague Union shall consist of the General Rules of Procedure of WIPO, supplemented and amended by the provisions set forth hereinafter.

Rule 2: Decisions When a Quorum is Not Reached
(1) In the case referred to in Article 2(3)(c) of the Complementary Act of Stockholm of 1967, the Director General shall immediately communicate those decisions which have not yet taken effect to the States members of the Assembly of the Hague Union which were not represented at the session, together with the report of the session and whatever additional explanations may be necessary.
(2) The period of three months allowed to them to express their vote or abstention shall run from the date on which the communication was sent. Replies shall be taken into consideration only if they reach the International Bureau within the period allowed.
(3) Replies shall come from the Ministry of Foreign Affairs or the competent authority of the State in question.

Rule 2bis: Adoption and Amendment of Certain Provisions of the Regulations
Only the States bound by the 1960 Act shall have the right to vote on the adoption or on any amendment of the provisions of the Regulations under the Hague Agreement which concern the implementation of the said 1960 Act.

Rule 3: Publication of the Report
The report on the work of each session, or a summary drawn up by the International Bureau, shall be published in the reviews **La Propriété industrielle** and **Industrial Property**.

12. HAGUE UNION CONFERENCE OF REPRESENTATIVES

I.

RESOLUTION ESTABLISHING THE CONFERENCE OF REPRESENTATIVES
adopted on September 27, 1976

The countries members of the Special Union for the International Deposit of
Industrial Designs (Hague Union) which are not members of the Assembly of the said
Union,

Meeting in Geneva from September 27, 1976 to October 5, 1976,

1. Resolve to establish a Conference of Representatives of the Hague Union;

2. Decide that the members of the said Conference of Representatives shall be those
member countries of the Hague Union which are not members of the Assembly of the
Hague Union, and that any member country of the Hague Union which, in the future, shall
become a member of the Assembly of the Hague Union shall automatically cease to be a
member of the Conference of Representatives;

3. Decide further that the Conference of Representatives

(i) may examine the Management Reports of the International Bureau of
WIPO as far as the Hague Union is concerned and may make observations
thereon to the Director General of WIPO or the Government of the Swiss
Confederation or both,

(ii) may examine the draft budgets of the Hague Union presented to it by
the Director General of WIPO and may make observations thereon to the
Director General of WIPO or the Government of the Swiss Confederation or
both,

(iii) may modify, on the proposal of the Director General of WIPO or the
Government of the Swiss Confederation, the amounts of the fees to be
charged under the Hague Agreement the fixing of which is not within the
jurisdiction of the Assembly; decision on such modification shall require
the majority of the votes of the countries members of the Conference of
Representatives; the procedure provided for in the Additional Act of Monaco
of 1961, Article 3, may be applied as an alternative procedure,

(iv) shall, in connection with the working capital fund of the Hague Union, have,
in respect of the countries members of the Conference of Representatives,
rights analogous to those which the Assembly has in respect of the countries
members of the Assembly and shall, by analogy, apply the relevant provisions of the Complementary Act of Stockholm (1967) in respect of the said
fund,

(v) shall establish its own rules of procedure.

II.

RULES OF PROCEDURE
adopted on September 27, 1976,
and amended on May 28, 1979,
and on September 28, 1979

Rule 1: Application of the General Rules of Procedure

The Rules of Procedure of the Conference of Representatives of the Hague Union shall
consist of the General Rules of Procedure of WIPO, supplemented and amended by the
provisions set forth hereinafter.

Rule 2: Representatives of Member States
(1) Each delegate may represent one State only.
(2) The expenses of each delegation shall be borne by the Government which has appointed it.

Rule 3: Sessions
(1) The Conference of Representatives of the Hague Union shall meet once in every second calendar year in ordinary session upon convocation by the Director General during the same period and at the same place as the Assembly of the Hague Union.
(2) It shall meet in extraordinary session at the request of one-fourth of its members or at the request of the Government of the Swiss Confederation, or on the initiative of the Director General.

Rule 4: Matters of General Interest
With respect to matters which are of interest also to other Unions, the Conference of Representatives of the Hague Union shall make its decisions after having heard the advice of the Coordination Committee.

Rule 4bis: Adoption and Amendment of Certain Provisions of the Regulations
The Member States of the Conference of Representatives of the Hague Union shall not have the right to vote on the adoption or on any amendment of the provisions of the Regulations under the Hague Agreement which concern the implementation of the 1960 Act.

Rule 5: Majority
The Conference of Representatives of the Hague Union shall, subject to the Resolution of September 27, 1976, establishing the said Conference, make its decisions by a majority of two-thirds of the votes cast. This rule shall not apply to decisions on procedure.

Rule 6: Publication of the Report
The report on the work of each session, or a summary drawn up by the International Bureau, shall be published in the reviews **La Propriété industrielle** and **Industrial Property**.

13. NICE UNION ASSEMBLY

RULES OF PROCEDURE
adopted on September 28, 1970

Rule 1: Application of the General Rules of Procedure
The Rules of Procedure of the Assembly of the Nice Union shall consist of the General Rules of Procedure of WIPO, supplemented and amended by the provisions set forth hereinafter.

Rule 2: Decisions When a Quorum is Not Reached
(1) In the case referred to in Article 5(3)(c) of the Nice Agreement, the Director General shall immediately communicate those decisions which have not yet taken effect to the States members of the Assembly of the Nice Union which were not represented at the session, together with the report of the session and whatever additional explanations may be necessary.
(2) The period of three months allowed to them to express their vote or abstention shall run from the date on which the communication was sent. Replies shall be taken into consideration only if they reach the Director General within the period allowed.
(3) Replies shall come from the Ministry of Foreign Affairs or the competent authority of the State in question.

Rule 3: Publication of the Report
The report on the work of each session, or a summary drawn up by the International Bureau, shall be published in the reviews **La Propriété industrielle** and **Industrial Property**.

14. NICE UNION CONFERENCE OF REPRESENTATIVES

I.
RESOLUTION
ESTABLISHING THE CONFERENCE OF REPRESENTATIVES
adopted on September 28, 1970,
and amended on September 28, 1979

The countries members of the International Union Concerning the International Classification of Goods and Services for the Purposes of the Registration of Marks (Nice Union) which are not members of the Assembly of the said Union,

Meeting in Geneva from September 21 to 28, 1970,
1. Resolve to establish a Conference of Representatives of the Nice Union;
2. Decide that the members of this Conference shall be those member countries of the Nice Union which are not members of the Assembly of the Nice Union, and that any member country of the Nice Union which, in the future, shall become a member of the Assembly of the Nice Union shall automatically cease to be a member of the Conference of Representatives;
3. Decide that the Conference of Representatives shall meet every two years in ordinary session in order to draw up, for each two-year period to come, a report on the foreseeable expenditure of the International Bureau as far as the Nice Union is concerned, and to consider questions relating to the protection and the development of the said Union;
4. Resolve that the Conference of Representatives may modify, by unanimous decision, the maximum annual amount of the expenditure of the International Bureau as far as the countries members of the Conference of Representatives are concerned, provided that it meets as a Conference of Plenipotentiaries upon convocation by the Government of the Swiss Confederation;
5. **Resolve** that the Conference of Representatives shall establish its own rules of procedure.

II.
RULES OF PROCEDURE
adopted on September 28, 1970

Rule 1: Application of the General Rules of Procedure
The Rules of Procedure of the Conference of Representatives of the Nice Union shall consist of the General Rules of Procedure of WIPO, supplemented and amended by the provisions set forth hereinafter.

Rule 2: Representatives of Member States
(1) Each delegate may represent one State only.
(2) The expenses of each delegation shall be borne by the Government which has appointed it.

Rule 3: Sessions
(1) The Conference of Representatives of the Nice Union shall meet during the same period and at the same place as the Assembly of the Nice Union.
(2) It shall meet in extraordinary session at the request of one-fourth of its members or the Government of the Swiss Confederation, or on the initiative of the Director General.

Rule 4: Matters of General Interest
With respect to matters which are of interest also to other Unions, the Conference of Representatives of the Nice Union shall make its decisions after having heard the advice of the Coordination Committee.

Rule 5: Majority
Subject to the provisions of paragraph 4 of the Resolution of September 28, 1970, the Conference of Representatives of the Nice Union shall make its decisions by a majority of two-thirds of the votes cast. This rule shall not apply to decisions on procedure.

Rule 6: Publication of the Report
The report on the work of each session, or a summary drawn up by the International Bureau, shall be published in the reviews **La Propriété industrielle** and **Industrial Property**.

15.   LISBON UNION ASSEMBLY
RULES OF PROCEDURE
adopted on November 27, 1973

Rule 1: Application of the General Rules of Procedure
The Rules of Procedure of the Assembly of the Lisbon Union shall consist of the General Rules of Procedure of WIPO, supplemented and amended by the provisions set forth hereinafter.

Rule 2: Decisions When a Quorum is Not Reached
(1) In the case referred to in Article 9(3)(c) of the Stockholm Act of the Lisbon Agreement, the Director General shall immediately communicate those decisions which have not yet taken effect to the States members of the Assembly of the Lisbon Union which were not represented at the session, together with the report of the session and whatever additional explanations may be necessary.
(2) The period of three months allowed to them to express their vote or abstention shall run from the date on which the communication was sent. Replies shall be taken into consideration only if they reach the Director General within the period allowed.
(3) Replies must come either from the Ministry of Foreign Affairs or from the competent authority of the State in question.

Rule 3: Publication of the Report
The report on the work of each session, or a summary drawn up by the International Bureau, shall be published in the reviews **La Propriété industrielle** and **Industrial Property**.

16.   LISBON UNION COUNCIL
I.
EXCERPT FROM THE LISBON AGREEMENT (1958)
ARTICLE 9
"(1) A Council composed of representatives of all the countries party to the special Union shall be set up, at the International Bureau, for the implementation of this Agreement. (2) This Council shall draw up its own statutes and rules of procedure and coordinate them with the organs of the Union for the Protection of Industrial Property and with those of international organizations which have concluded agreements for cooperation with the International Bureau."

II.

STATUTES
adopted on November 27, 1973

Article 1: Definitions

1. "Agreement" shall mean the Lisbon Agreement for the Protection of Appellations of Origin and their International Registration, of October 31, 1958.
2. "Special Union" shall mean the Union created by the Agreement.
3. "International Bureau" shall mean the International Bureau of Intellectual Property as defined in the Convention Establishing the World Intellectual Property Organization functioning under Article 21(3)(a) of that Convention as the United International Bureau for the Protection of Industrial, Literary and Artistic Property.
4. "Regulations" shall mean the Regulations for carrying out the Agreement, adopted at the same time and place as the Agreement.

Article 2: Composition of the Council

The Council, set up in accordance with Article 9(1) of the Agreement, is composed of representatives of all the countries members of the Special Union which are not members of the Assembly of the Special Union.

Article 3: Functions of the Council

The Council
   (i) may modify the amount of the registration fee (Article 7(2) of the Agreement and Article 7(2) of the Regulations);
   (ii) shall examine, subject to the competence of the Government of the Swiss Confederation in its capacity of Supervisory Authority of the International Bureau, the special annual management reports on the Service for the International Registration of Appellations of Origin (Article 7(1) of the Regulations), as well as the budget of that Service.

RULES OF PROCEDURE
adopted on November 27, 1973,
and amended on September 28, 1979

Rule 1: Application of the General Rules of Procedure

The Rules of Procedure of the Council of the Lisbon Union shall consist of the General Rules of Procedure of WIPO, supplemented and amended by the provisions set forth hereinafter.

Rule 2: Representatives of Member States

(1) Each delegate may represent one State only.
(2) The expenses of each delegation shall be borne by the Government which has appointed it.

Rule 3: Sessions

(1) The Council shall meet in ordinary session every two years, during the same period and at the same place as the Assembly of the Lisbon Union.
(2) It shall meet in extraordinary session at the request of one-fourth of its members or the Government of the Swiss Confederation, or on the initiative of the Director General.

Rule 4: Matters of General Interest
With respect to matters which are of interest also to other Unions, the Council shall make its decisions after having heard the advice of the Coordination Committee of the World Intellectual Property Organization.

Rule 5: Majority
Subject to the provisions of Article 7(2) of the Lisbon Agreement, the Council shall make its decisions by a simple majority.

Rule 6: Publication of the Report
The report on the work of each session, or a summary drawn up by the International Bureau, shall be published in the reviews **La Propriété industrielle** and **Industrial Property**.

17.   **LOCARNO UNION ASSEMBLY**
RULES OF PROCEDURE
adopted on October 2, 1971

Rule 1: Application of the General Rules of Procedure
The Rules of Procedure of the Assembly of the Locarno Union shall consist of the General Rules of Procedure of WIPO, supplemented and amended by the provisions set forth hereinafter.

Rule 2: Decisions When a Quorum is Not Reached
(1) In the case referred to in Article 5(3)(c) of the Locarno Agreement, the Director General shall immediately communicate those decisions which have not yet taken effect to the States members of the Assembly of the Locarno Union which were not represented at the session, together with the report of the session and whatever additional explanations may be necessary.
(2) The period of three months allowed to them to express their vote or abstention shall run from the date on which the communication was sent. Replies shall be taken into consideration only if they reach the Director General within the period allowed.
(3) Replies must come either from the Ministry of Foreign Affairs or from the competent authority of the State in question.

Rule 3: Publication of the Report
The report on the work of each session, or a summary drawn up by the International Bureau, shall be published in the reviews **La Propriété industrielle** and **Industrial Property**.

18.   **IPC (INTERNATIONAL PATENT CLASSIFICATION) UNION ASSEMBLY**
RULES OF PROCEDURE
adopted on October 9, 1975

Rule 1: Application of the General Rules of Procedure
The Rules of Procedure of the Assembly of the IPC Union (hereinafter called "the Assembly") shall consist of the General Rules of Procedure of WIPO, supplemented and amended by the provisions of the Strasbourg Agreement of 1971, by the resolution of the Assembly of October 7, 1975, and by the provisions set forth hereinafter.

Rule 2: Decisions When a Quorum is Not Reached
(1) In the case referred to in Article 7(3)(c) of the Strasbourg Agreement of 1971, the Director General shall immediately communicate those decisions which have not yet taken

effect to the States members of the Assembly which were not represented at the session, together with the report of the session and whatever additional explanations may be necessary.

(2) The period of three months allowed to them to express their vote or abstention shall run from the date on which the communication was sent. Replies shall be taken into consideration only if they reach the International Bureau within the period allowed.

(3) Replies shall come from the Ministry of Foreign Affairs or the competent authority of the State in question.

Rule 3: Special Observers

(1) Any State member of the Paris Union which is not a member of the IPC Union but which has pledged special contributions to defray the expenses of the IPC Union in a given year shall, during that year, have the status of special observer in all sessions of the Assembly and of any committee or working group established by the Assembly.

(2) Any special observer shall have the right to make proposals in any of the sessions referred to in paragraph (1).

Rule 4: Publication of the Report

The report on the work of each session, or a summary drawn up by the International Bureau, shall be published in the reviews **La Propriété industrielle** and **Industrial Property**.

19.   PCT (PATENT COOPERATION TREATY) UNION ASSEMBLY
RULES OF PROCEDURE
adopted on April 10, 1978,
and amended on February 3, 1984

Rule 1: Application of the General Rules of Procedure

The Rules of Procedure of the Assembly of the International Patent Cooperation (PCT) Union shall consist of the General Rules of Procedure of WIPO, supplemented and amended by the provisions set forth hereinafter.

Rule 2: Special Observers

Intergovernmental authorities having the power to grant patents effective in one or more States members of the PCT Union shall be invited as "special observers" to all sessions of the Assembly. They shall have the same rights in the sessions of the Assembly as States members of the Assembly, except the right to vote.

Rule 3: Draft Agenda

The draft agenda of each session shall be drawn up by the Director General. In the case of ordinary sessions, such draft shall follow the instructions of the Executive Committee once the Executive Committee is established (see PCT Articles 53(9) and 54(6)(a)). In the case of extraordinary sessions, the said draft shall include the item or items mentioned in the request referred to in Article 53(11)(c) of the Patent Cooperation Treaty.

Rule 4: Publication of the Report

The report on the work of each session, or a summary drawn up by the International Bureau, shall be published in the **Gazette** of the PCT Union and in the reviews of the World Intellectual Property Organization **La Propriété industrielle** and **Industrial Property**.

20. BUDAPEST UNION ASSEMBLY
RULES OF PROCEDURE
adopted on September 22, 1980

Rule 1: Application of the General Rules of Procedure
The Rules of Procedure of the Assembly of the Union for the International Recognition of the Deposit of Microorganisms for the Purposes of Patent Procedure (Budapest Union) shall consist of the General Rules of Procedure of WIPO, supplemented and amended by the provisions set forth hereinafter.

Rule 2: Publication of the Report
The report on the work of each session of the Assembly referred to in Rule 1, or a summary drawn up by the International Bureau, shall be published in the reviews **La Propriété industrielle** and **Industrial Property**.

21. VIENNA UNION ASSEMBLY
RULES OF PROCEDURE
adopted on October 1, 1985

Rule 1: Application of the General Rules of Procedure
The Rules of Procedure of the Assembly of the Vienna Union shall consist of the General Rules of Procedure of WIPO, supplemented and amended by the provisions set forth hereinafter.

Rule 2: Decisions When a Quorum is Not Reached
(1) In the case referred to in Article 7(3)(c) of the Vienna Agreement, the Director General shall immediately communicate those decisions which have not yet taken effect to the States members of the Assembly of the Vienna Union which were not represented at the session, together with the report of the session and whatever additional explanations may be necessary.

(2) The period of three months allowed to them to express their vote or abstention shall run from the date on which the communication was sent. Replies shall be taken into consideration only if they reach the Director General within the period allowed.

(3) Replies must come either from the Ministry of Foreign Affairs or from the competent authority of the State in question.

Rule 3: Publication of the Report
The report on the work of each session of the Assembly, or a summary drawn up by the International Bureau, shall be published in the reviews **La Propriété industrielle** and **Industrial Property**.

Appendix 5: Special Rules of Procedure for WIPO Committees

This appendix contains the text of Special Rules of Procedure adopted by Member States for the SCP, SCCR, SCT, IGC, ACE and CDIP, and a summary of the state of play on proposals for special rules for the PBC and CWS.

5.1. Standing Committee on the Law of Patents (SCP)

The rules of procedure applicable to the Standing Committee on the Law of Patents (SCP) were adopted at its first session, first part, held in Geneva from June 15 to 19, 1998 (see document SCP/1/2, paragraph 5), and were amended subsequently at its second session, held in Geneva from April 12 to 23, 1999 (see document SCP/2/2), and then in December 2011 at its seventeenth session (see document SCP/17/13). The Special Rules of Procedure are as follows:

1. Membership of the SCP is Member States of the Paris Union for the Protection of Industrial Property that are not Member States of WIPO, and observer status is extended to Member States of the United Nations that are not Member States of WIPO or the Paris Union.[1]

---

1 This decision was proposed in SCP/1/2 and adopted by the Committee. For the proposal, see WIPO, *Organizational Matters and Overview of the Issues to be Considered by the Standing Committee on the Law of Patents: Memorandum prepared by the International Bureau, Standing Committee on the Law of Trademarks, Industrial Designs and Geographical Indications, First Session, 13 to 17 June 1998* SCT/1/2 (Geneva: WIPO 1998). For the decision to approve the rules, see WIPO, *Report: Prepared by the International Secretariat, First Session of the Standing Committee on the Law of Patents, June 15–19,* SCP/1/7 (WIPO 1998) 4. The Committee also made decisions on working arrangements described in paragraphs 6 to 10 of that document with the following understandings: (i) the question of languages (para. 7 of document SCP/1/2) would be revisited at a future meeting of the Standing Committee in the light of any decision taken by the Assemblies of the Member States of WIPO on that issue; (ii) The summary of the conclusions of the Standing Committee provided by the chair at the conclusion of each session would be in writing, and presented prior to the end of the session; (iii) In the process of circulating the draft report for comments following the sessions of the Standing Committee (para. 8 of document SCP/1/2), the International Bureau would, if possible, circulate the first draft within one week of the meeting, and would make arrangements for participants to have the opportunity to comment on proposed changes to the report. Until the Committee decides otherwise, the revised report would be submitted to the Standing Committee at the next meeting for adoption; and (iv) The question of languages and funding for participation of delegates at any future working group of the Standing Committee (para. 10 of document SCP/1/2) would follow any procedures decided by the Assemblies of the Member States of WIPO on those issues, and meetings of the working group would be scheduled, if possible, on dates adjoining the dates of a meeting of the Standing Committee.

2. As invited in paragraph 5 of document SCP/2/2,[2] the Standing Committee adopted two special rules of procedure concerning the term and re-election of the Chair and the two Vice-Chairs. According to these two special rules, and in order to allow for the greatest continuity in their work, the Chair and Vice-Chairs will be elected for one year, and shall be immediately eligible for re-election to the offices which they have held.[3]

3. The working documents of the SCP be prepared in the six official languages of the United Nations (Arabic, Chinese, English, French, Russian and Spanish) in accordance with the WIPO language policy, effective as of January 2012.[4]

5.2. Standing Committee on Copyright and Related Rights (SCCR)

The Committee decided in 1998 that the General Rules of Procedure of WIPO shall apply to the Standing Committee on Copyright and Related Rights, subject to two Special Rules of Procedure as follows:[5]

1. All WIPO Member States, as well as Member States of the Berne Union that are not Member States of WIPO, shall be members of the SCCR. In addition, the European Community shall be a member of the SCCR, provided that it shall not have the right to vote.

2. Member States of the United Nations that are neither Member States of WIPO nor Member States of the Berne Union shall have observer status in the SCCR.

5.3. Standing Committee on the Law of Trademarks, Industrial Designs and Geographical Indications (SCT)

At its first session, which was held in Geneva from July 13 to 17, 1998, the Standing Committee osn the Law of Trademarks, Industrial Designs and Geographical Indications (SCT) adopted the following special rules of procedure (see document SCT/1/6, paragraphs 12 to 22), namely:

1. The extension of Membership of the SCT to Member States of the Paris Union that are not Member States of WIPO, and that observer status be extended to Member States of the United Nations that are not Member States of WIPO or the Paris Union.[6]

---

2 WIPO, *Rules of Procedure: Memorandum Prepared by the Secretariat, Standing Committee on the Law of Patents, Second Session, Geneva April 12 to 23, 1999* WIPO SCP/2/2 (WIPO 1999).

3 WIPO, *Report Adopted by the Standing Committee, Standing Committee on the Law of Patents, Second Session* SCP/2/13 (WIPO 1999) 3.

4 The Rules were proposed in WIPO, *Revised Rules of Procedure: Document Prepared by the Secretariat, Standing Committee on the Law of Patents, Seventeenth Session, Geneva, December 5 to 9, 2011* SCP/17/6.REV. (WIPO 2011) available at http://www.wipo.int/edocs/mdocs/scp/en/scp_17/scp_17_6.pdf accessed 1 August 2015. For the decision to approve the Special Rules, see WIPO, *Report, Standing Committee on the Law of Patents, Seventh Session, Geneva* SCP/17/13 (WIPO 2011) available at http://www.wipo.int/edocs/mdocs/scp/en/scp_17/scp_17_13.pdf accessed 1 August 2015.

5 WIPO, *Report: Adopted by the Standing Committee, Standing Committee on Copyright and Related Rights (SCCR), First Session, Geneva, November 2–10, 1998* SCCR/1/9, Annex 1 (WIPO 1998).

6 WIPO, *Organizational Matters and Overview of the Issues to be Considered by the Standing Committee on the Law of Trademarks, Industrial Designs and Geographical Indications, Standing Committee on the Law of Trademarks, Industrial Designs and Geographical Indications, First Session, Geneva, July 13 to 17, 1998* SCT/1/2 (WIPO 1998), see para. 5 on page 3. For documentation of their adoption, see WIPO, *Report Prepared by the International Bureau,*

2. Extension of Membership to the European Communities, provided that it shall not have the right to vote.

In addition, Members of the SCT adopted two further Special Rules of Procedure in 1999 as follows:[7]

3. In order to allow for the greatest possible continuity in the work of the officers of the Standing Committee, the Standing Committee shall elect the Chair and the two Vice-Chairs for one year.

4. The outgoing Chair and Vice-Chairs shall be immediately eligible for re-election to the offices which they have held.

5.4. Intergovernmental Committee on Intellectual Property and Genetic Resources, Traditional Knowledge and Folklore (IGC)

In 2001, the Committee approved Special Rules of Procedure as follows:

1. Extension of membership in the Intergovernmental Committee to Member States of the Paris Union for the Protection of Industrial Property (the Paris Union) that are not Member States of WIPO, and extension of observer status to Member States of the United Nations that are not Member States of WIPO or the Paris Union.

2. To allow for the greatest continuity in the work of the officers of the Intergovernmental Committee, the election of the Chair and the two Vice-Chairs for one year and the immediate eligibility for the outgoing Chair and Vice-Chairs for re-election to the offices which they have held.[8]

Members of the Committee also approved a Special Rule of Procedure as follows:

3. The extension of membership (without the right to vote) to the European Communities.[9]

5.5. WIPO Advisory Committee on Enforcement (ACE)

In 2002, in addition to a number of decisions on working methods, the General Assembly adopted the following Special Rules of Procedure for the Advisory Committee on Enforcement:[10]

Standing Committee on the Law of Trademarks, Industrial Designs and Geographical Indications, First Session, Geneva, July 13 to 17, 1998 SCIT/1/6 (WIPO 1998).

7 WIPO, *Rules of Procedure: Memorandum Prepared by the Secretariat, Standing Committee on the Law of Trademarks, Industrial Designs and Geographical Indications, Second Session, First Part, Geneva, March 15 to 17, 1999* SCT/2/2 (WIPO 1999), paragraphs 12 to 22.

8 For the proposed rules, see WIPO, *Rules of Procedure: Memorandum Prepared by the Secretariat, Intergovernmental Committee on Intellectual Property and Genetic Resources, Traditional Knowledge and Folklore, First Session, Geneva, April 30 to May 3, 2001* WIPO/GRTKF/IC/1/2 (WIPO 2001) as well as WIPO/GRTKF/IC/1/2 Rev. and WIPO/GRTKF/IC/1/2 Add.

9 WIPO, *Report Adopted by the Committee, Intergovernmental Committee on Intellectual Property and Genetic Resources, Traditional Knowledge and Folklore, First Session, Geneva, April 30 to May 3, 2001* WIPO/GRTKF/IC/1/13 (WIPO 2001) 5, available at http://www.wipo.int/edocs/mdocs/tk/en/wipo_grtkf_ic_1/wipo_grtkf_ic_1_13.pdf accessed 15 July 2015.

10 The proposals were contained in paragraphs 8 to 14 of the following document. WIPO, *Matters Concerning the Status of the Advisory Committee(s) on Enforcement: Document Prepared by the Secretariat, WIPO General Assembly, Twenty-Eighth (13th Extraordinary) Session, September 23 to October 1, 2002* WO/GA/28/4 (WIPO 2002) paragraphs 8 to 14. For documentation of their approval, see WIPO, *Report Adopted by the Assembly, WIPO General Assembly, September 23 to October 1, 2002* WO/GA/28/7 (WIPO 2002) 25–6, available at http://www.wipo.int/edocs/mdocs/govbody/en/wo_ga_28/wo_ga_28_7.pdf accessed 1 August 2015.

1. Membership would be extended to Member States of the Paris Union that were not Member States of WIPO, and that observer status be extended to Member States of the United Nations that were not Member States of WIPO or the Paris Union.
2. The Chair and the two Vice-Chairs should serve a term of one year and would immediately be eligible for re-election to the offices that they had held at the expiration of that term.

5.6.   Committee on Development and Intellectual Property (CDIP)

In 2008, the Committee on Development and Intellectual Property adopted the following Special Rules of Procedure:[11]
1. Application of the General Rules of Procedure: The Rules of Procedure of the Committee on Development and Intellectual Property ("the Committee") shall consist of the "WIPO General Rules of Procedure", supplemented by the provisions set forth hereinafter.
2. Composition: The Committee shall be composed of all Member States of WIPO and shall be open to the participation, as observers, of all intergovernmental and non-governmental organizations having permanent observer status in WIPO, and of other intergovernmental and non-governmental organizations admitted by the Committee on an *ad hoc* basis.
3. Officers: In the first meeting of a calendar year, the Committee shall elect a Chair and two Vice-Chairs to serve for one year. They shall remain in office until the election of new officers. Any outgoing Chair or Vice-Chair may be immediately re-elected to the same office which they have held, subject to a maximum of three consecutive years in office.

5.7.   WIPO Program and Budget Committee (PBC)

Members of the PBC have not adopted Special Rules of Procedure. In 2006, Members adopted a Program and Budget Mechanism (see Figure 6.4), which includes arrangements for the timing and frequency of meetings related to the approval of the Program and Budget (for decisions and practices with regard to the selection and rotation of the PBC membership and mandate, see Chapter 6).

5.8.   Committee on WIPO Standards (CWS)

As of end-2015, WIPO Member States have not reached agreement on Special Rules of Procedure for the CWS, the first proposals for which were submitted by the Secretariat at the first session of the CWS in 2010.[12] The absence of agreement occurred in the context of the suspension of the Committee's work since 2014, largely due to different views among Members on the Committee's mandate and on how and whether the work of the CWS, and

---

11 WIPO, *Procedural and Organizational Matters: Adopted by the Meeting, Committee on Development and Intellectual Property (CDIP), First Session, Geneva, March 3 to 7, 2008* CDIP/1/1 Rev. Annex (WIPO 2008).

12 For the original proposed special rules of procedure, see WIPO, *Organizational Matters and Special Rules of Procedure: Prepared by the Secretariat, Committee on WIPO Standards, First Session, Geneva, October 25 to 29, 2010* CWS/1/2 (WIPO 2010). For revised proposed rules of procedure, see WIPO, *Organizational Matters and Special Rules of Procedure: Prepared by the Secretariat, Committee on WIPO Standards, First Session, Geneva, April 30 to May 4, 2010* CWS/2/2 (WIPO 2010) available at http://www.wipo.int/edocs/mdocs/cws/en/cws_2/cws_2_2. pdf accessed 31 October 2015.

its special rules of procedure, should specifically address issues related to the implementation of the WIPO Development Agenda, and report on such actions to the General Assembly in light of the Development Agenda Coordination Mechanism.[13]

---

13 The fourth session of the CWS meeting, which was due to be reconvened in June 2015, was postponed due to lack of agreement among Member States on the agenda and on organizational/procedural matters. Debate on the resumption of the suspended work of the CWS continued at the 2015 WIPO Assemblies. See WIPO Circular CWS 52–02, *Postponement of the Reconvening of the Fourth Session of the Committee on WIPO Standards (CWS)*, March 24, 2015. For the state of play as of May 2014, see WIPO, *Decision of the 44th Session of the WIPO General Assembly in Relation to the CWS: Document Prepared by the Secretariat* CWS/4/2 (WIPO 2014). Also see WIPO, *Summary by the Chair, Fourth Session, 12 to 16 May 2014* CWS/4/15 (WIPO 2014).

Appendix 6: Example of Rules of Procedure for a Diplomatic Conference: Marrakesh Treaty

Rules of Procedure of the Diplomatic Conference to Conclude a Treaty to Facilitate Access to Published Works by Visually Impaired Persons and Persons with Print Disabilities.

Marrakesh, June 17 to 28, 2013
as adopted on June 18, 2013 by the Diplomatic Conference.

CHAPTER I: OBJECTIVE, COMPETENCE, COMPOSITION AND SECRETARIAT OF THE CONFERENCE

Rule 1: Objective and Competence of the Conference

(1) The objective of the Diplomatic Conference to Conclude a Treaty to Facilitate Access to Published Works by Visually Impaired Persons and Persons with Print Disabilities (hereinafter referred to as "the Conference") is to Conclude the Treaty to Facilitate Access to Published Works for Persons who are Blind, Visually Impaired or Otherwise Print Disabled (hereinafter referred to as "the Treaty") pursuant to the mandate contained in the General Assembly document (WO/GA/42/3).

(2) The Conference, meeting in Plenary, shall be competent to:

    (i) adopt the Rules of Procedure of the Conference (hereinafter referred to as "these Rules") and to make any amendments thereto;

    (ii) adopt the agenda of the Conference;

    (iii) decide on credentials, full powers, letters or other documents presented in accordance with Rules 6, 7 and 8 of these Rules;

    (iv) adopt the Treaty;

    (v) adopt any recommendation, resolution or agreed statement within the terms of the objective in paragraph (1);

    (vi) adopt any final act of the Conference;

    (vii) deal with all other matters referred to it by these Rules or appearing on its agenda.

Rule 2: Composition of the Conference

(1) The Conference shall consist of:

    (i) delegations of the States members of the World Intellectual Property Organization (hereinafter referred to as "the Member Delegations"),

    (ii) the special delegation of the European Union (hereinafter referred to as "the Special Delegation"),

    (iii) the delegations of States members of the United Nations other than the States members of the World Intellectual Property Organization invited to the Conference as observers (hereinafter referred to as "the Observer Delegations"), and

(iv) representatives of intergovernmental and non-governmental organizations and others invited to the Conference as observers (hereinafter referred to as "the Observers").

(2) References in these Rules of Procedure to "Member Delegations" shall be considered, except as otherwise provided (see Rules 11(2), 33 and 34), as references also to the Special Delegation.

(3) References in these Rules of Procedure to "Delegations" shall be considered as references to the three kinds (Member, Special and Observer) of Delegations but not to Observers.

Rule 3: Secretariat of the Conference

(1) The Conference shall have a Secretariat provided by the International Bureau of the World Intellectual Property Organization (hereinafter referred to as "the International Bureau" and "WIPO", respectively).

(2) The Director General of WIPO and any official of the International Bureau designated by the Director General of WIPO may participate in the discussions of the Conference, meeting in Plenary, as well as in any committee or working group thereof and may, at any time, make oral or written statements, observations or suggestions to the Conference, meeting in Plenary, and any committee or working group thereof concerning any question under consideration.

(3) The Director General of WIPO shall, from among the staff of the International Bureau, designate the Secretary of the Conference and a Secretary for each committee and for each working group.

(4) The Secretary of the Conference shall direct the staff required by the Conference.

(5) The Secretariat shall provide for the receiving, translation, reproduction and distribution of the required documents, for the interpretation of oral interventions and for the performance of all other secretariat work required for the Conference.

(6) The Director General of WIPO shall be responsible for the custody and preservation in the archives of WIPO of all documents of the Conference. The International Bureau shall distribute the final documents of the Conference after the closing of the Conference.

CHAPTER II: REPRESENTATION

Rule 4: Delegations

(1) Each Delegation shall consist of one or more delegates and may include advisors.

(2) Each Delegation shall have a Head of Delegation and may have a Deputy Head of Delegation.

Rule 5: Observers

An Observer may be represented by one or more representatives.

Rule 6: Credentials and Full Powers

(1) Each Delegation shall present credentials.

(2) Full powers shall be required for signing the Treaty. Such powers may be included in the credentials.

Rule 7: Letters of Appointment

The representatives of Observers shall present a letter or other document appointing them.

Rule 8: Presentation of Credentials, etc.
The credentials and full powers referred to in Rule 6 and the letters or other documents referred to in Rule 7 shall be presented to the Secretary of the Conference, preferably not later than twenty-four hours after the opening of the Conference.

Rule 9: Examination of Credentials, etc.
(1) The Credentials Committee referred to in Rule 11 shall examine the credentials, full powers, letters or other documents referred to in Rules 6 and 7, respectively, and shall report to the Conference, meeting in Plenary.
(2) The decision on whether a credential, full powers, letter or other document is in order shall be made by the Conference, meeting in Plenary. Such decision shall be made as soon as possible and in any case before the adoption of the Treaty.

Rule 10: Provisional Participation
Pending a decision upon their credentials, letters or other documents of appointment, Delegations and Observers shall be entitled to participate provisionally in the deliberations of the Conference as provided in these Rules.

CHAPTER III: COMMITTEES AND WORKING GROUPS

Rule 11: Credentials Committee
(1) The Conference shall have a Credentials Committee.
(2) The Credentials Committee shall consist of seven Member Delegations elected by the Conference, meeting in Plenary, from among the Member Delegations, except that the Special Delegation shall not be eligible for membership in the Credentials Committee.

Rule 12: Main Committees and Their Working Groups
(1) The Conference shall have two Main Committees. Main Committee I shall be responsible for proposing for adoption by the Conference, meeting in Plenary, the substantive law provisions of the Treaty and any recommendation, resolution or agreed statement referred to in Rule 1(2)(v) and (vi). Main Committee II shall be responsible for proposing for adoption by the Conference, meeting in Plenary, any administrative and the final clauses of the Treaty.
(2) Each Main Committee shall consist of all the Member Delegations.
(3) Each Main Committee may create working groups. In creating a working group, the Main Committee creating it shall specify the tasks of the Working Group, decide on the number of the members of the Working Group and elect such members from among the Member Delegations.

Rule 13: Drafting Committee
(1) The Conference shall have a Drafting Committee.
(2) The Drafting Committee shall consist of 17 elected members and two *ex officio* members. The elected members shall be elected by the Conference, meeting in Plenary, from among the Member Delegations. The Presidents of the two Main Committees shall be the *ex officio* members.
(3) The Drafting Committee shall prepare drafts and give advice on drafting as requested by either Main Committee. The Drafting Committee shall not alter the substance of the texts submitted to it. It shall coordinate and review the drafting of all texts submitted to it by the Main Committees, and it shall submit the texts so reviewed for final approval to the competent Main Committee.

Rule 14: Steering Committee

(1) The Conference shall have a Steering Committee.

(2) The Steering Committee shall consist of the President and Vice-Presidents of the Conference, the President of the Credentials Committee, the Presidents of the Main Committees and the President of the Drafting Committee. The meetings of the Steering Committee shall be presided over by the President of the Conference.

(3) The Steering Committee shall meet from time to time to review the progress of the Conference and to make decisions for furthering such progress, including, in particular, decisions on the coordinating of the meetings of the Plenary, the committees and the working groups.

(4) The Steering Committee shall propose the text of any final act of the Conference (see Rule 1(2)(vi)), for adoption by the Conference, meeting in Plenary.

CHAPTER IV: OFFICERS

Rule 15: Officers and Their Election; Precedence among Vice-Presidents

(1) The Conference shall have a President and seven Vice-Presidents.

(2) The Credentials Committee, each of the two Main Committees and the Drafting Committee shall have a President and two Vice-Presidents.

(3) Any Working Group shall have a President and two Vice-Presidents.

(4) The Conference, meeting in Plenary, and presided over by the Director General of WIPO, shall elect its President, and, then, presided over by its President shall elect its Vice-Presidents and the officers of the Credentials Committee, the Main Committees and the Drafting Committee.

(5) The officers of a Working Group shall be elected by the Main Committee that establishes that Working Group.

(6) Precedence among the Vice-Presidents of a given body (the Conference, the Credentials Committee, the two Main Committees, any Working Group, the Drafting Committee) shall be determined by the place occupied by the name of the State of each of them in the list of Member Delegations established in the alphabetical order of the names of the States in French. The Vice-President of a given body who has precedence over all the other Vice-Presidents of that body shall be called "the ranking" Vice-President of that body.

Rule 16: Acting President

(1) If the President is absent from a meeting, the meeting shall be presided over, as Acting President, by the ranking Vice-President of that body.

(2) If all the officers of a body are absent from any meeting of the body concerned, that body shall elect an Acting President.

Rule 17: Replacement of the President

If the President becomes unable to perform his or her functions for the remainder of the duration of the Conference, a new President shall be elected.

Rule 18: Vote by the Presiding Officer

(1) No President, whether elected as such or acting (hereinafter referred to as "the Presiding Officer"), shall take part in voting. Another member of his or her Delegation may vote for that Delegation.

(2) Where the Presiding Officer is the only member of his or her Delegation, he or she may vote, but only in the last place.

CHAPTER V: CONDUCT OF BUSINESS

Rule 19: Quorum
(1) A quorum shall be required in the Conference, meeting in Plenary; it shall, subject to paragraph (3), be constituted by one-half of the Member Delegations represented at the Conference.
(2) A quorum shall be required for the meetings of each Committee (the Credentials Committee, the two Main Committees, the Drafting Committee and the Steering Committee) and any working group; it shall be constituted by one-half of the members of the Committee or working group.
(3) The quorum at the time of the adoption of the Treaty by the Conference, meeting in Plenary, shall be constituted by one-half of the Member Delegations whose credentials were found in order by the Conference meeting in Plenary.

Rule 20: General Powers of the Presiding Officer
(1) In addition to exercising the powers conferred upon Presiding Officers elsewhere by these Rules, the Presiding Officer shall declare the opening and closing of the meetings, direct the discussions, accord the right to speak, put questions to the vote, and announce decisions. The Presiding Officer shall rule on points of order and, subject to these Rules, shall have complete control of the proceedings at any meeting and over the maintenance of order thereat.
(2) The Presiding Officer may propose to the body over which he or she presides the limitation of time to be allowed to each speaker, the limitation of the number of times each Delegation may speak on any question, the closure of the list of speakers or the closure of the debate. The Presiding Officer may also propose the suspension or the adjournment of the meeting, or the adjournment of the debate on the question under discussion. Such proposals of the Presiding Officer shall be considered as adopted unless immediately rejected.

Rule 21: Speeches
(1) No person may speak without having previously obtained the permission of the Presiding Officer. Subject to Rules 22 and 23, the Presiding Officer shall call upon persons in the order in which they ask for the floor.
(2) The Presiding Officer may call a speaker to order if the remarks of the speaker are not relevant to the subject under discussion.

Rule 22: Precedence in Receiving the Floor
(1) Member Delegations asking for the floor are generally given precedence over Observer Delegations asking for the floor, and Member Delegations and Observer Delegations are generally given precedence over Observers.
(2) The President of a Committee or working group may be given precedence during discussions relating to the work of the Committee or working group concerned.
(3) The Director General of WIPO or his representative may be given precedence for making statements, observations or suggestions.

Rule 23: Points of Order
(1) During the discussion of any matter, any Member Delegation may rise to a point of order, and the point of order shall be immediately decided by the Presiding Officer in accordance with these Rules. Any Member Delegation may appeal against the ruling of the Presiding Officer. The appeal shall be immediately put to the vote, and the Presiding Officer's ruling shall stand unless the appeal is approved.

(2) The Member Delegation that has risen to a point of order under paragraph (1) may not speak on the substance of the matter under discussion.

Rule 24: Limit on Speeches
In any meeting, the Presiding Officer may decide to limit the time allowed to each speaker and the number of times each Delegation and Observer may speak on any question. When the debate is limited and a Delegation or Observer has used up its allotted time, the Presiding Officer shall call it to order without delay.

Rule 25: Closing of List of Speakers
(1) During the discussion of any given question, the Presiding Officer may announce the list of participants who have asked for the floor and decide to close the list as to that question. The Presiding Officer may nevertheless accord the right of reply to any speaker if a speech, delivered after the list of speakers has been closed, makes it desirable.
(2) Any decision made by the Presiding Officer under paragraph (1) may be the subject of an appeal under Rule 23.

Rule 26: Adjournment or Closure of Debate
Any Member Delegation may at any time move the adjournment or closure of the debate on the question under discussion, whether or not any other participant has asked for the floor. In addition to the proposer of the motion to adjourn or close the debate, permission to speak on that motion shall be given only to one Member Delegation seconding and two Member Delegations opposing it, after which the motion shall immediately be put to the vote. The Presiding Officer may limit the time allowed to speakers under this Rule.

Rule 27: Suspension or Adjournment of the Meeting
During the discussion of any matter, any Member Delegation may move the suspension or the adjournment of the meeting. Such motions shall not be debated, but shall immediately be put to the vote.

Rule 28: Order of Procedural Motions; Content of Interventions on Such Motions
(1) Subject to Rule 23, the following motions shall have precedence in the following order over all other proposals or motions before the meeting:
      (i) to suspend the meeting,
     (ii) to adjourn the meeting,
    (iii) to adjourn the debate on the question under discussion,
    (iv) to close the debate on the question under discussion.
(2) Any Member Delegation that has been given the floor on a procedural motion may speak on that motion only, and may not speak on the substance of the matter under discussion.

Rule 29: Basic Proposal; Proposals for Amendment
(1)
    (a) Documents [documents prepared in accordance with Rule 1 will be specified here] shall constitute the basis of the discussions in the Conference, and the text of the draft Treaty contained in those documents shall constitute the "Basic Proposal."
    (b) Where, for any given provision of the draft Treaty there are two or three alternatives in the Basic Proposal, consisting of either two or three texts, or one or two texts and an alternative that there should be no such provision, the alternatives shall be designated with the letters A, B and, where applicable, C, and shall have equal status. Discussions shall take place simultaneously on the alternatives and, if voting is

necessary and there is no consensus on which alternative should be put to the vote first, each Member Delegation shall be invited to indicate its preference among the two or three alternatives. The alternative supported by more Member Delegations than the other one or two alternatives shall be put to the vote first.

(c) Wherever the Basic Proposal contains words within square brackets, only the text that is not within square brackets shall be regarded as part of the Basic Proposal, whereas words within square brackets shall be treated as a proposal for amendment if presented as provided in paragraph (2).

(2) Any Member Delegation may propose amendments to the Basic Proposal.

(3) Proposals for amendment shall, as a rule, be submitted in writing and handed to the Secretary of the body concerned. The Secretariat shall distribute copies to the Delegations and the Observers. As a general rule, a proposal for amendment cannot be taken into consideration and discussed or put to the vote at a meeting unless copies of it have been distributed not later than three hours before it is taken into consideration. The Presiding Officer may, however, permit the taking into consideration and discussion of a proposal for amendment even though copies of it have not been distributed or have been distributed less than three hours before it is taken into consideration.

Rule 30:   Decisions on the Competence of the Conference

(1) If a Member Delegation moves that a duly seconded proposal should not be taken into consideration by the Conference because it is outside the latter's competence, that motion shall be decided upon by the Conference, meeting in Plenary, before the proposal is taken into consideration.

(2) If the motion referred to in paragraph (1), above, is made in a body other than the Conference, meeting in Plenary, it shall be referred to the Conference, meeting in Plenary, for a ruling.

Rule 31: Withdrawal of Procedural Motions and Proposals for Amendment

Any procedural motion and any proposal for amendment may be withdrawn by the Member Delegation that has made it, at any time before voting on it has commenced, provided that no amendment to it has been proposed by another Member Delegation. Any motion or proposal thus withdrawn may be reintroduced by any other Member Delegation.

Rule 32: Reconsideration of Matters Decided

When any matter has been decided by a body, it may not be reconsidered by that body unless so decided by the majority applicable under Rule 34(2)(ii). In addition to the proposer of the motion to reconsider, permission to speak on that motion shall be given only to one Member Delegation seconding and two Member Delegations opposing the motion, after which the motion shall immediately be put to the vote.

CHAPTER VI: VOTING

Rule 33: Right to Vote

(1) Each Member Delegation shall have the right to vote. A Member Delegation shall have one vote, may represent itself only and may vote in its name only.

(2) The Special Delegation has no right to vote and, for the purposes of paragraph (1) of this Rule and Rule 34, the Special Delegation is not covered by the term "Member Delegations".

(3) The Special Delegation may, under the authority of the European Union, exercise the rights to vote of the Member States of the European Union which are represented at the Diplomatic Conference, provided that:

(i) the Special Delegation shall not exercise the rights to vote of the Member States of the European Union if the Member States exercise their rights to vote and vice versa, and

(ii) the number of votes cast by the Special Delegation shall in no case exceed the number of Member States of the European Union that are represented at the Diplomatic Conference and that are present at and entitled to participate in the vote.

Rule 34: Required Majorities

(1) All decisions of all bodies shall be made as far as possible by consensus.

(2) If it is not possible to attain consensus, the following decisions shall require a majority of two-thirds of the Member Delegations present and voting:

(i) adoption by the Conference, meeting in Plenary, of these Rules, and, once adopted, any amendment to them,

(ii) decision by any of the bodies to reconsider, under Rule 32, a matter decided,

(iii) adoption by the Conference, meeting in Plenary, of the Treaty,

whereas all other decisions of all bodies shall require a simple majority of the Member Delegations present and voting.

(3) "Voting" means casting an affirmative or negative vote; express abstention or non-voting shall not be counted.

Rule 35: Requirement of Seconding; Method of Voting

(1) Any proposal for amendment made by a Member Delegation shall be put to a vote only if seconded by at least one other Member Delegation.

(2) Voting on any question shall be by show of hands unless a Member Delegation, seconded by at least one other Member Delegation, requests a roll-call, in which case it shall be by roll-call. The roll shall be called in the alphabetical order of the names in French of the States, beginning with the Member Delegation whose name shall have been drawn by lot by the Presiding Officer.

Rule 36: Conduct During Voting

(1) After the Presiding Officer has announced the beginning of voting, the voting shall not be interrupted except on a point of order concerning the actual conduct of the voting.

(2) The Presiding Officer may permit a Member Delegation to explain its vote or its abstention, either before or after the voting.

Rule 37: Division of Proposals

Any Member Delegation may move that parts of the Basic Proposal or of any proposal for amendment be voted upon separately. If the request for division is objected to, the motion for division shall be put to a vote. In addition to the proposer of the motion for division, permission to speak on that motion shall be given only to one Member Delegation seconding and two Member Delegations opposing it. If the motion for division is carried, all parts of the Basic Proposal or of the proposal for amendment that have been separately approved shall again be put to the vote, together, as a whole. If all operative parts of the Basic Proposal or of the proposal for amendment have been rejected, the Basic Proposal or the proposal for amendment shall be considered rejected as a whole.

Rule 38: Voting on Proposals for Amendment

(1) Any proposal for amendment shall be voted upon before the text to which it relates is voted upon.

(2) Proposals for amendment relating to the same text shall be put to the vote in the order of their substantive remoteness from the said text, the most remote being put to the vote first and the least remote being put to the vote last. If, however, the adoption of any proposal for amendment necessarily implies the rejection of any other proposal for amendment or of the original text, such other proposal or text shall not be put to the vote.

(3) If one or more proposals for amendment relating to the same text are adopted, the text as amended shall be put to the vote.

(4) Any proposal the purpose of which is to add to or delete from a text shall be considered a proposal for amendment.

Rule 39: Voting on Proposals for Amendment on the Same Question

Subject to Rule 38, where two or more proposals relate to the same question, they shall be put to the vote in the order in which they have been submitted, unless the body concerned decides on a different order.

Rule 40: Equally Divided Votes

(1) Subject to paragraph (2), if a vote is equally divided on a matter that calls only for a simple majority, the proposal shall be considered rejected.

(2) If a vote is equally divided on a proposal for electing a given person to a given position as officer and the nomination is maintained, the vote shall be repeated, until either that nomination is adopted or rejected or another person is elected for the position in question.

CHAPTER VII: LANGUAGES AND MINUTES

Rule 41: Languages of Oral Interventions

(1) Subject to paragraph (2), oral interventions made in the meetings of any of the bodies shall be in Arabic, Chinese, English, French, Portuguese, Russian or Spanish, and interpretation shall be provided by the Secretariat into Arabic, Chinese, English, French, Russian and Spanish.

(2) Any of the Committees and any working group may, if none of its members objects, decide to dispense with interpretation or to limit interpretation to some only of the languages that are referred to in paragraph (1).

Rule 42: Summary Minutes

(1) Provisional summary minutes of the meetings of the Conference, meeting in Plenary, and of the Main Committees shall be drawn up by the International Bureau and shall be made available as soon as possible after the closing of the Conference to all speakers, who shall, within two months after the minutes have been made available, inform the International Bureau of any suggestions for changes in the minutes of their own interventions.

(2) The final summary minutes shall be published in due course by the International Bureau.

Rule 43: Languages of Documents and Summary Minutes

(1) Any written proposal shall be presented to the Secretariat in Arabic, Chinese, English, French, Russian or Spanish. Such proposal shall be distributed by the Secretariat in Arabic, Chinese, English, French, Russian and Spanish.

(2) Reports of the Committees and any working group shall be distributed in Arabic, Chinese, English, French, Russian and Spanish. Information documents of the Secretariat shall be distributed in English and French and, whenever practicable, also in Arabic, Chinese, Russian and Spanish.

(3)
    (a) Provisional summary minutes shall be drawn up in the language used by the speaker if the speaker has used English, French or Spanish; if the speaker has used another language, the intervention shall be rendered in English or French at the choice of the International Bureau.
    (b) The final summary minutes shall be made available in English and French and, whenever practicable, also in Arabic, Chinese, Russian and Spanish.]

CHAPTER VIII: OPEN AND CLOSED MEETINGS

Rule 44: Meetings of the Conference and of the Main Committees
The meetings of the Conference, meeting in Plenary, and of the Main Committees shall be open to the public unless the Conference, meeting in Plenary, or the interested Main Committee, decides otherwise.

Rule 45: Meetings of Other Committees and of Working Groups
The meetings of the Credentials Committee, the Drafting Committee, the Steering Committee and any working group shall be open only to the members of the Committee or the working group concerned and to the Secretariat.

CHAPTER IX: OBSERVER DELEGATIONS AND OBSERVERS

Rule 46: Status of Observers
(1) Observer Delegations may attend and make oral statements in the Plenary meetings of the Conference and the meetings of the Main Committees.
(2) Observers may attend the Plenary meetings of the Conference and the meetings of the Main Committees. Upon the invitation of the Presiding Officer, they may make oral statements in those meetings on questions within the scope of their activities.
(3) Written statements submitted by Observer Delegations or by Observers on subjects for which they have a special competence and which are related to the work of the Conference shall be distributed by the Secretariat to the participants in the quantities and in the languages in which the written statements were made available to it.

CHAPTER X: AMENDMENTS TO THE RULES OF PROCEDURE

Rule 47: Possibility of Amending the Rules of Procedure
With the exception of the present Rule, these Rules may be amended by the Conference, meeting in Plenary.

CHAPTER XI: FINAL ACT

Rule 48: Signing of the Final Act
If a final act is adopted, it shall be open for signature by any Delegation.

Appendix 7: WIPO Financial Regulations and Rules (selected excerpts on oversight and audit)

Source: WIPO, *WIPO Financial Regulations and Rules* (WIPO 2014) as amended by the WIPO General Assembly in October 2015, see WIPO, *Proposed Revision of the Terms of Reference of the WIPO Independent Advisory Oversight Committee (IAOC): Document Prepared by the Secretariat, Program and Budget Committee Twenty-Fourth Session, 14–18 September* 2015 WO/PBC/24/4 Annex 1 (WIPO 2015).

Note: Annex III below reflects the WIPO General Assembly's approval in October 2015 of revisions to the terms of reference for the IAOC proposed in WO/PBC/24/4/, which thus updated the 2014 version of the WIPO Financial Regulations and Rules.

CHAPTER 7: INTERNAL OVERSIGHT CHARTER

Internal Oversight Charter

Regulation 7.1
There shall be an Internal Oversight Division (IOD) to conduct independent internal audits, inspections and investigations in accordance with the provisions of the WIPO Internal Oversight Charter appended to the present Financial Regulations (Annex I).

CHAPTER 8: EXTERNAL AUDITOR

Appointment of the External Auditor

Regulation 8.1
The External Auditor, who shall be the Auditor-General (or official holding the equivalent title) of a Member State, shall be appointed by the General Assembly, in the manner decided by the Assembly.

Tenure of office of the External Auditor

Regulation 8.2
The External Auditor shall be appointed for a term of office of six years non-renewable consecutively.

Regulation 8.3
If the External Auditor ceases to hold office as Auditor-General (or equivalent title) in his or her own country, his or her tenure of office shall thereupon be terminated and he or she shall be succeeded as External Auditor by his or her successor as Auditor-General. The External Auditor may not otherwise be removed during his or her tenure of office except by the General Assembly.

Audit standards, scope and operations

Regulation 8.4
The audit shall be conducted in conformity with generally accepted common international auditing standards and, subject to any special directions of the General Assembly, in accordance with the terms of reference set out in the annex to the present Regulations (Annex II).

Regulation 8.5
The External Auditor may make observations with respect to the efficiency of the financial procedures, the accounting system, the internal financial controls and, in general, the administration and management of the Organization.

Regulation 8.6
The External Auditor shall be completely independent and solely responsible for the conduct of the audit.

Regulation 8.7
The General Assembly may request the External Auditor to perform certain specific examinations and issue separate reports on the results.

Facilities

Regulation 8.8
The Director General shall provide the External Auditor with the facilities they may require in the performance of the audit.

Special examination

Regulation 8.9
For the purpose of making a local or special examination or of effecting economies in the audit cost, the External Auditor may engage the services of any national Auditor-General (or official holding the equivalent title) or commercial public auditors of known repute or any other person or firm which, in the opinion of the External Auditor, is technically qualified.

Reporting

Regulation 8.10
The External Auditor shall issue an opinion on the annual financial statements for each calendar year of the financial period, which shall include such information as the External Auditor deems necessary with regard to matters referred to in Regulation 8.5 and in the annex to the present Regulations referred to in Regulation 8.4.

Regulation 8.11
The reports of the External Auditor on the annual financial statements, together with reports from other audits, shall be transmitted to the General Assembly, to other Assemblies of WIPO Member States and of the Unions through the Program and Budget Committee, together with the audited annual financial statements, in accordance with any directions given by the General Assembly, other Assemblies of WIPO Member States and of the Unions. The Program and Budget Committee shall examine the annual financial statements and the

audit reports and shall forward them to the General Assembly, to other Assemblies of WIPO Member States and of the Unions, with such comments and recommendations as it deems appropriate.

CHAPTER 9: INDEPENDENT ADVISORY OVERSIGHT COMMITTEE

Regulation 9.1

There shall be an Independent Advisory Oversight Committee to assist Member States in their role of oversight and for better exercise of their governance responsibilities with respect to the various operations of WIPO. The Independent Advisory Oversight Committee shall operate as an independent, expert advisory and external oversight body. The General Assembly shall approve the WIPO Independent Advisory Oversight Committee's terms of reference upon recommendation by the Program and Budget Committee. These terms of reference shall be appended to the present Financial Regulations (Annex III).

ANNEX I. WIPO INTERNAL OVERSIGHT CHARTER*

A.   INTRODUCTION

1. This Charter constitutes the framework for the Internal Oversight Division (IOD) of the World Intellectual Property Organization (WIPO) and establishes its mission: to examine and evaluate, in an independent manner, WIPO's control and business systems and processes in order to identify good practices and to provide recommendations for improvement. IOD thus provides assurance as well as assistance to Management in the effective discharge of their responsibilities and the achievement of WIPO's mission, goals and objectives. The purpose of this Charter is also to help strengthen accountability, value for money, stewardship, internal control and corporate governance in WIPO.

2. The internal oversight function in WIPO comprises internal audit, evaluation and investigation.

B.   INTERNAL OVERSIGHT DEFINITIONS AND STANDARDS

3. In accordance with the definition adopted by the Institute of Internal Auditors (IIA), internal auditing is an independent, objective assurance and consulting activity designed to add value and improve an organization's operations. It helps an organization to accomplish its objectives by bringing a systematic, disciplined approach to evaluate and improve the effectiveness of risk management, control, and governance processes.

4. The internal audit function in WIPO shall be carried out in accordance with the International Standards for the Professional Practice of Internal Auditing and the Code of Ethics promulgated by IIA and adopted by the Representatives of Internal Audit Services of the United Nations Organizations, Multilateral Financial Institutions and Associated Intergovernmental Organizations (RIAS).

5. An evaluation is a systematic, objective and impartial assessment of an ongoing or completed project, program or policy, its design, implementation and results. The aim is to determine the relevance and fulfilment of objectives, its efficiency, effectiveness, impact and sustainability. An evaluation should contribute to learning and accountability and provide credible, evidence-based information, enabling the incorporation of findings and recommendations into the decision-making processes of WIPO.

6. Evaluations in WIPO shall be carried out in accordance with the standards developed and adopted by the United Nations Evaluation Group (UNEG).

---

*   Amended on 29 September 2010, 9 October 2012 and 30 September 2014.

7. An investigation is a formal fact-finding inquiry to examine allegations of or information concerning misconduct and other wrongdoing in order to determine whether they have occurred and if so, the person or persons responsible.

8. Investigations in WIPO shall be carried out in accordance with the Uniform Principles and Guidelines for Investigations adopted by the Conference of International Investigators and with WIPO's regulations and rules.

C. MANDATE

9. The internal oversight function provides the Management of WIPO with independent, objective assurance, analyses, appraisals, recommendations, lessons learned, advice and information, through the undertaking of internal audits, evaluations and investigations. Its objectives include:

(a) Identifying means for improving WIPO's relevance, effectiveness, efficiency, and economy of the internal procedures and use of resources,

(b) Assessing whether cost-effective controls are in place, and

(c) Assessing compliance with WIPO's Financial Regulations and Rules, Staff Regulations and Rules, relevant General Assembly decisions, the applicable accounting standards, the Standards of Conduct for the International Civil Service, as well as good practice.

D.   AUTHORITY AND RESPONSIBILITY

10. The Director, IOD reports administratively to the Director General but is not part of operational management. The Director, IOD enjoys functional and operational independence from Management in the conduct of his/her duties. In the exercise of his/her functions, he/she takes advice from the WIPO Independent Advisory Oversight Committee (IAOC). He/she has the authority to initiate, carry out and report on any action, which he/she considers necessary to fulfil his/her mandate.

11. The Director, IOD and oversight staff shall be independent of all WIPO programs, operations and activities, to ensure impartiality and credibility of the work undertaken.

12. The Director, IOD and oversight staff shall conduct oversight work in a professional, impartial and unbiased manner and in accordance with good practice, standards and norms generally accepted and applied by the United Nations system organizations, as detailed in Section B above.

13. For the performance of his/her duties, the Director, IOD shall have unrestricted, unlimited, direct and prompt access to all WIPO records, officials or personnel, holding any WIPO contractual status, and to all the premises of WIPO. The Director, IOD shall have access to the Chairs of the General Assembly, the Coordination Committee, the Program and Budget Committee and the IAOC.

14. The Director, IOD shall maintain facilities for the submission of complaints by individual staff members as well as any other internal or external parties, concerning alleged misconduct, wrongdoing or irregularities including but not limited to: fraud and corruption, waste, abuse of privileges and immunities, abuse of authority, and violation of WIPO regulations and rules. Notwithstanding the foregoing, the mandate of the Director, IOD normally does not extend to those areas for which separate provision has been made for review, including workplace-related conflicts and grievances, personnel grievances arising from administrative decisions affecting a staff member's terms of appointment, and performance issues and performance-related disagreements. It rests with the Director, IOD to determine whether such matters may involve wrongdoing and should be handled by IOD or whether they should be referred to other internal bodies.

15. The right of all staff and personnel to communicate confidentially with, and provide information to the Director, IOD, without fear of reprisal, shall be guaranteed by the

Director General. This is without prejudice to measures that may be taken under WIPO Staff Regulations and Rules regarding claims which are intentionally and knowingly false or misleading or made with reckless disregard for accuracy of the information.

16. The Director, IOD shall respect the confidential nature of, and protect from unauthorized disclosure, any information gathered or received in the course of an internal audit, evaluation, or investigation, and shall use such information only in so far as it is necessary for the performance of his/her duties.

17. The Director, IOD shall liaise regularly with all other internal and external providers of assurance services to ensure the proper coordination of activities (External Auditor, Risk Officer, Compliance Officer). The Director, IOD shall also periodically liaise with the Chief Ethics Officer and with the Ombudsperson.

E. CONFLICT OF INTEREST

18. In the performance of their oversight work, the Director, IOD and oversight staff shall avoid perceived or actual conflicts of interest. The Director, IOD shall report any significant impairment to independence and objectivity, including conflicts of interest, for due consideration of the IAOC.

19. Notwithstanding the foregoing, where allegations of misconduct concern the staff of IOD, the Director, IOD shall inform and seek the advice of the IAOC on how to proceed.

20. Allegations of misconduct against the Director, IOD shall be reported to the Director General, who shall inform the Chairs of the Coordination Committee and IAOC and may, in consultation with them, decide to refer the matter to an independent external investigative authority.

21. Allegations of misconduct against the Director General shall be reported by the Director, IOD to the Chair of the General Assembly with a copy to the Chairs of the Coordination Committee and the IAOC. The Director, IOD shall seek the advice of the IAOC on how to proceed further.

F. DUTIES AND MODALITIES OF WORK

22. The internal oversight function contributes to the efficient management of the Organization and the accountability of the Director General to the Member States.

23. To carry out his/her mandate, the Director, IOD shall conduct audits, evaluations, and investigations. The types of audits should include, but not be limited to, performance audits, financial audits, and compliance audits.

24. To effectively implement WIPO's internal oversight functions, the Director, IOD shall:

   (a) Establish long and short term internal oversight work plans in coordination with the External Auditor. The annual work plan shall be based, where relevant, on a risk assessment to be carried out at least annually, on which basis work would be prioritized. In preparing the annual work plan, the Director, IOD shall take into account any suggestions received from Management, the IAOC or from Member States. Prior to finalizing the internal oversight plan, the Director, IOD shall submit the draft plan to the IAOC for its review and advice.

   (b) In consultation with Member States, establish policies for all oversight functions, i.e., internal audit, evaluation, and investigation. The policies shall provide rules and procedures on the access to reports while ensuring rights to due process and the preservation of confidentiality.

   (c) Prepare, for review by the IAOC, and issue an internal audit manual, an evaluation manual, and an investigation manual. Such manuals shall include the terms of reference of the individual oversight functions and a compilation of applicable procedures. They shall be reviewed every three years or earlier.

(d) Establish and maintain follow-up systems to determine whether effective action has been taken in response to oversight recommendations, within a reasonable time. The Director, IOD shall periodically report in writing to Member States, the IAOC and the Director General on situations where adequate, timely corrective action has not been implemented.

(e) Liaise and coordinate with the External Auditor and monitor the follow-up of their recommendations.

(f) Develop and maintain a quality assurance/improvement program covering all aspects of internal audit, evaluation and investigation, including periodic internal and external reviews and ongoing self-assessments in accordance with the applicable standards. Independent external assessments shall be conducted at least once every five years.

(g) Liaise and cooperate with the internal oversight or similar services of other organizations of the United Nations system and of Multilateral Financial Institutions, and represent WIPO in relevant inter-agency meetings.

25. In particular, the Director, IOD shall assess:

(a) The reliability, effectiveness and integrity of WIPO's internal control mechanisms.

(b) The adequacy of organizational structures, systems and processes to ensure that the results WIPO produces are consistent with the objectives established.

(c) The effectiveness of WIPO in meeting its objectives and achieving results and, as required, recommending better ways of achieving such results, taking into account good practices and lessons learned.

(d) Systems aimed at ensuring compliance with WIPO's regulations, rules, policies and procedures.

(e) The effective, efficient and economical use, and the safeguarding of human, financial and material resources of WIPO.

(f) Significant exposure of WIPO to risk and contributing to the improvement of risk management.

26. The Director, IOD shall also undertake investigations into allegations of misconduct and other wrongdoing. The Director, IOD may decide to proactively initiate investigations based on risks identified.

G.   REPORTING

27. At the completion of each audit, evaluation or investigation, the Director, IOD shall issue a report, which shall present the objectives, scope, methodology, findings, conclusions, remedial action or recommendations of the specific activity concerned and include, if applicable, recommendations for improvements and lessons learned from the activity. The Director, IOD shall ensure completeness, timeliness, fairness, objectivity and accuracy in the reporting of internal audits, evaluations and investigations.

28. Draft internal audit and evaluation reports shall be presented to the program manager and other relevant officials directly responsible for the program or activity that has been the object of the internal audit or evaluation, who shall be given the opportunity to respond within a reasonable time to be specified in the draft report.

29. Final internal audit and evaluation reports shall reflect any relevant comments from the managers concerned and, if applicable, the related management action plans and timetables. Should the Director, IOD and the program manager be unable to agree on the findings of a draft audit and evaluation report, the final report shall contain the opinion of both the Director, IOD and of the managers concerned.

30. The Director, IOD shall submit final internal audit and evaluation reports to the Director General with a copy to the IAOC and the External Auditor. Upon request, the External

Auditor shall be provided with any supporting documentation of internal audit and evaluation reports.

31. The Director, IOD shall publish internal audit and evaluation reports, as well as Management Implication Reports resulting from investigations, on the WIPO website within 30 days of their issuance. If required to protect security, safety or privacy, the Director, IOD may, at his/her discretion, withhold a report in its entirety or redact parts of it.

32. The Director, IOD shall submit final investigation reports to the Director General. For final investigation reports involving WIPO personnel at the Deputy Director General and Assistant Director General levels, the Director, IOD shall provide a copy of the report to the Chairs of the General Assembly and the Coordination Committee, with copies to the Chair of the IAOC and to the External Auditor. Final investigation reports concerning the Director General shall be submitted to the Chairs of the General Assembly and Coordination Committee for any action deemed appropriate, and copied to the IAOC, and to the External Auditor.

33. The External Auditor and the IAOC shall have access to investigation reports.

34. All investigation reports, drafts, materials, findings, conclusions and recommendations are fully confidential, unless disclosure is authorized by the Director, IOD or the Director General.

35. For oversight matters of a minor or routine nature, which do not require formal reporting, the Director, IOD may issue communications to any concerned WIPO manager.

36. The Director General is responsible for ensuring that all recommendations made by the Director, IOD are responded to promptly, indicating actions taken by Management regarding specific report findings and recommendations. In cases where investigation report findings and/or recommendations apply to the Director General, the IAOC shall, at the earliest opportunity, report to Member States that such findings and/or recommendations have been made.

37. The Director, IOD shall submit, on an annual basis, a report to the Director General, with a copy to the IAOC, regarding the implementation of recommendations made by the External Auditor.

38. The Director, IOD shall submit, on an annual basis, a summary report to the WIPO General Assembly, through the Program and Budget Committee (Annual Report). The Director General and the IAOC shall be provided with a draft version of the Annual Report for their comments, if any. The Annual Report shall give an overview on the internal oversight activities conducted during the reporting period, including the scope and objectives of such activities, the schedule of work undertaken and progress on the implementation of internal oversight recommendations. The Director General may submit comments on the final Annual Report in a separate report as deemed appropriate.

39. The Annual Report shall include the following, *inter alia*:

(a) A description of significant issues and deficiencies relating to WIPO's activities in general, or a program or operation in particular, disclosed during the period.

(b) A description, including the financial impacts, if any, of those investigative cases found to be substantiated and their disposition, such as disciplinary measures, referral to national law enforcement authorities, and other sanctions taken.

(c) A description of all high priority internal oversight recommendations made by the Director, IOD during the reporting period.

(d) A description of all recommendations which were not accepted by the Director General, together with his/her explanations for not doing so.

(e) An identification of high priority recommendations in previous reports on which corrective action has not been completed.

(f) Information concerning any significant management decision which in the view of the Director, IOD constitutes a serious risk for the Organization.

(g) A summary of any instance where IOD's access to records, personnel and premises was restricted.

(h) A summary of the report submitted by the Director, IOD to the Director General regarding the status of implementation of external audit recommendations.

(i) Confirmation of the operational independence of the internal oversight function and shall comment on the scope of his/her activities and the adequacy of resources for the purposes intended.

H. RESOURCES

40. In presenting Program and Budget proposals to the Member States, the Director General shall take into account the need to ensure the operational independence of the internal oversight function and shall provide the necessary resources to enable the Director, IOD to achieve the objectives of his/her mandate. The allocation of financial and human resources including in- sourcing, outsourcing or co-sourcing of services shall be clearly identified in the Program and Budget proposal, which will take into account the advice of the IAOC.

41. The Director, IOD shall ensure that IOD comprises staff, appointed in accordance with WIPO Staff Regulations and Rules, which collectively possess the knowledge, skills and other competencies needed to perform the internal oversight functions. He/she shall promote continuing professional development to meet the requirements of this Charter.

I. APPOINTMENT, PERFORMANCE APPRAISAL AND DISMISSAL OF THE DIRECTOR, IOD

42. The Director, IOD shall be a person with high qualifications and competence in oversight functions. The recruitment of the Director, IOD shall be based on an open, transparent international selection process to be conducted by the Director General in consultation with the IAOC.

43. The Director, IOD shall be appointed by the Director General after endorsement by the IAOC and the Coordination Committee. The Director, IOD shall have a non-renewable fixed term of office of six years. On completion of the fixed term of office he/she shall not be eligible for any further employment in WIPO. Steps should be taken, where possible, to ensure that the start of the terms of the Director, IOD should not be the same as that of a new External Auditor.

44. The Director General may dismiss the Director, IOD only on specific and documented grounds and after endorsement by the IAOC and the Coordination Committee.

45. The performance appraisal of the Director, IOD shall be made by the Director General after receiving input from and in consultation with the IAOC.

J. REVISION CLAUSE

46. This Charter shall be reviewed by the Director, IOD and the IAOC, every three years or earlier, if necessary. Any proposed amendments by the Secretariat to the Charter shall be reviewed by the IAOC and the Director General and shall be submitted to the Program and Budget Committee for approval.

ANNEX II. TERMS OF REFERENCE GOVERNING EXTERNAL AUDIT*

1. The External Auditor shall perform such audit of the accounting records of WIPO and of the Unions administered by WIPO, including all trust funds and special accounts, as he/she deems necessary in order to assure himself:

(a) that the annual financial statements are in accord with the books and records of WIPO;

(b) that the financial transactions reflected in the annual financial statements have been in accordance with the rules and regulations, the budgetary provisions and other applicable directives;

(c) that the securities and monies on deposit and on hand have been verified by certificate received direct from WIPO's depositaries or by actual count;

(d) that the internal controls are adequate in the light of the extent of reliance placed thereon;

(e) that procedures satisfactory to him have been applied to the recording of all assets, liabilities, surpluses and deficits.

2. The External Auditor shall be the sole judge as to the acceptance in whole or in part of certifications and representations by the Director General and may proceed to such detailed examination and verification as he/she chooses of all financial records including those relating to supplies and equipment.

3. The External Auditor and his/her staff have free access at all convenient times to all books, records and other documentation which are, in the opinions of the External Auditor, necessary for the performance of the audit. Information classified as privileged and which the Director General (or his designated senior official) agrees is necessary for the purposes of the audit and information classified confidential shall be made available on application. The External Auditor and his/her staff shall respect the privileged and confidential nature of any information so classified which has been made available and shall not make use of it except in direct connection with the performance of the audit. The External Auditor may draw the attention of the Governing Bodies concerned of WIPO and all interested Unions, and of the WIPO Independent Advisory Oversight Committee, to any denial of information classified as privileged which in his/her opinion was required for the purpose of the audit.

4. The External Auditor shall have no power to disallow items in the accounting records but shall draw to the attention of the Director General for appropriate action any transaction concerning which he/she entertains doubt as to legality or propriety. Audit objections to these or any other transactions arising during the examination of the accounting records shall be immediately communicated to the Director General.

5. The External Auditor shall express and sign an opinion on the annual financial statements of WIPO. The opinion shall include the following basic elements:

(a) the identification of the annual financial statements audited;

(b) a reference to the responsibility of WIPO's management and the responsibility of the External Auditor;

(c) a reference to the audit standards followed;

(d) a description of the work performed;

(e) an expression of opinion on the annual financial statements as to whether:

(i) the annual financial statements present fairly the financial position as at the end of the calendar year and the results of the operations for the calendar year;

---

* Amended on 9 October 2012.

      (ii) the annual financial statements were prepared in accordance with the stated accounting policies; and

      (iii) the accounting policies were applied on a basis consistent with that of the preceding calendar year.

(f) an expression of opinion on the compliance of transactions with the Financial Regulations and legislative authority;

(g) the date of the opinion;

(h) the External Auditor's name and position; and

      (i) should it be necessary, a reference to the report of the External Auditor on the annual financial statements.

6. The Report of the External Auditor on the financial operations of the calendar year should mention:

(a) the type and scope of his/her examination;

(b) matters affecting the completeness or accuracy of the accounting records, including where appropriate:

      (i) information necessary to the correct interpretation of the accounting records;

      (ii) any amounts which ought to have been received but which have not been brought to account;

      (iii) any amounts for which a legal or contingent obligation exists and which have not been recorded or reflected in the annual financial statements;

      (iv) expenditures not properly substantiated;

      (v) whether proper books of accounts have been kept. Where, in the presentation of the annual financial statements, there are deviations of a material nature from the generally accepted accounting principles applied on a consistent basis, these should be disclosed;

(c) other matters which should be brought to the notice of the Governing Bodies concerned of WIPO and all interested Unions, such as:

      (i) cases of fraud or presumptive fraud;

      (ii) wasteful or improper expenditure of WIPO's money or other assets (notwithstanding that the accounting for the transaction may be correct);

      (iii) expenditure likely to commit WIPO to further outlay on a large scale;

      (iv) any defect in the general system or detailed regulations governing the control of receipts and disbursements or of supplies and equipment;

      (v) expenditure not in accordance with the intention of the Governing Bodies concerned of WIPO and all interested Unions after making allowance for duly authorized transfers within the budget;

      (vi) expenditure in excess of appropriations as amended by duly authorized transfers within the budget;

      (vii) expenditure not in conformity with the authority which governs it;

(d) the accuracy or otherwise of the supplies and equipment records as determined by stock-taking and examination of the records.

In addition, the reports may contain reference to:

(e) transactions accounted for in a previous year concerning which further information has been obtained or transactions in a later year concerning which it seems desirable that the Governing Bodies concerned of WIPO and all interested Unions should have early knowledge.

7. The External Auditor may make such observations with respect to his/her findings resulting from the audit and such comments on the Director General's financial report as he/she

deems appropriate to the Governing Bodies concerned of WIPO and all interested Unions or the Director General.

8. Whenever the scope of audit of the External Auditor is restricted, or whenever the External Auditor is unable to obtain sufficient evidence, he/she shall refer to the matter in his/her opinion and report, making clear the reasons for his/her comments and the effect on the financial position and the financial transactions as recorded.

9. In no case shall the External Auditor include criticism in his/her Report without first allowing the Director General an adequate opportunity of explanation on the matter under observation.

ANNEX III. TERMS OF REFERENCE OF THE WIPO INDEPENDENT ADVISORY OVERSIGHT COMMITTEE

A. PREAMBLE

1. In September 2005, the WIPO General Assembly approved the establishment of a WIPO Audit Committee. In September 2010, the WIPO General Assembly approved a change to the title of the Committee to the Independent Advisory Oversight Committee and amended its composition and rotation procedures.

B. FUNCTIONS AND RESPONSIBILITIES

2. The IAOC, a subsidiary body of the General Assembly and of the Program and Budget Committee, is an independent, expert advisory and external oversight body established to provide assurance to Member States on the adequacy and effectiveness of internal controls and of internal and external oversight at WIPO. It aims to assist Member States in their role of oversight and in exercising their governance responsibilities with respect to the various operations of WIPO. Its mandate is as follows:

   (a) Promoting internal control by:

   (i) Systematically appraising management's actions to maintain and operate appropriate and effective internal controls;

   (ii) Contributing, through its scrutiny function, to maintaining the highest possible standards of financial management and addressing any irregularities;

   (iii) Reviewing the effectiveness of the Financial Rules and Regulations;

   (iv) Reviewing management's assessment of and approach to risk;

   (v) Reviewing and advising on the fraud and corruption prevention policies and on the ethics function, including the code of ethics, financial disclosure, and whistleblower protection.

   (b) Providing assurance to the General Assembly by:

   (i) Reviewing and monitoring the effectiveness and operational independence of WIPO's internal audit, evaluation and investigation functions;

   (ii) Reviewing and providing advice on the proposed annual work plans of the Internal Oversight Division and of the Ethics Office;

   (iii) Exchanging information and views with the External Auditor, including his/her audit plan;

   (iv) Promoting effective coordination between the internal and external audit function and reviewing the collective coverage of various WIPO functions, including the Internal Oversight Division, the Office of the Ombudsman, the Ethics Office and the Office of the Controller;

   (v) Confirming that oversight functions have been carried out to provide reasonable assurance to the General Assembly;

(vi) Providing input to the performance appraisals of the Director, Internal Oversight Division, as provided for in paragraph 45 of the Internal Oversight Charter, and of the Ethics Officer;

(vii) Advising the Director General on the appointment and dismissal, if any, of the Director, Internal Oversight Division, as provided for in paragraph 44 of the Internal Oversight Charter, and of the Ethics Officer.

(c) Overseeing compliance with internal and external oversight recommendations by:

(i) Monitoring the timeliness, effectiveness and adequacy of management responses to audit, evaluation and investigation recommendations;

(ii) Monitoring the implementation of oversight recommendations.

(d) Monitoring the delivery and content of financial statements in accordance with the requirements of the Financial Regulations.

(e) Overseeing and supporting investigations:

(i) In cases of significant impairment to independence and objectivity, including conflicts of interest, the IAOC shall provide advice to the Director, Internal Oversight Division on how to proceed;

(ii) In accordance with the Internal Oversight Charter, the IAOC shall provide advice to the Director IOD, on how to proceed in cases of allegations of misconduct against the Director General (DG). If the Director IOD, on grounds of conflict of interest, is unable to evaluate or investigate, the IAOC shall review the allegations and provide advice to the Chair of the General Assembly with a copy to the Chair of the Coordination Committee on how to proceed;

(iii) In cases of allegations of misconduct against the Director IOD, the IAOC shall review the allegations and provide advice to the DG and/or the Chair of the Coordination Committee, with a copy to the Chair of the General Assembly, on how to proceed. No investigative proceedings into allegations against the Director IOD shall be initiated without the concurrence of the IAOC.

(f) The Program and Budget Committee may from time to time request the IAOC to review or oversee particular activities and projects.

(g) The IAOC shall make recommendations to the Program and Budget Committee on issues within the terms of reference, as it considers appropriate and:

(i) Review, periodically, the content of the Financial Regulations and Rules including its Annexes "WIPO Internal Oversight Charter" (Annex I), "Terms of Reference Governing External Audit" (Annex II), and "Terms of Reference of the WIPO Independent Advisory Oversight Committee" (Annex III), for compliance with Generally Accepted Standards and with best practice and make recommendations to the Program and Budget Committee;

(ii) Review the quality assurance and improvement program of the internal oversight function and the results of its internal self-assessments and independent external reviews, in accordance with the Internal Oversight Charter.

C. MEMBERSHIP AND QUALIFICATIONS

3. The IAOC shall be composed of seven members, from each of the seven geographical regions of WIPO Member States. The seven members will be nominated by the Program and Budget Committee following a selection process carried out by a Selection Panel set up by the Committee for this purpose, to be assisted by the current IAOC.

4. The rotation mechanism for the IAOC members will be as follows:

(i) All members of the IAOC shall be nominated for a term of three years, renewable once. No member of the IAOC shall serve for more than six years in aggregate;

(ii) Each member of the IAOC would be replaced by a candidate from the same geographical region that he or she belongs to. If the departing member belongs to a Group that already has another representative, he/she will be replaced by a member originating from the Group(s) not represented in the Committee. However, in case there is no candidate available from the region concerned, who meets the criteria established by the Selection Panel in accordance with the General Assembly decision (recorded in paragraph 30, of document WO/GA/39/14) as contained in paragraphs 14, 15, 21, 22 and 26 of document WO/GA/39/13, then the position would be filled in by the highest ranking candidate irrespective of his or her regional representation;

(iii) The selection process as described in paragraph 28 of document WO/GA/39/13 shall apply;

(iv) In case of resignation or demise of a member of the IAOC while serving his or her term, a roster/pool of experts identified during the selection process may be used.

5. The Selection Panel, in recommending candidates for nomination by the Program and Budget Committee shall ensure that the candidates possess relevant qualifications and experience, for example, in auditing, evaluation, accounting, risk management, legal affairs, information technology, human resources management and other financial and administrative matters. Expertise as well as geographical distribution and rotation should guide the selection process. In making its final recommendations to the Program and Budget Committee, the Selection Panel will try to ensure collegiality, the right mix of skills and expertise, and gender balance in the overall composition of the Committee. Due consideration shall be given to the availability, commitment, professionalism, integrity and independence of the candidates. Candidates must possess a demonstrated working knowledge of WIPO official languages, in particular English or French. When making its recommendations to the Program and Budget Committee the Selection Panel shall provide redacted curricula vitae for all individuals being nominated for appointment to the Independent Advisory Oversight Committee.

6. The IAOC should collectively possess the following competencies:

(a) Technical or specialist knowledge of issues pertinent to the Organization's business;

(b) Experience of managing organizations of similar size and complexity;

(c) Understanding of the wider relevant environments in which the Organization operates, including its objectives, culture and structure;

(d) Detailed understanding of the Organization's governance environment and accountability structures;

(e) Oversight or management experience at senior level in the United Nations system;

(f) International and/or intergovernmental experience.

7. New members should have or should acquire by a structured induction program organized by the WIPO Secretariat in consultation and with the participation of Member States an understanding of the objectives of the Organization, its structure and its culture, and the relevant rules governing it.

8. Members shall serve in their personal capacity; they cannot delegate their duties and may not be represented by any other person in the sessions of the Committee. In performing their duties, members shall not seek or receive instructions from any Government or any other party.

9. Members of the IAOC shall sign a statement of disclosure of interest.

10. Members of the IAOC and their immediate family members shall not be eligible for employment at WIPO either directly or indirectly during their mandate period and for up to five years after their mandate period.

D.   CHAIRPERSONSHIP

11. The members of the IAOC shall elect annually a Chairperson and a Vice- Chairperson. In the event of the chairpersonship becoming vacant during the term, the Vice-Chairperson shall assume the office of the Chairperson until the expiration of the predecessor's term and members shall elect another Vice-Chairperson. In the event of both the Chairperson and the Vice-Chairperson being absent, the remaining members may designate an Acting Chairperson from among themselves to conduct the meeting or the entire session.

E.   REIMBURSEMENT OF COSTS

12. Members will not be remunerated for activities undertaken in their capacity as members of the Committee. However, WIPO shall reimburse Committee members, in accordance with WIPO Financial Regulations and Rules, for any travel and subsistence costs that are necessarily incurred in relation to participation in Committee and other official meetings.

F.   INDEMNITY OF MEMBERS

13. Committee members will be indemnified from actions taken against them as a result of activities performed in the course of exercising their responsibilities as members of the Committee, as long as such activities are performed in good faith and with due diligence.

G.   MEETINGS AND QUORUM

14. The IAOC will meet regularly every quarter in formal session at WIPO headquarters. In exigent circumstances, the Committee may decide to consider issues through virtual consultations and come to conclusions that will have the same force as conclusions arrived at during its regular sessions.

15. A minimum of four members of the IAOC are required to be present for a meeting of the Committee to be quorate.

16. The IAOC may invite officials of the WIPO Secretariat or others to attend its sessions.

17. The IAOC shall meet at least once a year in private sessions with the Director, Internal Oversight Division, the Ethics Officer, the Ombudsperson and the External Auditor, respectively.

H.   REPORTING AND REVIEW

18. The IAOC shall keep Member States informed of its work on a regular basis. In particular, following each of its formal sessions the Committee shall organize an information meeting with representatives of WIPO Member States and submit a report to the Program and Budget Committee.

19. Based on its review of the internal oversight and external audit functions of WIPO and its interactions with the Secretariat, the IAOC shall submit an annual report to the Program and Budget Committee and to the WIPO General Assembly.

20. The IAOC shall consider the reports of the External Auditor presented to the Program and Budget Committee and provide comments for consideration by the Program and Budget Committee to facilitate its report to the General Assembly as provided for in Financial Regulation 8.11. To this end, the IAOC shall receive a signed copy of the External Auditor's Report at least four weeks prior to the session of the Program and Budget Committee.

21. The Chairperson or other members designated by the Chairperson shall attend ex officio, relevant meetings of the General Assembly and of the Program and Budget Committee. At the invitation of other WIPO committees, the Chairperson or other members designated by the Chairperson may attend meetings of such committees.

I.   SELF-ASSESSMENT

22. The IAOC shall perform, at least every two years, a self-assessment relative to the Committee's purpose and mandate to ensure it is operating effectively.

J.   THE SECRETARY OF THE COMMITTEE

23. The WIPO Secretariat shall designate a Secretary to the IAOC who shall provide logistical and technical assistance to the Committee.

24. Such assistance entails preparing for and attending the sessions of the Committee and assisting with preparing draft reports or any correspondence. Such assistance may also entail research and background position papers in preparation for the sessions of the Committee, as may be requested by the Committee.

25. The performance appraisal of the IAOC Secretary shall be done with input from and in consultation with the Chairperson of the IAOC.

K.   BUDGET

26. WIPO shall include in its biennial budget a specific allocation for the IAOC, providing for the costs associated with the Committee's mandated activities, namely four formal sessions of four to five days each in principle, attendance by IAOC members at Program and Budget Committee sessions, at the General Assembly, and at other meetings as required, support by the IAOC Secretary, and, as required, external consultancies.

L.   INFORMATION REQUIREMENTS

27. Well in advance of each formal meeting, the WIPO Secretariat shall provide the Independent Advisory Oversight Committee with documents and information related to its Agenda, and any other relevant information. The Committee shall have unhindered access to all staff and consultants of the Organization, as well as access to records.

M.   AMENDMENTS TO THE TERMS OF REFERENCE

28. Previous revisions to these Terms of Reference have been approved by the WIPO General Assembly in September 2007, September 2010, September 2011, andOctober 2012. The latest revision (contained in document WO/PBC/24/4) has been approved by the WIPO General Assembly in October 2015.

29. Member States will review, every three years, the mandate, functioning, membership, selection and rotation of the IAOC. However, Member States retain the possibility to ask for this review to be put on the agenda of any session of the Program and Budget Committee.

Appendix 8: WIPO Staff Regulations and Rules (selected excerpts relevant to governance)

Source: WIPO, *Staff Regulations and Rules* (Geneva: WIPO 2014) as amended by the WIPO Coordination Committee at the 2015 Annual Assemblies, see WIPO, *Amendments to Staff Regulations and Rules: Document Prepared by the Director General* WO/CC/71/4 Rev. (WIPO 2015) and subject to exceptions noted in WIPO, *List of Decisions: Document Prepared by the WIPO Secretariat* A/55/INF/11 (WIPO 2015) 19.

Note: This Appendix provides excerpts from a sample of those WIPO Staff Regulations and Rules deemed by this author to be particularly relevant to the organisation's governance. The Appendix thus does not include reference to all Chapters and Regulations nor to all Rules under each Regulation. The footnotes provided in this Appendix are those contained in the 2014 version of the Staff Regulations and Rules; several footnotes have also been added by the author to signal those Regulations updated in 2015. The numbering of footnotes thus does not match the numbering in the 2014 version of the Staff Regulations and Rules.

CHAPTER I: DUTIES, OBLIGATIONS AND PRIVILEGES

Regulation 1.1: Status of Staff Members
The staff members of the International Bureau are international civil servants; their obligations are not national but exclusively international. By accepting appointment they pledge themselves to discharge their functions and regulate their conduct only with the interests of the International Bureau in view.

Regulation 1.4: Instructions from External Sources
In the performance of their duties with the International Bureau, staff members shall neither seek nor accept instructions or assistance from any government or from any other authority outside the International Bureau.

Regulation 1.5: Conduct
   (a) Staff members shall conduct themselves at all times in a manner befitting their status as international civil servants. They shall not engage in any activity which is incompatible with the proper discharge of their duties with the International Bureau. They shall avoid any action, and in particular any public pronouncement, which may adversely reflect on the international civil service or which is incompatible with the integrity, independence and impartiality required by their status. While they are not expected to disregard their national sentiments or their political or religious convictions, they shall at all times act with the reserve and tact incumbent on them by reason of their international status.
   (b) Staff members shall exhibit respect for all cultures; they shall not discriminate against any individual or group of individuals or otherwise abuse the power and authority vested in them.

(c) The Standards of Conduct of the International Civil Service, promulgated by the International Civil Service Commission (ICSC), shall apply to all staff members.[1]

(d) Disciplinary procedures as set out in Chapter X of the Staff Regulations and Rules may be applied to a staff member who fails to comply with his or her obligations as detailed in this Regulation.

Rule 1.5.1 – Discrimination or Harassment
Any form of discrimination or harassment, including sexual or gender harassment, as well as physical or verbal abuse in the workplace or in connection with official functions, is prohibited.

Rule 1.5.2 – Use of Property and Assets
Staff members shall use the property and assets of the International Bureau only for official purposes and shall exercise reasonable care when utilizing such property and assets. Reasonable personal use of the International Bureau's property by staff members is permitted.

Regulation 1.6: Activities and Interests outside the International Bureau[2]
(a) Staff Members:

(1) shall not engage, without the prior authorization of the Director General, in a continuous or intermittent manner, in any occupation or employment, remunerated or not, outside the International Bureau;

(2) may be authorized by the Director General to engage in an outside occupation or employment, whether remunerated or not, if such occupation or employment:

(i) is not incompatible with the proper discharge of their duties with the International Bureau and does not conflict with the staff member's official functions or their status as an international civil servant;

(ii) is not in conflict with the interests of the International Bureau; and

(iii) is permitted by domestic law at the duty station or where the occupation or employment occurs.

(b) Apart from their duties with the International Bureau, staff members shall not engage in any activity, or have any financial interest whatever, in any enterprise dealing with intellectual property. They shall not accept any benefits, gratuities or favors from firms or private individuals dealing with intellectual property or having commercial relations with the International Bureau.

(c) A staff member shall not be associated with the management of, or hold a financial interest directly or indirectly in, any business or other concern, if it is possible for the staff member, business or other concern to benefit from such association or financial interest by reason of the staff member's position with the International Bureau.

(d) If, in the course of their duties, staff members are involved with a matter involving a business or other concern in which their spouse or a dependent family member holds a financial interest, they shall inform the Director General of the extent of that interest. If staff members have knowledge that a non-dependent child, parent or

---

1 The revised standards of conduct for the International Civil Service have been adopted by the Sixty-Seventh (44th Ordinary) Session of the WIPO Coordination Committee, effective January 1, 2014.

2 Amended with effect from January 1, 2014 (please refer to Office Instruction No. 43/2013).

sibling holds a financial interest in such a business or other concern, they shall also inform the Director General of that interest.

(e) The ownership of shares in a company shall not be held to constitute a financial interest within the meaning of paragraph (d), above, unless such ownership gives the staff member, or the staff member's spouse or dependent family member, or non-dependent child, parent or sibling, any form of control over the company's activities.

(f) Staff members shall not, except in the normal course of official duties or with the prior authorization of the Director General, engage in any one of the following activities if they relate to the objectives, activities or interests of the International Bureau:

    (1) make statements to the press, radio or other information media;

    (2) accept public speaking engagements;

    (3) take part in film, theater, radio or television productions;

    (4) submit articles, books or other material for publication;

    (5) be a member of an association or non-governmental organization dealing with intellectual property;

    (6) provide professional services to third parties.

(g) All staff members at the level of D-1 and above, as well as other designated categories, shall be required to file a declaration in a designated form and disclosing designated types of interests for themselves, their spouses and designated family members. Such declarations shall be filed upon appointment and at designated intervals. Such declarations shall remain confidential.

(h) Authorizations which the Director General may grant under the provisions of this Regulation may be made subject to such conditions as he or she deems appropriate, including, where necessary, the requirement to file a declaration as prescribed in paragraph (g), above.

(i) The Director General shall prescribe procedures for requests for authorization and for the filing of disclosure declarations under this Regulation.

Regulation 1.7: Communication of Information[3]

(a) Staff members shall exercise the utmost discretion in all matters relating to official business. Except in the course of their official duties or with the permission of the Director General, they shall not communicate to any person any information known to them by reason of their official position which has not been made public. They shall not at any time use such information to their own advantage. These obligations do not cease upon separation from the International Bureau.

(b) A staff member who in good faith reports information concerning the possible existence of wrongdoing in the International Bureau regarding administrative, personnel and other similar matters shall be able to do so anonymously. The International Bureau shall enact provisions for protection from retaliatory action such as by way of adverse administrative decision or verbal harassment.

(c) Such a report shall be made through any of the following established channels: to a hierarchical supervisor, the Office of the Director General, the Director of the Internal Audit and Oversight Division or the chair of the Coordination Committee, who shall preserve the anonymity of the reporting staff member. Provisions for the reporting of wrongdoing shall be enacted by the International Bureau.

---

3 Amended in October 2015 by the WIPO Coordination Committee with effect from 1 January 2016 (footnote added by author).

(d) Protection by the International Bureau against retaliation will be extended to staff members provided that the staff member has made the report through established internal channels, unless there is an exceptional and demonstrable reason indicating that the use of established internal channels carries the risk of aggravation of the wrongdoing (including the failure to act on the report in a reasonable time or concealment of the wrongdoing), threatens the preservation of the staff member's anonymity or there is a justifiable apprehension of retaliation.

(e) Reports, statements or claims which are intentionally and knowingly false or misleading or made with reckless disregard for accuracy of the information shall be regarded as serious misconduct.

(f) Paragraphs (b), (c), (d) and (e) above shall be applied without prejudice to the staff member's obligations prescribed in paragraph (a) above and Rule 1.7.1 below.

Rule 1.7.1 – Confidential Documents, Information or Material
Where, by virtue of the provisions of any international agreement administered by the International Bureau, the International Bureau is entrusted with the task of maintaining the confidential nature of any document, information or material of any kind, the Director General may issue special instructions specifying the duties of staff members with respect to the custody of and access to such documents, information or material, and the means of identifying staff members authorized to handle the said materials. All confidential materials shall be placed under the exclusive control of staff members designated by the Director General, shall be used only within the International Bureau and shall not be made accessible to any non-designated WIPO employees, persons or authority outside the International Bureau.

Regulation 1.8: Honors and Gifts
(a) No staff member shall accept any honor, decoration, favor, gift or remuneration from any source external to the International Bureau, without first obtaining the approval of the Director General. Approval shall be granted only where such honor, decoration, favor, gift or remuneration is not incompatible with the staff member's status as an international civil servant. The Director General shall prescribe guidelines for the interpretation of the present Regulation through an Office Instruction.

(b) Where the Director General is involved, the approval shall be granted by the Coordination Committee.

(c) Staff members shall neither offer nor promise any favor, gift, remuneration, or any other personal benefit to another staff member or to any third party with an intent to cause him or her to perform, fail to perform, or delay the performance of any official act. Similarly, staff members shall neither seek nor accept any favor, gift, remuneration or any other personal benefit from another staff member or from any third party in exchange for performing, failing to perform, or delaying the performance of any official act.

Regulation 1.9: Political Activities
Staff members may not engage in any political activity which is incompatible with or might reflect upon the independence and impartiality required by their status as international civil servants.

Regulation 1.10: Privileges and Immunities
  (a) Staff members in Geneva shall enjoy the privileges and immunities specified in the Headquarters Agreement and those provided for in any agreement concluded to that end between the Republic and Canton of Geneva and the Director General.
  (b) Staff members in New York shall enjoy the privileges and immunities specified in any United States law and regulation relating to international organizations, and, to the extent applicable, the privileges and immunities specified in the Agreement between the United Nations and the United States of America regarding the Headquarters of the United Nations.
  (c) Staff members, where applicable, shall enjoy the privileges and immunities specified in the 1947 Convention on the Privileges and Immunities of the Specialized Agencies.
  (d) These privileges and immunities shall be conferred in the interests of the International Bureau. They shall not provide staff members with an excuse for not meeting their private obligations or complying with laws and police regulations. In all cases where these privileges and immunities are involved, the staff member concerned shall immediately inform the Director General, who shall decide whether or not they should be waived.

Regulation 1.11: Oath or Declaration
  (a) On taking up their duties staff members shall make and sign the following oath or declaration:
      "I solemnly swear (alternatively: undertake, affirm, promise) to exercise in all loyalty, discretion and conscience the functions entrusted to me as a staff member of the International Bureau, to discharge these functions and to regulate my conduct only with the interest of the International Bureau in view, and in accordance with the International Civil Service Commission Standards of Conduct of the International Civil Service, without seeking or accepting instructions or assistance from any Government or other authority outside the International Bureau in regard to the accomplishment of my duties."
  (b) The oath shall be taken (or the declaration made) in the presence of the Director General or his or her authorized representative; the document relating thereto shall be signed in his or her presence or in the presence of his or her authorized representative and placed in the file of the staff member. A new declaration shall be made after a break in service that exceeds three months. The Director General shall take the oath or make the declaration of loyalty before the General Assembly.

Regulation 1.12: Compliance with Local Laws and Private Legal Obligations
Staff members must comply with local laws and honor their private legal obligations.

Regulation 1.13: Information Requested of Staff Members and Obligation to Supply Such Information
On appointment, staff members shall be responsible for providing the Director General with the information necessary to determine their status and entitlements under the Staff Regulations and Rules, or to take the administrative measures required by their appointment.

Rule 1.13.1 – Information to be Supplied by Staff Members
  (a) Staff members shall be responsible for informing the Director General promptly in writing of any change which might affect their status and entitlements under the Staff Regulations and Rules.

(b) Staff members who intend to acquire the status of permanent resident in a country other than that of their nationality, or who intend to change their nationality, shall inform the Director General before such change of status or nationality becomes final.

(c) Staff members who are arrested or charged with an offense other than a minor traffic violation, or are defendants in a criminal action, or are convicted, fined or imprisoned for any offense other than a minor traffic violation, shall inform the Director General as soon as possible.

(d) The Director General may at any time request a staff member to supply information concerning facts prior to appointment which are relevant to his or her suitability, or concerning facts which are relevant to his or her integrity, conduct and service as a staff member.

CHAPTER IV PRINCIPLES GOVERNING RECRUITMENT, APPOINTMENT AND PROMOTION

Regulation 4.1: General Principles
The paramount consideration in the recruitment and appointment of staff members shall be the need to secure the highest standards of efficiency, competence and integrity. Recruitment and appointment of staff members shall be made without distinction as to race, ethnicity, gender, sexual orientation, disability, religion, age, political affiliation, or social status.

Regulation 4.2: Geographical Distribution and Gender Balance[4]
(a) Due regard shall be paid to the importance of recruiting staff members on as wide a geographical basis as possible, recognizing also the need to take into account considerations of gender balance.

(b) Recruitment on as wide a geographical basis as possible, in accordance with the requirements of paragraph (a) above, shall not apply to staff members appointed to "language" positions (namely positions of translators, interpreters, editors and revisers) or to staff members appointed to positions in the General Service and National Professional Officer categories.

Regulation 4.7: Nationality
(a) For the purpose of these Regulations and Rules, the International Bureau shall recognize only one nationality for each staff member.

(b) For the purpose of these Regulations and Rules, a staff member having several nationalities shall be regarded as a national of the country to which he or she is bound by the closest ties.

Regulation 4.8: Authority for Appointment
(a) All staff members shall be appointed by the Director General. The Deputy Directors General shall be appointed after approval by the WIPO Coordination Committee. The Assistant Directors General shall be appointed taking into account the advice of the WIPO Coordination Committee. The Director, Internal Audit and Oversight Division, shall be appointed taking into account the advice of the WIPO Coordination Committee and the WIPO Independent Audit and Oversight Committee.

---

4 Amended with effect from 1 Novermber 2014 (please refer to Office Instruction No. 55/2014).

Regulation 4.9: Recruitment

[. . .]

Rule 4.9.2 – Appointments under Funds-in-Trust and other Special Agreements[5]

(a) When certain services in the Professional category and also specific posts in the General Service and National Professional Officer categories are envisaged under Funds-in-Trust or co-operation agreements between the International Bureau and national and regional intellectual property offices, or Member State governments, the Director General may proceed with appointments without having recourse to a competition. Staff members recruited according to this procedure shall be granted fixed-term appointments not exceeding three years, which shall not be extended or converted to a continuing appointment.

(b) During their service, staff members appointed under a Funds-in-Trust agreement may apply for any vacancies at the International Bureau as external candidates.

(c) This Rule shall not apply to temporary staff members.

Regulation 4.15: Types of Appointment

(a) Staff members in the Professional and Higher and General Service categories shall be granted either temporary, fixed-term, continuing, or permanent appointments.

(b) Staff members in the National Professional Officer category shall be granted either temporary, fixed-term, or continuing appointments.

(c) Deputy Directors General and Assistant Directors General shall be granted fixed-term appointments.

Regulation 4.20: Accountability and Performance Management[6]

All staff members, including Deputy Directors General and Assistant Directors General, shall be accountable to the Director General for the proper discharge of their functions. Their performance shall be evaluated periodically to ensure that the required standards of performance are met.

Rule 4.20.1 – Performance Appraisal of Staff Members on Fixed-term, Continuing and Permanent Appointments[7]

(a) Performance appraisal is fundamental to the professional development of staff members, as well as ensuring their accountability. Staff members shall be evaluated through performance appraisal mechanisms that shall assess their performance at such intervals as the work situation or the individual performance requires. Supervisors shall regularly provide feedback to the staff member on his or her performance, and make specific suggestions for improvement in performance and conduct as necessary.

(b) The Director General shall seek to ensure that appropriate learning, development, and recognition programs are available for the benefit of staff members.

(c) This Rule shall not apply to staff members on initial fixed-term appointments while they are on probation, in accordance with Regulation 4.17(b). It shall also not apply

---

5 Amended with effect from 1 November 2014 (please refer to Office Instruction No. 55/2014).

6 Amended in October 2015 by the WIPO Coordination Committee, with effect from 1 January 2016 (footnote added by author).

7 Amended with effect from 1 January 2016.

to temporary staff members, with the exception of those who were granted temporary appointments before January 1, 2013.

CHAPTER VIII STAFF RELATIONS

Regulation 8.1. Staff Council
The staff shall have the right of association. The interests of the staff shall be represented before the Director General and his representatives by a Staff Council elected by the staff members.

Rule 8.1.1 – Staff Council
   (a) The Staff Council shall be composed in such a way as to afford equitable representation to staff at all levels and to all groups of staff members with common interests.
   (b) The Staff Council shall be consulted on questions relating to staff welfare and personnel administration, in particular principles governing appointment, promotion and termination, and on questions pertaining to salaries and entitlements. The Staff Council shall be entitled to make proposals on such questions to the Director General on behalf of the staff.
   (c) Except in emergency cases, general administrative instructions or directions on questions within the scope of paragraph (b) above shall be brought to the notice of the Staff Council in advance for consideration and comment before being put into effect.
   (d) Provisions concerning the representation of staff interests shall be entirely without prejudice to the right of individual staff members to make representations to the Director General on matters affecting them as individuals.
   (e) Staff representatives shall exercise their functions in a manner that is consistent with the standards of conduct of the ICSC.
   (f) Staff representatives shall be protected against discriminatory or prejudicial treatment based on their status or activities as staff representatives, both during their term of office and after it has ended.

Regulation 8.2. Advisory Body[8]
The Director General shall establish an advisory body with staff participation. The advisory body shall advise the Director General on any personnel or administrative matters which he or she wishes to refer to it, including provisions of the Staff Regulations and Rules or Office Instructions. The advisory body may also give advice to the Director General on its own initiative on such matters.

Rule 8.2.1 – Joint Advisory Group[9]
   (a) The advisory body provided for in Regulation 8.2 shall be called the Joint Advisory Group and be composed as follows:
      (1) three members and three alternates elected by the staff members of the International Bureau, from among the said staff members, according to a procedure established by the Director General;
      (2) three members and three alternates designated by the Director General from among the staff members of the International Bureau;

---

8 Amended with effect from 1 January 2014 (please refer to Office Instruction No. 43/2013).
9 Amended with effect from 1 January 2014 (please refer to Office Instruction No. 43/2013).

(3) ex officio, as Secretary of the Group, the Director of HRMD [Human Resources Management and Development] or his or her alternate.

(b) The Director General shall appoint a chair and one alternate chair who shall sit in the Group when the chair is unable to do so, from among the group members.

(c) The members of the Joint Advisory Group and their alternates shall be elected or designated for two years. They shall be eligible for re-election or re-designation, and shall remain in office until their successors are elected or designated.

(d) Meetings of the Joint Advisory Group shall be convened as necessary, either upon convocation by the Director General, the Director of HRMD, the Chair, at the request of at least two of its members, or at the request of at least fifty (50) staff members.

(e) The Joint Advisory Group shall prepare an annual report to the Director General, setting out a summary of the matters referred to it redacting the names of any individual staff members. The Director General shall make such report available to staff.

Rule 8.2.2 – Petition by Staff Members[10]

Staff members may directly petition the Joint Advisory Group to consider and give advice or recommendations to the Director General on any matter concerning personnel administration or staff welfare, provided that a minimum number of fifty (50) staff members sign such petition, indicating their full name. The petition shall be addressed to the Joint Advisory Group with copies to the Director General, the Director of HRMD and the Staff Council. The petition shall identify and clearly explain the matter being referred to the Joint Advisory Group. The Joint Advisory Group should, as far as practicable, issue recommendations or advice within thirty (30) calendar days from receipt of such petition, which shall be addressed to the Director General with copies to the petitioning staff members, the Director of HRMD and the Staff Council. Following the advice or recommendation of the Joint Advisory Group, the Director General shall respond by general email to all staff members concerning the matter subject of the petition.

CHAPTER IX SEPARATION FROM SERVICE

Regulation 9.2: Termination[11]

(a) The Director General, giving his or her reasons therefor, may terminate the appointment of a staff member who holds a fixed-term appointment, a permanent appointment, or a continuing appointment for any of the following reasons:

(1) if the exigencies of the service require abolition of the post or a reduction in staff;

(2) if for reasons of health the staff member concerned is unable to perform his or her duties;

(3) if the staff member's performance or conduct prove unsatisfactory;

(4) if facts anterior to the appointment of the staff member and relevant to his or her suitability come to light that, if they had been known at the time of his or her appointment, should have precluded his or her appointment;

(5) if the staff member abandons his or her post;

---

10 Rule added as an amendment with effect from 1 January 2014 (please refer to Office Instruction No. 43/2013).

11 Amended by the Coordination Committee in October 2015, with effect from 1 January 2016 (footnote added by author).

(6) if such action is in the interests of the good administration of the Organization, and provided the action is not contested by the staff member concerned;

(7) if the staff member no longer has a post as a result of a reclassification:

    (i) fixed-term staff members whose appointments are terminated as a result of reclassification shall be terminated and given a termination indemnity pursuant to Regulation 9.8(a)(1);

    (ii) permanent or continuing staff members whose appointments are terminated as a result of reclassification shall be terminated and given a termination indemnity pursuant to Regulation 9.8(a)(6).

(b) The Director General may also terminate the appointment of a staff member who holds a fixed-term appointment for such other reason as may be specified in the letter of appointment.

(c) Before termination of the appointment of an Assistant Director General or a Deputy Director General, the Coordination Committee shall be consulted; the Director General shall take due account of the advice of that Committee.

(d) On the advice of the Coordination Committee, the General Assembly may terminate the appointment of the Director General if for reasons of health he or she is no longer able to perform his or her duties, if his performance or conduct prove unsatisfactory, or for such other reason as may be specified in his or her letter of appointment.

(e) If the exigencies of the service require the abolition of posts or a reduction in staff, and if suitable posts are available in which their services can be effectively used, staff members shall be retained in the following order of preference, provided that due regard shall be given in all cases to relative competence, efficiency, conduct and length of services:

    (1) staff members holding permanent appointments;

    (2) staff members holding continuing appointments;

    (3) staff members holding fixed-term appointments.

(f) Any staff member whose permanent or continuing appointment is terminated as a result of the abolition of a post shall normally be offered an appointment to another suitable post for which he or she has applied, and for which he or she is considered to possess the necessary qualifications if such a post becomes vacant within a period of two years after the date on which the termination becomes effective.

(g) The Director General shall report all cases of termination to the Coordination Committee.

(h) The subject matter of this Regulation and the rules thereunder shall not apply to temporary staff members unless otherwise prescribed by Rule 9.2.2 entitled "Termination of Appointments of Temporary Staff Members."

Rule 9.2.2 – Termination of Appointments of Temporary Staff Members[12]

(a) Rule 9.2.1, "Definition of Termination", shall apply to temporary staff members.

(b) The Director General, giving his or her reasons therefor, may terminate the appointment of a staff member who holds a temporary appointment for any of the following reasons:

    (1) during the probation period at any time;

    (2) if the exigencies of the service require a reduction in staff;

---

12 Amended with effect from 1 January 2016.

(3) if for reasons of health the staff member concerned is unable to perform his or her duties;

(4) if the staff member's performance or conduct prove unsatisfactory;

(5) if facts anterior to the appointment of the staff member and relevant to his or her suitability come to light that, if they had been known at the time of his or her appointment, should have precluded his or her appointment;

(6) if such action is in the interests of the good administration of the International Bureau, and provided the action is not contested by the staff member concerned.

(c) The Director General may also terminate the appointment of a staff member who holds a temporary appointment for such other reason as may be specified in the letter of appointment.

(d) If the exigencies of the service require a reduction in staff, staff members holding permanent, continuing or fixed-term appointments shall be retained in preference to those holding temporary appointments.

(e) Appointments shall be terminated with due regard to competence, efficiency, conduct and length of service.

Regulation 9.7: Notice of Termination[13]

(a) A staff member whose appointment is terminated pursuant to Regulation 9.2 or 9.4 shall be given such notice as is provided for in his or her letter of appointment or contract and such indemnity as provided for under the Staff Regulations and Rules.

(b) A staff member whose permanent or continuing appointment is terminated shall be given not less than three months' written notice of such termination.

(c) A staff member whose fixed-term appointment is terminated shall be given not less than thirty days' written notice of such termination or such notice as may be stipulated in his or her letter of appointment.

(d) In lieu of notice, the Director General may authorize payment to a staff member whose appointment is terminated of compensation calculated on the basis of the salary and allowances which the staff member would have received had the termination taken effect at the end of the notice period.

(e) Notwithstanding paragraph (a) above, no termination notice or compensation in lieu thereof shall be given in case of summary dismissal.

(f) The subject matter of this Regulation and the rules thereunder shall not apply to temporary staff members unless otherwise prescribed by Rule 9.7.1 entitled "Notice of Termination for Temporary Staff Members."

Rule 9.7.1 – Notice of Termination for Temporary Staff Members

(a) A staff member holding a temporary appointment of six months whose appointment is terminated shall be given 30 days' written notice. A staff member holding a temporary appointment of less than six months whose appointment is terminated shall be given 10 working days' written notice. In lieu of the notice period, the Director General may authorize compensation equivalent to salary, applicable post adjustment and allowances corresponding to the relevant notice period at the rate in effect on the last day of service.

(b) No termination notice or compensation in lieu thereof shall be given in case of termination for misconduct.

---

13 Amended by the WIPO Coordination Committee in October 2015, effective from 1 January 2016 (footnote added by author).

CHAPTER X DISCIPLINARY MEASURES

Regulation 10.1: Disciplinary Measures
- (a) A staff member who fails to observe the Staff Regulations and Rules, the standards of conduct required of an international civil servant or any other obligation of staff members of the International Bureau may be subject to disciplinary measures.
- (b) Any disciplinary measure applied to a staff member shall be proportionate to the nature and gravity of his or her misconduct.
- (c) No disciplinary measure shall be applied to a staff member without giving him or her an opportunity to present his or her defense.

Rule 10.1.1 – Disciplinary Measures
- (a) Disciplinary measures may take one or more of the following forms only:
    - (1) written reprimand;
    - (2) delayed advancement, for a specified period of time, to the next salary step;
    - (3) relegation to a lower salary step within the same grade;
    - (4) demotion to a lower grade for a specified period of time;
    - (5) dismissal; and
    - (6) summary dismissal for serious misconduct.
- (b) Measures other than those listed under Rule 10.1.1(a) shall not be considered to be disciplinary measures within the meaning of the present Rule.

[. . .]

CHAPTER XI CONFLICT RESOLUTION[14]

Regulation 11.1: Respectful Workplace
All staff members have a duty to contribute to a respectful and harmonious workplace.

Regulation 11.2: Independence, Impartiality, Conflict of Interest and Confidentiality
- (a) All persons entrusted with a function in informal and formal conflict resolution shall at all times act in an independent and impartial manner and shall avoid actual, potential or apparent conflicts of interest.
- (b) They shall in all instances uphold confidentiality in their dealings. All communications initiated or received in connection with the performance of that function shall be confidential.
- (c) The Director General may prescribe provisions relating to the disclosure and resolution of conflicts of interest by Office Instruction.

Regulation 11.3: Informal Conflict Resolution
A staff member who:
- (i) believes that he or she has been subjected to discrimination and/or harassment; or
- (ii) wishes to rebut his or her performance appraisal; or
- (iii) wishes to file a request for review of an administrative decision other than a disciplinary measure,

---

14 Chapter amended with effect from 1 January 2014 (please refer to Office Instruction No. 43/2013).

is strongly encouraged to resolve the matter through informal conflict resolution, without prejudice to the right to request a review of the matter in accordance with Regulation 11.4. Resort to informal resolution of conflicts shall not in any way affect the deadlines relating to the formal resolution of conflicts, which remain intact unless expressly suspended or extended in accordance with the provisions of Chapter XI.

Rule 11.3.1 – Means of Informal Conflict Resolution

(a) A staff member who wishes to resolve any of the matters referred to in Regulation 11.3 by way of informal conflict resolution may seek the assistance of the following:
    (1) the Office of the Ombudsperson;
    (2) HRMD or a higher level supervisor;
    (3) any other informal conflict resolution mechanism established by the Director General.
(b) There shall be no formal record of any of the informal processes referred to above.
(c) The Director General may establish by Office Instruction measures to support a respectful and harmonious workplace.

Rule 11.3.2 – Office of the Ombudsperson

(a) The Ombudsperson shall assist with the fair resolution of workplace-related conflicts or grievances. He or she shall act as a neutral interlocutor, who mediates in conflicts between individual staff members or with management towards reaching amicable solutions to workplace-related difficulties. In all of his or her actions, the Ombudsperson shall act in an independent and impartial manner and shall in all instances uphold confidentiality in his or her dealings. All communications with the Ombudsperson shall be considered privileged.
(b) Provisions concerning the mandate of the Ombudsperson, the applicable procedures and reporting shall be prescribed by the Director General by Office Instruction.

Regulation 11.4: Formal Conflict Resolution[15]

(a) A staff member who:
    (i) believes that he or she has been subjected to discrimination and/or harassment; or
    (ii) wishes to rebut his or her performance appraisal; or
    (iii) wishes to file a request for review of an administrative decision
        shall have the right to request a review of the matter in accordance with the procedures set out hereunder.
(b) The Director General shall review and take a decision on any matter referred to in subparagraph (a) above in respect of which he or she has already taken a decision. The Director General may delegate his or her authority to review and take a decision on such matters. The Director of HRMD shall review and take a decision on any matter referred to in subparagraph (a) above in respect of which the Director General has not already taken a decision.
(c) The initiation of formal conflict resolution procedures shall not preclude recourse to informal conflict resolution at any time.

[. . .]

---

15 Amended with effect from 1 November 2014 (please refer to Office Instruction No. 55/2014).

Regulation 11.5: Internal Appeal

The Director General shall establish an administrative body with staff participation to advise him or her whenever a staff member, a former staff member or a duly qualified beneficiary to the rights of a deceased staff member, appeals against a decision taken under Regulation 11.4, or a disciplinary decision taken under Rule 10.1.2.

Rule 11.5.1 – Appeal Board[16]

    (a) The administrative body provided for in Regulation 11.5 shall be called the WIPO Appeal Board.

    (b) The Appeal Board shall be composed as follows:

        (1) A Chair and a Deputy Chair designated by the WIPO Coordination Committee on a proposal made by the Director General after consultation with the Staff Council, from among persons having experience in the law of the international civil service or equivalent experience in applicable administrative law, who are not staff members or former staff members for the past 10 years of the International Bureau. Subject to the eligibility criteria provided above, the Director General shall make an interim appointment of the Chair and the Deputy Chair, after consultation with the Staff Council, pending designation by the WIPO Coordination Committee on the proposal made by the Director General. The interim appointments shall expire on the date that the WIPO Coordination Committee decides on the designations for these functions.

        (2) Two members designated by the Director General from among the staff members of the International Bureau.

        (3) Two members elected by the staff members of the International Bureau from among the staff members, according to a procedure to be established, after consultation with the Staff Council, by the Director General.

    (c) For each of the members referred to in subparagraphs (b)(2) and (b)(3) above, one alternate, who shall sit on the Appeal Board when the member is unable to do so, shall be designated or elected in the same way as the member.

    (d) No member or former member for the past three years of the Joint Advisory Group, the Office of the Legal Counsel, the Internal Audit and Oversight Division, HRMD or the Staff Council may serve as a member of the Appeal Board.

    (e) The Chair and Deputy Chair shall be designated for a term of five years, renewable once. The other members shall be designated, renewable once, or elected for a period of two years and shall be eligible for re-election.

    (f) Should the post of Chair fall vacant between two sessions of the WIPO Coordination Committee, the Deputy Chair shall fulfill the function of Chair until a new Chair is designated by the Coordination Committee, on a proposal made by the Director General, after consultation with the Staff Council, from among persons meeting the conditions set forth in subparagraph (b)(1) above.

    (g) Each appeal shall be considered by a Panel consisting of the Chair or Deputy Chair, one member referred to in subparagraph (b)(2) above and one member referred to in subparagraph (b)(3) above. The Panel members shall be selected by the Chair. Panels may sit in parallel.

    (h) The Deputy Chair shall assume the functions of the Chair when the Chair is unable to do so.

---

16 Amended with effect from 1 January 2016.

(i) The Director General shall designate a Secretary and an alternate Secretary to the Appeal Board. No member of the Joint Advisory Group, the Office of the Legal Counsel, the Internal Audit and Oversight Division, HRMD or the Staff Council may serve as a Secretary or alternate Secretary of the Appeal Board. The Secretary, or Alternate Secretary, shall attend the meetings of the Board but shall not take part in its deliberations.

(j) The Chair of the Appeal Board may make proposals to the Director General for supplementary rules of procedure or for amendments to the existing rules of procedure.

(k) The Appeal Board may decide to join appeals involving similar facts and raising similar issues of law, if it deems that this is in accordance with the principle of economy and the good administration of justice.

(l) The Appeal Board shall have two periods of annual recess, from December 24 to January 4, over the holiday season, and from July 15 to August 15, over the summer period. During the Appeal Board's recess, all time limits before the Appeal Board are suspended for the duration of the recess.

Regulation 11.6: Litigious Appeal
After having exhausted all means available to him or her under Regulation 11.5, a staff member shall have the right to appeal to the Administrative Tribunal of the International Labour Organization ("Tribunal") in accordance with the conditions set forth in the Statute of that Tribunal.

Rule 11.6.1 – Administrative Tribunal

(a) Any staff member, former staff member or a duly qualified beneficiary of the rights of a deceased official of the International Bureau shall have the right to appeal to the Tribunal, which is also competent to deal with cases affecting staff members of the International Bureau. Such appeals shall be made in accordance with the conditions set forth in the Statute of the Tribunal and in the agreement concluded between the Tribunal and WIPO.

(b) The Tribunal shall be competent to hear complaints alleging non-observance, in substance or in form, of the terms of appointment of officials and the provisions of the Staff Regulations and Rules.

(c) No appeal shall be made to the Tribunal before the appeal procedure within the International Bureau has been exhausted.

CHAPTER XII GENERAL PROVISIONS

Regulation 12.6: Delegation of Authority[17]
The Director General may delegate the authority vested in him or her by the Staff Regulations and Rules under such terms as he or she deems desirable.

---

17 Regulation added as an amendment with effect from 1 November 2014 (please refer to Office Instruction No. 55/2014).

Appendix 9: WIPO Investigation Policy

First Edition, January 22, 2014

1. INTRODUCTION AND PURPOSE

1. The WIPO Investigation Policy (hereinafter the Policy) provides the framework and establishes governing principles for the investigation function within the World Intellectual Property Organization (WIPO).

2. The Policy is established in consultation with Member States, pursuant to the WIPO Internal Oversight Charter.[1]

3. The Policy is consistent with WIPO regulations, rules, and related administrative issuances, and has been prepared in accordance with generally accepted investigation standards, taking account of the Uniform Guidelines for Investigations[2] and good practices of organizations of the United Nations system.[3]

4. The Policy aims to:
   (a) protect the rights and reaffirm the duties of WIPO staff members involved in investigative activities, including subjects of investigations, in accordance with relevant WIPO regulations and rules, and principles of fairness;
   (b) enhance the ability of the Director, Internal Audit and Oversight Division (IAOD) to carry out effectively and independently the oversight function of investigation entrusted to him/her by the Member States, and thereby protect the interests of WIPO; and
   (c) promote accountability, a culture of ethics and integrity, and good governance within WIPO.

5. To implement this Policy, ensure the objectivity, impartiality, and quality of IAOD investigative activities, and guide WIPO staff in understanding the investigation function within WIPO, the Director, IAOD may establish written procedures and guidelines, including the WIPO Investigation Procedures Manual.[4]

2. SCOPE AND AUTHORITY

6. Investigation is a formal fact-finding inquiry to examine allegations of misconduct and other wrongdoing in order to determine whether they have occurred and if so, the person or persons responsible.[5]

---

1 See Internal Oversight Charter, para. 13(b). The last version of the Internal Oversight Charter was approved by the WIPO General Assembly at its Forty-First Session in October 2012 (WO/GA/41/10 Rev. and WO/GA/41/18). The Investigation Policy was submitted to the Member States for consultations from 19 August to 18 October 2013.

2 As endorsed by the 10th Conference of International Investigators, 2009.

3 See Internal Oversight Charter, para. 2(a) and para. 5.

4 Ibid., para. 13(c).

5 Ibid., para. 2(c).

7. The Director, IAOD has overall authority and responsibility for investigating possible instances of misconduct, wrongdoing or malfeasance within WIPO falling within his/her mandate.[6]

8. This Policy applies to all WIPO staff members as defined in the Staff Regulations and Rules.

9. The Policy normally does not extend to those areas for which separate provision has been made for review, including:

   (a) workplace-related conflicts and grievances;[7]

   (b) personnel grievances arising from administrative decisions affecting a staff member's terms of appointment;[8] and

   (c) performance issues and performance-related disagreements.[9]

10. Formal complaints of discrimination and/or harassment should be submitted to the Director of the Human Resources Management Department (HRMD).[10] Complaints of retaliation for reporting possible misconduct or cooperating with an oversight activity should be addressed to the Ethics Office.[11] However, the Director, HRMD or the Ethics Office may later refer the matter to IAOD for investigation in accordance with their respective terms of reference.

11. An investigation is administrative in nature. It is a fact-finding exercise, not a punitive undertaking. The investigation function is part of WIPO's internal justice system, which is based on the Organization's internal regulations and rules, not on national laws. Disciplinary proceedings are initiated by way of a charge letter sent by the Director, HRMD pursuant to Rule 10.1.2 of the Staff Regulations and Rules. The separation of functions between investigation and disciplinary action provides necessary checks and balances for the proper administration of justice.

3. REPORTING MISCONDUCT

12. WIPO staff members have a duty to report possible misconduct.[12]

13. In accordance with Staff Regulation 1.7, staff members shall address reports of possible misconduct to:

   (a) a hierarchical supervisor,

   (b) the Office of the Director General, or

   (c) the Chair of the Coordination Committee,

any of whom upon receiving such report shall inform the Director, IAOD.[13]

---

6 Ibid., paras 12 and 14(h).

7 See Staff Regulations and Rules, Chapter XI, 'Conflict Resolution', in particular Staff Regulation 11.4 and Staff Rule 11.4.1, 'Administrative Resolution of Workplace-Related Conflicts and Grievances'; see Staff Regulation 11.3 and related Staff Rules, and Office Instruction on 'The Office of the Ombudsperson' (as may be amended from time to time).

8 See Staff Regulations and Rules, Chapter XI, 'Conflict Resolution', in particular Staff Regulation 11.4 and Staff Rule 11.4.3, 'Administrative Resolution of Requests for Review of Other Administrative Decisions'.

9 See Staff Regulations and Rules, Chapter XI, 'Conflict Resolution', in particular Staff Regulation 11.4 and Staff Rule 11.4.2, 'Administrative Resolution of Rebuttal of Performance Appraisals'.

10 See Staff Regulation 11.4 and Staff Rule 11.4.1.

11 See Office Instruction on the 'Policy to Protect against Retaliation for Cooperating in an Oversight Activity or Reporting Misconduct or Other Wrongdoing ("Whistleblower Protection Policy")' (as may be amended from time to time).

12 See Standards of Conduct for the International Civil Service (2013), para. 20. See also Whistleblower Protection Policy, and Uniform Guidelines for Investigations, para. 14 (as may be amended from time to time).

13 See also Whistleblower Protection Policy.

14. The Director, IAOD shall also be available to receive directly from individual staff members reports of possible misconduct, including complaints or information concerning the possible existence of fraud, waste, abuse of authority, non-compliance with regulations and rules of WIPO in administrative, personnel and other matters or other irregular activities relevant to the mandate of the Director, IAOD.[14]

15. Reports of possible misconduct shall be received on a confidential basis and may also be submitted anonymously.

16. The Director, IAOD shall acknowledge receipt in writing of those reports made by identifiable sources.

17. Where allegations of misconduct concern the staff of IAOD, the Director, IAOD will inform the Independent Advisory Oversight Committee (IAOC), who will make the appropriate recommendations. Allegations of misconduct concerning the Director, IAOD shall be reported to the Director General, who will immediately inform the Chairs of the Coordination Committee and IAOC and may refer the matter to an alternative external investigative authority.

4. INITIATING INVESTIGATIONS

18. Upon receipt of a report of possible misconduct, IAOD will carry out a preliminary evaluation of the information available, the purpose of which is to determine whether:
  (a) the alleged behavior, if established, would constitute misconduct;
  (b) the matter is not appropriate for a full investigation because of a lack of credibility, materiality and/or verifiability; and/or
  (c) a more appropriate or less formal remedy is available, or the matter falls within the purview of another body.[15]

19. IAOD will endeavor to complete the preliminary evaluation within 60 working days. Based on the outcome of the preliminary evaluation, the Director, IAOD may decide to initiate a full investigation or to close the matter. The Director, IAOD shall document the reason(s) for his or her decision whether or not to initiate a full investigation.

5. GOVERNING PRINCIPLES

20. IAOD investigative activities include all fact-finding inquiries conducted both during the preliminary evaluation and the full investigation. They aim at gathering and reviewing the evidence available, both inculpatory and exculpatory, that is, evidence that either substantiates or disproves an allegation. Investigative findings and conclusions are determined through an impartial, objective, and independent process of information gathering and analysis, which may include reasonable inferences, and are only based on substantiated facts and evidence.

21. The Director, IAOD and the investigators he/she may designate shall have unrestricted, unlimited, direct and prompt access to all WIPO records, property, officials or staff, and to all the premises of WIPO.[16]

22. WIPO staff members have a duty to cooperate unreservedly with investigative activities conducted by IAOD and to respond promptly and fully to IAOD requests for information.[17]

23. No one shall interfere with an ongoing investigation or otherwise attempt to influence or stop such investigation.

---

14 See Internal Oversight Charter, para. 8.

15 See Uniform Guidelines, paras 29–31.

16 See Internal Oversight Charter, para. 7.

17 Ibid. See also Whistleblower Protection Policy, and Uniform Guidelines for Investigations, para. 15.

24. The right of WIPO staff members to communicate confidentially with, and provide information to, the Director, IAOD, without fear of reprisal, is guaranteed by the Director General.[18]

25. Notwithstanding the foregoing, making allegations or providing information that are known to be false or misleading or that recklessly disregard the accuracy of the information constitutes serious misconduct[19] and may result in disciplinary or other appropriate administrative action.

26. Investigative activities must preserve confidentiality, respect the individual rights and obligations of WIPO staff members and be conducted with strict regard for fairness, impartiality and the presumption of innocence.

27. Confidentiality must be maintained with respect to all investigative matters by the Director, IAOD, designated investigators, and all others involved.[20] IAOD shall keep confidential the identity of the source of the initial report of possible misconduct and disclose it on a need to know basis only where required by the legitimate needs of the investigation and/or any subsequent proceedings. IAOD will protect from unauthorized disclosure the information gathered in the course of its investigative activities. WIPO staff members shall not release publicly the details or the fact itself of an investigation. Breach of confidentiality in relation to IAOD investigative activities may amount to misconduct.

28. In the performance of their investigative functions, the Director, IAOD and designated investigators will consider the impact on staff members who might be negatively affected by the appearance of being investigated, and take reasonable steps to protect the reputation of such staff members.

29. Once the preliminary evaluation has been completed and if the Director, IAOD determines that a full investigation is warranted, the Director, IAOD shall notify a staff member whose conduct is under examination for possible misconduct (hereinafter the subject) that he/she is under investigation. The notification will take place as soon as this is feasible without jeopardizing the effectiveness or integrity of the investigative process and will provide information on the general nature of the allegations under investigation and on the subject's rights and obligations.

30. The subject of an investigation shall be given a fair and reasonable opportunity to explain or justify the conduct being examined and present evidence on his/her behalf prior to the issuance of an adverse finding against him/her. The subject will normally be provided such an opportunity at two different stages before the completion of the investigation. First, during the interview, the subject will be provided details of the allegations and of the evidence in support thereof and he/she will be afforded the opportunity to respond and to provide countervailing evidence. Subsequently, the subject will normally be given an opportunity to review and comment on relevant excerpts of the draft investigation report.

31. The subject of an investigation may be accompanied to his/her interview by a suitable third party, who will act as an observer, provided the third party undertakes to respect the confidentiality of the investigation, is reasonably available, and is not connected to the matter under investigation. The presence of an observer shall not relieve the subject of the obligation to respond personally in the matter under investigation.

---

18 See Internal Oversight Charter, para. 9; Staff Regulation 1.7; and Whistleblower Protection Policy.

19 See Staff Regulation 1.7(d).

20 See Internal Oversight Charter, paras 10, 13(b) and 21.

6.   REPORTS

32. Investigation reports, including findings, conclusions and recommendations, are fully confidential, unless disclosure is authorized by the Director, IAOD or the Director General.[21]

33. The Director, IAOD shall submit final investigation reports to the Director General.[22] The Director, IAOD will endeavor to submit such reports within four months of the date of initiating the full investigation, unless circumstances warrant a longer period.

34. For final investigation reports involving WIPO staff at the Deputy Director General and Assistant Director General levels, the Director, IAOD may also send a copy to the Chair of the General Assembly, to the Chair of the IAOC and to the External Auditors. Should the investigation concern the Director General, the final report shall be submitted by the Director, IAOD, to the Chair of the General Assembly, for any action deemed appropriate, and copied to the Chairs of the Coordination Committee and the IAOC and to the External Auditors.[23]

35. The foregoing is without prejudice to the specific provisions that may be applicable with respect to final investigation reports issued further to a referral from the Director, HRMD pursuant to Staff Rule 11.4.1.

36. Should the Director, IAOD consider it appropriate, he/she will make recommendations that are derived from investigation findings.

7.   REVIEW OF THE POLICY

37. The Policy will be reviewed on a regular basis, preferably at least every three years from the date of its issuance.

[Annex I follows]

ANNEX I: REFERENCE DOCUMENTS

1. WIPO Internal Oversight Charter (Annex I to the Financial Regulations and Rules)
2. Uniform Guidelines for Investigations (2nd edition, 2009)
3. IAOD Investigation Procedures Manual (2nd edition, 2013)
4. Chapter X, "Disciplinary Measures," of the Staff Regulations and Rules
5. Chapter XI, "Conflict Resolution," of the Staff Regulations and Rules
6. Office Instruction on the "Policy to Protect against Retaliation for Cooperating in an Oversight Activity or Reporting Misconduct or Other Wrongdoing ('Whistleblower Protection Policy')" (as may be amended from time to time)
7. Office Instruction on "The Office of the Ombudsperson" (as may be amended from time to time)

---

21 See Internal Oversight Charter, paras 19 and 21.

22 Ibid., para. 22.

23 Ibid., para. 22.

Bibliography

Abbott, F, 'Distributed Governance at the WTO-WIPO: An Evolving Model for Open-Architecture Integrated Governance' (2000) 3(1) *Journal of International Economic Law* 63

Abbott, F, Gurry, F and Cottier, T, *The International Intellectual Property System: Commentary and Materials* (The Hague: Kluwer Law 1999)

Abdel Latif, A, 'Developing Country Coordination in International Intellectual Property Standard-Setting' *TRADE Working Paper 24* (Geneva: South Centre 2005)

Anderfelt, U, *International Patent Legislation and Developing Countries* (The Hague: Martinus Nijhoff 1971)

Ashton-Hart, N, 'Inside Views: How to Reboot WIPO' *Intellectual Property Watch* (12 September 2014)

Barnett, M and Finnemore, M, *Rules for the World: International Organizations in Global Politics* (Ithaca: Cornell University Press 2004)

Barnett, M and Finnemore, M, 'The Politics, Power and Pathologies of International Organizations' (1999) 53(4) *International Organization* 699–732

Beier, F-K, 'One Hundred Years of International Cooperation: The Role of the Paris Convention in the Past, Present and Future' (1984) 15(1) *International Review of Industrial Property and Copyright Law* 1–20

Blagescu, M, de las Casas, L and Lloyd, R, *Pathways to Accountability: The GAP Framework* (London: One World Trust 2011)

Bogsch, Á, *Brief History of the First 25 Years of the World Intellectual Property Organization* (Geneva: WIPO 1992)

Boyle, J, 'A Manifesto on WIPO and the Future of Intellectual Property' (2004) 9 *Duke Law and Technology Review* 1–12

Braithwaite, J and Drahos, P, *Global Business Regulation* (Cambridge: Cambridge University Press 2000)

CIEL, *A Citizens' Guide to WIPO* (Geneva: Centre for International Environmental Law 2007)

Civil Society Coalition, 'Geneva Declaration on the Future of the World Intellectual Property Organization' (2004) <http://www.futureofwipo.org/futureofwipodeclaration.pdf> accessed 7 July 2015

Correa, C (ed), *Research Handbook on the Protection of Intellectual Property under WTO Rules* (Cheltenham, UK and Northampton, MA, USA: Edward Elgar Publishing 2010)

Deere, C, 'Reforming Governance to Advance the WIPO Development Agenda', in de Beer, J (ed.), *Implementing WIPO's Development Agenda* (Waterloo Canada: Wilfrid Laurier University Press 2009)

Deere Birkbeck, C, *Governing the World Intellectual Property Organization: The Power Politics of Institutional Crisis and Reform* (Abingdon, Oxford: Routledge forthcoming 2016)

Deere Birkbeck, C, *Independent Strategic Review of the WIPO Academy*, Internal document of the WIPO Secretariat (Geneva: WIPO 2013)

Deere Birkbeck, C, 'Inside View: Strengthening WIPO's Governance for the Next 50 Years: A Time for Action' *Intellectual Property Watch* (26 September 2014)

Deere Birkbeck, C and Roca, S, *Independent External Review of WIPO Technical Assistance in the Area of Cooperation for Development* CDIP/8/INF/1 (Geneva: WIPO 2011)

Dinwoodie, G, 'The Architecture of the International Intellectual Property System' (2002) 77(3) *Chicago-Kent Law Review* 993–1014

Dinwoodie, G. and R. Dreyfuss, 'Designing a Global Intellectual Property System Responsive to Change: The WTO, WIPO and Beyond' (2009) 46(4) *Houston Law Review* 1187–234

Flynn, S, 'Inside Views: WIPO Treaty for the Blind Shows that Transparency Can Work (and Is Necessary)' *Intellectual Property Watch* (26 June 2013)

Gaultier, G, 'The History of AIPPI' in General Secretariat of AIPPI, *1897–1997 Centennial Edition: AIPPI and the Development of Industrial Property Protection 1897–1997* (Basel: AIPPI Foundation 1997)

Geneva Group, 'About the Geneva Group' <http://www.thegenevagroup.net/cms/home/about-the-geneva-group.html> accessed 15 October 2014

Gervais, D (ed.), *International Intellectual Property: A Handbook of Contemporary Research* (Cheltenham, UK: Edward Elgar Publishing 2015)

Gervais, D, "Rethinking the International Intellectual Property System: What Role for WIPO?' *Rethinking International Intellectual Property Law: What Institutional Environment for the Development and Enforcement of IP Law? Global Perspectives and Challenges for the Intellectual Property System, Issue 1* (Geneva and Strasbourg: ICTSD and CEIPI 2015)

Global Agenda Council on Institutional Governance Systems, *Effective Leadership in International Organizations* (Geneva and Oxford: World Economic Forum and Blavatnik School of Government 2015)

Gross, R, 'World Intellectual Property Organisation (WIPO): Institutional Overviews' (2007) *Global Information Society Watch* <http://www.giswatch.org> accessed 30 October 2014

Gurry, F, 'The Dispute Resolution Service of the World Intellectual Property Organization' (1999) 2(2) *Journal of International Economic Law* 385–98

Halbert, D, 'The World Intellectual Property Organization: Past, Present and Future' (2005) 54(1) *Journal of the Copyright Society of the USA* 253–84

Hale, T, 'Transparency, Accountability and Global Governance' (2008) 14(1) *Global Governance* 73–94

ICSC, *Standards of Conduct in the International Civil Service* (New York: International Civil Service Commission 2013)

ILO, 'ILO Administrative Tribunal' <http://www.ilo.org/public/english/tribunal/about/index.htm> accessed 15 September 2015

Interpol–WIPO, 'Co-operation Agreement between the International Criminal Police Organization and the World Intellectual Property Organization' <http://www.inter pol.int/content/download/9466/69442/version/6/file/WorldIntellectualPropertyOrg anization(WIPO).pdf> accessed 26 October 2015

JIU, 'About Us' <https://www.unjiu.org/en/about-us/Pages/default.aspx> accessed 1 October 2014

JIU, *Accountability Frameworks in the United Nations System* JIU/REP/2011/5 (New York: UN Joint Inspection Unit 2011)

JIU, *Analysis of the Evaluation Function in the United Nations System* JIU/REP/2014/6 (New York: UN Joint Inspection Unit 2014)

JIU, *Review of Management and Administration in the World Intellectual Property Organization (WIPO)* JIU/REP/2014/2 (New York: UN Joint Inspection Unit 2014)

JIU, *Review of the Management and Administration in WIPO: Budget, Oversight and Related Issues* JIU/REP/2005/1 (New York: UN Joint Inspection Unit 2005)

JIU, *South-South and Triangular Cooperation in the United Nations System* JIU/REP/2011/3 (New York: UN Joint Inspection Unit 2011)

JIU, *Strategic Planning in the United Nations System* JIU/REP/2012/12 (New York: UN Joint Inspection Unit 2012)

Joachim, J, Reinalda, B and Verbeek, B, *International Organizations and Implementation: Enforcers, Managers, Authorities?* (Abingdon, Oxford: Routledge 2008)

Knowledge Ecology International, 'Transparency of Negotiating Documents in Selected Fora' (Washington, D.C.: KEI 2009) <http://www.keionline.org/misc-docs/4/attach ment2_transparency_ustr.pdf> accessed 15 August 2014

Kotthapally, N, 'From World Intellectual Property Organization (WIPO) to World Innovation Promotion Organization (WIPO): Whither WIPO?' (2011) 3(1) *The WIPO Journal* 56–71

Kwakwa, E, 'Some Comments on Rule Making at the World Intellectual Property Organization' (2002) 12(1) *Duke Journal of Comparative and International Law* 179–95

Kwakwa, E and Rols, M-L, 'The Privileges and Immunities of the World Intellectual Property Organization: Practice and Challenges', in Blokker, N and Schrijver, N (eds), *Immunity of International Organizations* (Leiden: Brill Nijhoff 2015)

Malcolm, J, 'Public Interest Representation in Global IP Policy Institutions' *Program on Information Justice and Intellectual Property (PIJIP) Research Paper No. 6*, (Washington, D.C: American University Washington College of Law 2010)

Mathiason, J, *Invisible Governance: International Secretariats in Global Politics* (Bloomfield, CT, United States: Kumarian Press 2007)

May, C, *The World Intellectual Property Organization: Resurgence and the Development Agenda* (Abingdon, Oxford: Routledge 2006)

Monagle, C, *Observer Status and Access to Documents: Comparative Analysis across Selected International Organizations* (Berne: Berne Declaration and Development Fund 2011).

Musungu, S and Dutfield, G, *Multilateral Agreements and a TRIPS-Plus World: The World Intellectual Property Organisation* TRIPS Issues Paper 3 (Geneva: Quaker United Nations Office (QUNO) and Quaker International Affairs Program (QIAP) 2003)

New, W, 'India Joins Opposition to Casablanca Meeting Outcome' *Intellectual Property Watch* (4 October 2005)

New, W, 'Special Feature: Differences over GIs Threaten 2016/17 WIPO Budget Approval' *Intellectual Property Watch* (30 July 2015)

Okediji, R, 'The International Relations of Intellectual Property: Narratives of Developing Country Participation in the Global Intellectual Property System' (2003) 7 *Singapore Journal of International and Comparative Law* 315–85

Okediji, R, 'WIPO–WTO Relations and the Future of Global Intellectual Property Norms' (2008) 39 *Netherlands Yearbook of International Law* 69–125

Permanent Mission of India to the United Nations Geneva, 'World Intellectual Property Organisation (WIPO)' <pmindiaun.org/pages.php?id=326> accessed 8 July 2015

Saez, C, 'At WIPO, A Singular Explanation of a "Non-Unitary" Budget' *Intellectual Property Watch* (8 October 2015)

Saez, C, 'New Proposal to Keep Indigenous Peoples on WIPO Traditional Knowledge Committee, *Intellectual Property Watch* (26 August 2014)

Saez, C, 'United States Hopeful Lisbon Members Will Open Diplomatic Conference to All' *Intellectual Property Watch* (7 May 2015)

Salmon, P, 'Cooperation between the World Intellectual Property Organization and the World Trade Organization' (2003) 17 *St. John's Journal of Legal Commentary* 429–42

Secretan, J, 'L'évolution de structure des unions internationaux pour la protection de la propriété intellectuelle' in BIRPI, *Les Unions Internationale pour la protection de la propriété industrial, littéraire et artistique, 1883–1963* (Geneva: BIRPI 1962)

Sell, S, 'Everything Old Is New Again: The Development Agenda Now and Then' (2011) 3(1) *The WIPO Journal* 17–23

South Centre, 'Integrating Development into WIPO Activities and Processes: Strategies for the 2004 WIPO Assemblies' *South Centre Analytical Note* (Geneva: South Centre 2004).

Stack, A, *International Patent Law: Cooperation, Harmonization and an Institutional Analysis of WIPO and the WTO* (Cheltenham, UK and Northampton, MA, USA: Edward Elgar Publishing 2011)

UN, *United Nations Common System: Report of the International Civil Service Commission, Resolution Adopted by the General Assembly on 12 April 2013* A/RES/67/257 (New York: UN 2013), <http://icsc.un.org/resources/pdfs/general/standardsE.pdf> accessed 26 October 2015

UN ECOSOC, *Information Received from the United Nations System and Other Intergovernmental Organizations: Secretariat on the Convention on Biological Diversity and WIPO* E/C.19/2008/4.Add.13 (New York: UN 2008)

UN ECOSOC, *Recommendations of the Permanent Forum: Comprehensive Dialogue with the World Intellectual Property Organization* E/C.19/2012/L.4 (New York: UN 2012)

UNESCO, 'UNESCO Universal Copyright Convention 1954' <http://portal.unesco.org/en/ev.php-URL_ID=15381&URL_DO=DO_TOPIC&URL_SECTION=201.html> accessed 30 October 2015

UN General Assembly, *Towards an Accountability System in the United Nations* A/RES/64/259 (New York: UN 2010)

UPOV, 'About UPOV' <http://www.upov.int/about/en> accessed 1 September 2015

Visser, C, 'The Policy-Making Dynamics in Intergovernmental Organizations: A Comment on the Remarks of Geoffrey Yu' (2007) 82 *Chicago-Kent Law Review* 1457–8

Wechsler, A, 'WIPO and the Public–Private Web of Global Intellectual Property Governance' in Hermann, C, Krajewski, M and Terhechte, J (eds), *2013 European Yearbook of International Economic Law* (Berlin, Heidelberg: Springer 2013) 413–40

Weiss, T and Wilkinson, R (eds), *International Organisation and Global Governance* (Abingdon, Oxford: Routledge 2013)

Woods, N, 'Good Governance in International Organizations' (1999) 5(1) *Global Governance* 39–61

World Customs Organization, 'Capacity Building Cooperation with WTO and WIPO' <http://www.wcoomd.org/en/media/newsroom/2011/january/capacity-building-cooperation-with-wto-and-wipo.aspx> accessed 26 October 2015

WTO, 'TRIPS: Agreement on Trade-Related Aspects of Intellectual Property Rights 1994' <https://www.wto.org/english/docs_e/legal_e/27-trips.pdf> accessed 30 October 2015

Yu, G, 'The Structure and Process of Negotiations at the World Intellectual Property Organization' (2007) 82 *Chicago-Kent Law Review* 1443–53

Yu, P, 'A Tale of Two Development Agendas' (2008) 35 *Ohio Northern University Law Review* 466–573

WIPO sources

BIRPI, *Joint Meeting of the Permanent Bureau of the Paris Union and the Permanent Committee of the Berne Union* (Geneva: BIRPI 1962)

BIRPI, *Observations of BIRPI on their Draft Reorganisation*, BPCP/I/2 (Geneva: BIRPI 1962)

BIRPI, *Report of the Working Group on the Plan of Reorganisation of BIRPI* (Geneva: BIRPI 1962)

Madrid Union, *Draft Report: Prepared by the International Bureau, Forty-Ninth Session of the Assembly of the Special Union for the International Registration of Marks (Madrid Union), 5 to 14 October 2015* MM/A/49/5 Prov. (Geneva: WIPO 2015)

Madrid Union, *Matters Concerning the Madrid and Lisbon Unions: Proposal of the United States of America to the Madrid Assembly* MM/A/49/4 (Geneva: WIPO 2015)

Nice Union, *Draft Revised Rules of Procedure of the Committee of Experts of the Nice Union* CLIM/WG/3/2 (Geneva: WIPO 2009)

PCT, 'Applicability of 90% Reduction in Certain PCT Fees' (WIPO 2015) <http://www.wipo.int/export/sites/www/pct/en/fees/fee_reduction.pdf> accessed 1 November 2015

PCT, 'PCT Regulations' (WIPO 2015) <http://www.wipo.int/export/sites/www/pct/en/texts/pdf/pct_regs/pdf> accessed 1 November 2015

PCT, 'Schedule of Fees' (WIPO 2015) <http://www.wipo.int/pct/en/texts/rules/rtax.htm> accessed 1 November 2015

PCT Union, *Draft Report: Prepared by the International Bureau, International Patent Cooperation Union (PCT Union) Assembly, Forty-Seventh Session, 5 to 14 October 2015* WIPO, PCT/A/48/9 Prov. (Geneva: WIPO 2015)

PCT Union, *Matters Concerning the Lisbon Union: Proposal of the United States of America to the Patent Cooperation Treaty Assembly* PCT/A/47/8 (Geneva: WIPO 2015)

PCT Union, *Report Adopted by the Assembly of the 36th Session* PCT/A/36/13 (Geneva: WIPO 2007)

WIPO, *2012 PCT Yearly Review: The International Patent System* Publication No. 901E/2012 (Geneva: WIPO 2012)

WIPO, *A Users' Guide: An Introduction to the Organization for Delegates* Publication No. 1040 (Geneva: WIPO 2012)

WIPO, 'About WIPO Lex' <http://www.wipo.int/wipolex/en/about.html> accessed 7 July 2015

WIPO, *Accountability Framework* WO/PBC/22/12 (Geneva: WIPO 2014)

WIPO, *Address of the Director General: WIPO Assemblies 2014* (Geneva: WIPO 2014)

WIPO, *Admission of Observers: Assemblies of the Member States of WIPO, 37th Series of Meetings* A/37/8 (Geneva: WIPO 2002)

WIPO, *Agreement between the United Nations and the World Intellectual Property Organization* WIPO Publication No. 111 (Geneva: WIPO 1975)

WIPO, *Annual Financial Report and Financial Statements 2014: prepared by the Secretariat* A/55/7 (Geneva: WIPO 2015)

WIPO, *Amendments to Staff Regulations and Rules: Document Prepared by the Director General* WO/CC/71/4 Rev. (Geneva: WIPO 2015)

WIPO, *Annual Report 2002* WIPO Publication No. 441(E) (Geneva: WIPO 2003)

WIPO, *Annual Report by the Director of the Internal Oversight Division: Prepared by the Secretariat* WO/GA/47/4 (Geneva: WIPO 2015)

WIPO, *Annual Report on Human Resources, Prepared by the Director General* WO/CC/71/2 Rev. (Geneva: WIPO 2015)

WIPO, *Annual Report: Report of the Director General to the WIPO Assemblies* (Geneva: WIPO 2015)

WIPO, *Appointment of Deputy Directors General and Assistant Directors General: Document prepared by the Director General* WO/CC/70/2 (Geneva: WIPO 2014)

WIPO, *Arrears of Contributions of the Least Developed Countries: Text Issued by the Informal Working Group Consisting of Germany, Argentina, France, India, Sudan and the United Kingdom, 22nd Series of Meetings of the Governance Bodies of WIPO and the Unions Administered by WIPO* AB/XXII/20 (Geneva: WIPO 1991)

WIPO Circular CWS 52–02, *Postponement of the Reconvening of the Fourth Session of the Committee on WIPO Standards (CWS),* March 24, 2015 (Geneva: WIPO 2015)

WIPO, 'Code of Conduct for WIPO Suppliers' <http://www.wipo.int/export/sites/www/procurement/en/docs/code_of_conduct_for_wipo_suppliers.pdf> accessed 15 July 2015

WIPO, *Composition of the Program and Budget Committee: Document Prepared by the Secretariat* WO/GA/40/1 (Geneva: WIPO 2014)

WIPO, *Constitutional Reform, First Session of the Working Group, 22 to 24 March* WO/GA/WG-CR/2 (Geneva: WIPO 2000)

WIPO, *Constitutional Reform: Memorandum of the Secretariat* A/33/3 (Geneva: WIPO 1998)

WIPO, *Constitutional Reform: Memorandum of the Secretariat, Assemblies of the Member States of WIPO, 34th Series of Meetings, 20 to 29 September 1999* A/34/9 (Geneva: WIPO 1999)

WIPO, 'Contribution Classes of States Members of WIPO and/or the Paris and/or the Berne Unions' <http://www.wipo.int/treaties/en/contribution_classes.html#f2> accessed 8 July 2015

WIPO, Convention Establishing the World Intellectual Property Organization (WIPO Convention) 1967 (amended 1979)

WIPO, 'Coordination Mechanisms and Monitoring, Assessing and Reporting Modalities' <http://www.wipo.int/ip-development/en/agenda/coordination_mechanisms.html> accessed 1 September 2014

WIPO, *Coordination Mechanisms and Monitoring, Assessing and Reporting Modalities: Annex II of the Report of the CDIP* WO/GA/39/7 (Geneva: WIPO 2010)

WIPO, *Decision of the 44th Session of the WIPO General Assembly in Relation to the CWS: Document Prepared by the Secretariat* CWS/4/2 (Geneva: WIPO 2014)

WIPO, *Decision on the Committee on Development and IP (CDIP) Matters: Document Prepared by the Secretariat* WO/GA/46/10 (Geneva: WIPO 2014)

WIPO, *Description of the Contribution of the Relevant WIPO Bodies to the Implementation of the Respective Development Agenda Recommendations: Document Prepared by the Secretariat* WO/GA/46/4 (Geneva: WIPO 2014)

WTO, 'Dispute Settlement' <www.wto.org/english/tratop_e/dispu_e/dispu_e.htm> accessed 30 October 2015

WIPO, *Draft Consolidated and Annotated Agenda* W/54/1 PROV.4 (Geneva: WIPO 2014)

WIPO, *Draft General Report: Prepared by the Secretariat* A/54/13/PROV (Geneva: WIPO 2014)

WIPO, *Draft Program and Budget 1998–99* A/32/2 (Geneva: WIPO 1998)

WIPO, *Draft Report: Prepared by the Secretariat, Committee on Development and Intellectual Property (CDIP) Seventh Session, 2 to 6 May 2011* CDIP/7/8 PROV. (Geneva: WIPO 2011)

WIPO, *Draft Report: Prepared by the Secretariat, 47th Session of the WIPO General Assembly, 5 to 14 October 2015* WO/GA/47/19 Prov. (Geneva: WIPO 2015)

WIPO, *Draft General Report: Prepared by the Secretariat, Assemblies of the Member States of WIPO, 55th Series of Meetings,* A/55/13 PROV. (Geneva: WIPO 2015)

WIPO, *Draft Report: Prepared by the Secretariat, 46th Session of the WIPO General Assembly* WO/GA/46/12 Prov. (Geneva: WIPO 2014)

WIPO, 'Evaluations' <http://www.wipo.int/about-wipo/en/oversight/iaod/evaluation> accessed 1 October 2015

WIPO, *Final Recommendations of the WIPO General Assembly Working Group on Constitutional Reform* A/37/5 (Geneva: WIPO 2002)

WIPO, *Final Report of the Desk-to-Desk Assessment of the Human and Financial resources of the World Intellectual Property Organization: prepared by the Secretariat,* WO/GA/34/1 (Geneva: WIPO 2007)

WIPO, *Final Texts of Proposed Amendments to the Convention Establishing the World Intellectual Property Organization: Document Prepared by the Secretariat,* 39th *Assemblies of the Member States of WIPO, 22 September to 1 October 2003* A/39/2 (Geneva: WIPO 2003)

WIPO, *Final Texts of Proposed Amendments to the Paris Convention and Other WIPO-Administered Treaties, 39th Assemblies of the Member States of WIPO, 22 September to 1 October 2003* A/39/3 (Geneva: WIPO 2003)

WIPO, *Financial Management Report for the 2012/13 Biennium* WO/PBC/22/6 (Geneva: WIPO 2014)

WIPO, *Financial Regulations and Rules* (1 November 2014 edition) <www.wipo.int/about-wipo/en/pdf/wipo_financial_regulations.pdf> accessed 1 October 2015

WIPO, *General Report Adopted by the Governing Bodies, Twenty-Second Series of Meetings of the Governance Bodies of WIPO and the Unions Administered by WIPO* AB/XXII/22 (Geneva: WIPO 1991)

WIPO, *General Report: adopted by the Assemblies, 51st Series of Meetings of the Member States of WIPO,* A/51/20 (Geneva: WIPO 2013)

WIPO. *General Report: adopted by the Assemblies, 54th Series of Meetings of the Member States of WIPO,* A/54/13 (Geneva: WIPO 2014)

WIPO, *General Report: WIPO Assemblies of Member States, 35th Series of Meetings* A/35/15 (Geneva: WIPO 2000)

WIPO, *General Report: WIPO Assemblies of Member States, 37th Series of Meetings* A/37/14 (Geneva: WIPO 2002)

WIPO, *General Report,* WIPO Assemblies of Member States, 43rd *Series of Meetings* A/43/16 (Geneva: WIPO 2007)

WIPO, *General Report: WIPO Assemblies of Member States, 48th Series of Meetings* A/48/15 (Geneva: WIPO 2010)

WIPO, *Governance at WIPO: Report Prepared by the WIPO Independent Advisory Oversight Committee* WO/PBC/19/26 (Geneva: WIPO 2012)

WIPO, *Hague Yearly Review: International Registration of Industrial Designs* (Geneva: WIPO 2015)

WIPO, *Intergovernmental Committee on Intellectual Property and Genetic Resources, Traditional Knowledge and Folklore: Report Prepared by the Secretariat* WIPO/GRTKF/IC/5/15 (Geneva: WIPO 2003)

WIPO, *Internal Oversight Division: Evaluation Policy (Draft) Second Edition* IOD/EP/2015 (Geneva: WIPO: 2015)

WIPO, *Internal Oversight Division: Report Publication Policy, First Edition* IOD/PP/2015 (Geneva: WIPO: 2015)

WIPO, *Introduction to WIPO: Objectives, Organization Structure and Activities, Development Cooperation Program* WIPO/ACAD/E/94/2 (Geneva: WIPO 1994)

WIPO, *Investigation Policy: First Edition, Internal Audit and Oversight Division* IAOD/IP/2014, 22 January 2014 (Geneva: WIPO 2014)

WIPO, 'ISA and IPEA Agreements' http://www.wipo.int/pct/en/access/isa_ipea_agree
ments.html> accessed 31 October 2015

WIPO, 'Japan Funds-in-Trust for Industrial Property: Africa & LDCS' <http://www.
wipo.int/cooperation/en/funds_in_trust/japan_fitip/> accessed 31 October 2015

WIPO, *Joint Inspection Unit Report 'Review of Management and Administration in the
World Intellectual Property Organization' (JIU/REP/2014/2) Progress Report on the
Implementation of Recommendations: Document Prepared by the Secretariat* WO/
PBC/23/4 (Geneva: WIPO 2015)

WIPO, *Joint Resolution Concerning Provisions of Well-Known Marks* A/34/13 (Geneva:
WIPO 1999)

WIPO, *List of Decisions: Document Prepared by the Secretariat, Assemblies of the
Member States of WIPO, Fifty-Fifth Series of Meetings, 5–14 October 2015* A/55/
INF/11 (Geneva: WIPO 2015)

WIPO, *List of Decisions: Document Prepared by the Secretariat, Program and Budget
Committee, Twenty-Fourth Session, 14 to 18 September 2015* WO/PBC/24/17
(Geneva: WIPO 2015)

WIPO, *List of Decisions: Prepared by the Secretariat, 23rd Session of the Program and
Budget Committee, 5 to 14 October 2015* WO/PBC/23/9 (Geneva: WIPO 2015)

WIPO, *Matters Concerning Intellectual Property and Genetic Resources, Traditional
Knowledge and Folklore* WO/GA/26/6 (Geneva: WIPO 2000)

WIPO, *Matters Concerning the Status of the Advisory Committee(s) on Enforcement:
Document Prepared by the Secretariat, WIPO General Assembly Twenty-Eighth (13th
Extraordinary) Session* WO/GA/28/4 (Geneva: WIPO 2002)

WIPO, *Medium Term Strategic Plan for WIPO, 2010–15* A/48/3 (Geneva: WIPO 2010)

WIPO, 'Member, WIPO Independent Advisory Oversight Committee (IAOC)' <https://
erecruit.wipo.int/public/hrd-cl-vac-view.asp?jobinfo_uid_c=27167&vaclng=en>
accessed 8 August 2014

WIPO, 'Member States' <http://www.wipo.int/members/en/> accessed 26 October 2015

WIPO, 'Multi-Stakeholder Platforms' <http://www.wipo.int/cooperation/en/multi_
stakeholder_platforms/> accessed 25 October 2015

WIPO, *Note on Technical and Legal Assistance of WIPO Relevant to the Implementation
of the Agreement on TRIPs* (Geneva: WIPO 2010)

WIPO, 'Observers' <http://www.wipo.int/members/en/admission/observers.html>
accessed 25 October 2015

WIPO, *Office Instruction on the 'Policy to Protect against Retaliation for Cooperating in
an Oversight Activity or Reporting Misconduct or Other Wrongdoing ("Whistleblower
Protection Policy")' (As May Be Amended from Time to Time)* Office Instruction
58/2012 (Geneva: WIPO 2012)

WIPO, *Options for the Financial Sustainability of the Lisbon Union: Document Prepared
by the Secretariat, Program and Budget Committee, Twenty-Fourth Session, Geneva,
14 to 18 September 2015* WO/PBC/24/16 (Geneva: WIPO 2015)

WIPO, *Organizational Matters and Overview of the Issues to be Considered by the Standing
Committee on the Law of Patents: Memorandum prepared by the International Bureau,
Standing Committee on the Law of Trademarks, Industrial Designs and Geographical
Indications, First Session, 13 to 17 June 1998* SCT/1/2 (Geneva: WIPO 1998)

WIPO, *Organizational Matters and Overview of the Issues to be Considered by the Standing Committee on the Law of Trademarks, Industrial Designs and Geographical Indications, Standing Committee on the Law of Trademarks, Industrial Designs and Geographical Indications, First Session, 13 to 17 July 1998* SCT/1/2 (Geneva: WIPO 1998)

WIPO, *Organizational Matters and Special Rules of Procedure: Prepared by the Secretariat, Committee on WIPO Standards, First Session* CWS/1/2 (Geneva: WIPO 2010)

WIPO, *Organizational Matters and Special Rules of Procedure: Prepared by the Secretariat, Committee on WIPO Standards, First Session* CWS/2/2 (Geneva: WIPO 2010)

WIPO, 'Oversight' <http://www.wipo.int/about-wipo/en/oversight> accessed 4 October 2014

WIPO, *Patent Cooperation Treaty Yearly Review: The International Patent System 2014* WIPO Publication No. 901_2014 (Geneva: WIPO 2015)

WIPO, 'Patentscope' <http://www.wipo.int/patentscope/search/en/search.jsf> accessed 7 July 2015

WIPO, 'Performance Management and Staff Development System Guidelines' <www.wipo.int/export/sites/www/about-wipo/en/strategic_realignment/pdf/pmsds_guidelines.pdf> accessed 1 September 2014

WIPO, *Policies and Practices for the Nomination and Appointment of Directors General* WO/GA/23/6 (Geneva: WIPO 1998)

WIPO, *Policy Advisory Commission and Industry Advisory Commission* WO/GA/24/6 (Geneva: WIPO 1999)

WIPO, 'Policy Advisory Commission: World Intellectual Property Declaration' <http://www.wipo.int/about-wipo/en/pac/ip_declaration.htm> accessed 26 October 2015

WIPO, *Policy on Languages at WIPO* WO/PBC/18/15 (Geneva: WIPO 2011)

WIPO, *Procedural and Organizational Matters: Adopted by the Meeting, Committee on Development and Intellectual Property (CDIP), First Session* CDIP/1/1 Rev. Annex (Geneva: WIPO 2008)

WIPO, *Program and Budget 2010/11* (Geneva: WIPO 2009)

WIPO, *Program and Budget 2014/15* WO/PBC/21/8 (Geneva: WIPO 2013)

WIPO, *Progress Report on the Implementation of the Joint Inspection Unit (JIU) Recommendations for the Review of WIPO Legislative Bodies: Prepared by the Secretariat, Twenty-Fourth Session of the Program and Budget Committee, 14 to 18 September 2015* WO/PBC/24/7 (Geneva: WIPO 2015)

WIPO, *Progress Report on the Implementation of WIPO Language Policy: Prepared by the Secretariat* WO/PBC/21/15 (Geneva: WIPO 2013)

WIPO, *Progress Report on the New Construction Project and the New Conference Hall Project: Prepared by the Secretariat,* A/54/11 (Geneva: WIPO 2014)

WIPO, *Proposal on a Revised WIPO Policy Related to Reserves: Document Prepared by the Secretariat, Annex 1, 23rd Session of the Program and Budget Committee, 13 to 17 July 2015* WO/PBC/23/8 (Geneva: WIPO 2015)

WIPO, *Proposal to Amend the Policy on Investments: Document Prepared by the Secretariat* WO/PBC/22/19 (Geneva: WIPO 2014)

WIPO, *Proposals on a New Mechanism to Further Involve Member States in the Preparation and Follow Up of the Program and Budget: Document Prepared by the Secretariat* WO/PBC/10/5 (Geneva: WIPO 2006)

WIPO, *Proposed Joint Recommendation Concerning Provisions on the Protection of Marks, and Other Industrial Property Rights in Signs, on the Internet* A/36/8 (Geneva: WIPO 2001)

WIPO, *Proposed Program and Budget for the 2016/17 Biennium* A/55/5 Rev. (Geneva: WIPO 2015)

WIPO, *Proposed Revision of the Terms of Reference of the WIPO Independent Advisory Oversight Committee (IAOC): Document Prepared by the Secretariat, Program and Budget Committee 24th Session, 14–18 September* 2015 WO/PBC/24/4 Annex 1 (Geneva: WIPO 2015)

WIPO, *Proposed Revisions to the WIPO Internal Oversight Charter: The Terms of Reference Governing External Audit and the Terms of Reference of the WIPO IAOC* WO/GA/41/10 Rev. (Geneva: WIPO 2012)

WIPO, *Q & A: Proposed Program and Budget 2016/17 (and Other PBC Documents): Document Prepared by the Secretariat, Program and Budget Committee, 24th Session, 14 to 18 September 2015* 9 (Geneva: WIPO 2015)

WIPO, 'Recommended WIPO Contract Clauses and Submission Agreements' <http://www.wipo.int/amc/en/clauses/> accessed 30 October 2015

WIPO, *Report: Adopted by the Coordination Committee* WO/CC/63/8/ (Geneva: WIPO 2010)

WIPO, *Report: Adopted by the Coordination Committee, 22 to 30 September 2014* WO/CC/70/5 (Geneva: WIPO 2014)

WIPO, *Report: Adopted by the Assemblies of the 42nd Series of Meetings* A/42/14 (Geneva: WIPO 2006)

WIPO, *Report: Adopted by the General Assembly, 23rd Session* WO/GA/23/7 (Geneva: WIPO 1998)

WIPO, *Report: Adopted by the General Assembly, 26th Session* WO/GA/26/10 (Geneva: WIPO 2000)

WIPO, *Report: Adopted by the General Assembly, 28th Session* WO/GA/28/7 (Geneva: WIPO 2002)

WIPO, *Report: Adopted by the Committee, 70th Session of the Coordination Committee* WO/CC/70/5 (Geneva: WIPO 2015) 4

WIPO, *Report: Adopted by the Committee, Intergovernmental Committee on Intellectual Property and Genetic Resources, Traditional Knowledge and Folklore, First Session, Geneva, April 30 to May 3, 2001* WIPO/GRTKF/IC/1/13 (Geneva: WIPO 2001)

WIPO, *Report: Adopted by the Standing Committee, Standing Committee on Copyright and Related Rights (SCCR) First Session* SCCR/1/9 Annex 1 (Geneva: WIPO 1998)

WIPO, *Report Adopted by the Standing Committee, Standing Committee on the Law of Patents, Second Session* SCP/2/13 (Geneva: WIPO 1999)

WIPO, *Report Adopted by the WIPO General Assembly, 34th Session* WO/GA/34/16 (Geneva: WIPO 2007)

WIPO, *Report by the WIPO Independent Advisory Oversight Committee (IAOC), Prepared by the Secretariat* A/43/5 (Geneva: WIPO 2013)

WIPO, *Report of the Director General to the WIPO Assemblies: The Year in Review* WIPO Publication 1040/14 (Geneva: WIPO 2014)

WIPO, *Report of the Fifth Session of the Working Group, 18 to 22 February* WO/GA/WG-CR/5/4 (Geneva: WIPO 2002)

WIPO, *Report of the First Session of the Working Group, 22 to 24 March* WO/GA/WG-CR/3 (Geneva: WIPO 2000)

WIPO, *Report of the Fourth Session of the Working Group, 11 to 14 September* WO/GA/WG-CR/4/4 (Geneva: WIPO 2001)

WIPO, *Report of the Second Session of the Working Group* WO/GA/WG-CR/2/8 (Geneva WIPO 2000)

WIPO, *Report of the Selection Panel for the Appointment of the WIPO External Auditor* WO/GA/40/3 (Geneva: WIPO 2011)

WIPO, *Report of the Sixth Session of the Working Group, 24 to 28 June* WO/GA/WG-GCR/6/3 (Geneva: WIPO 2002)

WIPO, *Report of the Third Session of the Working Group, 3 to 6 March 2001* WO/GA/WG-CR/3/6 (Geneva: WIPO 2001)

WIPO, *Report of the WIPO Audit Committee since 2008* WO/GA/38/2 (Geneva: WIPO 2009)

WIPO, *Report on, and Recommendations Adopted by, the Ninth and Tenth Sessions of the Program and Budget Committee* A/42/9 (Geneva: WIPO 2006)

WIPO, *Report on the Outcome of the Marrakesh Diplomatic Conference to Conclude a Treaty to Facilitate Access to Published Works by Visually Impaired Persons and Persons with Print Disabilities* WO/GA/43/9 (Geneva: WIPO 2013)

WIPO, *Report Prepared by the International Bureau, Standing Committee on the Law of Trademarks, Industrial Designs and Geographical Indications, First Session Geneva, July 13 to 17, 1998* SCIT/1/6 (Geneva: WIPO 1998)

WIPO, *Report: Prepared by the International Secretariat, First Session of the Standing Committee on the Law of Patents, June 15–19* SCP/1/7 (Geneva: WIPO 1998)

WIPO, *Report, Standing Committee on the Law of Patents, Seventh Session, Geneva,* SCP/17/13 (Geneva: WIPO 2011)

WIPO, *Resolutions and Decisions of the United Nations: Report by the Director General, WIPO General Assembly 16th Session* WO/GA/XVI/3 (Geneva: WIPO 1995)

WIPO, *Resolutions and Decisions of the United Nations: Report by the Director General, WIPO General Assembly 21st Session* WO/GA/XXI/6 (Geneva: WIPO 1997)

WIPO, *Resolutions and Decisions of the United Nations, the Administrative Committee on Coordination and the Joint Inspection Unit: Report by the Director General, WIPO General Assembly 24th Session* WO/GA/24/3 (Geneva: WIPO 1999)

WIPO, *Review of WIPO's Financial Situation and its Policies Related to Reserves: Document Prepared by the Secretariat* WO/PBC/22/28 (Geneva: WIPO 2014)

WIPO, *Revised Policy on Investments: Prepared by the Secretariat, Program and Budget Committee, Twenty-Fourth Session, 14 to 18 September 2015* WO/PBC/24/10 (Geneva: WIPO 2015)

WIPO, *Revised Rules of Procedure: Document Prepared by the Secretariat, Standing Committee on the Law of Patents, Seventeenth Session, Geneva, 5 to 9 December 2011* SCP/17/6.REV (Geneva: WIPO 2011)

WIPO, *Revised Terms of Reference of the WIPO Audit Committee: Revised WIPO Internal Audit Charter* WO/GA/34/15 (Geneva: WIPO 2007)

WIPO, *Rules of Procedure: As Adopted on 11 May 2015 by the Diplomatic Conference, Diplomatic Conference for the Adoption of a New Act of the Lisbon Agreement for the Protection of Appellations of Origin and their International Registration* LI/DC/2 (Geneva: WIPO 2015)

WIPO, *Rules of Procedure of the Diplomatic Conference, Prepared for the Diplomatic Conference to Conclude a Treaty to Facilitate Access to Published Works by Visually Impaired Persons and Persons with Print Disabilities* VIP/DC/2 (Geneva: WIPO 2013)

WIPO, *Rules of Procedure: Memorandum Prepared by the Secretariat, Intergovernmental Committee on Intellectual Property and Genetic Resources, Traditional Knowledge and Folklore, First Session* WIPO/GRTKF/IC/1/2 (Geneva: WIPO 2001)

WIPO, *Rules of Procedure: Memorandum Prepared by the Secretariat, Standing Committee on the Law of Patents, Second Session* WIPO SCP/2/2 (Geneva: WIPO 1999)

WIPO, *Rules of Procedure: Memorandum Prepared by the Secretariat, Standing Committee on the Law of Trademarks, Industrial Designs and Geographical Indications, Second Session, First Part* SCT/2/2 (Geneva: WIPO 1999)

WIPO, *Special Rules of Procedure of the Governing Bodies: Compilation Prepared by the International Bureau, 24th Series of Meetings* AB/XXIV/INF/2 (Geneva: WIPO 1993)

WIPO, *Special Rules of Procedure of the Governing Bodies: Compilation Prepared by the International Bureau, 25th Series of Meetings* AB/XXV/INF/2 (Geneva: WIPO 1994)

WIPO, *Staff Regulations and Rules* (Geneva: WIPO 2014)

WIPO, *Standing Committee on Information Technology: Document Prepared by the Secretariat* WO/GA/38/10 (Geneva: WIPO 2009)

WIPO, *Status of the Payment of Contributions as at June 30, 2014: Document Prepared by the Secretariat* WO/PBC/22/7 (Geneva: WIPO 2014)

WIPO, *Status of the Payment of Contributions as at September 1, 2015: Document Prepared by the Secretariat* A/55/8 (Geneva: WIPO 2015) 8

WIPO, *Summary by the Chair, Fourth Session* CWS/4/15 (Geneva: WIPO 2014)

WIPO, *Summary of Recommendations Made by the Program and Budget Committee* A/48/24 (Geneva: 2010 WIPO)

WIPO, 'Summary Table of Membership of the World Intellectual Property Organization (WIPO) and the Treaties Administered by WIPO, plus UPOV, WTO and UN' <http://www.wipo.int/treaties/en/summary.jsp> accessed 31 October 2015

WIPO, *Taking the Initiative: WIPO Strategic Realignment Program* (Geneva: WIPO 2012)

WIPO, 'Technical Assistance: Business Software Solutions for IP Offices' <http://www.wipo.int/global_ip/en/activities/technicalassistance> accessed 21 July 2015

WIPO, 'The 45 Adopted Recommendations under the WIPO Development Agenda' <http://www.wipo.int/ip-development/en/agenda/recommendations.html> accessed 30 October 2015

WIPO, *The First Twenty Years of the Japan Funds-in-Trust for Industrial Property at WIPO (1987–2007)* (Geneva: WIPO 2009)

WIPO, *The Governance Structure of WIPO: Memorandum of the International Bureau* A/32/INF/2 (Geneva: WIPO 1998)

WIPO, *The Measurement of the Millennium Development Goals (MDGs) in Other United Nations Agencies and the Contribution of WIPO to the MDGs: Prepared by the Secretariat* CDIP/12/8 (Geneva: WIPO 2013)

WIPO, *The WIPO Voluntary Fund: A Stronger Voice for Indigenous and Local Communities in WIPO's Work on Traditional Knowledge, Traditional Cultural Expressions and Genetic Resources* WIPO Publication No. 936(E) (Geneva: WIPO 2007)

WTO, 'The WTO and World Intellectual Property Organization' <https://www.wto.org/english/thewto_e/coher_e/wto_wipo_e.htm> accessed 15 October 2015

WIPO, *Understanding of the United States on the Unitary Contribution System and the Unitary Budget as they Relate to the Lisbon Agreement: Document Prepared by the Secretariat* A/55/INF/10 (Geneva: WIPO 2015)

WIPO, *Unitary Contribution System for the Six Contribution-Financed Unions and Alignment of the Contributions of Non-Union States* AB/XXIV/5, 31 May 1993 (Geneva: WIPO 2015)

WIPO, 'Webcasting' <www.wipo.int/webcasting/en> accessed 28 October 2014

WIPO, *Webcasting at WIPO: Document Prepared by the Secretariat* WO/PBC/18/19 (Geneva: WIPO 2011)

WIPO, 'WHO, WIPO, WTO Trilateral Cooperation on Public Health, IP and Trade' <http://www.wipo.int/globalchallenges/en/health/trilateral_cooperation.html> accessed 15 October 2015

WIPO, *WIPO Code of Ethics* Office Instruction 84/2012 (Geneva: WIPO 2012)

WIPO, 'WIPOCOS: Software for Collective Management of Copyright and Related Rights' <http://www.wipo.int/copyright/en/initiatives/wipocos.html> accessed 21 July 2015

WIPO, 'WIPO Director General Francis Gurry to Chair the UN High-Level Committee on Management' *WIPO News Archive* (19 April 2012) <http://www.wipo.int/portal/en/news/2012/article_0021.html> accessed 15 September 2014

WIPO, *WIPO Financial Management Report 2012/2013* WO/PBC/22/6 (Geneva: WIPO 2014)

WIPO, *WIPO Financial Regulations and Rules* (Geneva: WIPO 2014)

WIPO, *WIPO: Financial Supervision Audit Relating to Construction Projects and New Security Measures, Report of the External Auditor: Swiss Federal Audit Office* WO/PBC/19/18 Appendix (Geneva: WIPO 2012)

WIPO, *WIPO General Rules of Procedure* WIPO Publication 339 Rev. 3 (Geneva: WIPO 1998)

WIPO, *WIPO Governance Structure* WO/PBC/18/20 (Geneva: WIPO 2011)

WIPO, *WIPO Governance Structure: Document Prepared by the Secretariat* WO/PBC/17/2.Rev. (Geneva: WIPO 2011)

WIPO, 'WIPO Guide to the Uniform Domain Name Dispute Resolution Policy (UDRP)' <http://www.wipo.int/amc/en/domains/guide/> accessed 30 October 2015

WIPO, 'WIPO Independent Advisory Oversight Committee' <http://www.wipo.int/about-wipo/en/oversight/iaoc/> accessed 31 October 2015

WIPO, *WIPO Intellectual Property Handbook: Policy, Law and Use* (Geneva: WIPO 2004)

WIPO, 'WIPO International Classifications' <http://www.wipo.int/classifications/en> accessed 30 October 2015

WIPO, *WIPO: Making IP Work* (Geneva: WIPO 2014)

WIPO, 'WIPO Organigram' < http://www.wipo.int/export/sites/www/about-wipo/en/pdf/organigram/_visio-org_en.pdf> accessed 1 December 2015

WIPO, *WIPO Overview* WIPO Publication No. 1007/E/11 (Geneva: WIPO 2011)

WIPO, *WIPO Strategic Realignment Program Roadmap* (Geneva: WIPO 2011)

WIPO, *World Intellectual Property Organization: 1992–2007* (Geneva: WIPO 2003)

WIPO/EPO, 'EPO and WIPO Sign Agreement to Enhance Co-operation' WIPO/EPO Press Release, 3 May 2012 <http://www.wipo.int/pressroom/en/articles/2012/article_0008.html> accessed 26 October 2015

WTO, 'WTO–WIPO Cooperation Agreement 1995' <http://www.wto.org/english/tratop_e/trips_e/wtowip_e.htm> accessed 30 October 2015

Index

access to documents *see* external relations and transparency; WIPO website
Access to Research for Development and Innovation (ARDI) 31
Access to Specialised Patent Information (ASPI) 31
Accessible Books Consortium (ABC) 30–31
accountability 2, 49, 66, 157–65 *see also* transparency
    of WIPO Secretariat 51, 123, 157–65 *see* WIPO Secretariat and control mechanisms
    of Member States 47
    to stakeholders 47, 196
Ad Hoc Committee of Experts 186
Administrative Tribunal (ILO) 164, 175, 179
Advisory Committee on Enforcement (ACE) 79, 93
Advisory Committee on Investments 136
African regional group 96 *see also* regional groups
African Regional Intellectual Property Organization (ARIPO) 102, 180–81
Agreement between the United Nations and the World Intellectual Property Organization (1974) 31
    Article 1 8–9, 177–8
    Article 3 178
    Article 4 178
    Article 5 178
    Article 6 179
    full text of 210–15
    as legal foundation 58–60

alternative dispute resolution (ADR) 29
American Intellectual Property Law Association (AIPLA) 180
Annual Meeting of the Assemblies 70, 73–6, 85, 140, 159
Appeal Board 175
appellations of origin 78–9 *see also* geographical indications
appendices 198–296
    Agreement between the United Nations and the World Intellectual Property Organization (1974) 210–15
    Convention establishing the World Intellectual Property Organization (1967) 198–209
    Financial Regulations and Rules 262–76
    General Rules of Procedure 216–26
    Investigation Policy 292–6
    Marrakesh Treaty (Example of Rules of Procedure for a Diplomatic Conference) 252–61
    Special Rules of Procedure for WIPO Committees 247–51
    Special Rules of Procedure of the Governing Bodies 227–46
    Staff Regulations and Rules 277–91
Arab countries
    WIPO cooperation with 41, 96
Arbitration and Mediation Center 29, 148, 181
arrears 128–9 *see also* Program and Budget process
Asian regional group 96 *see also* regional groups
Assemblies of the Unions 56, 59, 81, 143

assessment, evaluation and impact studies
   (Development Agenda Cluster D)
   60, 64 *see also* evaluation.
Assistant Director General (ADG) 40, 42,
   72–3 *see also* leadership
Association of South East Asian Nations
   (ASEAN) 103
audits *see* WIPO Secretariat and control
   mechanisms and External Auditor

Beijing Audiovisual Treaty (2012)
   member states (table) 14–27
   scope of 12, 29
Berne Convention for the Protection
   of Literary and Artistic Works
   (1886)
   amendments to 56
   chairpersons of 86
   contribution class of members 124–6
   and Coordination Committee 72
   Executive Committee 68, 72–5, 86
   member states (table) 10, 14–27
   and origins of WIPO 7
   Union of, 55, 70, 72–5, 86, 88, 91, 123
Bodenhausen, Georg 39
Bogsch, Árpád 39, 60, 123
Brazil
   contribution class 124, 128
   donations by 144–5
Brussels Convention (1974) 12, 28
Budapest Treaty (1977) 13, 29

capacity building 2, 10, 30–31, 56, 60–62,
   66, 79, 97, 101, 103–4, 144, 163, 179
   181–2, 184, 190, 194,
   technical assistance and capacity
      building (Development Agenda
      Cluster A) 61
   see WTO–WIPO Cooperation
      Agreement
Central Asian and East European States
   regional group 96
Central Europe and Baltic States regional
   group (CEBs) 96
Chair of the General Assembly 71, 75–6,
   85–7, 142
Chairpersons *see* chairs

Chairs
   election of 50, 53, 75, 85–7, 97 *see also*
      officers, election of and Chair of
      the General Assembly
   role of 75–6, 84–5, 87, 97–8, 142, 186,
Chief Economist *see* Office of Chief
      Economist
Chief Ethics Officer 176
China
   contribution class 124, 128
   intervenes in WIPO debates 103
   as own WIPO regional group 96
   PCT applications 109–10
circulars 105
civil society 52, 65–6, 68, 70, 78, 80,
      100, 186–90 *see also* NGOs,
      stakeholders
Clusters of Development Agenda
      recommendations 60–66
Code of Ethics 166
   full text of 172–4
Committee on Development and
      Intellectual Property (CDIP) 66, 79,
      87, 93, 189
Committee on WIPO Standards (CWS)
      79–80, 93
Committees 76–9, 83–4
Committees of Experts 50, 67, 76, 80, 186
complaints *see* Administrative Tribunal
      (ILO); WIPO Secretariat and
      control mechanisms; Staff
      Association; Whistleblower policy;
      Ethics Office
consensus 73, 87, 105, 142, 156, 191
   and consensus-building 49–50, 53,
      87–90, 95–7, 190 *see also* regional
      groups, informal consultations
      and Secretariat, role in Member
      State deliberations
constitutional reform 48, 56, 126,
      146–7 *see also* Working Group on
      Constitutional Reform
Contribution class, 51, 56, 124, 127–8 *see
      also* Unitary Contribution System
Contribution-financed Unions 146–56
   allocation of income and budgeted
      expenditure 148–56

budget by program (2016/17) 150, 152, 154
introduction 146–7
control mechanisms *see* WIPO Secretariat and control mechanisms
Controller 130, 134–5
Convention establishing the World Intellectual Property Organization (1967) 3, 7
  amendments to 56, 71, 127, 145–6
  Article 4 31, 55–6
  Article 9 31–2, 40, 56–8
  Article 13 180
  full text of 198–209
  governance system 69, 99
  as legal foundation 55–8
  member states (table) 14–27
  New Contribution System amendment 56, 127, 146 *see also* Unitary Contribution System
  Preamble (excerpt) 8
  voting and consensus 87–8
Convention on Privileges and Immunities of Specialized Agencies of the United Nations (1947) 44
cooperation agreements 181–2 *see also* Memoranda of Understanding and WTO-WIPO Cooperation Agreement
Coordination Committee
  amendments to Staff Regulations and Rules 174–5
  approves agreements with intergovernmental organisations 180 *see also* Memoranda of Understanding
  approves DDG nominations 40
  chairpersons of 86
  membership of 69, 72
  nominates Director General 70
  scope of 69–73, 92–5
  voting and consensus 87–9
copyright 30, 78
Copyright Management System (WIPOCOS) 30
Copyright Treaty *see* WIPO Copyright Treaty (1996)

corruption 43, 51, 167, 175–6
  see also Code of Ethics
counterfeiting 79
cybersquatting 29

daily subsistence allowance (DSA) 100
decision-making structure 67–105
  Annual Meeting of the Assemblies 70, 73–6, 85
  Committees 76–9, 83–4
  Committees of Experts 80
  complexity of (diagram) 10, 68
  Coordination Committee 69–70, 72–3, 86–9, 92–5
  Diplomatic Conferences 81–3, 101
  General Assembly 69–73, 77, 81–2, 87–9, 93–5
  General Rules of Procedure 83–6, 88, 90
  governing bodies of the Unions 73–6
  introduction 49–51
  Member State representation 99–105
  and observer delegations 10, 78, 80, 83–4, 87, 97
  regional groups, informal consultations and consensus-building 87–8, 95–7
  role of Secretariat in Member State deliberations 98–9
  rule-making processes for treaties and soft law 90–92
  Special Rules of Procedure for WIPO Committees 75–6
  Special Rules of Procedure of the Governing Bodies 83, 85–7
  voting and consensus 87–90
  WIPO Conference 69, 71–2, 87–9, 142, 145
  Working Groups 80–81
  see also Program and Budget Committee, *individual governing bodies and committees*
Deputy Director General (DDG) 40, 42, 72, 180
developing countries
  contribution classes 124, 127–8
  and Development Agenda 2–3, 93

use of voting by 88, 90
WIPO finances costs of meeting
    attendance 100–101
Development Agenda 2–3, 31
    adoption of 9
    clusters of recommendations 60–66
    implementation by CDIP 79, 93
    importance to developing countries
        2–3, 93
Development Agenda Coordination and
    Monitoring Mechanism 66, 92–5
Development Agenda Group (DAG)
    103 see Group of Friends of
    Development
Development cooperation see capacity
    building
Diplomatic Conferences 81–3, 101, 155–6,
    252–61
Director General 98
    consensus building 53
    and Coordination Committee 72
    coordination with UN 177–8
    election and selection of 40, 50–51, 89
    and Ethics Office 175–6
    financial responsibilities of 130–32, 134,
        136, 139–40, 142–4
    general responsibilities of 32–3, 39–40,
        42–3, 54, 104–5
    IOD reports to 159
    limitation of terms 56
    listing of persons 39
    and observers of Ad Hoc Committee of
        Experts 186
    oversight responsibilities 162
    powers of 54, 167, 174
    prepares Memoranda of
        Understanding (MOUs) 180–81

Egypt
    proposes roll-call vote in CDIP
        meeting 90
Electronic Forum 79
Ethics Office 175–6
    see also Code of Ethics
Eurasian Patent Organization 102
European Communities
    WIPO Committee membership for 87

European Patent Office (EPO) 102
European Patent Organisation 181
European Union
    voting rights of 103
    and WIPO regional groups 96
Evaluation 49, 51–2, 95, 131, 158–60,
    162–3, 175, 194–5 see also
    IOD Evaluation Policy and
    responsibilities
    and capacity building 61, 64, 66, 144
    culture, lack of 182
Executive committee see Executive
    Committees of Berne and Paris
    Unions
Executive boards (in international
    organisations) 69
External Auditor 77–8, 89, 132, 135, 158–9
external relations and transparency
    177–94
    ad hoc relations with other
        international organisations
        181–3
    guidelines on observers 186–90
    introduction 49, 52
    and NGO accreditation 187–90
    relations with private sector
        stakeholders 184–5
    relations with UN system 177–81
    transparency and access to documents
        190–94
    Trilateral Cooperation on Public
        Health, IP and Trade 182–3
    Wi-Fi availability in buildings 191

fee-paid services see Program and Budget
    process
financial arrangements see Program and
    Budget process
Financial Regulations and Rules
    Director General's oversight
        responsibilities 162
    external audits 158
    full text of 262–76
    Internal Oversight Charter 158–60
    and Program and Budget process 109,
        130–35, 137, 139, 142–4
Foreign Affairs Ministries 99, 102

France
  contribution class 124, 128
  PCT applications 110
Fund-in-Trust (FITs) 129–30, 139, 144–5

General Assembly
  appoints Director General 32
  approves UN-WIPO agreement 59
  authority over Program and Budget 139
  chairpersons of 71, 75–6, 85–6, 142
  and Coordination Committee 69–73
  creates CDIP 66
  and Development Agenda
    coordination 93–5
  and Diplomatic Conferences 81–2
  and Financial Regulations and Rules
    130, 132
  and IAOC 157–8
  meetings of 56
  and PBC membership 77
  reports of 75–6
  use of reserve funds 134
  voting and consensus 87–9, 142
General Report of the Assemblies 75–6
General Rules of Procedure
  and decision-making structure 83–6,
    88, 90
  full text of 216–26
  and informal practices 53
  joint meetings 140, 142
  and Legal Counsel assistance 164
  observers 186
genetic resources, traditional knowledge
  and folklore 79 *see also* IGC
Geneva Group 104–5
geographical indications 78, 82 *see also*
  appellations of origin
Germany
  contribution class 124, 128
  PCT applications 110
gifts and donations to WIPO 143–5 *see
  also* Funds-in-Trust (FITs)
Global Brands Database 30
Global Innovation Index 163
governance system 47–54
  accountability 49, 51–2
  decision-making structure 49–51,

68; *see also* decision-making
  structure
demands on (1970-2015) 10
external relations and transparency 49,
  52; *see also* external relations and
  transparency
financing 49, 51, 106–30 *see also*
  Program and Budget process
introduction 2–6
key components of 50–52
mandate and purpose 49–50
reports on (1998-2014) 48
stakeholder influence on 109–10, 177,
  184–7, 196
see also WIPO Secretariat and control
  mechanisms
green technologies 30
Group B (developed countries) 96
Group of Friends of Development 103 *see
  also* Development Agenda Group
Group of Least Developed Countries
  (LDCs) *see also* least-developed
  countries
  as regional group 103
group of 77 103
Gurry, Francis 39–40

Hague Agreement (1925)
  fee-based budget for 147–8, 151, 153
  member states (table) 14–27
  scope of 13, 29
  share of fee income 109
  top design corporate/country
    applicants (2014) 114
  top ten corporate users 110
Hong Kong Trade and Development
  Council 181

Idris, Kamil 39–40
IGO observers *see* observers
income sources *see* Program and Budget
  process
Independent Advisory Oversight
  Committee (IAOC) 77–8, 131–2,
  157–9
India
  contribution class 128

indigenous and local community
representatives as observers 189
industrial designs 78
Industrial Property Automation System
(IPAS) 30
industry 185, 187 *see also* private sector
stakeholders
Industry Advisory Commission (IAC)
185
informal processes 73, 77, 88, 98, 101,
104 *see* regional groups, informal
consultations and consensus-
building
Information Meetings 190
INSEAD
Global Innovation Index 163
institutional culture 2–4, 42, 53, 162, 165,
167, 172, 196
see also headings at WIPO Secretariat
institutional matters including mandate
and governance (Development
Agenda Cluster E) 60, 64–6
Intellectual Property Watch (news media)
6
Intergovernmental Committee on
Intellectual Property and Genetic
Resources, Traditional Knowledge
and Folklore (IGC) 79, 87, 93, 189
Internal Oversight Charter 52, 130,
158–60, 175
Internal Oversight Division (IOD) 41, 52,
68, 143, 158–60, 162–3, 175
Evaluation Policy and responsibilities
158–60, 162–3, 175
Investigation Policy 159, 175, 292–6
Report Publication Policy 159–60
Validation reports 51, 143, 163
International Bureau 7, 31 *see* WIPO
Secretariat
International Civil Service 165, 175
International Civil Service Commission
(ICSC) 165
International Court of Justice 179
International Criminal Police
Organization (Interpol) 181–2
International Labour Organization (ILO)
28, 164, 175, 179

International Public Sector Accounting
Standards (IPSAS) 132, 136
International Searching and International
Preliminary Examining Authorities
181
International Union for the Protection of
New Varieties of Plants (UPOV)
member states (table) 14–27
relationship to WIPO 11, 28
Internet Corporation for Assigned Names
and Numbers (ICANN) 181
Investigation Policy 52, 159, 175,
292–6
investments *see* Program and Budget
process
IP applicants and right-holders *see* private
sector stakeholders

Japan
contribution class 125, 128
Fund-in-Trust (FITs) 145
and IP rights-holders 184–5
PCT applications 110

Korea, Republic of
donations by 144
PCT applications 110

laissez-passer travel document (UN) 60,
179
languages
official UN 87
WIPO policy on 53, 85, 192–3 *see also*
translation
Latin American and Caribbean regional
group (GRULAC) 96
Leadership
executive head 32, 39–40
misconduct 39
performance review 39
powers of 54
quality of 53, 196
relations with UN system 60
rotation in 73, 97
staff association, 175
and staffing 32, 39–44, 175
see also decision-making structure;

individual leadership positions;
   Senior Management Team
least-developed countries (LDCs) *see
   also* Group of Least Developed
   Countries (LDCs)
   capacity building for, 61–4, 182–3
   TRIPS Agreement 182–4
   waiver of arrears (1991) 128–9
legal counsel *see* Office of the Legal
   Counsel
legal foundations 55–66
   Convention ratification dates 57–8
   UN-WIPO agreement 58–60
   WIPO Convention 55–8
   *see also individual conventions and
   agreements*
Lisbon Agreement (1958)
   appellations of origin 78–9
   budget by program (2016/17) 151, 153
   fee-based budget for 147–8, 154–6
   Geneva Act diplomatic conference
      81–3
   member states (table) 14–27
   scope of 13, 29
   share of fee income 109
lobbying 104, 184–5
   and Member State influence on
      Secretariat 105
   and private sector influence, 184–5, 196
   and Secretariat influence 53–4
   by stakeholders, 185, 196
Locarno Agreement (1968)
   member states (table) 14–27
   scope of 13

Madrid Union (Agreement/1891 and
   Protocol/1989)
   budget by program (2016/17) 150, 152,
      154
   fee-based budget for 109, 147–8, 156
   member states (table) 14–27
   scope of 12–13, 29
   WIPO finances costs of meeting
      attendance 100
Marrakesh Treaty (Example of Rules
   of Procedure for a Diplomatic
   Conference) 252–61

member states (table) 14–27
   scope of 12
*Medium Term Strategic Plan for WIPO,
   2010–15* (MTSP) 137–8
Member States (WIPO)
   abolishment of WIPO Conference 71
   adoption of Development Agenda
      Coordination Mechanism 66
   adoption of 'Guiding Principles
      Regarding WIPO External
      Offices' (2015) 45
   amendments to Staff Regulations and
      Rules 174–5
   approves Industry Advisory
      Commission (IAC) 185
   approves Policy Advisory Commission
      (PAC) 185
   contribution classes 124–6
   and decision-making structure 10, 68,
      99–105
   and Diplomatic Conferences 81–3
   and General Rules of Procedure
      84–5
   income sources from 123–9
   interaction among 103–4
   interaction with WIPO Secretariat
      98–9, 102, 104–5, 163–4
   national representation of 99–102
   number of 8
   Policy on Languages 192–3
   and regional groups 87–8, 95–7
   and treaty membership (table) 14–27
   and UN Joint Inspection Unit (JIU)
      161–2
   voting and consensus 87–9
Memoranda of Understanding (MOUs)
   52, 144, 180–82 *see also* cooperation
   agreements
Mexico
   donations by 144–5
Millennium Development Goals (MDGs)
   178
mismanagement 167
Morocco, Government of 101

Nairobi Treaty (1981) 12
national representation 99–102

Netherlands
  PCT applications 110
NGOs *see also* civil society, stakeholders
  access to documents 190–94
  accreditation 187–90 *see also* observers
  civil society *see* civil society
  observers *see* observers
  participation 190 *see also* observers
    and stakeholders
  private sector NGOs *see also* private
    sector stakeholders
  public interest NGOs *see* civil society
Nice Agreement (1957)
  member states (table) 14–27
  scope of 12
norm-setting, flexibilities, public policy
    and public domain (Development
    Agenda Cluster B) 60, 62–3
norm-setting process *see* rule-making
    processes for treaties and soft law
note verbale 105

observers
  ad hoc observer status 187, 189
  and decision-making structure 10, 78,
    80, 83–4, 87, 97
  guidelines on 186–90
  IGOs 68, 76, 78, 186
  indigenous and local community
    representatives as 189
  NGOs 52, 68, 70, 78, 80, 100, 186–90
  permanent observer status 10, 68,
    187–9
  private sector stakeholders as 184
  UN agencies as WIPO observers 178
Office Instruction documents 43, 51, 131,
    166, 175–6
Office of Chief Economist 163
Office of the Legal Counsel 71–2, 84, 90,
    163–4
officers, election of 85–7, 97 *see also*
    chairs, election of
Ombudsperson's Office 41, 43, 170, 175
organisation culture *see* institutional
    culture
Organisation for Economic Co-operation
    and Development (OECD) 96

organisational change initiatives 51–3,
    167–8, 196 *see also* Strategic
    Realignment Program and
    constitutional reform
oversight 2, 6, 10, 47, 49, 52
  Member State responsibilities *see*
    WIPO Secretariat and control
    mechanisms

Paris Convention for the Protection of
    Industrial Property (1883)
  amendments to 56
  chairpersons of 86
  contribution class of members 124–6
  and constitutional reform 56
  and Coordination Committee 72
  Executive Committee 68, 74, 88
  and its Union 55, 74–5, 86, 91, 133
  member states (table) 14–27
  and origins of WIPO 7
  and WIPO membership 8, 70
Patent Cooperation Treaty (PCT) (1970)
  budget by program (2016/17) 150, 152
  cooperation agreements 181
  fee-based budget for 147–8, 154–6
  member states (table) 14–27
  PCT Yearly Review 163
  reserve accounts 134
  scope of 13, 29
  share of fee income 107, 109–10
  top fifty corporate/country applicants
    (1995–2014) 111–13
  top fifty corporate/country applicants
    (2014) 115–17
  top fifty university applicants (2014)
    118–20
  top ten country applicants (2014) 110
  top thirty government and research
    institution applications (2014)
    121–2
  Union Assembly 81, 89–90
  WIPO finances costs of meeting
    attendance 100
  working capital funds 133
Patent Law Treaty (2000)
  member states (table) 14–27
  scope of 12, 29

Patent Scope (database) 30
patents 78
  see also Standing Committee on
    the Law of Patents; *individual
    treaties, offices and organisations*
PCT Yearly Review 163
Performance Management and Staff
  Development System (PMSDS) 166
Performances and Phonograms Treaty
  (1996)
  member states (table) 14–27
  scope of 12, 29
Permanent Committee on Cooperation
  for Development related to IP
  (PCDIP) 71
permanent observer status *see* observers
personal promotions 42
Phonograms Convention (1971) 12, 28
piracy 79 *see also* counterfeiting
plant variety protection *see* International
  Union for the Protection of New
  Varieties of Plants (UPOV)
Policy Advisory Commission (PAC) 185
political appointments 40, 42, 72 *see also*
  personal promotions
power politics 1, 5, 53–4, 73, 174, 196
private sector stakeholders 184–5, 196
  and ACE initiatives 79
  and decision-making structure 10,
    195–6
  and financing of WIPO 109–30
  governance structure 68
  influence *see also* lobbying
  as observers 184, 187
  as partners *see also* public-private
    partnerships
  private sector NGOs
  and transparency 52, 184–5
  use of Re:Search 30
Program and Budget Committee (PBC)
  amendments to Staff Regulations and
    Rules 174–5
  and Development Agenda
    coordination 93
  and Financial Regulations and Rules
    130, 132
  and IAOC 158

meetings of 77–8
membership of 77
and Program and Budget Mechanism
  139–40
responsibilities of 76–7
right to vote 89
Program and Budget process 69–70,
  106–56
  aligned to Strategic Goals 137–9, 144,
    146
  budget by program and Union
    (2016/17) 150–55
  and committee coordination 92
  contribution classes 124–9
  Contribution-financed Unions 146–56
  and Controller 134–5
  external offices 45
  extra-budgetary contributions, gifts
    and donations 143–5
  extra-budgetary income and Funds-in-
    Trust 129–30, 139, 144–5
  Financial Management Reports
    132–4
  Financial Regulations and Rules 109,
    130–35, 137, 139, 142–4
  general fund 133
  income (2002-2017) 108
  income sources from fees 107, 109,
    113–30
  income sources from Member States,
    Unitary Contribution System,
    and arrears 123–9
  introduction 3, 49, 51, 71–2, 106–7
  investment policy 49, 51, 106, 134–6
  reserve policy 49, 51, 106, 134, 136, 147,
    155–6
  private sector income *see* income
    sources from fees
  Program and Budget Mechanism
    139–43
  Program Performance Reports 51, 95,
    141, 143, 163, 194
  proposed budget (2016/17) 107
  and regional groups 97
  reporting requirements 143
  results-based management (RBM) 32,
    45, 137–8, 143–4, 146, 163–5

and expected results 138, 148, 163, 194
  see also Strategic Goals
trust funds and special accounts 134
Unitary Contribution System 123–9,
  145–6
working capital funds 133
Program Performance Reports 143, 163
public interest
  balance between IP protection and
    62
  constituents 185, 187
  and Development Agenda 196
  NGOs 10, 100, 187
  research centres 68
public-private partnerships (PPPs) 2, 10,
  30, 32
publishing in accessible formats 30–31

quorum
  for approval of the Program and
    Budget 71, 85
  for Coordination Committee 88–9
  for General Assembly 88–9, 142
  for WIPO Conference 71, 142

Recommendation Concerning the
  Provisions on the Protection
  of Marks, and Other Industrial
  Property Rights in Signs, on the
  Internet (2000) 91–2
reform of international organisations
  approaches to 2–3, 52–3
  need for scholarly review 5
  and staffing 165
  see also organisational change
    initiatives; UN Joint Inspection
    Unit (JIU); Working Group on
    Constitutional Reform
Regional Center for Book Development
  in Latin America and the Caribbean
  (CERLALC) 180
regional group coordinators 97
regional groups, informal consultations
  and consensus-building 87–8, 95–7
Resolution Concerning Provisions on the
  Protection of Well-Known Marks
  (1999) 91

right-holders *see* private sector
  stakeholders
Rome Convention (1961)
  member states (table) 14–27
  scope of 12, 28
rule-making processes for treaties and
  soft law 90–92 *see also* diplomatic
  conferences
Rules of Procedure for the Diplomatic
  Conference 81–2

secret ballots 73, 88–90 *see also* voting
Secretariat *see* WIPO Secretariat
Senior management 54, 104–5, 140, 165,
  167
  Senior Management Team (SMT) 40,
    42–3, 51, 54,
Singapore Treaty on the Law of
  Trademarks (2006) 12, 29
soft law IP norms 90–92
Special Rules of Procedure for WIPO
  Committees
  and decision-making structure 75–6
  full text of 247–51
  and Language Policy 192
Special Rules of Procedure of the
  Governing Bodies
  and decision-making structure 83,
    85–7, 164
  full text of 227–46
Staff Association 52, 175
Staff Regulations and Rules 3, 40, 51,
  165–71, 174–5, 277–91
Standing Committee on Copyright and
  Related Rights (SCCR) 78, 93
Standing Committee on the Law of
  Patents (SCP) 78, 93
Standing Committee on Trademarks,
  Industrial Designs and Geographical
  Indications (SCT) 78–9, 82, 93
Strasbourg Agreement (1971) 13
Strategic Goals 32, 39, 137–8, 144, 146,
  162
Strategic Realignment Program 51, 137–8,
  172
Sweden
  PCT applications 110

Switzerland
  as *ex officio* member of PBC 77
  PCT applications 110

technical assistance *see* capacity building
technical assistance and capacity building
  (Development Agenda Cluster A)
  60–62 *see also* capacity building
technology transfer, information and
  communication technologies
  (ICT) and access to knowledge
  (Development Agenda Cluster C)
  60, 63–4 *see also* capacity building
Trademark Law Treaty (1994)
  member states (table) 14–27
  scope of 12
trademarks 78
  see also Standing Committee on
    Trademarks, Industrial Designs
    and Geographical Indications;
    individual treaties
training *see* capacity building
translation 52, 85, 182–3, 193–4 *see also*
  languages
transparency 2, 6, 49, 54, 66–7, 160, 177,
  190–94 *see also* external relations
  and transparency
travel expenses 100
treaties
  and Diplomatic Conferences 81–3
  member states (table) 14–27
  purpose and ratification of (table)
    12–3
  rule-making processes for 90–92
  see also individual treaties
Trilateral Cooperation on Public Health,
  IP and Trade 182–3

UN Chief Executives Board (CEB) 177
UN Economic and Social Commission for
  Asia and the Pacific (ESCAP) 180
UN Economic and Social Council 178
UN Food and Agriculture Organization
  (FAO) 180
UN General Assembly 59, 178–9
UN High-Level Committee on
  Management (HLCM) 177–8

UN Industrial Development Organization
  (UNIDO) 180
UN Joint Inspection Unit (JIU)
  on cross-referencing of WIPO
    documents 193
  oversight responsibilities 68, 160–62,
    164, 179
  on WIPO governance 2–3, 67
UNITAID 182
Unitary Contribution System 56, 123–9,
  145–6 *see* Program and Budget
  process
United International Bureaux for the
  Protection of Intellectual Property
  (BIRPI) 7
United Kingdom (UK)
  contribution class 126, 128
  PCT applications 110
United Nations Conference on Trade and
  Development (UNCTAD) 96
United Nations Educational, Scientific
  and Cultural Organization
  (UNESCO)
  Universal Copyright Convention 28
United Nations (UN)
  creation of WIPO Group B and
    UNCTAD 96
  and Geneva Group 104
  laissez-passer travel document 60, 179
  MOUs with UN agencies
  observer status of UN agencies
  official languages of 192
  UN Safety and Security System 166
  UN-WIPO agreement *see* Agreement
    between the United Nations and
    the World Intellectual Property
    Organization (1974)
  and WIPO staff accountability 165–71
  see also individual UN organisations
United States of America
  contribution class 126, 128
  and IP rights-holders 184–5
  objection to Diplomatic Conference on
    Lisbon Agreement 82, 155–6
  PCT applications 110
Universal Copyright Convention
  (UNESCO) 28

Vienna Agreement (1973) 13
voting 87–90 *see also* decision-making
    processes and secret ballots

Waldheim, Kurt 60
Washington Treaty (1989) 12
webcasting of meetings 190–91
website *see* WIPO website
Whistleblower Protection Policy 52,
    175–6
Wi-Fi availability 191
WIPO Conference 69, 71–2, 87, 142
WIPO Copyright Treaty (1996)
    member states (table) 14–27
    scope of 12, 29
WIPO Green (online marketplace) 30
WIPO Lex (database) 30
WIPO Re:Search (consortium) 30
WIPO Secretariat 31–46
    cooperation agreements 181–2
    and decision-making structure
        (diagram) 10, 68
    Director General *see* Director General
        and individual leadership
        positions
    drafts agenda for Annual Meeting of
        the Assemblies 75–6, 85
    drafts General Report of the
        Assemblies 75
    financial responsibilities of 109, 132–3,
        140, 143–5
    general responsibilities of 9–11, 28–31
    headquarters and offices 44–5
    interaction with Member States 98–9,
        102, 104–5, 163–4
    internal organisation 45–6
    leadership and staffing 32, 39–44
    Medium Term Strategic Plan for WIPO,
        2010–15 (MTSP) 137–8
    Program and Budget (2010-2017)
        32–8
    Senior Management Team *see* senior
        management
    on purpose of WIPO 2, 9
    and regional groups 97
    reports to UN 179
    reports to WTO 182–3

role in Member State deliberations
    98–9
voting and consensus 87–8
WIPO Secretariat and control
    mechanisms 157–76
    access to documents by 190–94
    audit and oversight mechanisms
        157–62
    Code of Ethics 172–4
    internal accountability mechanisms
        164–5
    introduction 49, 51–2
    Investigation Policy 159, 175, 292–6 *see*
        also IOD
    IOD Evaluation Policy and
        responsibilities 158–60, 162–3, 175
        see also IOD
    and Office of the Legal Counsel 163–4
    staff accountability 165–71, 174–5
    Staff Regulations and Rules 3, 40, 51,
        165–71, 174–5, 277–91
    transparency 2, 6, 49, 54, 66–7, 160,
        177, 190–94
    and UN Joint Inspection Unit (JIU)
        2–3, 67–8, 160–62, 164, 179
    Whistleblower Protection Policy 52,
        175–6
WIPO website
    improvement process for 193–4
    internal audit reports 159–60
    Observatory (Member State-only
        access) 143
    online databases 30, 194
    Secretariat reports 76, 191
    stakeholder consultation and input
        191–2
    treaty negotiations 191–2
    video recordings of meetings 78, 191
    webcasting of meetings 190–91
Working Group on Constitutional Reform
    48, 123, 146 *see also* constitutional
    reform and organisational reform
Working Groups 50, 67, 74, 80–81, 97–8,
    186, 192
World Customs Organization (WCO)
    182
World Health Organization (WHO) 182

World Intellectual Property Declaration
185
World Intellectual Property Organization
(WIPO)
agreements 11; *see also* appendices;
treaties; *individual agreements*
decision-making *see* decision-making
structure
Development Agenda 2–3, 9, 31,
60–66, 79
diagram of organisation 41
external relations *see* external relations
and transparency
financial arrangements *see* Program
and Budget process
functions of 9–31
governance *see* governance system
introduction 1–6
legal foundations *see* legal foundations
literature review 4–5
member states and treaties (table)
14–27
mission of 9

number of member states 8
origins of 7–8
purpose of 8–9
Secretariat *see* headings at WIPO
Secretariat
summary conclusion 195–7
treaties *see* treaties; *individual treaties*
see also individual committees
World Intellectual Property Report 163
World Trade Organization (WTO)
Agreement on Trade-related Aspects
of Intellectual Property Rights
(TRIPS) 28–30, 183–4
member states (table) 14–27
negotiations on geographical
indications 82
and WIPO Trilateral Cooperation
on Public Health, IP and Trade
182
WTO-WIPO Cooperation Agreement
182–3
WTO-WIPO Cooperation Agreement
182–3